AF361693

Energy Transport at the Micro/Nanoscale

Energy Transport at the Micro/Nanoscale

Editor

Xinwei Wang

MDPI • Basel • Beijing • Wuhan • Barcelona • Belgrade • Manchester • Tokyo • Cluj • Tianjin

Editor
Xinwei Wang
Department of
Mechanical Engineering
Iowa State University
Ames, IA, USA

Editorial Office
MDPI
St. Alban-Anlage 66
4052 Basel, Switzerland

This is a reprint of articles from the Special Issue published online in the open access journal *Nanomaterials* (ISSN 2079-4991) (available at: https://www.mdpi.com/journal/nanomaterials/special_issues/energy_trans_micro_nano).

For citation purposes, cite each article independently as indicated on the article page online and as indicated below:

LastName, A.A.; LastName, B.B.; LastName, C.C. Article Title. *Journal Name* **Year**, *Volume Number*, Page Range.

ISBN 978-3-0365-7910-8 (Hbk)
ISBN 978-3-0365-7911-5 (PDF)

Cover image courtesy of Xinwei Wang.

Contents

About the Editor . . . . **vii**

Preface to "Energy Transport at the Micro/Nanoscale" . . . . **ix**

Xinwei Wang
Perspectives on Energy Transport at the Micro/Nanoscale
Reprinted from: *Nanomaterials* **2023**, *13*, 1746, doi:10.3390/nano13111746 . . . . **1**

Chenfei Xu, Shen Xu, Zhi Zhang and Huan Lin
Research on In Situ Thermophysical Properties Measurement during Heating Processes
Reprinted from: *Nanomaterials* **2023**, *13*, 119, doi:10.3390/nano13010119 . . . . **5**

Jing Liu, Pei Li, Shen Xu, Yangsu Xie, Qin Wang and Lei Ma
Temperature Dependence of Thermal Conductivity of Giant-Scale Supported Monolayer
Graphene
Reprinted from: *Nanomaterials* **2022**, *12*, 2799, doi:10.3390/nano12162799 . . . . **15**

**Cheng Deng, Menglong Jiang, Di Wang, Yongqiang Yang, Vyacheslav Trofimov, Lianxi Hu
and Changjun Han**
Microstructure and Superior Corrosion Resistance of an In-Situ Synthesized NiTi-Based
Intermetallic Coating via Laser Melting Deposition
Reprinted from: *Nanomaterials* **2022**, *12*, 705, doi:10.3390/nano12040705 . . . . **27**

**Willian G. Nunes, Aline M. Pascon, Bruno Freitas, Lindomar G. De Sousa, Débora V. Franco,
Hudson Zanin and Leonardo M. Da Silva**
Electrochemical Behavior of Symmetric Electrical Double-Layer Capacitors and
Pseudocapacitors and Identification of Transport Anomalies in the Interconnected Ionic
and Electronic Phases Using the Impedance Technique
Reprinted from: *Nanomaterials* **2022**, *12*, 676, doi:10.3390/nano12040676 . . . . **41**

Qin Wang, Yu Wu, Xin Deng, Liping Xiang, Ke Xu, Yongliang Li and Yangsu Xie
Preparation and Bolometric Responses of MoS_2 Nanoflowers and Multi-Walled Carbon
Nanotube Composite Network
Reprinted from: *Nanomaterials* **2022**, *12*, 495, doi:10.3390/nano12030495 . . . . **65**

Huan Lin, Jinbo Xu, Fuhua Shen, Lijun Zhang, Shen Xu, Hua Dong and Siyi Luo
Effects of Current Annealing on Thermal Conductivity of Carbon Nanotubes
Reprinted from: *Nanomaterials* **2022**, *12*, 83, doi:10.3390/nano12010083 . . . . **83**

Huan Lin, Fuhua Shen, Jinbo Xu, Lijun Zhang, Shen Xu, Na Liu and Siyi Luo
Thermal Transport in Extremely Confined Metallic Nanostructures: TET Characterization
Reprinted from: *Nanomaterials* **2023**, *13*, 140, doi:10.3390/nano13010140 . . . . **99**

Mohammad Hassan Kalantari and Xian Zhang
Thermal Transport in 2D Materials
Reprinted from: *Nanomaterials* **2023**, *13*, 117, doi:10.3390/nano13010117 . . . . **109**

Jianjun Zhou, Shen Xu and Jing Liu
Review of Photothermal Technique for Thermal Measurement of Micro-/Nanomaterials
Reprinted from: *Nanomaterials* **2022**, *12*, 1884, doi:10.3390/nano12111884 . . . . **141**

Huanyu Dai and Ridong Wang
Methods for Measuring Thermal Conductivity of Two-Dimensional Materials: A Review
Reprinted from: *Nanomaterials* **2022**, *12*, 589, doi:10.3390/nano12040589 . . . . **153**

Jing Liu, Pei Li and Hongsheng Zheng
Review on Techniques for Thermal Characterization of Graphene and Related 2D Materials
Reprinted from: *Nanomaterials* **2021**, *11*, 2787, doi:10.3390/nano11112787 . . . . **173**

About the Editor

Xinwei Wang

Dr. Xinwei Wang is an Anson Marston Distinguished Professor and Wilkinson Professor in Interdisciplinary Engineering at Iowa State University (http://web.me.iastate.edu/wang). He obtained his Ph.D. from the School of Mechanical Engineering, Purdue University in 2001 and his M.S. (1996) and B.S. (1994) from the University of Science and Technology of China. Over the past 20 years, he has led his laboratory to develop new techniques for the characterization of energy transport at the micro/nanoscale, including the TET, ET-Raman, TD-Raman, and FR-Raman techniques. His lab reported the first study that distinguished optical and acoustic phonon temperatures under intense photon excitation and determined their energy coupling factor. His work on conjugated phonon and hot carrier transport represents the first accomplishment in distinguishing these two physical processes and quantifying their transport diffusivities. The thermal reffusivity theory developed in his lab provides a novel way to characterize a material's structure domain size, similar to that measured via X-ray diffraction, but it has unique applications for nanomaterials. He received the inaugural Viskanta Fellow Award of Purdue University in recognition of his pioneering and independent work in thermal sciences. He has been the recipient of the Mid-career Award for Research (2014) and Award for Outstanding Achievement in Research (2018) from ISU. He is a Fellow of ASME and Associate Fellow of AIAA. He serves as the associate editor/editor/senior editor of five international journals and is on the editorial board of six international journals.

Preface to "Energy Transport at the Micro/Nanoscale"

With the rapid development of micro/nanoscale materials in the last two decades, there is now substantial demand for improvements in their thermophysical properties, especially thermal conductivity, thermal diffusivity and interface thermal conductance, as they are strongly affected by micro/nanoscale structures. The measurement of these properties is a significant task and requires new scientific and engineering developments. This Special Issue targets the state-of-art research in this area and is anticipated to provide timely reviews and research advancements which will benefit researchers and engineers in materials science, engineering, physics, etc.

Xinwei Wang
Editor

Editorial

Perspectives on Energy Transport at the Micro/Nanoscale

Xinwei Wang

Department of Mechanical Engineering, Iowa State University, Ames, IA 50011, USA; xwang3@iastate.edu;
Tel.: +1-515-294-8023

Over the last two decades, with the fast development of micro/nanomaterials, including micro/nanoscale and micro/nanostructured materials, significant attention has been attracted to study the energy transport in them [1–3]. This energy transport can be sustained by electrons and phonons, whose transport is strongly affected by micro/nanoscale structure scattering. Numerous computer models based on first-principle, molecular dynamics, and lattice Boltzmann transport have been reported [4–6]. Also tremendous efforts have been reported on development of new technologies to characterize the thermophysical properties at the micro/nanoscale [7,8]. Examples of such properties include thermal conductivity, thermal diffusivity, and specific heat [9–11].

Thermophysical characterization at the micro/nanoscale is extremely challenging due to the very small size of the sample under study. It is a non-trivial job to apply a very well defined heat flux along the sample and characterize the temperature drop over it. To overcome this challenge, new transient techniques have been developed by applying transient Joule or photon heating, and track the material's thermal response using electrical or optical methods. Examples include the transient electro-thermal (TET), transient photo-electro-thermal (TPET), pulsed laser-assisted thermal relaxation (PLTR), time domain differential Raman (TD-Raman), frequency-resolved Raman (FR-Raman), and energy transport state-resolved Raman (ET-Raman) techniques [7,8,12–16]. These techniques provide quick and high-level measurement of thermal diffusivity/conductivity of 1D and 2D materials down to atomic-level thickness [17].

This special issue includes some recent work on micro/nanoscale energy transport, including research progress reports and reviews. These reviews are in great technical detail since the authors have tremendous experience and expertise in the topics under review. In the paper by Lin et al. [18], the TET technique was reviewed thoroughly, especially about the differential TET concept. The TET technique measures 1D material's voltage/resistance change under step-current heating and can be used to measure thermal diffusivity, conductivity, and specific heat. The differential concept is especially useful in measuring materials of nm-thickness which is too thin to suspend between two electrodes. The energy transport in 2D materials features very unique characteristics due to the extreme phonon confinement and scattering. The review by Kalantari and Zhang [19] provides excellent coverage, discussions, and perspectives on computer modeling and experimental characterization. The works by Dai and Wang [20] and Liu et al. [21] are great additions to the review by Mohammad and Xian, with focus on detailed experimental development. The work by Zhou et al. [22] provides sound technical details on the photothermal technique for measuring the thermal conductivity and interface thermal resistance of coatings. This work covers the fundamental physical principles, mathematical solutions for data processing, and typical examples of measurement.

Of the research progress reports covered by this Special Issue, the work by Xu et al. provides inspiring measurement technique and knowledge about the dynamic thermal diffusivity evolution during fast heating of corn leaves and ultra-high-molecular-weight polyethylene (UHMW-PE) micro-fibers [23]. This indeed significantly extends the capability of the TET technique and provides unprecedented knowledge about thermal diffusivity evolution during fast heating. The work by Liu et al. presents pioneering efforts in studying

Citation: Wang, X. Perspectives on Energy Transport at the Micro/Nanoscale. *Nanomaterials* **2023**, *13*, 1746. https://doi.org/10.3390/nano13111746

Received: 21 May 2023
Accepted: 24 May 2023
Published: 26 May 2023

the thermal conductivity variation of giant-scale graphene depending on temperature [24]. This work is very challenging since the thermal expansion mismatch between graphene and the poly(methyl methacrylate) (PMMA) substrate could easily break the graphene layer when temperature goes down. The experimental work by Wang et al. on the bolometric response of MoS_2 nanoflowers and multi-walled carbon nanotube composite [25], and work on the effect of current annealing on thermal conductivity of carbon nanotubes by Lin et al. [26] present welcome efforts on studying the structural and temperature effects on energy transport. Nanoscale energy transport has tremendous applications in materials synthesis. The work by Deng et al. [27] reports the microstructure and superior corrosion resistance of NiTi-based intermetallic coatings. Such coating synthesis uses laser melting deposition, which is a strong energy transport-controlled process. The work by Nunes et al. reported detailed study of electrochemical behavior related to charge transport in double-layer capacitors and pseudocapacitors [28]. An understanding of the physics of such transport phenomenon is critical to the design and optimization of capacitor performance.

Energy transport at the micro/nanoscale is still a very active research area, and current research is very diverse, including study of detailed phonon dynamics, structure, and behaviors, material design to either enhance or suppress energy transport, and new technology development to overcome challenges in characterizing special materials [29,30].

Funding: This research was funded by the US National Science Foundation (CBET1930866 and CMMI2032464).

Conflicts of Interest: The author declares no conflict of interest.

References

1. Xie, Y.; Xu, S.; Xu, Z.; Wu, H.; Deng, C.; Wang, X. Interface-mediated extremely low thermal conductivity of graphene aerogel. *Carbon* **2016**, *98*, 381–390. [CrossRef]
2. Feng, T.; Zhong, Y.; Shi, J.; Ruan, X. Unexpected high inelastic phonon transport across solid-solid interface: Modal nonequilibrium molecular dynamics simulations and Landauer analysis. *Phys. Rev. B* **2019**, *99*, 045301. [CrossRef]
3. Feng, T.; Yao, W.; Wang, Z.; Shi, J.; Li, C.; Cao, B.; Ruan, X. Spectral analysis of nonequilibrium molecular dynamics: Spectral phonon temperature and local nonequilibrium in thin films and across interfaces. *Phys. Rev. B* **2017**, *95*, 195202. [CrossRef]
4. Zhong, Z.; Wang, X.; Xu, J. Equilibrium Molecular Dynamics Study of Phonon Thermal Transport in Nanomaterials. *Numer. Heat Transf. Part B Fundam.* **2004**, *46*, 429–446. [CrossRef]
5. Zhang, J.; Huang, X.; Yue, Y.; Wang, J.; Wang, X. Dynamic response of graphene to thermal impulse. *Phys. Rev. B* **2011**, *84*, 235416. [CrossRef]
6. Xu, J.; Wang, X. Simulation of ballistic and non-Fourier thermal transport in ultra-fast laser heating. *Phys. B Condens. Matter* **2004**, *351*, 213–226. [CrossRef]
7. Guo, J.; Wang, X.; Geohegan, D.B.; Eres, G.; Vincent, C.C. Development of pulsed laser-assisted thermal relaxation technique for thermal characterization of microscale wires. *J. Appl. Phys.* **2008**, *103*, 113505. [CrossRef]
8. Guo, J.Q.; Wang, X.W.; Wang, T. Thermal characterization of microscale conductive and nonconductive wires using transient electrothermal technique. *J. Appl. Phys.* **2007**, *101*, 063537. [CrossRef]
9. Deng, C.; Sun, Y.; Pan, L.; Wang, T.; Xie, Y.; Liu, J.; Zhu, B.; Wang, X. Thermal Diffusivity of a Single Carbon Nanocoil: Uncovering the Correlation with Temperature and Domain Size. *ACS Nano* **2016**, *10*, 9710–9719. [CrossRef]
10. Deng, C.; Cong, T.; Xie, Y.; Wang, R.; Wang, T.; Pan, L.; Wang, X. In situ investigation of annealing effect on thermophysical properties of single carbon nanocoil. *Int. J. Heat Mass Transf.* **2020**, *151*, 119416. [CrossRef]
11. Gao, J.; Zobeiri, H.; Lin, H.; Xie, D.; Yue, Y.; Wang, X. Coherency between thermal and electrical transport of partly reduced graphene paper. *Carbon* **2021**, *178*, 92–102. [CrossRef]
12. Wang, T.; Wang, X.; Guo, J.; Luo, Z.; Cen, K. Characterization of thermal diffusivity of micro/nanoscale wires by transient photo-electro-thermal technique. *Appl. Phys. A* **2007**, *87*, 599–605. [CrossRef]
13. Xu, S.; Wang, T.; Hurley, D.; Yue, Y.; Wang, X. Development of time-domain differential Raman for transient thermal probing of materials. *Opt. Express* **2015**, *23*, 10040–10056. [CrossRef]
14. Wang, T.; Xu, S.; Hurley, D.H.; Yue, Y.; Wang, X. Frequency-resolved Raman for transient thermal probing and thermal diffusivity measurement. *Opt. Lett.* **2016**, *41*, 80–83. [CrossRef]
15. Yuan, P.; Wang, R.; Tan, H.; Wang, T.; Wang, X. Energy Transport State Resolved Raman for Probing Interface Energy Transport and Hot Carrier Diffusion in Few-Layered MoS_2. *ACS Photonics* **2017**, *4*, 3115–3129. [CrossRef]
16. Lin, H.; Xu, S.; Wang, X.; Mei, N. Thermal and Electrical Conduction in Ultra-thin Metallic Films: 7 nm down to Sub-nm Thickness. *Small* **2013**, *9*, 2585–2594. [CrossRef]

17. Liu, J.; Wang, T.; Xu, S.; Yuan, P.; Xu, X.; Wang, X. Thermal conductivity of giant mono- to few-layered CVD graphene supported on an organic substrate. *Nanoscale* **2016**, *8*, 10298–10309. [CrossRef]
18. Lin, H.; Shen, F.; Xu, J.; Zhang, L.; Xu, S.; Liu, N.; Luo, S. Thermal Transport in Extremely Confined Metallic Nanostructures: TET Characterization. *Nanomaterials* **2023**, *13*, 140. [CrossRef]
19. Kalantari, M.H.; Zhang, X. Thermal Transport in 2D Materials. *Nanomaterials* **2023**, *13*, 117. [CrossRef]
20. Dai, H.; Wang, R. Methods for Measuring Thermal Conductivity of Two-Dimensional Materials: A Review. *Nanomaterials* **2022**, *12*, 589. [CrossRef]
21. Liu, J.; Li, P.; Zheng, H. Review on Techniques for Thermal Characterization of Graphene and Related 2D Materials. *Nanomaterials* **2021**, *11*, 2787. [CrossRef] [PubMed]
22. Zhou, J.; Xu, S.; Liu, J. Review of Photothermal Technique for Thermal Measurement of Micro-/Nanomaterials. *Nanomaterials* **2022**, *12*, 1884. [CrossRef] [PubMed]
23. Xu, C.; Xu, S.; Zhang, Z.; Lin, H. Research on In Situ Thermophysical Properties Measurement during Heating Processes. *Nanomaterials* **2023**, *13*, 119. [CrossRef] [PubMed]
24. Liu, J.; Li, P.; Xu, S.; Xie, Y.; Wang, Q.; Ma, L. Temperature Dependence of Thermal Conductivity of Giant-Scale Supported Monolayer Graphene. *Nanomaterials* **2022**, *12*, 2799. [CrossRef] [PubMed]
25. Wang, Q.; Wu, Y.; Deng, X.; Xiang, L.; Xu, K.; Li, Y.; Xie, Y. Preparation and Bolometric Responses of MoS2 Nanoflowers and Multi-Walled Carbon Nanotube Composite Network. *Nanomaterials* **2022**, *12*, 495. [CrossRef]
26. Lin, H.; Xu, J.; Shen, F.; Zhang, L.; Xu, S.; Dong, H.; Luo, S. Effects of Current Annealing on Thermal Conductivity of Carbon Nanotubes. *Nanomaterials* **2022**, *12*, 83. [CrossRef]
27. Deng, C.; Jiang, M.; Wang, D.; Yang, Y.; Trofimov, V.; Hu, L.; Han, C. Microstructure and Superior Corrosion Resistance of an In-Situ Synthesized NiTi-Based Intermetallic Coating via Laser Melting Deposition. *Nanomaterials* **2022**, *12*, 705. [CrossRef]
28. Nunes, W.G.; Pascon, A.M.; Freitas, B.; De Sousa, L.G.; Franco, D.V.; Zanin, H.; Da Silva, L.M. Electrochemical Behavior of Symmetric Electrical Double-Layer Capacitors and Pseudocapacitors and Identification of Transport Anomalies in the Interconnected Ionic and Electronic Phases Using the Impedance Technique. *Nanomaterials* **2022**, *12*, 676. [CrossRef]
29. Wang, R.; Hunter, N.; Zobeiri, H.; Xu, S.; Wang, X. Critical problems faced in Raman-based energy transport characterization of nanomaterials. *Phys. Chem. Chem. Phys.* **2022**, *24*, 22390–22404. [CrossRef]
30. Zobeiri, H.; Hunter, N.; Xu, S.; Xie, Y.; Wang, X. Robust and high-sensitivity thermal probing at the nanoscale based on resonance Raman ratio (R3). *Int. J. Extrem. Manuf.* **2022**, *4*, 035201. [CrossRef]

 *nanomaterials*

Article

Research on In Situ Thermophysical Properties Measurement during Heating Processes

Chenfei Xu [1], Shen Xu [1,2,*], Zhi Zhang [1] and Huan Lin [3]

[1] School of Mechanical and Automotive Engineering,
   Shanghai University of Engineering Science, Shanghai 201620, China
[2] Mechanical Industrial Key Laboratory of Boiler Low-Carbon Technology, Shanghai University of Engineering Science, Shanghai 201620, China
[3] School of Environmental and Municipal Engineering, Qingdao University of Technology,
   Qingdao 266033, China
* Correspondence: shxu16@sues.edu.cn

Abstract: Biomass pyrolysis is an important way to produce biofuel. It is a chemical reaction process significantly involving heat, in which the heating rate will affect the yield and composition (or quality) of the generated biofuel. Therefore, the heat transfer inside the biomass pellets is important for determining the rate of temperature rise in the pellets. The accurate knowledge of the thermophysical properties of biomass pellets is required to clarify the process and mechanism of heat transfer in the particles and in the reactor. In this work, based on the transient thermoelectric technology, a continuous in situ thermal characterization method for a dynamic heating process is proposed. Multiple thermophysical properties, including thermal conductivity and volumetric heat capacity for corn leaves, are measured simultaneously within a heating process. In temperatures lower than 100 °C, the volumetric heat capacity slightly increases while the thermal conductivity decreases gradually due to the evaporation of water molecules. When the temperature is higher than 100 °C, the organic components in the corn leaves are cracked and carbonized, leading to the increase in the thermal conductivity and the decrease in the volumetric heat capacity against temperature.

Keywords: heating process transient electrothermal technique; thermal conductivity

Citation: Xu, C.; Xu, S.; Zhang, Z.; Lin, H. Research on In Situ Thermophysical Properties Measurement during Heating Processes. *Nanomaterials* **2023**, *13*, 119. https://doi.org/10.3390/nano13010119

Academic Editors: Lyudmila M. Bronstein and Diego Cazorla-Amorós

Received: 28 November 2022
Revised: 20 December 2022
Accepted: 22 December 2022
Published: 26 December 2022

1. Introduction

Biomass energy is the fourth largest energy source in the world after coal, oil and natural gas in terms of total energy consumption [1], with the dual attributes of being renewable and environmentally friendly. The rapid depletion of fossil fuel reserves makes biomass energy the most promising renewable energy source. Agricultural and forestry residues are the main source of biomass. Many rural areas often burn these agricultural and forestry residues directly as conventional fuels, which are poorly utilized, pollute the environment and endanger human health. Biomass pyrolysis is a key technology for achieving biomass energy utilization [2–4]. The process involves rapid heating of biomass under anoxic conditions to obtain high calorific value products, such as oil and natural gas.

During the pyrolysis process, the heating rate of biomass pellets determines the process of the pyrolysis reaction and the quality of the product. Rapid heating can increase the yield of oil and gas products. However, at the same time, the chemical structure in biomass pellets is degraded to form structural defects that hinder the heat transfer inside the biomass pellets, which is an important factor in determining the heating rate [5,6]. The biomass pellets are composed of several biomass material fragments, such as corn leaves, stalks, woods, etc. The in-plane heat conduction of these fragments, rather than the out-of-plane heat transfer among the fragments, contributes to the heat conduction inside the pellets since the loose contact between the fragments will raise a large thermal contact resistance and hinder the heat transfer crossing them. Thus, the in-plane heat conduction is more critical when determining the temperature rise, temperature distribution, and the possible chemical reactions in the fragment. Also, when many researchers [7,8] proposed computational models to elucidate the complexity of biomass pyrolysis, they found that thermal conductivity of the fragments is an important parameter for model building. Obtaining in situ real-time thermophysical properties (thermal conductivity, volumetric heat capacity, etc.) of biomass in pyrolysis reactions has become particularly important to study the heat transfer and temperature dynamic distribution in biomass pellets. Therefore, we endeavor to measure the in-plane thermal conductivity and other thermophysical properties of dried corn leaves undergoing the heating process (mimicking pyrolysis in vacuum).

Various transient methods for quickly measuring thermophysical properties have been successfully developed, including 3ω method [9], microfabricated suspended device method [10], optical heating and electrical thermal sensing (OHETS method) [11] and transient electrothermal (TET) technique [12], etc. These transient methods can measure the thermophysical properties of materials in a very short time and are widely applied to thermal measurement in dynamic processes. Among them, the TET method has the advantages of high measurement accuracy, fast measurement speed and short measurement period, which makes it widely used. It is effective to measure the thermal diffusivity of solid materials (including conductive, semi-conductive or non-conductive one-dimensional structures). The TET method has been used to successfully measure the thermal diffusivity of ultra-thin metal films [13,14], silk [15], DNA fibers [16], graphene [17], etc. The method exhibits the strong measurement ability for measuring the sample of different size ranging from nanometer to millimeter.

In this work, the measurement of the thermophysical properties of dried corn leaves in the heating process by using a continuous in situ thermal characterization method was developed from the TET technique [12]. Furthermore, only a small piece of a corn leaf sample is needed to fulfill thermal measurement and totally exclude the space effect in a packed sample. Section 2 details the mechanism of the TET method and the continuous in situ thermal characterization method for measuring the variation of thermal diffusivity, thermal conductivity, and volumetric heat capacity against temperature. Section 3 describes the verification of the method and investigation on a corn leaf sample and discusses the results.

2. Method for Continuous Thermal Properties Measurement for Biomass Particles

2.1. Measurement Principle of the TET Method

The TET technique utilizes electrical heating to introduce uniform heating over a whole suspended fiber, gathers the transient temperature variation based on voltage/resistance, and determines the in-plane thermophysical properties based on a one-dimensional heat transfer model (Figure 1a) [12]. By applying the TET technique, one can measure the in-plane thermal diffusivity of a tape-like sample with a millimeter length quickly, typically in several seconds. Specifically, the measurement principle is: Before measurement, non-electrical conductive samples should be first coated with a thin metal coating (e.g., iridium (Ir) coating, gold (Au) coating, etc.), so that it can be electrically conductive. A step current then passes through the sample, which causes Joule heating in the metal coating. The temperature rise of the sample can be measured by recording the overall resistance variation of the metal coating, which also works as a temperature sensor based on the effect of temperature on resistance in metal. Because the metal coating is very thin, usually around several tenths of nanometers, the rate of the temperature-rise process of the sample is related to the sample's thermal diffusivity. For example, when the thermal diffusivity of the sample is small, the temperature raises slowly, so it takes a long time to reach the stable temperature. Applying a constant current after the current is on, the transient temperature rise from the beginning to the thermally steady state is characterized by recording the voltage change at both ends of the sample. Figure 1b shows a theoretical variation of the voltage between both ends of the sample with time in the TET measurement. In most cases, metal has a constant resistance–temperature coefficient, and thus, one can monitor the voltage change of the sample to measure its temperature change. By fitting the normalized average temperature rise of the sample according to the variation of the voltage, the thermal diffusivity of the sample can be obtained.

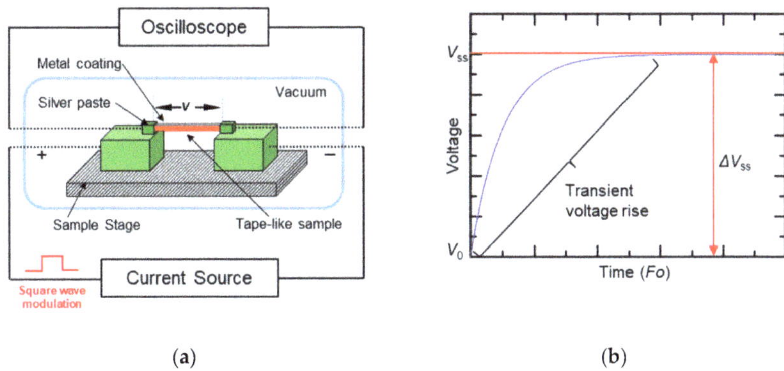

Figure 1. (**a**) Schematic of the experimental principle for the TET technique. (**b**) Voltage response to a step heating current through the sample.

2.2. One-Dimensional Heat Transfer Model

Since the length of the tape-like sample is much larger than its diameter, a one-dimensional heat transfer model along the axial direction (x direction) can be satisfied, and the heat transfer equation along the x direction can be expressed as Equation (1):

$$\frac{\partial \left(\rho c_p T\right)}{\partial t} = k\frac{\partial^2 T}{\partial x^2} + q_0, \tag{1}$$

where ρ, c_p and k are the density, specific heat, and thermal conductivity of the sample. T is the sample temperature. The effect of thermal convection is eliminated by employing a vacuum environment, and the radiation effect is included in the conduction properties and will be discussed and excluded later.

The initial condition is:

$$T(x, t = 0) = T_0, \tag{2}$$

and the boundary conditions are:

$$T(x = 0, t) = T(x = L, t) = T_0, \tag{3}$$

where T_0 and L are the room temperature and the length of the sample.

By solving Equation (1) using Green's function, the relationship between the normalized temperature rise θ^* [$\theta^* = (T - T_0)/(T_{ss} - T_0)$] of the sample and time t can be obtained as shown in Equation (4):

$$T^* = \frac{96}{\pi^4} \sum_{m=1}^{\infty} \frac{1 - \exp\left[-(2m-1)^2 \pi^2 \alpha t / l^2\right]}{(2m-1)^4}, \tag{4}$$

The TET thermophysical property measurement is carried out in a vacuum environment with a vacuum degree of 2×10^{-3} mbar, so the influence of convective heat transfer can be safely ignored. In addition, the thermal radiation between the tested sample and the environment and the metal coating on the non-conductive sample will affect the accuracy of the thermal diffusivity measurement. For details, please refer to literature [12,17].

The contribution to the measured thermal diffusivity from the thermal radiation is denoted by α_{rad} and can be expressed as Equation (5):

$$\alpha_{rad} = \frac{1}{\rho c_p} \frac{8\varepsilon_r \sigma T_0^3}{D} \frac{L^2}{\pi^2},\tag{5}$$

where ε_r is the effective emissivity of the sample, and $\sigma = 5.67 \times 10^{-8}$ W m^{-2} K^{-4} is the Stefan–Boltzmann constant. The contribution caused by the metal coating, $\alpha_{coating}$, can be expressed as:

$$\alpha_{coating} = \frac{L_{Lorenz} T \cdot L}{R A_W \rho c_p},\tag{6}$$

where A_W is the cross-sectional area of the sample before being coated; L_{Lorenz} is the Lorenz number for the metal coating; and R is the electrical resistance of the sample. After removing the influence of α_{rad} and $\alpha_{coating}$ from the measured thermal diffusivity, the actual thermal diffusivity α_{real} of the sample can be obtained as $\alpha_{real} = \alpha_{real} - \alpha_{rad} - \alpha_{coating}$.

Though the transient temperature rise contributes to the determination of the thermal diffusivity, the temperature increase at the thermal steady state can help to calculate the thermal conductivity directly, without the knowledge of other thermal properties, like specific heat. According to Equation (4), when t goes to infinite, the steady-state temperature has an expression as $T_{SS} = T_0 + q_0 l^2 / 12k$. One can determine the thermal conductivity k immediately with Equation (7):

$$k = I^2 R L \times (dR/dT)/(12 A_W \times \Delta R),\tag{7}$$

where I is the current; dR/dT is the electrical resistance–temperature coefficient of the metal coating; and ΔR is the change of the electrical resistance of the sample during Joule heating. Furthermore, from the definition of thermal diffusivity α: $\alpha = k/\rho \cdot c_p$, the volume-specific heat $\rho \cdot c_p$ of the sample can then be obtained. That is, the temperature T, thermal diffusivity α, thermal conductivity k and volumetric specific heat $\rho \cdot c_p$ of the sample can be obtained simultaneously in a single square wave period of the measurement.

2.3. Continuous Thermal Characterization Based on the TET

2.3.1. Mechanism of the Continuous in Situ Thermal Characterization

One important parameter in the TET method is the characterization time. From Equation (4), it is clear that the normalized temperature rise θ^* mainly depends on $\alpha t^2 / L$, which is a dimensionless parameter, Fourier number (Fo). Then, the characteristic time t_c has been defined when Fo equals to 0.2026. t_c ($=\sqrt{0.2026 L^2 / \alpha}$) indicates the spent time when the temperature of a specific sample (having a specific thermal diffusivity α) almost reaches the thermal steady-state temperature after being heated. Thus, one can estimate the possible time that one Joule heating and measurement may take. It depends on the thermal diffusivity and length of the sample, and in turn, t_c (as well as the TET measuring time) can be adjusted by selecting the desired length of the sample. Based on this mechanism, we cut samples into the suitable length, and the time for one TET measurement would be much shorter than the heating process, as shown in Figure 2a.

2.3.2. A typical Experimental Setup

Figure 2b shows a typical experimental setup. The tape-like sample is fixed on a lab-made sample stage. It is suspended between two electrodes, which are placed on a slide of glass. Then, the sample stage is placed on a heating plate. The heating plate is provided with a controllable heating source to generate a slow heating process. The temperature-rise rate can be adjusted by the power source connected to the heating plate. On the sample, another modulated square-wave current is fed to generate 'fast' Joule heating and a small temperature increase in the sample to acquire the thermal diffusivity of the sample. The oscilloscope is attached to the two ends of the sample and records the fast voltage variation due to Joule heating. A thermocouple is attached to the one electrode and close to the sample end to monitor the real-time temperature of the sample. It is necessary for calculating dR/dT of the nanometer thick coating, since the electrical properties of the coating may be greatly different from its bulk counterpart.

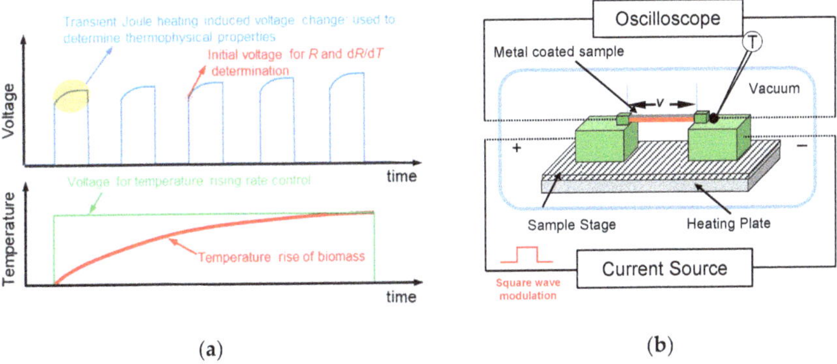

Figure 2. (a) Mechanism of the continuous in situ thermal characterization method. (b) A lab-developed, experimental setup for continuous thermal characterization.

3. Results and Discussions

3.1. Verification of the Method and Experimental Setup

First, an ultrahigh, molecular-weight, polyethylene (UHMW-PE) fiber is employed to verify the method and experimental setup. UHMW-PE fibers have a high crystalline content, >90%, so they work well in heat conduction along its axial direction. In previous studies, the similar fibers were investigated at the room temperature and reported to have a high thermal diffusivity of 1.1×10^{-5} m^2/s. According to this high thermal diffusivity and the definition of *Fo* (=0.2026) mentioned above, a one-millimeter fiber can almost reach the new thermal steady state in 0.02 s after Joule heating begins. In other words, the measurement duration is only about 0.02 s. Thus, we could set a heating process from room temperature to 90 °C with a time span of 200 s. During the 0.02 s- measurement duration, the temperature rise induced by the heating stage will be as low as 6.5×10^{-3} °C. It is safe to neglect the heating stage raised temperature rise and directly record the voltage variation and the temperature rise through the thermocouple to determine the thermophysical properties change against time.

We prepare a thin UHMW-PE fiber as a standard sample, which is about 909.5 µm long and 43.2 µm width, as shown in Figure 3a,b. It has been coated with 20 nm Ir film and fixed on a sample stage. Silver paste is applied to its two ends to guarantee a good electrical and thermal connection between the sample end and the electrode. In the measurement, the Joule heating current is 4 mA and modulation frequency is 10 Hz. The room temperature is around 23 °C. Figure 3c shows a typical voltage rising curve against time (bottom panel) and data fitting [18] (top panel) at a certain temperature during the Joule heating. The determined thermal diffusivity is 1.13 ± 0.03 m^2/s. The variation of thermal diffusivity for the UHMW-PE fiber is shown in Figure 3d. It linearly decreases against temperature.

Furthermore, it is important to note that we can obtain the electrical resistance of the sample at the very beginning of Joule heating, since the current is constant. That means the real temperature of the sample can be derived through this electrical resistance, and the relationship between the electrical resistance of the Ir coating against time can be recorded. As shown in the bottom panel in Figure 3d, the resistance of the coating increases linearly against temperature. The electrical resistance–temperature coefficient (dR/dT) is determined to be 0.737 Ω/°C. With the obtained thermal diffusivity and dR/dT, we can calculate the thermal conductivity and volumetric heat capacity, as shown in Figure 3d. The thermal conductivity decreases linearly against the rising temperature, and the volumetric heat capacity keeps almost constant in this temperature range. When the temperature is above 90 °C, the fiber begins to melt, and the coating is broken at the same time, which causes the loss of the voltage signal. However, before the melting of fiber, the measured thermal properties agree well with the value and the varying trend reported in previous work [19]. It verifies this method that the experimental setup works well for thermal characterization during the heating process.

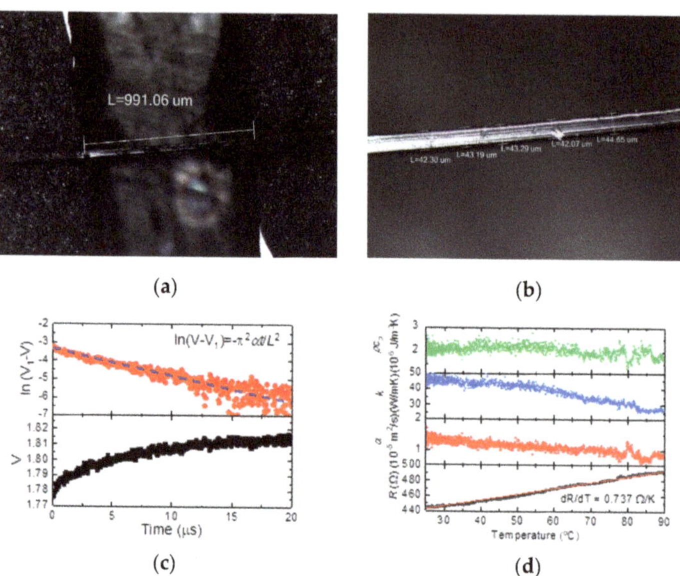

(a)

(b)

(c)

(d)

Figure 3. Verification of the method by using a UHMW-PE fiber. (**a**) Length and (**b**) width of the sample UHMW-PE fiber. (**c**) A typical measured voltage variation (bottom) and thermal diffusivity determination (top). (**d**) The variations of thermal diffusivity α, thermal conductivity k, volumetric heat capacity $\rho \cdot c_p$, and electrical resistance R for the UHMW-PE fiber against temperature.

3.2. Thermal Characterization for Corn Leaves during Heating

To investigate the thermophysical properties' variation in heating processes, a corn leaf is used as a typical biomass sample. The corn leaf is freeze-dried and cut into tape-like shape. Then, a layer of Ir film (40 nm thick) is coated on the leaf surface to make it conductive, and its two ends are fixed on the electrode with the silver paste as that in the UHMW-PE fiber sample preparation. However, obviously different from the UHMW-PE fiber, the corn leaf fiber has a low thermal conductivity/diffusivity. It needs more time to reach the criteria of $Fo = 0.2026$. To ensure that the heating stage temperature rise is negligible in the Joule heating duration, the sample is prepared into a short length, and it can quickly reach the thermal steady state during one Joule heating and measurement duration. The length of the corn leaf sample prepared as shown in Figure 3 is about 0.65 mm, and the time required for the sample to reach the thermal steady state is about 0.85 s. Different from the above, the UHMW-PE fiber having a round cross-section, the corn leaf is a flat film with a width of 0.45 mm. Its length is much larger than its thickness (less than 0.06 mm), and the time duration for Joule heat to propagate in the thickness direction and to reach, a thermal steady state (~0.02 s) will be much shorter than that required to propagate along the length and reach a thermal steady state (~0.85 s). Therefore, when applying the TET method to measure the corn leaf sample, it is reasonably assumed that the temperature is uniform along the thickness direction, and Joule heat mainly transfers along the length of the sample, which agrees well with the one-dimensional heat transfer model.

Under the condition of a heating rate of 0.87 °C/s, the measured thermal diffusivity of corn leaves is shown in Figure 4. At room temperature, the thermal diffusivity of corn is about 1.2×10^{-7} m^2/s, which is similar to the thermal diffusivity of biomass materials reported in the literature [20,21]. As the temperature increases, the variation of the thermal diffusivity of the corn leaf sample shows a trend of first decline and then rise, and reaches the lowest value near 110 °C. The electrical resistance–temperature coefficient of the 40 nm Ir coating on top of the corn leaf shows a good linearity in the temperature range from room temperature to 225 °C. Below 225 °C, dR/dT is fitted to be 0.01345 Ω/°C, while above 225 °C, the Ir coating may be broken by the chemical reaction in the corn leaf, and the electrical resistance becomes unstable. The value of dR/dT is abnormal, and the thermal conductivity and volumetric heat capacity cannot be defined then. The thermal conductivity k of the sample can be obtained below 225 °C, as shown in Figure 4b. The measured k here is lower than that reported in other literature. This is because the sample is dried in advance and is measured in the vacuum, where different environmental conditions may cause the lower k than others [22–24]. k has the same varying trend as that of the thermal diffusivity. When the temperature is lower than 100 °C, it decreases with the increase in temperature, which is mainly due to the small amount of water remaining in the corn leaf samples. Because the thermal conductivity of water is much higher than the organic components in corn leaves, heating and evaporation of water molecules reduces the overall thermal conductivity of the sample corn leaf. As the temperature further rises, the organic matter in the corn leaves is cracked, the carbonization gradually occurs at a lower heating rate, and the carbon in the solid residue increases. The thermal conductivity of carbon is higher than the organic components in corn leaves (including cellulose, hemicellulose, lignin, etc.), so the increment in carbon content will increase the thermal conductivity of the entire solid phase residue. Therefore, the overall k of the sample corn leaf increases [25].

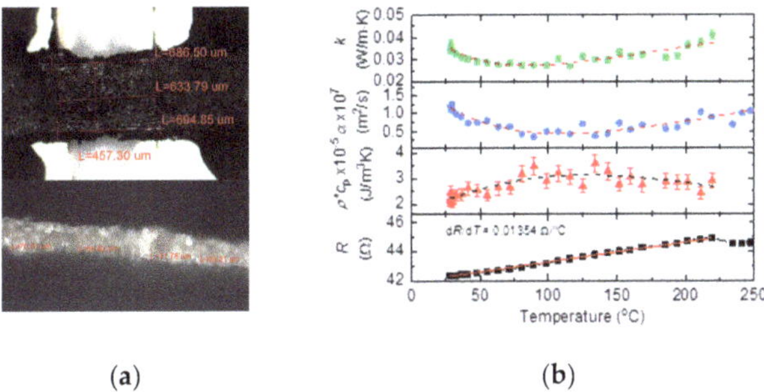

<table>
<tr><td>(a)</td><td>(b)</td></tr>
</table>

Figure 4. Continuous thermal characterization of corn leaves. (**a**) Length (top), width (top), and thickness (bottom) of the corn leaf sample with Ir coating. (**b**) The variations of thermal diffusivity α, thermal conductivity k, volumetric heat capacity $\rho \cdot c_\mathrm{p}$, and electric resistance R for the corn leaf sample against temperature. The dash lines show the varying of the properties.

Then the volumetric heat capacity of the corn leaf is calculated by using $\alpha = k/\rho \cdot c_\mathrm{p}$, and the result is shown in Figure 4b. $\rho \cdot c_\mathrm{p}$ first rises against temperature, and after the temperature is higher than 120 °C, it declines. Volatilization of a small amount of water has little effect on the density of solid-phase components in the initial heating stage, and $\rho \cdot c_\mathrm{p}$ shows a slight increasing trend against temperature. When the temperature is higher than 100 °C, due to carbonization of bio-organic molecules, small gas molecules are generated and leave the solid structure, which produces a loose porous structure in solid, reduces the density of the solid phase components, and results in a decrease in $\rho \cdot c_\mathrm{p}$ with temperature.

4. Conclusions

In this work, we have developed a continuous in situ thermal characterization method and established a corresponding experimental setup for the continuous thermal diffusivity, thermal conductivity, and volumetric heat capacity measurement for UHMW-PE fibers and corn leaves during heating processes. The verification by using the UHMW-PE fiber showed a good measurement ability of the method and the experimental setup. Furthermore, by applying the new method, the thermophysical properties' variation of corn leaves has been investigated in a slow heating process. In a vacuum, the thermal diffusivity first decreased from 1.2×10^{-7} m^2/s to 0.5×10^{-7} m^2/s below 100 °C and then increased to 1.2×10^{-7} m^2/s until the coating broke. The thermal conductivity showed the similar varying trend as the thermal diffusivity. It decreased from 0.035 W/m·K to 0.028 W/m·K and increased to 0.04 W/m·K. The volumetric heat capacity changed inversely. It increased first from 2.2×10^5 J/m^{3}K to 3.0×10^5 J/m^{3}K and then decreased to around 2.2×10^5 J/m^{3}K. Both dehydration and carbonization on the thermophysical properties of biomass materials contributed to these variations. However, the time resolution for the measurement of corn leaves was somehow limited by the sample size/characteristic time. In a sample with a much smaller size, further work could be conducted on faster heating processes, such as fast pyrolysis, in the future.

Author Contributions: Conceptualization, S.X.; writing—original draft preparation, C.X., Z.Z. and S.X.; writing—review and editing, S.X. and H.L.; supervision, S.X.; funding acquisition, S.X. All authors have read and agreed to the published version of the manuscript.

Funding: This research was funded by National Natural Science Foundation of China, grant number 52106220 (for S.X.).

Data Availability Statement: The data presented in this study are available on request from the corresponding author.

Conflicts of Interest: The authors declare no conflict of interest.

References

1. Saxena, R.C.; Adhikari, D.K.; Goyal, H.B. Biomass-based energy fuel through biochemical routes: A review. *Renew. Sustain. Energy Rev.* **2009**, *13*, 167–178. [CrossRef]
2. Wankhade, R.D.; Bhattacharya, T. Pyrolysis oil an emerging alternate fuel for future (Review). *J. Pharmacogn. Phytochem.* **2017**, *6*, 239–243.
3. Whalen, J.; Xu, C.C.; Shen, F.; Kumar, A.; Eklund, M.; Yan, J. Sustainable biofuel production from forestry, agricultural and waste biomass feedstocks. *Appl. Energy* **2017**, *198*, 281–283. [CrossRef]
4. Williams, C.L.; Westover, T.L.; Emerson, R.M.; Tumuluru, J.S.; Li, C. Sources of Biomass Feedstock Variability and the Potential Impact on Biofuels Production. *Bioenergy Res.* **2016**, *9*, 1–14. [CrossRef]
5. Mettler, M.S.; Vlachos, D.G.; Dauenhauer, P.J. Top ten fundamental challenges of biomass pyrolysis for biofuels. *Energy Environ. Sci.* **2012**, *5*, 7797–7809. [CrossRef]
6. Bridgwater, T. Challenges and Opportunities in Fast Pyrolysis of Biomass: Part I. *Johns. Matthey Technol. Rev.* **2018**, *62*, 118–130. [CrossRef]
7. Rezaei, H.; Sokhansanj, S.; Bi, X.; Lim, C.J.; Lau, A. A numerical and experimental study on fast pyrolysis of single woody biomass particles. *Appl. Energy* **2017**, *198*, 320–331. [CrossRef]
8. Zhang, K.; You, C.; Li, Y. Experimental and numerical investigation on the pyrolysis of single coarse lignite particles. *Korean J. Chem. Eng.* **2012**, *29*, 540–548. [CrossRef]
9. Lu, L.; Yi, W.; Zhang, D.L. 3ω method for specific heat and thermal conductivity measurements. *Rev. Sci. Instrum.* **2001**, *72*, 2996–3003. [CrossRef]
10. Kim, P.; Shi, L.; Majumdar, A.; McEuen, P.L. Thermal Transport Measurements of Individual Multiwalled Nanotubes. *Phys. Rev. Lett.* **2001**, *87*, 215502. [CrossRef]
11. Hou, J.; Wang, X.; Guo, J. Thermal characterization of micro/nanoscale conductive and non-conductive wires based on optical heating and electrical thermal sensing. *J. Phys. D Appl. Phys.* **2006**, *39*, 3362–3370. [CrossRef]
12. Guo, J.; Wang, X.; Wang, T. Thermal characterization of microscale conductive and nonconductive wires using transient electrothermal technique. *J. Appl. Phys.* **2007**, *101*, 063537. [CrossRef]
13. Lin, H.; Xu, S.; Li, C.; Dong, H.; Wang, X. Thermal and electrical conduction in 6.4 nm thin gold films. *Nanoscale* **2013**, *5*, 4652–4656. [CrossRef] [PubMed]
14. Lin, H.; Xu, S.; Wang, X.; Mei, N. Thermal and Electrical Conduction in Ultrathin Metallic Films: 7 nm down to Sub-Nanometer Thickness. *Small* **2013**, *9*, 2585–2594. [CrossRef]
15. Liu, G.; Xu, S.; Cao, T.T.; Lin, H.; Tang, X.; Zhang, Y.Q.; Wang, X. Thermally induced increase in energy transport capacity of silkworm silks. *Biopolymers* **2014**, *101*, 1029–1037. [CrossRef]

16. Xu, Z.; Wang, X.; Xie, H. Promoted electron transport and sustained phonon transport by DNA down to 10 K. *Polymer* **2014**, *55*, 6373–6380. [CrossRef]
17. Lin, H.; Xu, S.; Wang, X.; Mei, N. Significantly reduced thermal diffusivity of free-standing two-layer graphene in graphene foam. *Nanotechnology* **2013**, *24*, 415706. [CrossRef]
18. Karamati, A.; Hunter, N.; Lin, H.; Zobeiri, H.; Xu, S.; Wang, X. Strong linearity and effect of laser heating location in transient photo/electrothermal characterization of micro/nanoscale wires. *Int. J. Heat Mass Transf.* **2022**, *198*, 123393. [CrossRef]
19. Zhu, B.; Liu, J.; Wang, T.; Han, M.; Valloppilly, S.; Xu, S.; Wang, X. Novel Polyethylene Fibers of Very High Thermal Conductivity Enabled by Amorphous Restructuring. *ACS Omega* **2017**, *2*, 3931–3944. [CrossRef]
20. Pandecha, K.; Pongtornkulpanich, A.; Sukchai, S.; Suriwong, T. Thermal properties of corn husk fiber as insulation for flat plate solar collector. *Int. J. Renew. Energy* **2015**, *10*, 27–36.
21. Czajkowski, Ł.; Wojcieszak, D.; Olek, W.; Przybył, J. Thermal properties of fractions of corn stover. *Constr. Build. Mater.* **2019**, *210*, 709–712. [CrossRef]
22. Kustermann, M.; Scherer, R.; Kutzbach, H.D. Thermal conductivity and diffusivity of shelled corn and grain. *J. Food Process Eng.* **1981**, *4*, 137–153. [CrossRef]
23. Chang, C.S. Thermal Conductivity of Wheat, Corn, and Grain Sorghum as Affected by Bulk Density and Moisture Content. *Trans. ASAE* **1986**, *29*, 1447–1450. [CrossRef]
24. Hays, R.L. The thermal conductivity of leaves. *Planta* **1975**, *125*, 281–287. [CrossRef] [PubMed]
25. Williams, C.L.; Westover, T.L.; Petkovic, L.M.; Matthews, A.C.; Stevens, D.M.; Nelson, K.R. Determining Thermal Transport Properties for Softwoods Under Pyrolysis Conditions. *ACS Sustain. Chem. Eng.* **2017**, *5*, 1019–1025. [CrossRef]

Article

Temperature Dependence of Thermal Conductivity of Giant-Scale Supported Monolayer Graphene

Jing Liu [1], Pei Li [1], Shen Xu [2], Yangsu Xie [3], Qin Wang [3] and Lei Ma [1,*]

1   College of New Materials and New Energies, Shenzhen Technology University, Shenzhen 518116, China
2   School of Mechanical and Automotive Engineering, Shanghai University of Engineering Science, Shanghai 201620, China
3   College of Chemistry and Environmental Engineering, Shenzhen University, Shenzhen 518055, China
*   Correspondence: malei@sztu.edu.cn

Abstract: Past work has focused on the thermal properties of microscale/nanoscale suspended/supported graphene. However, for the thermal design of graphene-based devices, the thermal properties of giant-scale (~mm) graphene, which reflects the effect of grains, must also be investigated and are critical. In this work, the thermal conductivity variation with temperature of giant-scale chemical vapor decomposition (CVD) graphene supported by poly(methyl methacrylate) (PMMA) is characterized using the differential transient electrothermal technique (diff-TET). Compared to the commonly used optothermal Raman technique, diff-TET employs joule heating as the heating source, a situation under which the temperature difference between optical phonons and acoustic phonons is eased. The thermal conductivity of single-layer graphene (SLG) supported by PMMA was measured as 743 ± 167 W/(m·K) and 287 ± 63 W/(m·K) at 296 K and 125 K, respectively. As temperature decreased from 296 K to 275 K, the thermal conductivity of graphene was decreased by 36.5%, which can be partly explained by compressive strain buildup in graphene due to the thermal expansion mismatch.

Keywords: giant-scale graphene; thermal conductivity; supported by PMMA; compressive strain

Citation: Liu, J.; Li, P.; Xu, S.; Xie, Y.; Wang, Q.; Ma, L. Temperature Dependence of Thermal Conductivity of Giant-Scale Supported Monolayer Graphene. *Nanomaterials* **2022**, *12*, 2799. https://doi.org/10.3390/nano12162799

Academic Editors: Alberto Fina and Gyaneshwar P. Srivastava

Received: 16 July 2022
Accepted: 11 August 2022
Published: 15 August 2022

Publisher's Note: MDPI stays neutral with regard to jurisdictional claims in published maps and institutional affiliations.

1. Introduction

The discovery of graphene created explosive growth in research on the various properties of graphene [1–4]. Due to its high thermal conductivity (k) [5], ultrahigh electron mobility [6], and remarkable mechanical strength [7], graphene is regarded to have broad and promising applications including flexible electronics [8,9], photovoltaic devices [10], batteries [11], and so on [12]. With the increasing intense heat of electronics, graphene with super-high k has potential applications for the thermal management of microelectronics. A massive amount of work has focused on the experimental and theoretical calculation of the k of suspended and supported graphene, and great progress has been achieved [13–17]. The effect of various parameters such as system size [17], defects [18–20], substrates [21,22], and grain size [23–25] on the k of graphene has been deeply studied. Last but not least, since temperature affects the phonon propagation, the k of graphene shows strong temperature dependence. It has been reported that the k of supported graphene increases with increasing temperature, with the peak k appearing around 300 K [14]. When the temperature is lower than 300 K, the phonon-substrate scattering dominates the phonon scattering [14].

Thermal property measurement is critical to the application of graphene in thermal management. Since graphene is extremely thin, the commonly used thermal conductivity measurement techniques of graphene are optothermal Raman spectroscopy [26–28] and the micro-bridge method [14]. For optothermal Raman spectroscopy, the accuracy of the measured k depends on the absorbed laser power and the temperature coefficient of the Raman shift of the G peak [29]. Li et al. developed the laser-flash optothermal Raman technique, which eases the laser absorption coefficient uncertainty in the measurement of thermal conductivity [29,30]. It is assumed that optical phonons and acoustic phonons are in thermal equilibrium under intense laser irradiation. However, Ruan et al. first reported that the phonon branches were in strong thermal non-equilibrium by employing density functional perturbation theory. The temperature of out-of-plane acoustic phonons (ZA) is 14.8% lower than that of transverse optical phonons (TO) [31]. Under this situation, the k of graphene will be overestimated. Wang et al. first detected the lumped temperature difference between optical and acoustic phonons by nanosecond energy transport state-resolved Raman spectroscopy [32]. Seol et al. developed the micro-bridge method to measure the k of supported graphene. The micro-bridge method uses joule heating as the heating source. In the experiment, the graphene supported by SiO_2 acts as the thermal bridge between the heating part and the temperature-sensing part [14]. In principle, the micro-bridge method is feasible, but its measurement accuracy is guaranteed when the thermal resistance of the sample is comparable to that of the resistance thermometer in the experiment setup. In addition, it is technically challenging and time consuming to fabricate the whole measurement device [33].

So far, most thermal conductivity measurements of graphene focus on microscale samples. It is reported that the k of suspended graphene is size/geometry dependent. The k of graphene has a ~log L (L: sample length) dependence which was confirmed by experiments (up to 9 µm) [17] and theoretical simulations [34]. Although the k of supported graphene is less sensitive to the length size due to substrate coupling [21,35], the k of macroscale supported graphene is critical, since the edge-phonon scattering usually leads to a great reduction in k. Furthermore, graphene has important applications in the field of flexible electronics, which calls for the thermal properties of graphene supported by flexible materials. To date, seldom work has been conducted on the temperature dependence of the thermal conductivity of millimeter-scale graphene on soft substrates, yet such knowledge is essential to graphene-based device design and optimization.

In this work, the temperature dependence of the thermal conductivity of millimeter-scale SLG supported by poly(methyl methacrylate) (PMMA) is characterized by a differential transient thermoelectrical technique (diff-TET) [36]. The diff-TET employs self-heating as the heating source, which ensures the thermal equilibrium among phonon branches. The sample size is approximately 2–3 mm in width and 1–3 mm in length, which significantly suppresses the effect of size on thermal conductivity. The k of PMMA is much lower than that of graphene. Choosing extremely thin (~457 nm) PMMA as the substrate can ensure the contribution of graphene to the overall thermal conductivity is comparable to that of PMMA. Thus, it is feasible to measure the k of graphene with high accuracy. The k of supported SLG is reported to be 743 ± 167 W/(m·K) at 296 K, which is 23.8% higher than that of micro-scale SiO_2-supported graphene measured using the micro-bridge method [14]. The k of supported SLG is reduced to 287 ± 63 W/(m·K) when the temperature is 125 K, partly due to the strain-induced rips in the sample.

2. Sample Preparation and Characterization

2.1. Sample Preparation

SLG supported by PMMA characterized in this work was obtained from Jiangsu Xianfeng nanoscale materials company. The samples used in this experiment were fabricated using the chemical vapor deposition (CVD) method. The graphene is grown on a copper (Cu) in a controlled chamber pressure CVD system. At first, a clean Cu foil was annealed at 1077 °C with a H_2 flow rate of 500 sccm. Then, the H_2 flow rate and chamber pressure were adjusted to 70 sccm and 108 Torr, respectively. By introducing 0.15 sccm CH_4 into the chamber, the graphene starts to grow. The copper was etched off after PMMA was coated on the graphene. Finally, graphene supported by PMMA was transferred to a filter substrate. The layer number of graphene was provided in the product technical data.

The as-received graphene was cut into the desired size by scissors. Then, the experimental sample was suspended between two electrodes, as shown in Figure 1a. The effective k of these samples will be measured by diff-TET without any further processing. The thickness of PMMA (δ_p) is necessary to determine the k of graphene when subtracting the effect of PMMA. Atomic force microscopy (AFM) was used to determine the thickness of PMMA. The supported graphene was transferred to a silicon substrate; then, the thickness of PMMA was determined with AFM. Figure 1b shows the AFM image of the as-received supported graphene. The thickness of PMMA was determined to be 457 nm.

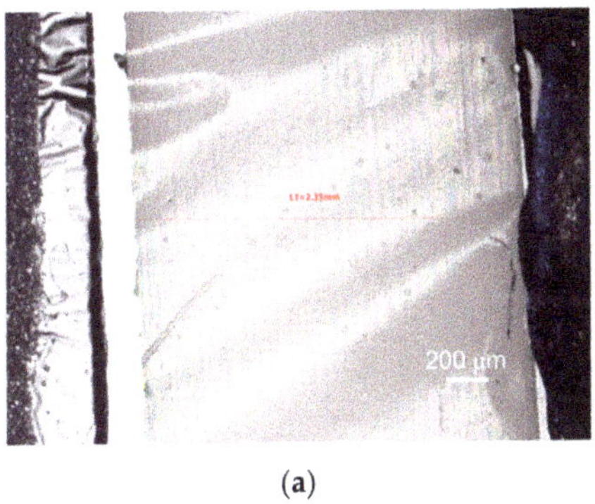

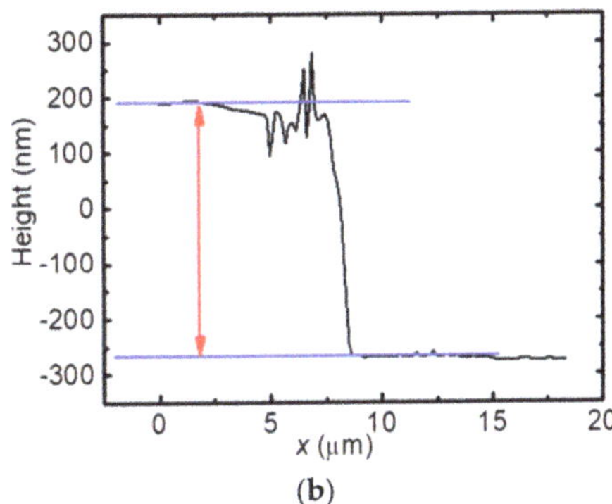

(a)

(b)

Figure 1. (**a**) Topology of S3 under microscope; (**b**) AFM image of the as-received SLG supported by PMMA.

2.2. Structure Study Based on Raman Spectroscopy

Even though the layer number of the as-received sample was given in the technical data sheet, the layer number of the as-received graphene on PMMA was verified with confocal Raman spectroscopy (Horiba, LabRam Odyssey). In total, 30 random spots were tested. In the Raman spectroscopy test, a 532 nm laser with ~0.45 mW was focused on the graphene under $50\times$ objective. The integration time was 10 s. Spectra of the as-received sample are shown in Figure 2. No D peak (~1340 cm^{-1}) can be observed in the Raman spectra, indicating that the supported graphene has rare D band-related defects. Peaks at 1588.3 cm^{-1} (G band) and 2681.5 cm^{-1} (2D band) can be observed. We used a ratio ($I_{\mathrm{G}}/I_{\mathrm{2D}}$) of the intensity of the G band to the intensity of 2D band to evaluate the layer number of the as-received sample [37]. It was found that the layer number of each tested spot is 1. Thus, we can verify that the layer number of graphene in the whole sample is 1, and the graphene distributes on the PMMA uniformly. Since the to-be-measured sample was cut from the as-received sample, we can confirm that the graphene layer number of each to-be-measured sample is 1. The PMMA thickness, graphene layer number, length, and width for the four samples are summarized in Table 1.

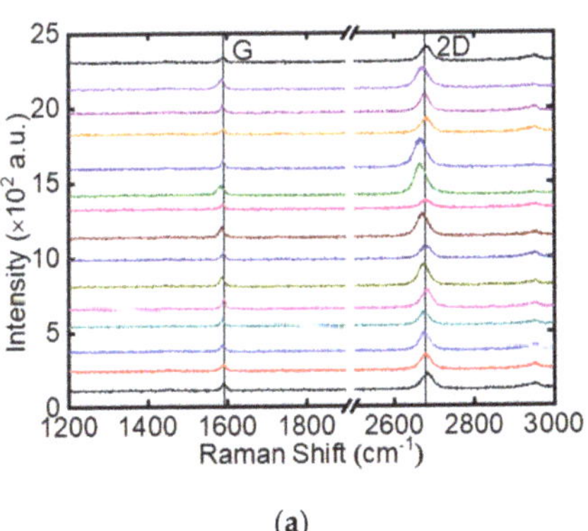

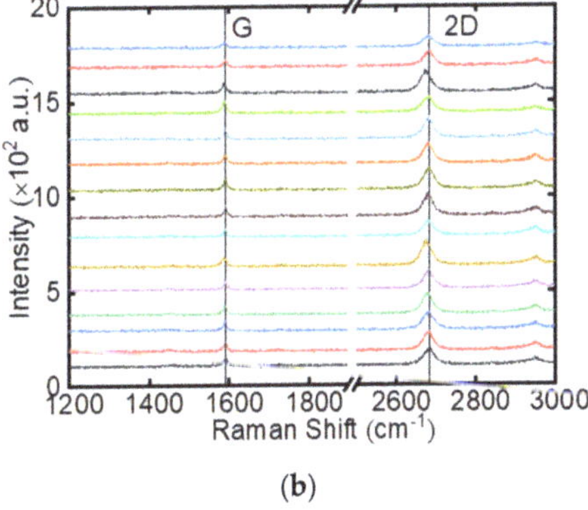

(a)

(b)

Figure 2. (**a**,**b**) Raman spectra of as-received sample.

Table 1. PMMA thickness, graphene layer number, length, and width of S1, S2, S3, S4, and S5.

Sample	S1	S2	S3	S4	S5
PMMA thickness(nm)	457	457	457	457	457
Graphene layer number	1	1	1	1	1
Length (mm)	1.73	1.53	2.35	2.25	2.09
Width (mm)	1.92	1.85	3.20	2.80	0.74

3. Thermal Transport Characterization of Giant-Scale Graphene Supported by PMMA

The thermal diffusivity of graphene supported by PMMA was characterized by diff-TET [36]. As shown in Figure 1a, the sample was suspended between two electrodes. Silver paste was used to eliminate the thermal contact resistance and electric contact resistance between the sample and the electrodes. The whole sample was placed in a vacuum chamber (Janis CCS-100/204N) to eliminate the convective effect on the measurement of the thermal diffusivity. During the experiment, a step current provided by Keithley 6221 was fed through the sample to induce joule heating. The rise of the temperature led to a change in resistance and voltage. The voltage evolution of the sample was recorded by an oscilloscope (Tektronix MDO32). The normalized temperature rise obtained from the experiment is determined as $T^* = (V - V_0)/(V_1 - V_0)$. Here, V_0 and V_1 are the initial voltage and steady-state voltage over the sample, respectively. The environmental temperature was controlled by the temperature controller which ranges from 7 K to 300 K. Since most of the samples were broken at 125 K with a sudden jump resistance to a very high value, we did the experiments from room temperature (RT) down to 125 K in 25 K steps. During the joule heating, the thermal transport in the sample can be regarded as one-dimensional, thus the energy governing equation can be expressed as:

$$\frac{\partial(\rho c_p T)}{\partial t} = k\frac{\partial^2 T}{\partial x^2} + \dot{q} \tag{1}$$

where ρ, c_p, and k are the density, specific heat capacity of the sample, respectively. $\dot{q}$ is the heating power per unit volume, which equals to $I^2 R_s / AL$. Here, A and L are the cross-sectional area and length of the sample, respectively. I and R_s are the fed-in current and the sample resistance, respectively. Since the two electrodes are much larger than the sample, the temperature of the two electrodes can be regarded as environmental temperature. Thus, the boundary conditions can be depicted as: $T(x = 0, x = L) = T_0$ (T_0: room temperature). The theoretical normalized temperature rise is defined as: $T^*(t) = [T(t) - T_0]/[T(t \to \infty) - T_0]$. The theoretical solution to Equation (1) is solved as:

$$T^* = \frac{48}{\pi^4}\sum_{m=1}^{\infty}\frac{1 - \exp\left[-(2m-1)^4\pi^2\alpha_{eff}t/L^2\right]}{(2m-1)^4} \tag{2}$$

A Matlab program created based on Equation (2) was used to fit the normalized temperature rise obtained by the experiments. The trial value of α_{eff} which gives the best fit of the experiment data was taken as the sample's effective thermal diffusivity. Figure 3b shows the normalized voltage evolutions and the fitting curves for S1 at 275, 200, and 125 K. Magnificent fitting was obtained. The TET technique has been rigorously proven to be a quick and effective method to measure the thermal diffusivity of various conductive and non-conductive micro/nanoscale samples. More details can be found in references [13,36].

The effective thermal diffusivity (α_{eff}) includes the radiation effect (α_{rad}) which can be expressed as:

$$\alpha_{rad} = 8\varepsilon k_B T^3 L^2 / (\pi^2 \delta \rho c_p) \tag{3}$$

where ε, k_B, and δ are emissivity, the Stefan–Boltzmann constant, and thickness of the sample, respectively. The emissivity of the sample is taken from [36] as 0.08. After obtaining the real thermal diffusivity (α_{real}), the effective thermal conductivity (k_{eff}) can be obtained as $k_{eff} = \alpha_{real} \cdot (\rho c_p)_p$. The volumetric heat capacity of PMMA was used for the whole sample with high accuracy due to the extremely low mass proportion of graphene. In part 2, the Raman spectroscopy study of graphene showed that the graphene is distributed on the PMMA uniformly and all the graphene in samples is found to be a single layer. The relationship between effective thermal conductivity and thermal conductivity of PMMA and graphene can be depicted as:

$$k_{eff} = \frac{k_g \delta_g + k_p \delta_p}{\delta_g + \delta_p} \tag{4}$$

Here, δ_p and δ_g are the thickness of PMMA and graphene, and are taken as 457 nm and 0.335 nm, respectively. k_p and k_g are thre thermal conductivities of PMMA and graphene, respectively. The temperature-dependent volumetric heat capacity and thermal conductivity of PMMA are taken from references [38,39]. The test methods of the heat capacity and k of PMMA are the vacuum calorimeter and the 3ω method, respectively [38,39]. The thermal conductivity of SLG supported by PMMA is obtained from the average graphene thermal conductivities of the four samples. Two critical points should be explained here. In thermal characterization, the graphene is first heated by the electrical current, then the thermal energy is transferred to the PMMA. Work by Liu et al., has proven that graphene and PMMA reached thermal equilibrium in the cross-sectional direction during thermal characterization [36]. Additionally, the interface thermal resistance ($\sim 10^{-2}$ K/W) between graphene and PMMA is neglectable in comparison to the thermal resistance ($\sim 10^{6}$ K/W) of PMMA. More details can be found in [36].

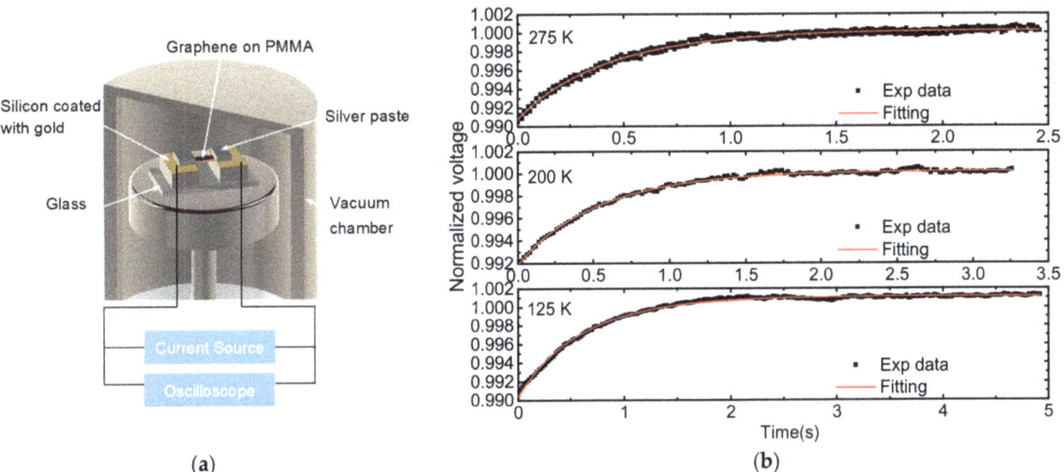

Figure 3. (a) Schematic setup of the TET measurement (not to scale); (b) Normalized voltage evolution and the fitting curve for S1 at 275, 200, and 125 K.

4. Results and Discussion

4.1. Abnormal Temperature Coefficient of Resistance for Graphene Supported by PMMA

The normalized resistance ($R^* = R/R_0$, R_0: resistance at RT) variation against the temperatures of S1, S2, S3, and S4 is presented in Figure 4a. The resistances of the four samples jump to very high values at 100 K, which indicates severe fractures in the sample. Thus, the normalized resistance is shown to be between RT and 125 K. It has been reported that the resistivity (ρ_e) of graphene is linearly proportional to T, as temperature is higher than the Bloch–Gruneisen temperature (Θ_{BG}) of graphene and is proportional to T^4 in the opposite case ($T < \Theta_{BG}$) [40]. However, the R^* of the four samples decreases slightly as temperature decreases, then increases as temperature is decreased from RT to 125 K.

The turning point is in the range of 250–275 K. The R^* of S2 and S4 is increased by 35% and 23%, while the R^* of S1 and S3 is decreased by 0.012% and 0.0075% as temperature changes from RT to 125 K. To obtain more details on the resistance of supported graphene, the temperature dependence of R^* of S5 was measured every 10–25 K for three rounds. Figure 4b shows the normalized resistance of three rounds for S5. As temperature decreases from RT to 150 K, the R^* trends of S5 are similar to that of S1 and S3. As temperature continues to decrease from 150 K, the R^* of S5_r1 and S5_r2 first decreases and then increases with temperature, while the R^* of S5_r3 continues to increase. Hinnefeld et al. studied the resistance of graphene supported by PDMS under strain and it was found that the tensile strain in the supported graphene can lead to rips in the graphene. These rips cause the resistance of the supported graphene to increase significantly with increased strain [41]. As temperature decreases, the graphene will expand and PMMA will contract. However, as the graphene is adhered to PMMA by van der Waals forces, the graphene will contract. The Raman spectra study of the experimental sample in the following part also confirms that the compressive strain builds in graphene as the temperature decreases from RT to 125.

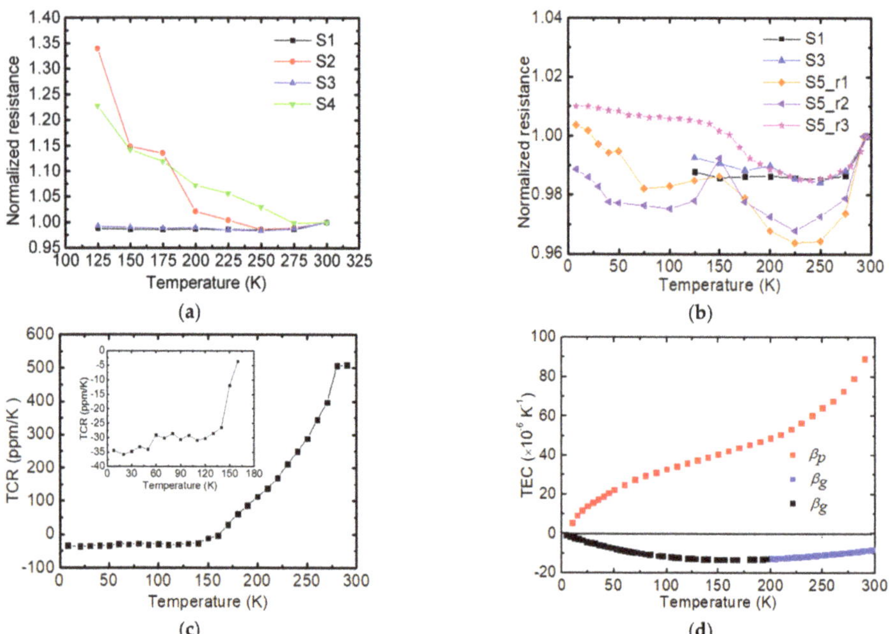

Figure 4. (**a**) Normalized resistance of S1, S2, S3, and S4. (**b**) Normalized resistance of S1, S3, S5_r1, S5_r2. and S5_r3. (**c**) Temperature coefficient of resistance of S5. The TCR was obtained based on the data of S5_r3. (**d**) Thermal expansion coefficient of PMMA (Reprinted/adapted with permission from Ref. [39]. Copyright 2013, Elsevier) and suspended graphene (Reprinted/adapted with permission from Ref. [40]. Copyright 2011, American Chemical Society). The data in blue square are obtained through experiment while the data shown in black square are estimated values.

The temperature coefficient of resistance (TCR) of graphene supported by PMMA is further discussed based on the data of S5_r3. The TCR of S5_r3 is shown in Figure 4c. The inset gives a close up to the TCR as temperature is in the range of 7–180 K. Apart from the intrinsic TCR of relaxed graphene, the overall TCR of the sample is affected by the thermal expansion of PMMA and graphene. The overall TCR of the whole sample can be described by the following equation: $TCR = TCR_i + (\beta_p - \beta_g)\gamma$. Here, TCR_i and γ are the intrinsic TCR of relaxed graphene and a positive constant, respectively. β_p and β_g are the thermal expansion coefficients (β) of PMMA and graphene, respectively. Figure 4d shows the TEC of graphene [40] and PMMA [39]. As graphene and PMMA are held together by van der Waals forces, the compressive strain/stress will build in graphene. As shown in Figure 4c, β_p decreases with decreasing temperature and remains positive when the temperature is above 0 K. β_g remains negative when temperature is lower than RT. In the entire temperature range, TCR_i remains negative [42,43]. When the temperature is close to RT, β_p is relatively large, which helps maintain a positive TCR in supported graphene. As temperature is decreased, the difference between β_p and β_g becomes smaller in comparison to the effect of TCR_i, causing the TCR of supported graphene to be negative.

4.2. Thermal Properties of SLG Supported by PMMA

The real thermal diffusivity without the effect of radiation of four samples is shown in Figure 5a. As temperature is decreased from RT, the α_{real} of S1, S2 and S4 decreases first, then the α_{real} of S2 remains constant while the α_{real} of S1 and S4 increases slightly. The change in the α_{real} of S3 is relatively small when compared to the other three samples. The k of SLG supported by PMMA is presented in Figure 5b. For comparison, the k of SLG supported by SiO_2 [14,27] and bilayer graphene with PMMA residue [42] are shown in Figure 5b. At RT, the k of supported SLG is 743 ± 167 W/(m·K), which is smaller than that of SiO_2-supported SLG (840 W/(m·K)) [27]. In [27], the k of supported graphene is measured by a comprehensive Raman optothermal method which eliminated the laser absorption uncertainty [27]. However, this work did not take the thermal non-equilibrium between different phonon branches into account. In this situation, the k of supported graphene is overestimated. The k in this work is larger than two literature values (~600 W/(m·K) for SiO_2-supported SLG [14] and 560 W/(m·K) for bilayer graphene with PMMA [42]). The differences in the k of our work and above two differences may be attributed to the different interface coupling strength.

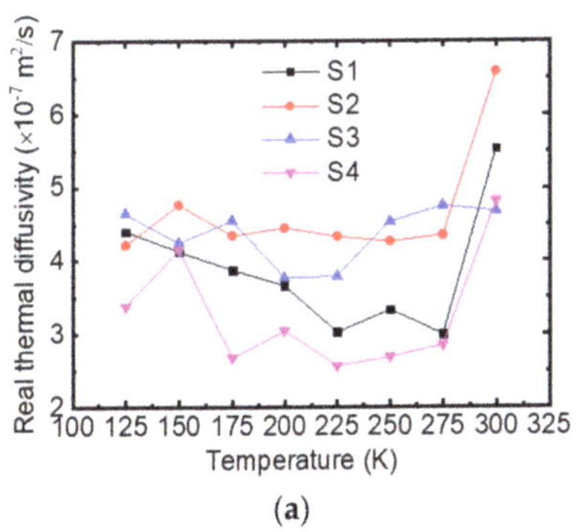
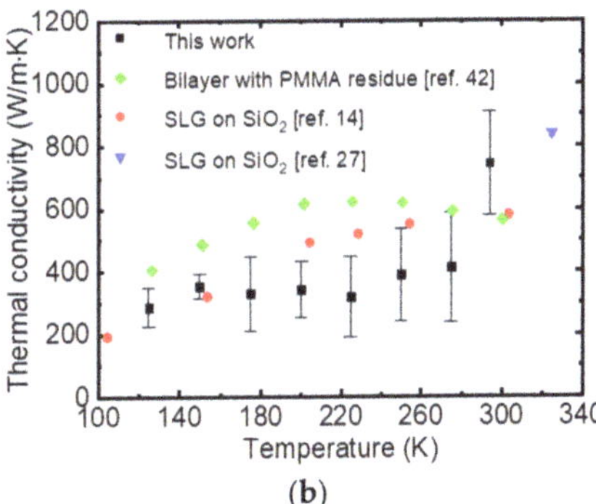

(a)   **(b)**

Figure 5. (a) Real thermal diffusivity without radiation effect for S1, S2, S3, and S4; (b) Thermal conductivity variation against temperature of SLG supported by PMMA. For comparison, the thermal conductivities of SLG supported by SiO_2 (Reprinted/adapted with permission from Ref. [14]. Copyright 2010, The American Association for the Advancement of Science) and bilayer graphene with PMMA residue (Reprinted/adapted with permission from Ref. [42]. Copyright 2011, American Chemical Society).

As temperature decreases from RT to 275 K, the k of supported SLG first decreases by 36.5%, which is much larger than the k reduction in [14,27]. As discussed in Section 4.1, there is compressive strain that builds in the graphene as temperature decreases from RT. There is limited work about the strain effect on the k of graphene supported by a flexible substrate. As such, we turn our attention to the effect on the k of suspended graphene. As reported in the literature, compressive strain in suspended graphene suppresses thermal conductivity [43]. This is attributed to the fluctuant structure created in graphene under compressive strain, under which the phonons can be scattered significantly more often [43,44]. With −0.05% strain in suspended graphene, it has been reported that the k can be reduced by 26% [43]. We speculate that the compressive strain induced by the TEC mismatch between graphene and PMMA results in a large k reduction when temperature decreases from RT to 275 K. Thus, Raman spectroscopy is used to investigate the G peak under different temperatures. The graphene sample suspended between two electrodes was placed in a cryogenic cell where the temperature can be controlled between 77 and 300 K. A confocal Raman is used to collect the Raman spectra of graphene under different temperatures.

Figure 6a shows the frequency shift of the G peak ($\Delta\omega_G$) of SLG on PMMA as a function of temperature. The G peak blueshifts as temperature goes down from RT. The temperature dependent frequency shift of the G peak is attributed to three parts: thermal expansion of the lattice ($\Delta\omega_G^E$); anharmonic effect ($\Delta\omega_G^A$), changing the phonon energy; and compressive strain ($\Delta\omega_G^S$), induced by the TEC mismatch between graphene and PMMA [45]. Thus, $\Delta\omega_G$ can be given by [45]:

$$\Delta\omega_G(T) = \Delta\omega_G^E(T) + \Delta\omega_G^A(T) + \Delta\omega_G^S(T) \tag{5}$$

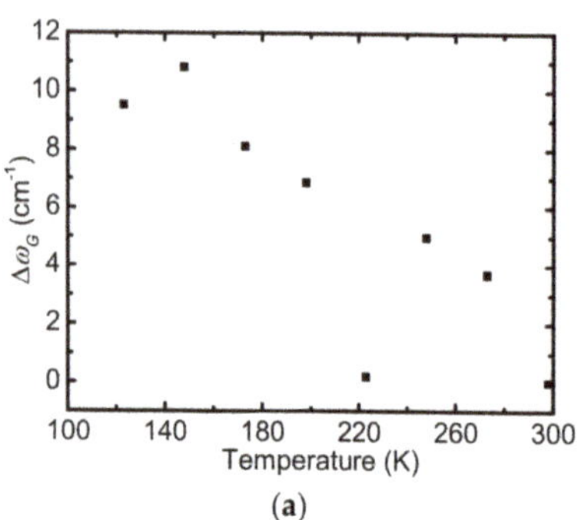
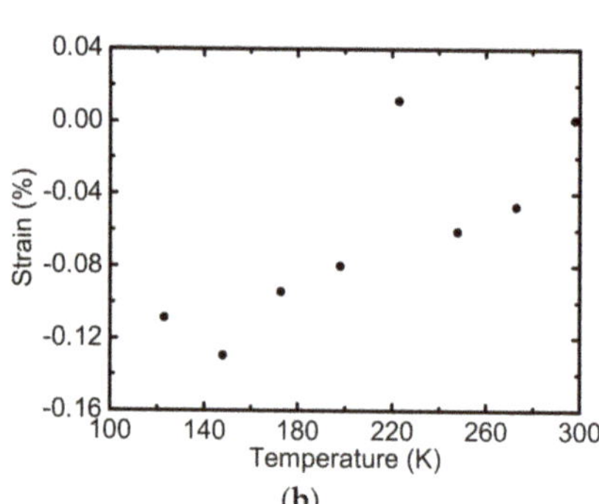

(a)
(b)

Figure 6. (**a**) Frequency shift of the G band of SLG supported by PMMA. (**b**) Temperature dependence of the strain buildup in graphene due to the TEC mismatch between graphene and PMMA.

The G-band frequency shift due to the strain induced by the TEC mismatch can be expressed as [45]:

$$\Delta\omega_G^S(T) = \beta\varepsilon(T). \tag{6}$$

where β is the biaxial strain coefficient of the G band. The biaxial strain coefficient of the G band has been determined to be around −70 cm^{-1}/% at RT [46]. Since the temperature dependence of the G-band frequency is more reliable than the TEC of graphene and PMMA, the G-band frequency shift due to temperature variation ($\Delta\omega_G^E + \Delta\omega_G^A$) obtained from theoretical calculations [47] are subtracted from $\Delta\omega_G$ to obtain $\Delta\omega_G^S(T)$. Strain buildup in graphene is calculated according to Equation (6). Figure 6b shows the temperature dependence of the strain buildup in graphene between graphene and PMMA. At 275 K, the strain is −0.047%, which indicates that compressive strain was built in graphene [46]. Li et al. reported that the k of suspended graphene can be reduced by 26% with −0.05% strain in graphene [43]. However, whether the −0.047% strain is sufficient to explain the large k reduction at 275 K is still doubtful. It also has been reported that the k of graphene nanoribbons are insensitive to compressive strain [48]. For graphene supported by flexible substrate, the effect of compressive strain on k still needs more theoretical calculations. As temperature continues decreasing from 275 K, the variation of k is not obvious, especially in the range of 150–225 K. We interpreted this trend from the structure of the sample. The SEM figure of S3 after cryogenic test is obtained and shown in Figure 7. A lot of micro-scale rips are observed. We speculate that there are micro-rips in the graphene when temperature is lower than 225 K. The rips suppress the k of graphene as compared to the k of supported graphene without any rips [14,42]. At lower temperatures, the effect of rips on thermal conductivity dominates, which keeps the changes in the k of graphene small.

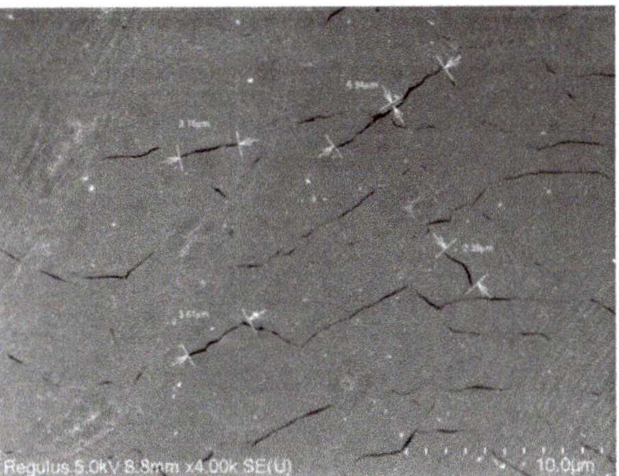

Figure 7. SEM figure of S3 after the cryogenic test. Many micro-scale rips can be observed.

5. Conclusions

In summary, we first reported the resistance–temperature relationship for supported graphene since this relationship is critical for explaining the behavior of graphene in thermal characterization. The TCR of our sample reduced from a positive value at RT to a negative value at low temperatures, while the free-standing graphene has a negative TCR throughout the entire temperature range. The abnormal R–T relationship is due to the TEC mismatch between graphene and PMMA and rips in graphene appearing at lower temperature. Using the diff-TET technique, the temperature dependence of the thermal conductivity of graphene supported by a flexible substrate is obtained. Through monitoring the blueshift of the Raman peak, compressive strain is confirmed to be built up in the graphene. The large reduction in k as temperature decreases from RT to 275 K is partly due to the compressive strain built up in graphene. This work can provide some guidance on the design of graphene-based electrothermal devices.

Author Contributions: Conceptualization, J.L. and L.M.; methodology, J.L., S.X. and Y.X.; validation, J.L., P.L.; investigation, P.L. and Q.W.; data curation, Y.X.; writing—original draft preparation, J.L.; writing—review and editing, J.L. and Y.X.; visualization, P.L.; supervision, J.L. and L.M.; project administration, J.L.; funding acquisition, J.L. and L.M. All authors have read and agreed to the published version of the manuscript.

Funding: Natural Science Foundation of Top Talent of SZTU 2019209; Guangdong Basic and Applied Basic Research Foundation 2020A1515110389; Project of Youth Innovative Talents in Higher Education Institutions of Guangdong 2020KQNCX069.

Institutional Review Board Statement: Not applicable.

Informed Consent Statement: Not applicable.

Data Availability Statement: The data presented in this study are available on request from the corresponding author.

Acknowledgments: Support of this work by the Natural Science Foundation of Top Talent of SZTU (2019209, to J.L.), the Guangdong Basic and Applied Basic Research Foundation (2020A1515110389, to J.L.), and the Project of Youth Innovative Talents in Higher Education Institutions of Guangdong (2020KQNCX069, to L.M.) is gratefully acknowledged.

Conflicts of Interest: The authors declare no conflict of interest.

References

1. Ghosh, S.; Calizo, I.; Teweldebrhan, D.; Pokatilov, E.P.; Nika, D.L.; Balandin, A.A.; Bao, W.; Miao, F.; Lau, C.N. Extremely high thermal conductivity of graphene: Prospects for thermal management applications in nanoelectronic circuits. *Appl. Phys. Lett.* **2008**, *92*, 151911. [CrossRef]
2. Geim, A.K. Graphene: Status and Prospects. *Science* **2009**, *324*, 1530–1534. [CrossRef] [PubMed]
3. Ni, G.X.; Yang, H.Z.; Ji, W.; Baeck, S.J.; Toh, C.T.; Ahn, J.H.; Pereira, V.M.; Ozyilmaz, B. Tuning Optical Conductivity of Large-Scale CVD Graphene by Strain Engineering. *Adv. Mater.* **2014**, *26*, 1081–1086. [CrossRef] [PubMed]
4. Novoselov, K.S.; Fal'ko, V.I.; Colombo, L.; Gellert, P.R.; Schwab, M.G.; Kim, K. A roadmap for graphene. *Nature* **2012**, *490*, 192–200. [CrossRef]
5. Gu, X.K.; Wei, Y.J.; Yin, X.B.; Li, B.W.; Yang, R.G. Colloquium: Phononic thermal properties of two-dimensional materials. *Rev. Mod. Phys.* **2018**, *90*, 041002. [CrossRef]
6. Bolotin, K.I.; Sikes, K.J.; Jiang, Z.; Klima, M.; Fudenberg, G.; Hone, J.; Kim, P.; Stormer, H.L. Ultrahigh electron mobility in suspended graphene. *Solid. State. Commun.* **2008**, *146*, 351–355. [CrossRef]
7. Lee, C.; Wei, X.D.; Kysar, J.W.; Hone, J. Measurement of the elastic properties and intrinsic strength of monolayer graphene. *Science* **2008**, *321*, 385–388. [CrossRef]
8. You, R.; Liu, Y.Q.; Hao, Y.L.; Han, D.D.; Zhang, Y.L.; You, Z. Laser Fabrication of Graphene-Based Flexible Electronics. *Adv. Mater.* **2020**, *32*, 1901981. [CrossRef]
9. Secor, E.B.; Lim, S.; Zhang, H.; Frisbie, C.D.; Francis, L.F.; Hersam, M.C. Gravure Printing of Graphene for Large-Area Flexible Electronics. *Adv. Mater.* **2014**, *26*, 1401052. [CrossRef] [PubMed]
10. Freitag, M.; Low, T.; Avouris, P. Increased Responsivity of Suspended Graphene Photodetectors. *Nano Lett.* **2013**, *13*, 1644–1648. [CrossRef] [PubMed]
11. Cai, X.Y.; Lai, L.F.; Shen, Z.X.; Lin, J.Y. Graphene and graphene-based composites as Li-ion battery electrode materials and their application in full cells. *J. Mater. Chem. A* **2017**, *5*, 15423–15446. [CrossRef]
12. Cai, C.L.; Wang, T.; Zhang, Y.X.; He, N.Y. Facile fabrication of ultra-large graphene film with high photothermal effect and thermal conductivity. *Appl. Surf. Sci.* **2021**, *563*, 150354. [CrossRef]
13. Cai, W.W.; Moore, A.L.; Zhu, Y.W.; Li, X.S.; Chen, S.S.; Shi, L.; Ruoff, R.S. Thermal Transport in Suspended and Supported Monolayer Graphene Grown by Chemical Vapor Deposition. *Nano Lett.* **2010**, *10*, 1645–1651. [CrossRef]
14. Seol, J.H.; Jo, I.; Moore, A.L.; Lindsay, L.; Aitken, Z.H.; Pettes, M.T.; Li, X.S.; Yao, Z.; Huang, R.; Broido, D.; et al. Two-Dimensional Phonon Transport in Supported Graphene. *Science* **2010**, *328*, 213–216. [CrossRef] [PubMed]
15. Ong, Z.Y.; Pop, E. Effect of substrate modes on thermal transport in supported graphene. *Phys. Rev. B* **2011**, *84*, 075471. [CrossRef]
16. Wei, Z.Y.; Yang, J.K.; Bi, K.D.; Chen, Y.F. Mode dependent lattice thermal conductivity of single layer graphene. *J. Appl. Phys.* **2014**, *116*, 153503. [CrossRef]
17. Xu, X.F.; Pereira, L.F.C.; Wang, Y.; Wu, J.; Zhang, K.W.; Zhao, X.M.; Bae, S.; Bui, C.T.; Xie, R.G.; Thong, J.T.L.; et al. Length-dependent thermal conductivity in suspended single-layer graphene. *Nat. Commun.* **2014**, *5*, 3689. [CrossRef] [PubMed]
18. Malekpour, H.; Ramnani, P.; Srinivasan, S.; Balasubramanian, G.; Nika, D.L.; Mulchandani, A.; Lake, R.K.; Balandin, A.A. Thermal conductivity of graphene with defects induced by electron beam irradiation. *Nanoscale* **2016**, *8*, 14608–14616. [CrossRef] [PubMed]
19. Hu, S.Q.; Chen, J.; Yang, N.; Li, B.W. Thermal transport transport in graphene with defect and doping: Phonon modes analysis. *Carbon* **2017**, *116*, 139–144. [CrossRef]
20. Li, M.Y.; Deng, T.Z.X.; Zheng, B.; Zhang, Y.; Liao, Y.G.; Zhou, H.M. Effect of Defects on the Mechanical and Thermal Properties of Graphene. *Nanomaterials* **2019**, *9*, 347. [CrossRef] [PubMed]
21. Chen, J.; Zhang, G.; Li, B.W. Substrate coupling suppresses size dependence of thermal conductivity in supported graphene. *Nanoscale* **2013**, *5*, 532–536. [CrossRef] [PubMed]
22. Li, M.; Zhang, J.C.; Hu, X.J.; Yue, Y. Thermal transport across graphene/SiC interface: Effects of atomic bond and crystallinity of substrate. *Appl. Phys. A* **2015**, *119*, 415–424. [CrossRef]
23. Liu, H.K.; Lin, Y.; Luo, S.N. Grain Boundary Energy and Grain Size Dependences of Thermal Conductivity of Polycrystalline Graphene. *J. Phys. Chem. C* **2014**, *118*, 24797–24802. [CrossRef]
24. Limbu, T.B.; Hahn, K.R.; Mendoza, F.; Sahoo, S.; Razink, J.J.; Katiyar, R.S.; Weiner, B.R.; Morell, G. Grain size-dependent thermal conductivity of polycrystalline twisted bilayer graphene. *Carbon* **2017**, *117*, 367–375. [CrossRef]
25. Lee, W.; Kihm, K.D.; Kim, H.G.; Shin, S.; Lee, C.; Park, J.S.; Cheon, S.; Kwon, O.M.; Lim, G.; Lee, W. In-Plane Thermal Conductivity of Polycrystalline Chemical Vapor Deposition Graphene with Controlled Grain Sizes. *Nano Lett.* **2017**, *17*, 2361–2366. [CrossRef] [PubMed]
26. Chen, S.; Li, Q.; Zhang, Q.; Qu, Y.; Ji, H.; Ruoff, R.S.; Cai, W. Thermal conductivity measurements of suspended graphene with and without wrinkles by microRaman mapping. *Nanotechnology* **2012**, *23*, 365701. [CrossRef] [PubMed]
27. Li, Q.Y.; Xia, K.L.; Zhang, J.; Zhang, Y.Y.; Li, Q.Y.; Takahashi, K.; Zhang, X. Measurement of specific heat and thermal conductivity of supported and suspended graphene by a comprehensive Raman optothermal method. *Nanoscale* **2017**, *9*, 10784–10793. [CrossRef]
28. Wang, R.D.; Wang, T.Y.; Zobeiri, H.; Li, D.C.; Wang, X.W. Energy and Charge Transport in 2D Atomic Layer Materials: Raman-Based Characterization. *Nanomaterials* **2020**, *10*, 1807. [CrossRef]

29. Li, Q.Y.; Katakami, K.; Ikuta, T.; Kohno, M.; Zhang, X.; Takahashi, K. Measurement of thermal contact resistance between individual carbon fibers using a laser-flash Raman mapping method. *Carbon* **2019**, *141*, 92–98. [CrossRef]

30. Li, Q.Y.; Zhang, X.; Takahashi, K. Variable-spot-size laser-flash Raman method to measure in-plane and interfacial thermal properties of 2D van der Waals heterostructures. *Int. J. Heat Mass Trans.* **2018**, *125*, 1230–1239. [CrossRef]

31. Vallabhaneni, A.K.; Singh, D.; Bao, H.; Murthy, J.; Ruan, X.L. Reliability of Raman measurements of thermal conductivity of single-layer graphene due to selective electron-phonon coupling: A first-principles study. *Phys. Rev. B* **2016**, *93*, 125432. [CrossRef]

32. Wang, R.D.; Zobeiri, H.; Xie, Y.S.; Wang, X.W.; Zhang, X.; Yue, Y.N. Distinguishing Optical and Acoustic Phonon Temperatures and Their Energy Coupling Factor under Photon Excitation in nm 2D Materials. *Adv. Sci.* **2020**, *7*, 2000097. [CrossRef]

33. Liu, J.; Li, P.; Zheng, H. Review on Techniques for Thermal Characterization of Graphene and Related 2D Materials. *Nanomaterials* **2021**, *11*, 2787. [CrossRef]

34. Wang, L.; Hu, B.B.; Li, B.W. Logarithmic divergent thermal conductivity in two-dimensional nonlinear lattices. *Phys. Rev. E* **2012**, *86*, 040101. [CrossRef] [PubMed]

35. Su, R.X.; Zhang, X. Size effect of thermal conductivity in monolayer graphene. *Appl. Therm. Eng.* **2018**, *144*, 488–494. [CrossRef]

36. Liu, J.; Xu, Z.L.; Cheng, Z.; Xu, S.; Wang, X.W. Thermal Conductivity of Ultrahigh Molecular Weight Polyethylene Crystal: Defect Effect Uncovered by 0 K Limit Phonon Diffusion. *ACS Appl. Mater. Inter.* **2015**, *7*, 27279–27288. [CrossRef]

37. Graf, D.; Molitor, F.; Ensslin, K.; Stampfer, C.; Jungen, A.; Hierold, C.; Wirtz, L. Spatially resolved raman spectroscopy of single- and few-layer graphene. *Nano Lett.* **2007**, *7*, 238–242. [CrossRef] [PubMed]

38. Putnam, S.A.; Cahill, D.G.; Ash, B.J.; Schadler, L.S. High-precision thermal conductivity measurements as a probe of polymer/nanoparticle interfaces. *J. Appl. Phys.* **2003**, *94*, 6785. [CrossRef]

39. Esposito, M.; Buontempo, S.; Petriccione, A.; Zarrelli, M.; Breglio, G.; Saccomanno, A.; Szillasi, Z.; Makovec, A.; Cusano, A.; Chhiuchiolo, A.; et al. and Giordano, M. Fiber Bragg Grating sensors to measure the coefficient of thermal expansion of polymers at cryogenic temperatures. *Sens. Actuators* **2013**, *189*, 195–203. [CrossRef]

40. D'Souza, R.; Mukherjee, S. First-principles study of the electrical and lattice thermal transport in monolayer and bilayer graphene. *Phys. Rev. B* **2017**, *95*, 085435. [CrossRef]

41. Hinnefeld, J.H.; Gill, S.T.; Zhu, S.; Swanson, W.J.; Li, T.; Mason, N. Reversible Mechanical and Electrical Properties of Ripped Graphene. *Phys. Rev. Appl.* **2015**, *3*, 014010. [CrossRef]

42. Pettes, M.T.; Jo, I.S.; Yao, Z.; Shi, L. Influence of Polymeric Residue on the Thermal Conductivity of Suspended Bilayer Graphene. *Nano Lett.* **2011**, *11*, 1195–1200. [CrossRef] [PubMed]

43. Li, X.B.; Maute, K.; Dunn, M.L.; Yang, R.G. Strain effects on the thermal conductivity of nanostructures. *Phys. Rev. B* **2010**, *81*, 245318. [CrossRef]

44. Guo, Z.X.; Zhang, D.; Gong, X.G. Thermal conductivity of graphene nanoribbons. *Appl. Phys. Lett.* **2009**, *95*, 163103. [CrossRef]

45. Yoon, D.; Son, Y.W.; Cheong, H. Negative Thermal Expansion Coefficient of Graphene Measured by Raman Spectroscopy. *Nano Lett.* **2011**, *11*, 3227–3231. [CrossRef]

46. Yoon, D.; Son, Y.W.; Cheong, H. Strain-Dependent Splitting of the Double-Resonance Raman Scattering Band in Graphene. *Phys. Rev. Lett.* **2011**, *106*, 155502. [CrossRef]

47. Bonini, N.; Lazzeri, M.; Marzari, N.; Mauri, F. Phonon anharmonicities in graphite and graphene. *Phys. Rev. Lett.* **2007**, *99*, 176802. [CrossRef]

48. Wei, N.; Xu, L.Q.; Wang, H.Q.; Zheng, J.C. Strain engineering of thermal conductivity in graphene sheets and nanoribbons: A demonstration of magic flexibility. *Nanotechnology* **2011**, *22*, 105705. [CrossRef]

 *nanomaterials*

Article

Microstructure and Superior Corrosion Resistance of an In-Situ Synthesized NiTi-Based Intermetallic Coating via Laser Melting Deposition

Cheng Deng [1], Menglong Jiang [1], Di Wang [1], Yongqiang Yang [1], Vyacheslav Trofimov [1], Lianxi Hu [2] and Changjun Han [1,*]

[1] School of Mechanical and Automotive Engineering, South China University of Technology, Guangzhou 510641, China; dengcheng@scut.edu.cn (C.D.); rong0610@mail.scut.edu.cn (M.J.); mewdlaser@scut.edu.cn (D.W.); meyqyang@scut.edu.cn (Y.Y.); trofimov@scut.edu.cn (V.T.)

[2] School of Materials Science and Engineering, Harbin Institute of Technology, Harbin 150001, China; hulx@hit.edu.cn

* Correspondence: cjhan@scut.edu.cn; Tel.: +86-13667208949

Abstract: A nickel–titanium (NiTi)-based intermetallic coating was in-situ synthesized on a Ti–6Al–4V (TC4) substrate via laser melting deposition (LMD) using Ni–20Cr and TC4 powders. Scanning electron microscopy, X-ray diffraction, a digital microhardness tester and an electrochemical analyzer were used to evaluate the microstructure, Vicker's microhardness and electrochemical corrosion resistance of the intermetallic coating. Results indicate that the microstructure of the intermetallic coating is composed of $NiTi_2$, NiTi and Ni_3Ti. The measured microhardness achieved is as high as ~850 $HV_{0.2}$, ~2.5 times larger than that of the TC4 alloy, which can be attributed to the solid solution strengthening of Al and Cr, dispersion strengthening of the intermetallic compounds, and grain refinement strengthening from the rapid cooling of LMD. During the electrochemical corrosion of 3.5% NaCl solution, a large amount of Ti ions were released from the intermetallic coating surface and reacted with Cl^- ions to form $[TiCl_6]^2$ with an increase in corrosion voltage. In further hydrolysis reactions, TiO_2 formation occurred when the ratio of $[TiCl_6]^{2-}$ reached a critical value. The in-situ synthesized intermetallic coating can achieve a superior corrosion resistance compared to that of the TC4 alloy.

Keywords: laser melting deposition; nickel–titanium coating; in-situ synthesis; corrosion resistance

Citation: Deng, C.; Jiang, M.; Wang, D.; Yang, Y.; Trofimov, V.; Hu, L.; Han, C. Microstructure and Superior Corrosion Resistance of an In-Situ Synthesized NiTi-Based Intermetallic Coating via Laser Melting Deposition. *Nanomaterials* **2022**, *12*, 705. https://doi.org/10.3390/nano12040705

Academic Editor: Giuseppe Lazzara

Received: 24 December 2021
Accepted: 16 February 2022
Published: 20 February 2022

Publisher's Note: MDPI stays neutral with regard to jurisdictional claims in published maps and institutional affiliations.

1. Introduction

Nickel–titanium (NiTi) alloys are widely used in aerospace, electric, chemical, and biological medicine applications due to their shape memory effect, high strength, good wear resistance, pseudo-elasticity and biocompatibility [1–4]. In particular, NiTi alloys exhibit excellent corrosion resistance because of the formation of a stable and dense titanium oxide passivation film on their surface to prevent further corrosion [5–7]. However, the passivation film is susceptible to damage and even being detached from NiTi alloys in a harsh corrosion environment (e.g., highly acidified chloride solutions) [8–11].

NiTi-based intermetallic coatings have been developed to improve the corrosion resistance of NiTi alloys and reduce the material costs by decreasing the usage of expensive NiTi alloys. For instance, Zhou et al. prepared NiTi-based intermetallic coatings on a Cu substrate by low pressure plasma spraying (LPPS) [12]. They found that the coatings were composed of NiTi, $NiTi_2$, Ni_3Ti, and Ti, and possessed higher anti-cavitation performance than coatings of pure Ti. Bitzer et al. prepared NiTi-based intermetallic coatings by LPPS on a $42CrMo_4$ steel and found that the NiTi-based intermetallic coatings were composed of NiTi, oxygen-containing $NiTi_2$ and Ni_4Ti_3 [13]. Such coatings showed significantly improved cavitation resistance compared with the UTP 730 stainless steel. However, defects, such as porosity and microcracks may deteriorate the corrosion resistance of LPPS-produced NiTi-based intermetallic coatings [14].

Laser surface modification techniques have been demonstrated to reduce the defects produced in NiTi-based coatings. Hiraga et al. produced dense NiTi-based intermetallic coatings using laser-plasma spraying hybrid cladding [14,15]. They found that the NiTi and Ni_3Ti intermetallic compounds formed in the $Ni_{50}Ti_{50}$ coating, while NiTi, Ni_3Ti and $NiTi_2$ appeared in the $Ni_{60}Ti_{40}$ coating. As a result, the corrosion resistance of the NiTi-based intermetallic coatings was ~40 times higher than that of the TC4 alloy. Cui et al. [16] studied the corrosion resistance of NiTi-based intermetallic coatings produced by laser remelting and laser gas nitriding. The corrosion resistance of the coatings were enhanced by the formation of a TiN phase on the coating surface. Moreover, Hu et al. [10] added TaC particles in $NiTi/NiTi_2$ composite coatings prepared by laser cladding for the enhancement of the corrosion resistance of the coatings. The TaC particles contributed to the formation of SiO_2 and Ta_2O_5 thereby hindering the further corrosion of the composite coatings.

In this paper, we report a laser melting deposition (LMD) method of preparing the in-situ synthesized NiTi-based intermetallic coatings for surface modification. We consider LMD as an innovative and effective process for producing high-performance NiTi-based intermetallic coatings. LMD, characterized by a rapid cooling rate up to 10^6–10^7 K/s, is a new and promising laser surface treatment technique for strengthening pure metals, alloys, and metal matrix composites [17,18]; it has been shown to be effective in improving the mechanical and wear properties of a number of metals and alloys because of its capability to impart desirable refined microstructures and reinforced phases through rapid solidification and chemical reactions. Another advantage for laser deposition would be the achievement of very complex geometries and customized designs [19]. Although some published works that did report that fine microstructure and superior wear resistance of NiTi-based intermetallic alloy coatings in-situ synthesized through LMD can be achieved [1,20], surprisingly few have reported on the electrochemical corrosion behavior of the in-situ synthesized NiTi-based intermetallic coatings.

In this work, Ni–20Cr and TC4 powders were utilized and mixed as the cladding materials to reduce the cost of raw powders. The microstructure and mechanics of a NiTi-based intermetallic coating in-situ synthesized by optimized LMD process were characterized using scanning electron microscopy, X-ray diffraction, and digital microhardness tester. Furthermore, for the first time, the corrosion behavior of the intermetallic coating was evaluated by electrochemical corrosion and immersion tests, and the underlying mechanism of the enhanced corrosion resistance of the in-situ synthesized NiTi-based coating was discussed.

2. Materials and Methods

2.1. Materials

A TC4 alloy with dimensions of $100 \times 60 \times 10$ mm^3 was used as the substrate for the coating. The chemical composition of the TC4 alloy is listed in Table 1. Ni–20Cr (wt%) and TC4 powders with a weight ratio of 4:1 were mechanically mixed at a speed of 300 rpm for 1 h in an alcohol atmosphere in a planetary ball mill (TJ-2L, procured from a company in Tianjin, China, TECHIN Ltd.). The powder-to-ball mass ratio was set as 1:3. The mixed powder was dried at 373 K for 2 h and then used as the cladding material.

Table 1. Chemical composition of TC4 powder used in this work.

Element	C	H	O	N	Fe	Al	V	Ti
Composition (wt%)	0.08	0.015	0.2	0.05	0.4	6.05	4.02	Bal.

2.2. LMD Coating Process

Prior to LMD, the surface of the TC4 substrate was polished and cleaned with alcohol. The LMD process was carried out using an IPG fiber laser with a wavelength of 1070 nm. A shielding of argon gas was used to protect the molten pool of LMD and deliver the mixed powders into the molten pool. A schematic configuration of LMD is depicted in Figure 1. The processing parameters were optimized to obtain the crack-free NiTi-based intermetallic coating by LMD: the laser power of 1 kW, the laser scanning speed of 600 mm/min, powder feeding rate of 0.8 g/min, the spot diameter of 2 mm, and overlapping rate of 50%. The height and width of NiTi-based intermetallic coating were ~1 mm and ~7 mm, respectively.

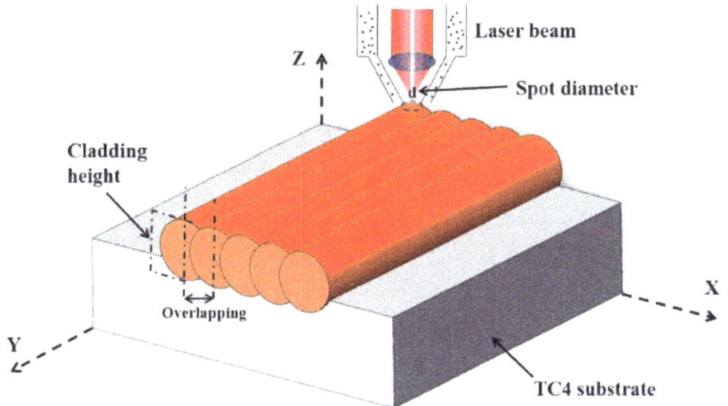

Figure 1. Schematic drawing of laser melting deposition.

After LMD, all the samples were cut from the substrate, polished, and then etched by Kroll's solution (10 mL HF, 15 mL HNO_3, and 75 mL H_2O). The microstructure of the NiTi-based intermetallic coating prepared by LMD was examined by field emission scanning electron microscopy (SEM, ZEISS Sigma 300) equipped with an X-ray energy-dispersive spectrometer (EDS). The phases were investigated by a D/MAX-2500 X-ray diffraction (XRD, Cu Kα at 40 kV and 40 mA, scanning rate of 0.02°/s). The microhardness of the intermetallic coating was tested using a HV-1000 Vickers digital microhardness tester with a load of 1.96 N and a dwelling time of 10 s. The reported microhardness was averaged from three samples for each condition.

The electrochemical corrosion resistance of the NiTi-based intermetallic coating was measured by a CHI604E electrochemical analyzer (Chenhua, Shanghai, China) in a 3.5 wt% NaCl solution. A standard three-electrode cell was composed of a working electrode made from a composite specimen with an exposed area of 1 cm^2, a platinum counter electrode, and a saturated calomel reference electrode. All the samples were immersed into the 3.5 wt% NaCl solution at room temperature for 1 h to stabilize the open circuit potential (OCP). Potentiodynamic polarization scanning was varied from −1.5 V to 4.0 V at a sweep rate of 5 mV/s. Electrochemical impedance spectroscopy (EIS) testing was performed at the OCP potentionstatically by scanning a frequency range from 10^{-2}~10^5 Hz with a voltage perturbation amplitude of 10 mV. The corresponding Nyquist and Bode plots were fitted by impedance spectrum data using Zsimpwin software. All potentials were measured at least three times.

Prior to immersion testing, the samples were ground with waterproof silicon carbide papers up to 2000 grits under running water, then cleaned in acetone, ethanol for 30 min using ultrasound, and finally dried at room temperature. The static immersion testing was conducted using 3.5% NaCl solution for 7 days at room temperature. Three samples were tested for each group.

3. Results and Discussion

3.1. Microstructure of the NiTi-Based Intermetallic Coating

Figure 2a shows the XRD pattern of the NiTi-based intermetallic coating in-situ synthesized by LMD. The results indicate that it consists of a dominant $NiTi_2$ phase with a face-centered cubic (fcc) structure, while the other two intermetallic phases of NiTi and Ni_3Ti have primitive hexagonal crystal structures (Figure 2a). The grain sizes of each phase can be determined from the Bragg peak width at half of the maximum intensity using the Scherrer formula [21]:

$$D = \frac{0.9\lambda}{B\cos\theta},$$ (1)

where D is the grain size, λ is the wavelength of the X-ray radiation, B is the peak width at half of the maximum intensity, and θ is the Bragg diffraction angle. The grain sizes of NiTi, $NiTi_2$ and Ni_3Ti were calculated as ~30 nm, ~17 nm and ~25 nm, respectively. According to the previous works [22,23], the volume fractions of the NiTi, $NiTi_2$ and Ni_3Ti phases can be calculated as ~20%, ~52% and ~28%, respectively, (as shown in Figure 2b).

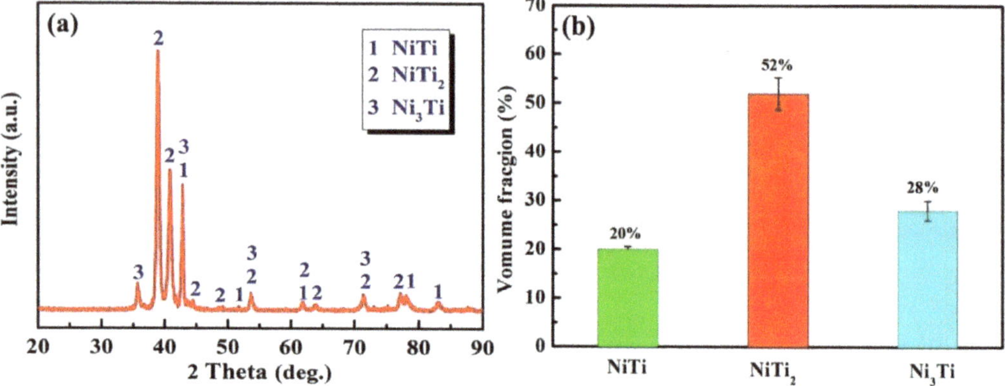

Figure 2. (**a**) X-ray diffraction (XRD) pattern; (**b**) The estimated volume fraction of phase constituents in the intermetallic coating.

Figure 3 shows the microstructure of the NiTi-based intermetallic coating in-situ synthesized by LMD. As shown in Figure 3a, the presence of three distinct regions (as marked by I, II and III) can be observed from the top to the bottom of the coating. The petal-like dendritic microstructure is formed in region I, with a grain size of a maximum of ~20 μm in length (marked as A). Based on the XRD results (Figure 2a) and EDS analysis (Table 2), the petal-like dendrites can be identified as NiTi, while the intermetallic (marked B) located between the petal-like dendrites is identified as Ni_3Ti. Moreover, region II is mainly composed of equiaxial or columnar dendrites (marked as C and D), which can be identified as $NiTi_2$. The length of the oriented dendrites is measured as ~80 μm and the main stems are angled ~30° toward the normal direction of the coating-substrate interface (marked as D).

Generally, thermocapillarity caused the violent stirring and convection in the molten pool [24], thus, increasing the longer lifespan in the center of the molten pool than that at the bottom of the molten pool; this, in turn, resulted in the non-uniform distribution of solutes and the temperature in front of the solid/liquid interface. Therefore, the growth direction of dendrites can deviate from the normal direction of the coating/substrate interface. However, coarse dendritic arms can be formed because of a relatively slow solidification speed at the bottom of the molten pool [25]. It is seen that large secondary dendritic arms appear at the bottom of region II (marked E), and the lateral growths of dendrites occur near the coating/substrate interface (marked F); these phenomena are attributed to a relatively larger specific surface area of the smaller dendritic arms, facilitating the growths of larger dendritic arms by way of consuming the smaller dendritic arms to reduce the total surface energy. The longer time the dendrites coarsening takes, the larger spacing the dendritic arms possess. Hence, an increase in the distance from the coating/substrate interface can decrease the spacing of secondary dendritic arms.

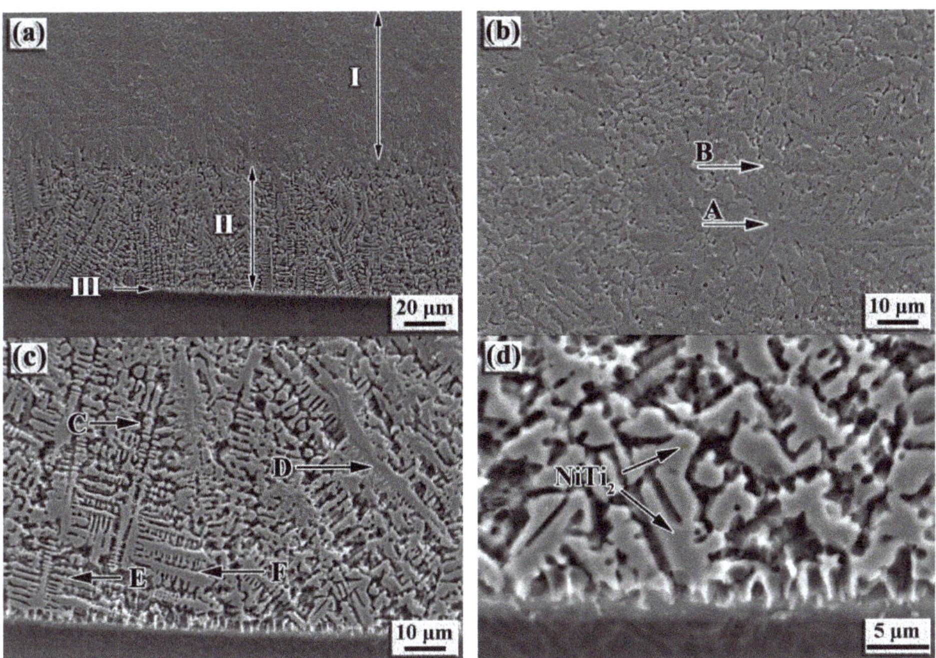

Figure 3. SEM images showing the microstructure of the in-situ synthesized NiTi-based intermetallic coating via LMD: (**a**) Cross-sectional morphology; (**b**) Region I; (**c**) Region II; (**d**) Region III.

Table 2. Element compositions of the intermetallic coating from EDS measurement.

Location	Composition (wt%)				
	Al	Ti	V	Cr	Ni
A	2.98	44.33	1.63	8.01	43.01
B	3.93	56.61	1.87	4.93	32.66
C	3.59	56.79	1.61	6.86	31.16
D	4.1	47.27	4.27	16.95	27.41
E	1.84	58.99	1.48	3.42	34.27
F	5.14	56.86	1.49	3.89	32.62

In addition, planar growths are seen at region III; such features indicate that the metallurgical bonding is generated at the coating/substrate interface. According to rapid solidification theory, the characteristics of the microstructure growths are related to the ratio G/R, where G is the temperature gradient and R is the solidification front rate. The R value is related to the laser scanning speed V_S directly and can be described as follows [26,27]:

$$R = V_s \cos \theta \tag{2}$$

where θ is the angle between V_S and R, h is the cladding height, and A is the spot diameter, as schematized in Figure 4. Prominently, R starts off with zero at the bottom of the molten pool but increases rapidly to the maximum value. However, G starts off with the largest value at the bottom of the molten pool while decreasing gradually toward the surface of the molten pool. Therefore, the G/R value approaches an infinite value at the bottom of the molten pool just corresponding to the planar growths. With the increasing distance far away from the coating/substrate interface, the G/R value decreases, inferring the presence of a constitutional supercooling ahead of the solidification front. Hence, the planar solid/liquid interface becomes unstable, resulting in the formation of dendrites (Figure 3d).

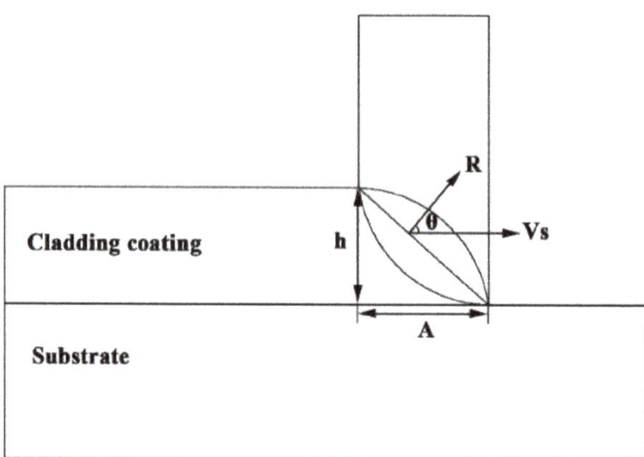

Figure 4. Schematic diagram of angle relationship between the solidification front rate and the laser scanning speed.

During LMD, there was a rapid phase transformation from the liquid phase to β-Ti for the cladding powders. According to the phase diagram of Ni-Ti alloy (Figure 5) [28], when the thermal diffusion continued, Ni₃Ti and NiTi formed with a eutectic reaction occurring in the liquid phase at a temperature of 1583 K.

$$L \rightarrow NiTi + Ni_3Ti \tag{3}$$

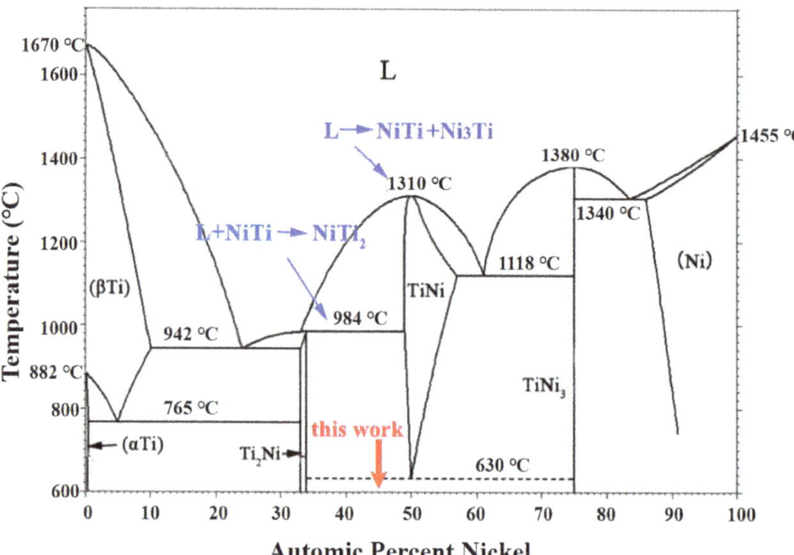

Figure 5. Phase diagram of Ni-Ti alloy showing phase transformation at different temperatures [28].

As the atom ratio of Ni to Ti is 77.99:86.33 (less than 1:1) in this work, a peritectic reaction between the liquid phase L$'$ and the formed NiTi in the titanium-rich side can proceed, resulting in the formation of another intermetallic compound $NiTi_2$ at a temperature of 1257 K [28–30]:

$$L' + NiTi \rightarrow NiTi_2 \tag{4}$$

For Ni-Ti binary system at different temperatures, NiTi (formation enthalpy $\Delta H = -67$ kJ/mol), $NiTi_2$ ($\Delta H = -83$ kJ/mol), Ni_3Ti ($\Delta H = -140$ kJ/mol) intermetallic compounds can be formed with exothermic reactions occurring [31–33]. Ni_3Ti can be formed firstly during LMD because of its minimum formation enthalpy. According to Equation (4), when cooling proceeds, $NiTi_2$ can be produced from the interaction between the formed NiTi and the residual liquid phase L$'$. This is the reason to explain the presence of dominant $NiTi_2$ phase constituent in the intermetallic coating (Figure 2).

The formation mechanism of the petal-like dendrites can be explained as follows. The intermetallic compounds (NiTi and Ni_3Ti) can grow rapidly at the initial stage of rapid solidification due to constitutional supercooling. Afterward, the Ni_3Ti grows rapidly into the coarse dendritic branch and the Ti atoms diffuse into the liquid phase. The supersaturated Ni-based phase containing rich Ti atoms is precipitated, as the subsequent phase transforms into a NiTi intermetallic and grows on the surface of the primary Ni_3Ti intermetallic. Consequently, the duplex phase nucleation sites with the interface of the intergrowth are formed, supplying the atoms for the neighboring phase to grow harmoniously, which depends on the diffusivity of the solute atoms, such as Ni, Cr and Ti to diffuse continually on the interface of Ni_3Ti and NiTi intermetallics. Moreover, the eutectic Ni_3Ti and NiTi phases are characterized by the non-facet growth of the unshaped interface. As such, the eutectics are formed by the intergrowth of Ni_3Ti and NiTi, both of which present different crystal structures (Figure 3b). Therefore, the petal-like eutectic intermetallics grow in terms of the intergrowth model of layer and slice during LMD.

3.2. Microhardness of NiTi-Based Intermetallic Coating

Figure 6 shows the microhardness of the NiTi-based intermetallic coating in-situ synthesized by LMD. It was observed that the average microhardness of the NiTi-based intermetallic coating is ~850 $HV_{0.2}$, which is ~2.5 times that of the substrate (~350 $HV_{0.2}$); this can be attributed to the formation of $NiTi_2$, dispersion strengthening, solid solution strengthening, and grain refinement strengthening. First, the very important factor is the presence of the dominant $NiTi_2$ phase in a face-centered cubic (fcc) structure with high hardness (HV700) and strong atomic bonds, thereby, increasing the overall hardness of NiTi-based intermetallic coating. In addition, these intermetallic compounds, such as NiTi and Ni_3Ti (Figure 2) derived from the in-situ reactions of Ni and Ti atoms during LMD of Ni-20Cr and TC4 powders, are dispersedly distributed in the NiTi-based intermetallic coating, creating the dispersion strengthening effect. Moreover, the diffusion of a large number of alloying elements, such as Al and Cr into the NiTi, NiTi2 and Ni3Ti, results in their lattice distortions and solid solution strengthening. Finally, the formation of fine-grained dendrites in the intermetallic coating due to rapid solidification is essential to increase the overall hardness as well.

3.3. Electrochemical Corrosion of the NiTi-Based Intermetallic Coating

Figure 7 shows the anodic polarization curves of the NiTi-based intermetallic coating and Ti6Al4V alloy in 3.5% NaCl solution at room temperature. A distinct passivation behavior can be observed between the intermetallic coating and TC4 alloy, and the passivation region of the TC4 alloy is significantly larger than that of the NiTi based intermetallic coating. The presence of a stable passivation platform for the TC4 alloy initiates from the corrosion voltage reaching around −0.3 V. However, the stable passivation of the intermetallic coating is formed at a corrosion voltage beyond 3 V, and a successive fluctuation of the curve in the range of −0.3 V to 3 V can be observed. This fluctuation can be attributed to the formation of different passivation films on the intermetallic coating surface, which is derived from different distributions of the intermetallic phases, such as NiTi$_2$, NiTi and Ni$_3$Ti. As a result, the polarization curve is changed from a passivation state to an active state, resulting in the instability of the passivation platform [34].

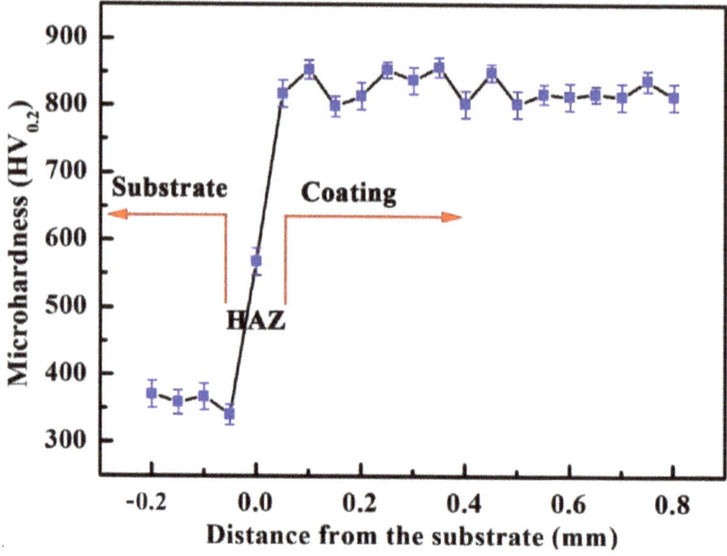

Figure 6. Microhardness of the NiTi-based intermetallic coating. HAZ represents heat affected zone.

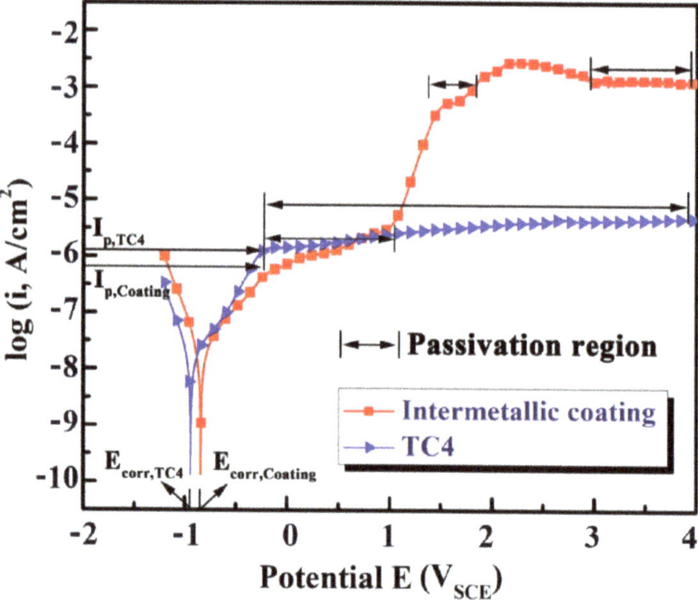

Figure 7. Potential dynamic curves of the NiTi-based intermetallic coating and TC4 alloy in the 3.5 wt% NaCl solution.

The corrosion potential E_{corr}, corrosion current density I_{corr}, and passivation current density I_p are the important parameters to evaluate the corrosion resistance of materials, as shown in Table 3. The E_{corr} value of the NiTi-based intermetallic coating is higher than that of the TC4 alloy, indicating much better stability of the passivation film formed in the coating [35,36]. The intermetallic coating obtains the I_{corr} value of 1.977×10^{-7} A/cm^2, which is slightly smaller than that of the TC4 alloy (2.068×10^{-7} A/cm^2). A lower I_{corr} indicates a smaller corrosion rate of the passivation film and better corrosion resistance [37,38]. In addition, when the corrosion voltage is less than 1 V, the I_p value of the intermetallic coating is smaller than that of the TC4 alloy. A larger I_p results in the faster dissolution of the passivation film. Therefore, the intermetallic coating is beneficial for improving the corrosion resistance of the TC4 alloy substrate.

Table 3. Corrosion parameters of the intermetallic coating and TC4 alloy in Figure 7.

Sample	E_{corr} (V)	I_{corr} (A/cm^2)	I_p (A/cm^2)
Immiscible coating	−0.854	1.977×10^{-7}	-6.2 ± 0.01
TC4 alloy	−0.943	2.068×10^{-7}	-5.8 ± 0.01

To further study the corrosion characteristics of the intermetallic coating and TC4 alloy, electrochemical impedance spectroscopy (EIS) was measured in a 3.5% NaCl solution. The Nyquist results of EIS are illustrated in Figure 8a. It is seen that a similar semicircle capacitive impedance loop exists in the Nyquist curves of both the intermetallic coating and TC4 alloy. However, the radii of the capacitive impedance loop of the intermetallic coating are larger than that of the TC4 alloy. The larger the radius of the capacitive impedance loop indicates the higher corrosion resistance [39,40]. Figure 8b,c show the Bode results of EIS. The maximum |Z| value of the intermetallic coating and TC4 alloy present a linear change with a slope of ~−1 in the low-frequency region (10^{-2}–10^0 Hz) and the intermediate frequency region (10^{-2}~10^3 Hz).

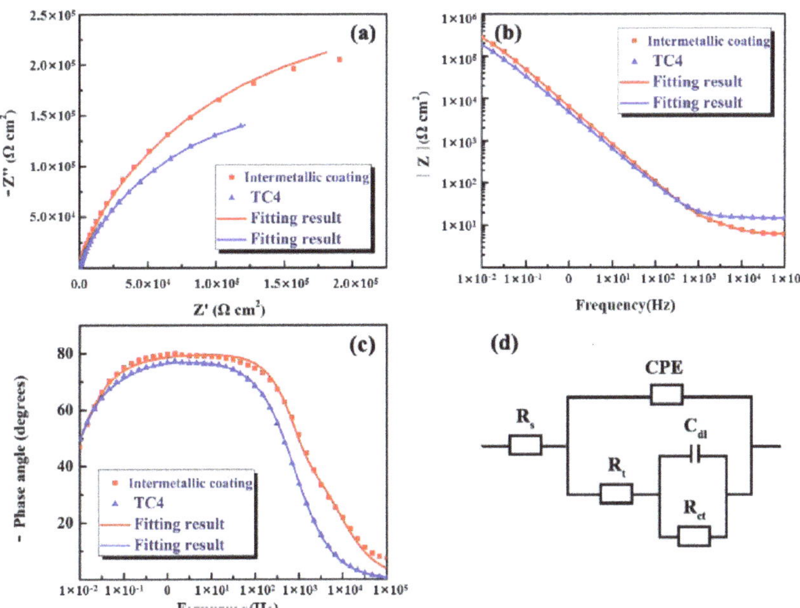

Figure 8. EIS results of the NiTi-based intermetallic composite coating and TC4 alloy in the 3.5 wt% NaCl solution: (**a**) Nyquist curves; (**b**,**c**) Bode curves; (**d**) Equivalent circuit.

The phase angles of the intermetallic coating and TC4 alloy increase, and the phase angle of the intermetallic coating (~90°) is slightly higher than that of TC4 alloy, indicating a typical capacitance behavior. The greater angle values of the coating indicate its better corrosion resistance, which is consistent with the results of polarization curves (Figure 7). This can be confirmed by the equivalent circuits shown in Figure 8d. To obtain the optimal fitting results, the equivalent circuits chosen χ^2 (chi-squared) must be in the range of 10^{-4}–10^{-3} and the results are listed in Table 4. As shown in Figure 8d, R_s can be regarded as the solution resistance, R_t is the resistance of the passivation film on the TC4 alloy surface during electrochemical corrosion, and R_{ct} is defined as the charge transfer resistance. The values of R_s and R_t of the intermetallic coating are smaller than those of the TC4 alloy, while the R_{ct} value of the intermetallic coating is much larger than that of the TC4 alloy. The higher R_{ct} indicates the higher charge transfer resistance and resultant better corrosion resistance.

Table 4. Electrochemical results obtained from equivalent circuits fitting of the intermetallic coating and TC4 alloy in the 3.5% NaCl solution.

Sample	R_S (Ω cm^2)	R_t (Ω cm^2)	R_{ct} (Ω cm^2)	C_{d1} (F cm^{-2})	Q1-Y_0 (Ω^{-1} cm^{2}s^n)	n_1	χ^2
NiTi-based coating	6.931	23.99	5.69×10^5	4.94×10^{-6}	2.63×10^{-5}	0.8628	8.6×10^{-4}
TC4 alloy	14.82	2.459×10^5	1.33×10^5	3.27×10^{-5}	4.29×10^{-5}	0.8548	1.2×10^{-4}

The equivalent circuit of the intermetallic coating is mainly composed of the double layer capacitance and constant phase angle. This indicates that double layer capacitance C_{dl} consists of the NaCl solution and coating, and the constant phase angle (CPE) is composed of the coating and TC4 substrate. Generally, CPE is defined as $Z_{CPE} = [Z_0(jw)^n]^{-1}$, where Z_0 is the constant of CPE, $j^2 = -1$ is imaginary, w is the angular frequency (w = $2\pi f$), and n is the index of CPE ($-1 \leq n \leq 1$) [41–43]. As shown in Table 4, the n value of the intermetallic coating (0.8628) is slightly greater than that of the TC4 alloy (0.8548), indicating that the passivation film on the intermetallic coating is denser than that on the TC4 alloy. Furthermore, the χ^2 (chi-squared) values of the intermetallic coating and the TC4 alloy are all in the order of ~10^{-4}, showing a good fitting result.

During electrochemical corrosion, the different concentrations of Cl$^-$ ions agglomerate together on the surface of the intermetallic coating to replace the internal O ions, resulting in pitting. The schematic of the pitting formation process is illustrated in Figure 9. The corrosion current density increases quickly following the pitting process. With an increase in the corrosion voltage, the passivation platform of the intermetallic coating is punctured and a large amount of Ti ions are released to react with Cl$^-$ ions and form [TiCl$_6$]$^{2-}$. When the corrosion voltage is increased to ~3 V, [TiCl$_6$]$^{2-}$ reaches a certain critical value in the solution, and hereby, TiO$_2$ is produced from the hydrolysis reaction to protect the intermetallic coating from further corrosion [5,44]. Moreover, slight pitting can be found on the surface of the intermetallic coating (Figure 10a), while it becomes serious on the surface of the TC4 alloy (Figure 10b). This confirms that the intermetallic coating has superior corrosion resistance than the TC4 alloy during the electrochemical corrosion of 3.5% NaCl solution.

The intermetallic coating and TC4 alloy were immersed into the 3.5 wt% NaCl solution for 7 days to validate the results of polarization curves and EIS. Figure 11 shows the surface morphology of the intermetallic coating and TC4 alloy after the immersion testing. The surface of the intermetallic coating is relatively smooth and only slight pitting can be observed on the surface of the intermetallic coating (Figure 11a). Comparatively, the sizes and amounts of the pits on the TC4 surface are much larger than those on the surface of the intermetallic coating (Figure 11b). Therefore, the immersion results also demonstrate better corrosion resistance for the intermetallic coating than that of the TC4 alloy, which is in good agreement with the results of polarization curves and EIS.

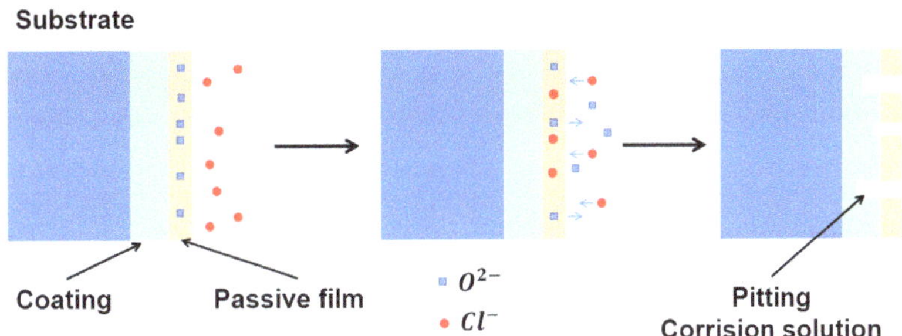

Figure 9. Schematic illustration of the pitting of the NiTi-based intermetallic coating in the 3.5 wt% NaCl solution.

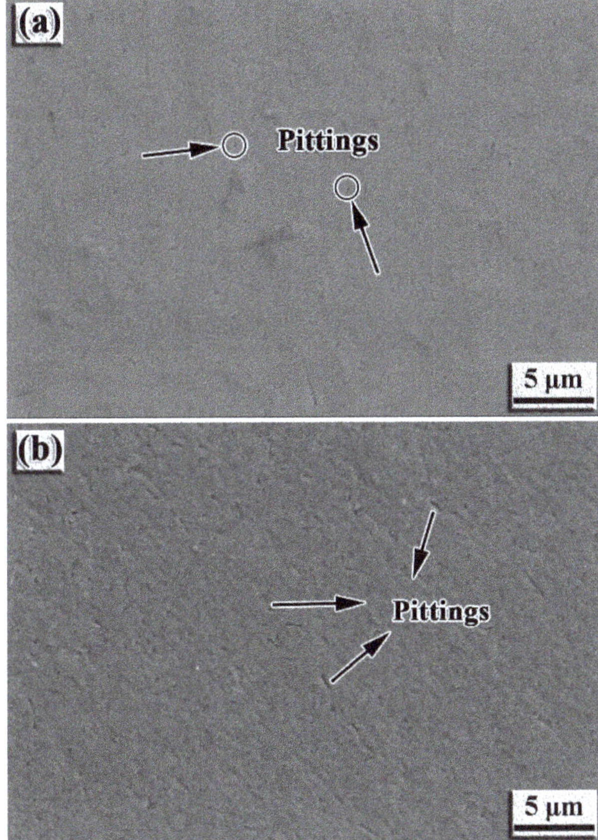

Figure 10. SEM images showing the morphology of the samples after electrochemical corrosion: (**a**) NiTi-based intermetallic coating; (**b**) TC4 alloy.

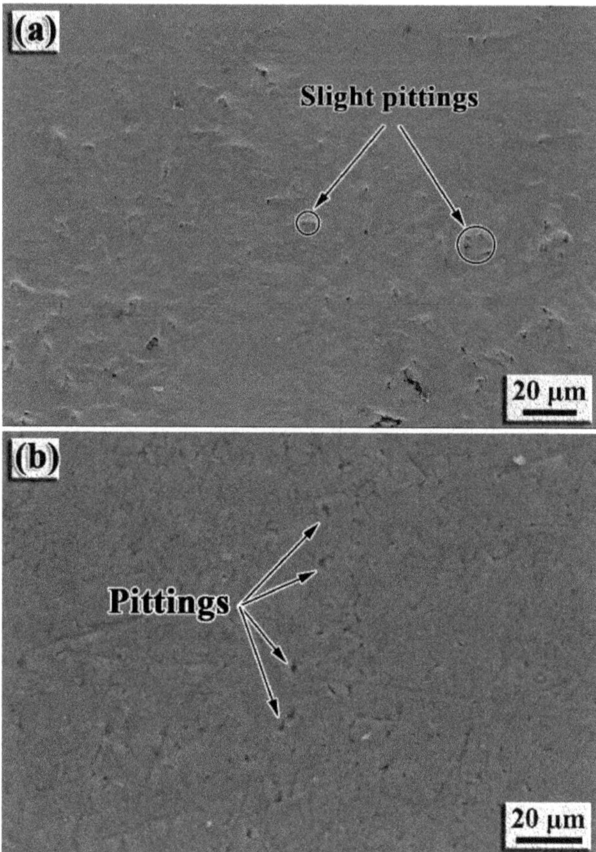

Figure 11. SEM images showing the morphology of the samples after immersing test in the 3.5 wt.% NaCl solution for 7 days at room temperature: (**a**) NiTi-based intermetallic coating; (**b**) TC4 alloy.

4. Conclusions

This work investigates the microstructure, mechanical properties, and electrochemical corrosion resistance of a NiTi-based intermetallic coating in-situ synthesized by LMD. The main findings are presented as follows.

(1) The NiTi-based intermetallic coating was in-situ synthesized on the TC4 substrate by LMD using a mixed powder of Ni-20Cr and TC4. The phases of the coating are composed of the intermetallic compounds of $NiTi_2$, $NiTi$, and Ni_3Ti, and their volume fractions are ~52%, ~20% and ~28%, respectively.

(2) The microhardness of the intermetallic coating is ~850 $HV_{0.2}$, which is ~2.5 times larger than that of the TC4 alloy. The high microhardness can be attributed to the solid solution strengthening of Al and Cr, dispersion strengthening of the intermetallic compounds, and grain refinement strengthening from the rapid solidification.

(3) The intermetallic coating exhibits better corrosion resistance than the TC4 alloy. With the increase in the corrosion voltage, a large amount of Ti ions react with the Cl^- ions to form $[TiCl_6]^{2-}$ in the solution. When $[TiCl_6]^{2-}$ reaches a certain critical value, TiO_2 is formed by hydrolysis reaction to protect the intermetallic coating from further corrosion. Slight pitting appears on the coating surface, while large pits can be observed on the TC4 surface.

Author Contributions: C.D.: Conceptualization, Methodology, Data curation, Formal analysis, Writing—original draft, Funding acquisition. M.J.: Methodology, Data curation, Formal analysis, Writing—review & editing. D.W.: Writing—review & editing. Y.Y.: Conceptualization, Resources, Funding acquisition, Writing—review & editing. V.T.: Writing—review & editing. L.H.: Writing—review & editing. C.H.: Conceptualization, Validation, Supervision, Writing—review & editing. All authors have read and agreed to the published version of the manuscript.

Funding: This research was funded by National Natural Science Foundation of China, grant number U2001218; the Guangdong Basic and Applied Basic Research Foundation, grant number 2020A1515110699; the Guangdong Basic and Applied Basic Research Foundation, grant number 2021A1515110527; National Engineering Research Center of Near-Net-Shape Forming for Metallic Materials Open Fund, SCUT, grant number 2020003.

Data Availability Statement: Not applicable.

Conflicts of Interest: The authors declare that they have no known competing financial interests or personal relationships that could have appeared to influence the work reported in this paper.

References

1. Gao, F.; Wang, H.M. Effect of TiNi in dry sliding wear of laser melt deposited $Ti_2Ni/TiNi$ alloys. *Mater. Charact.* **2008**, *59*, 1349–1354. [CrossRef]
2. Wang, L.; Xie, L.; Zhang, L.C.; Chen, L.; Ding, Z.; Lv, Y.; Zhang, W.; Lu, W.; Zhang, D. Microstructure evolution and superelasticity of layer-like NiTiNb porous metal prepared by eutectic reaction. *Acta Mater.* **2018**, *143*, 214–226. [CrossRef]
3. Wang, D.; Liu, L.Q.; Deng, G.W.; Deng, C.; Bai, Y.C.; Yang, Y.Q.; Wu, W.H.; Chen, J.; Liu, Y.; Wang, Y.G.; et al. Recent progress on additive manufacturing of multi-material structures with laser powder bed fusion. *Virtual Phys. Prototyp.* **2022**. [CrossRef]
4. Li, D.Y. Development of novel wear-resistant materials: TiNi-based pseudoelastic tribomaterials. *Mater. Des.* **2000**, *21*, 551–555. [CrossRef]
5. Alves, V.A.; Reis, R.Q.; Santos, I.C.B.; Souza, D.G.; Goncalves, T.d.; Pereira-da-Silva, M.A.; Rossi, A.; da Silva, L.A. In situ impedance spectroscopy study of the electrochemical corrosion of Ti and Ti–6Al–4V in simulated body fluid at 25 °C and 37 °C. *Corros. Sci.* **2009**, *51*, 2473–2482. [CrossRef]
6. Lu, H.Z.; Ma, H.W.; Cai, W.S.; Luo, X.; Wang, Z.; Song, C.H.; Yin, S.; Yang, C. Stable tensile recovery strain induced by a Ni4Ti3 nanoprecipitate in a $Ni_{50.4}Ti_{49.6}$ shape memory alloy fabricated via selective laser melting. *Acta Mater.* **2021**, *219*, 117261. [CrossRef]
7. Xue, L.; Atli, K.C.; Picak, S.; Zhang, C.; Zhang, B.; Elwany, A.; Arroyave, R.; Karaman, I. Controlling martensitic transformation characteristics in defect-free NiTi shape memory alloys fabricated using laser powder bed fusion and a process optimization framework. *Acta Mater.* **2021**, *215*, 117017. [CrossRef]
8. Zhou, Y.L.; Niinomi, M.; Akahori, T.; Fukui, H.; Toda, H. Corrosion resistance and biocompatibility of Ti–Ta alloys for biomedical applications. *Mater. Sci. Eng. A* **2005**, *398*, 28–36. [CrossRef]
9. Yu, F.; Addison, O.; Baker, S.J.; Davenport, A.J. Lipopolysaccharide inhibits or accelerates biomedical titanium corrosion depending on environmental acidity. *Int. J. Oral Sci.* **2015**, *7*, 179–186. [CrossRef]
10. Hu, L.F.; Li, J.; Tao, Y.F.; Lv, Y.H. Corrosion behaviors of $TiNi/NiTi_2$ matrix coatings in the environment rich in Cl ions. *Surf. Coat. Technol.* **2017**, *311*, 295–306. [CrossRef]
11. Man, H.C.; Cui, Z.D.; Yue, T.M. Corrosion properties of laser surface melted NiTi shape memory alloy. *Scr. Mater.* **2001**, *45*, 1447–1453. [CrossRef]
12. Zhou, K.S.; Wang, D.Z.; Liu, M. A study of the cavitation erosion behavior of a Ti-Ni alloy coating. *Surf. Coat. Technol.* **1987**, *34*, 79–87. [CrossRef]
13. Bitzer, M.; Rauhut, N.; Mauer, G.; Bram, M.; Vaben, R.; Buchkremer, H.P.; Stover, D.; Pohl, M. Cavitation-resistant NiTi coatings produced by low-pressure plasma spraying (LPPS). *Wear* **2015**, *328–329*, 369–377. [CrossRef]
14. Hiraga, H.; Inoue, T.; Shimura, H.; Matsunawa, A. Cavitation erosion mechanism of NiTi coatings made by laser plasma hybrid spraying. *Wear* **1999**, *231*, 272–278. [CrossRef]
15. Hiraga, H.; Inoue, T.; Kamado, S.; Kojima, Y.; Matsunawa, A.; Shimura, H. Fabrication of NiTi intermetallic compound coating made by laser plasma hybrid spraying of mechanically alloyed powders. *Surf. Coat. Technol.* **2001**, *139*, 93–100. [CrossRef]
16. Cui, Z.D.; Man, H.C.; Cheng, F.T.; Yue, T.M. Cavitation erosion–corrosion characteristics of laser surface modified NiTi shape memory alloy. *Surf. Coat. Technol.* **2003**, *162*, 147–153. [CrossRef]
17. Zhang, H.; Zhang, C.H.; Wang, Q.; Wu, C.L.; Zhang, S.; Chen, J.; Abdullah, A.O. Effect of Ni content on stainless steel fabricated by laser melting deposition. *Opt. Lasers Technol.* **2018**, *101*, 363–371. [CrossRef]
18. Li, B.; Han, C.; Lim, C.; Zhou, K. Interface formation and deformation behaviors of an additively manufactured nickel-aluminum-bronze/15-5 PH multimaterial via laser-powder directed energy deposition. *Mater. Sci. Eng. A* **2022**, *829*, 142101–142115. [CrossRef]

19. Mostafa, A.M.; Menazea, A.A. Laser-assisted for preparation ZnO/CdO thin film prepared by pulsed laser deposition for catalytic degradation. *Radiat. Phys. Chem.* **2020**, *176*, 109020. [CrossRef]

20. Gao, F.; Wang, H. Abrasion wear property of laser melting/deposition Ti_2Ni/TiNi intermetallic alloy. *Trans. Nonferrous Met. Soc. China* **2007**, *17*, 1358–1362. [CrossRef]

21. Suryanarayana, C. Mechanical alloying and milling. *Prog. Mater. Sci.* **2001**, *46*, 1–184. [CrossRef]

22. Ehtemam-Haghighi, S.; Liu, Y.; Cao, G.; Zhang, L.C. Phase transition, microstructure evolution and mechanical properties of Ti-Nb-Fe alloys induced by Fe addition. *Mater. Des.* **2016**, *97*, 279–286. [CrossRef]

23. Zhang, L.C.; Shen, Z.Q.; Xu, J. Glass formation in a (Ti,Zr,Hf)-(Cu,Ni,Ag)-Al high-order alloy system by mechanical alloying. *J. Mater. Res.* **2003**, *18*, 2141–2149. [CrossRef]

24. Zhou, S.; Zeng, X. Growth characteristics and mechanism of carbides precipitation in WC-Fe composite coatings by laser induction hybrid rapid cladding. *J. Alloys Compd.* **2010**, *505*, 685–691. [CrossRef]

25. Zhou, S.; Xiong, Z.; Dai, X.; Liu, J.; Zhang, T.; Wang, C. Microstructure and oxidation resistance of cryomilled NiCrAlY coating by laser induction hybrid rapid cladding. *Surf. Coat. Technol.* **2014**, *258*, 943–949. [CrossRef]

26. Gremaud, M.; Carrard, M.; Kurz, W. The microstructure of rapidly solidifed Al-Fe alloys subjected to laser surface treatment. *Acta Metall. Mater.* **1990**, *38*, 1587–1599. [CrossRef]

27. Zhong, M.; Liu, W.; Yao, K.; Goussain, J.C.; Mayer, C.; Becker, A. Microstructural evolution in high power laser cladding of Stellite 6+WC layers. *Surf. Coat. Technol.* **2002**, *157*, 128–137. [CrossRef]

28. Garay, J.E.; Anselmi-Tamburini, U.; Munir, Z.A. Enhanced growth of intermetallic phases in the Ni-Ti system by current effects. *Acta Mater.* **2003**, *51*, 4487–4495. [CrossRef]

29. Nagarajan, R.; Chattopadhyay, K. Intermetallic Ti_2Ni/TiNi nanocomposite by rapid solidification. *Acta Metall. Mater.* **1994**, *42*, 947–958. [CrossRef]

30. Liu, F.; Mao, Y.; Lin, X.; Zhou, B.; Qian, T. Microstructure and high temperature oxidation resistance of Ti-Ni gradient coating on TA2 titanium alloy fabricated by laser cladding. *Opt. Laser Technol.* **2016**, *83*, 140–147. [CrossRef]

31. Locci, A.M.; Orrù, R.; Cao, G.; Munir, Z.A. Field-activated pressure-assisted synthesis of NiTi. *Intermetallics* **2003**, *11*, 555–571. [CrossRef]

32. Li, B.Y.; Rong, L.J.; Li, Y.Y. Stress–strain behavior of porous Ni–Ti shape memory intermetallics synthesized from powder sintering. *Intermetallics* **2000**, *8*, 643–646. [CrossRef]

33. Neves, F.; Martins, I.; Correia, J.B.; Oliveira, M.; Gaffet, E. Reactive extrusion synthesis of mechanically activated Ti–50Ni powders. *Intermetallics* **2007**, *15*, 1623–1631. [CrossRef]

34. Guilemany, J.M.; Cinca, N.; Dosta, S.; Benedetti, A.V. Corrosion behaviour of thermal sprayed nitinol coatings. *Corros. Sci.* **2009**, *51*, 171–180. [CrossRef]

35. Dai, N.; Zhang, L.C.; Zhang, J.; Chen, Q.; Wu, M. Corrosion behavior of selective laser melted Ti-6Al-4V alloy in NaCl solution. *Corros. Sci.* **2016**, *102*, 484–489. [CrossRef]

36. Dai, N.; Zhang, L.C.; Zhang, J.; Zhang, X.; Ni, Q.; Cheng, Y.; Wu, M.; Yang, C. Distinction in corrosion resistance of selective laser melted Ti-6Al-4V alloy on different planes. *Corros. Sci.* **2016**, *111*, 703–710. [CrossRef]

37. Chen, Y.; Zhang, J.; Dai, N.; Qin, P.; Attar, H.; Zhang, L.C. Corrosion behavior of selective laser melted Ti-TiB biocomposite in simulated body fluid. *Electrochim. Acta* **2017**, *232*, 89–97. [CrossRef]

38. Chen, Y.; Zhang, J.; Gu, X.; Dai, N.; Qin, P.; Zhang, L.C. Distinction of corrosion resistance of selective laser melted Al-12Si alloy on different planes. *J. Alloys Compd.* **2018**, *747*, 648–658. [CrossRef]

39. Jia, Z.; Duan, X.; Qin, P.; Zhang, W.; Wang, W.; Yang, C.; Sun, H.; Wang, S.; Zhang, L.C. Disordered atomic packing structure of metallic glass: Toward ultrafast hydroxyl radicals production rate and strong electron transfer ability in catalytic performance. *Adv. Funct. Mater.* **2017**, *27*, 1702258. [CrossRef]

40. Dai, N.; Zhang, J.; Chen, Y.; Zhang, L.C. Heat treatment degrading the corrosion resistance of selective laser melted Ti-6Al-V alloy. *J. Electrochem. Soc.* **2017**, *164*, C428–C434. [CrossRef]

41. Handzlik, P.; Fitzner, K. Corrosion resistance of Ti and Ti–Pd alloy in phosphate buffered saline solutions with and without H_2O_2, addition. *Trans. Nonferrous Met. Soc. China* **2013**, *23*, 866–875. [CrossRef]

42. Obadele, B.A.; Olubambi, P.A.; Andrews, A.; Pityana, S.; Mathew, M.T. Electrochemical behaviour of laser-clad Ti6Al4V with CP Ti in 0.1 M oxalic acid solution. *J. Alloys Compd.* **2015**, *646*, 753–759. [CrossRef]

43. Verdian, M.M.; Raeissi, K.; Salehi, M. Corrosion performance of HVOF and APS thermally sprayed NiTi intermetallic coatings in 3.5% NaCl solution. *Corros. Sci.* **2010**, *52*, 1052–1059. [CrossRef]

44. González, J.E.G.; Mirza-Rosca, J.C. Study of the corrosion behavior of titanium and some of its alloys for biomedical and dental implant applications. *J. Electroanal. Chem.* **1999**, *471*, 109–115. [CrossRef]

Article

Electrochemical Behavior of Symmetric Electrical Double-Layer Capacitors and Pseudocapacitors and Identification of Transport Anomalies in the Interconnected Ionic and Electronic Phases Using the Impedance Technique

Willian G. Nunes [1], Aline M. Pascon [1], Bruno Freitas [1], Lindomar G. De Sousa [2], Débora V. Franco [2], Hudson Zanin [1,*] and Leonardo M. Da Silva [2,*]

[1]   Carbon Sci-Tech Labs, Center for Innovation on New Energies, Advanced Energy Storage Division, School of Electrical and Computer Engineering, University of Campinas, Av. Albert Einstein 400, Campinas 13083-852, SP, Brazil; nuneswillian40@gmail.com (W.G.N.); alinepascon@gmail.com (A.M.P.); brungaf@gmail.com (B.F.)

[2]   Laboratory of Fundamental and Applied Electrochemistry, Department of Chemistry, Federal University of Jequitinhonha e Mucuri's Valley, Rodovia MGT 367, Km 583, n° 5000, Alto da Jacuba, Diamantina 39100-000, MG, Brazil; lindogomes01@hotmail.com (L.G.D.S.); dvfranco@gmail.com (D.V.F.)

*   Correspondence: hzanin@unicamp.br (H.Z.); lsilvamorais@hotmail.com (L.M.D.S.)

Citation: Nunes, W.G.; Pascon, A.M.; Freitas, B.; De Sousa, L.G.; Franco, D.V.; Zanin, H.; Da Silva, L.M. Electrochemical Behavior of Symmetric Electrical Double-Layer Capacitors and Pseudocapacitors and Identification of Transport Anomalies in the Interconnected Ionic and Electronic Phases Using the Impedance Technique. *Nanomaterials* **2022**, *12*, 676. https://doi.org/10.3390/nano12040676

Academic Editor: Xinwei Wang

Received: 19 January 2022
Accepted: 14 February 2022
Published: 18 February 2022

Publisher's Note: MDPI stays neutral with regard to jurisdictional claims in published maps and institutional affiliations.

Abstract: A double-channel transmission line impedance model was applied to the study of supercapacitors to investigate the charge transport characteristics in the ionic and electronic conductors forming the electrode/solution interface. The macro homogeneous description of two closely mixed phases (Paasch–Micka–Gersdorf model) was applied to study the influence of disordered materials on the charge transport anomalies during the interfacial charge–discharge process. Different ex situ techniques were used to characterize the electrode materials used in electrical double-layer (EDLC) and pseudocapacitor (PC) devices. Two time constants in the impedance model were adequate to represent the charge transport in the different phases. The interfacial impedance considering frequency dispersion and blocked charge transfer conditions adequately described the charge storage at the interface. Deviations from the normal (Fickian) transport involving the ionic and electronic charge carriers were identified by the dispersive parameters (e.g., n and s exponents) used in the impedance model. The ionic and electronic transports were affected when the carbon-based electrical double-layer capacitor was converted into a composite with strong pseudocapacitive characteristics after the decoration process using NiO. The overall capacitance increased from 2.62 F g^{-1} to 536 F g^{-1} after the decoration. For the first time, the charge transport anomalies were unequivocally identified in porous materials used in supercapacitors with the impedance technique.

Keywords: impedance models; disordered electrode materials; anomalous charge transport; supercapacitors

1. Introduction

According to the literature [1–7], the electrochemical properties exhibited by different types of porous/nanostructured carbon-based materials used in supercapacitors can be considerably improved after their decoration using different transition metal oxides (TMOs) (e.g., NiO, Co_3O_4, Nb_2O_5, $NiCo_2O_4$, and MnO_2). However, as recently discussed by some of the present authors [1,8–12], the electrochemical characterization of composite materials containing different carbon structures and TMOs is not easy due to the porous/disordered nature of the electrode and the presence of reversible solid-state Faradaic reactions resulting in pseudocapacitive behavior (e.g., pseudocapacitors, PCs).

The use of electrochemical impedance spectroscopy (EIS) can be quite helpful for the study of complex electrode materials since some fundamental processes observed in the frequency domain cannot be accessed using the other electrochemical techniques [1]. Commonly, complex (e.g., porous/disordered) electrode materials exhibit distributed capacitance in the time and frequency domains due to hierarchically interconnected structural defects, which is usually modeled by an assembly of identical cylindrical pores (e.g., De Levie's model). Alternatively, different electrode materials can be studied using a "macro homogeneous description of two closely mixed phases" to account for the "disordered behavior" foreseen from different nanostructured materials (e.g., the Paasch et al. and Bisquert et al. models—see further discussion). Also, some interesting insights were recently reported regarding the influence of mass transport and ohmic resistances on capacitive behavior [13].

Unfortunately, in different literature reports, the study of porous/disordered electrodes, as is the case of those used in supercapacitors, is accomplished using the EIS technique based on ad hoc equivalent circuit analogs (ECs) containing the diffusive Warburg element (W), which fits the experimental data well but fails to provide a physical correspondence with the fundamental processes occurring at the electrode/electrolyte interface, as well as in the liquid and solid phases (e.g., the presence of anomalous transport characteristics) [1]. Modified versions of the Randles–Ershler circuit (e.g., $R_\Omega(C_{edl}[R_{ct}W])C$, $R_\Omega(C_{edl}[R_{ct}WC])$, etc.) are commonly used, with the incorporation of an additional capacitive element (in bold) to simulate the impedance response of a blocked electrode, as is the case with supercapacitors (SC). A typical misuse of irrational equivalent circuit analogs using the Warburg element in the absence of a charge transfer resistance was recently found in the literature [14] when a circuit containing only serial elements (e.g., L–R_o–Z_W) was used. This is nonsense since the Warburg impedance must always appear in series with the charge transfer resistance resulting in the Faradaic impedance (Z_F), which appears in parallel to the electrical double-layer capacitance [15]. Unfortunately, several speculative analyses using the EIS can be found in the literature [16]. This critical question was recently discussed by some of the present authors [1].

The main source of confusion in the EIS reports involving the diffusive elements comes from the mathematical equivalence existing between the distinct theoretical models proposed for studying the porous electrode behavior (e.g., De Levie's model for blocked interfaces where charge transfer is absent) and the diffusive mass transport coupled to Faradaic reactions (e.g., the Warburg and Kruger models for unblocked interfaces with a net charge transfer). These different models *predict the same impedance behavior* characterized by a phase angle of $\approx -45°$ since a mathematical equivalence arises from the general solution presented for second-order partial differential equations.

Physical interpretations of complex-plane (Nyquist) plots for EDLCs were recently presented by Mei et al. [17] using simulations accomplished based on the modified Poisson–Nernst–Planck (MPNP) model for binary and symmetric electrolytes. Good qualitative findings were achieved by these authors without the use of conventional circuit models. However, the porous nature of real EDLCs was not considered in the theoretical model. Even so, the impedance profiles obtained by these authors are practically the same as those simulated using other robust impedance models [18–21]. Therefore, choosing the appropriate theoretical impedance model is a great challenge in EIS studies.

Transmission lines (TLs) are special classes of equivalent circuits formally derived from fundamental laws according to particular transfer functions (TFs) representing the intrinsic properties of the studied system. Only after the pioneering TL model proposed by De Levie in 1963 [22] was a plausible physical meaning proposed for the dispersive capacitive effects verified at high frequencies for porous electrodes and characterized by a phase angle (φ) close to $-45°$. In this case, the accepted hypothesis is the dependency of the penetration depth of the sinusoidal wave inside the narrow pores with the applied frequency instead of a normal (Fickian) diffusive effect intrinsically coupled to a Faradaic reaction.

Outstanding contributions to the study of porous electrodes using the EIS were made in the last three decades by Lasia [18], Paasch et al. [19], Srinivasan and Weidner [20], Bisquert et al. [21], and other prominent authors [23–25]. A general literature survey of the impedance response of porous electrodes was recently reported by Huang et al. [26]. In particular, Bisquert et al. [21] proposed several impedance models to study different electrode materials considering the anomalous transport for the charge carriers in disordered media (e.g., semiconductors, some mixed oxides, and conducting polymers).

From the above considerations, we applied in this study a robust and generic impedance model for the study of complex electrochemical systems, which represents an effective macro homogeneous description of two closely mixed phases (Paasch–Micka–Gersdorf model) and provides a reliable description of the different physicochemical events occurring during the charge–discharge processes in porous electrodes used in SCs. The model contains two time constants (τ) representing the different events occurring in the liquid (Z_1) and solid (Z_2) phases, and a lumped impedance (Z_3) describing the charge storage process at the solid/liquid interface. As a result, we can identify fundamentally different events occurring in supercapacitors. It is worth mentioning that the formalism introduced to the impedance model proposed by Bisquert et al. [21] and used in this work does not depend on the particular pore geometry, as is the case with the De Levie's model [18], where evenly distributed identical cylinders compose the pores. It is worth mentioning that the influence of the physicochemical properties of porous electrode materials used in supercapacitors (e.g., intrinsic conductivities of the solid and liquid phases) was comprehensively incorporated by Srinivasan and Weidner in their well-known impedance model available in ZView® software (Scribner Associates Inc., Southern Pines, USA), coded as DX-Type #8 [19]. However, the latter impedance model has a drawback since it demands previous knowledge of different properties obtained in independent (complementary) studies. In addition, various combinations of the intrinsic materials' conductivity and capacitances can produce similar impedance spectra, leading to simulation findings that are difficult to interpret.

To the best of our knowledge, this is the first time that the Paasch–Micka–Gersdorf model has been used to study symmetric coin cells containing porous electrodes in the presence and absence of pronounced pseudocapacitance, considering the influence of the abnormal transport of the ionic and electronic charges. Using carbon nanofibers (CNF) and composite (CNF@NiO) electrodes housed in symmetric cells, we aim to instigate the charge transport in the electronic and ionic phases in intimate contact. At least in principle, the impedance model discussed in this work can be applied to different porous electrode materials used in SCs since the intrinsic chemical properties related to the electrode material are not incorporated in the present impedance model, i.e., only the structural material characteristics affecting the charge transport and frequency (capacitance) dispersion are relevant in the current context. Additional experiments were accomplished using cyclic voltammetry (CV) and galvanostatic charge–discharge (GCD) techniques to verify the internal consistency of the experimental findings.

2. Experimental Details

2.1. Preparation of the Composite Electrodes

The composite electrodes (model PC system) used in the symmetric coin cells consisted of carbon nanofibers grown by chemical vapor deposition on a porous carbon fabric substrate [27] and decorated with NiO particles using the incipient wetness impregnation method [8]. HexForce 3K carbon fabric fiber (Hexcel Co., Stamford, USA), composed of bundles containing carbon fibers with an average diameter of 7.5 μm, was applied as the current collector, which we used to grow carbon nanofibers. The pristine carbon fabric was cut into 5 cm × 3 cm pieces (e.g., ~1.0 g) and cleaned using a 63% (w/w) HNO_3 solution for 1.0 h to remove the residues from the fabrication process. After drying in air at 110 °C for 12 h, the material was immersed in a 10 g dm^{-3} $Ni(NO_3)_2{\cdot}6H_2O$ (Acros Co., New Jersey, USA), purity of 98%, alcoholic solution (e.g., 50% (v/v) ethanol-water) and subsequently dried for 12 h at 110 °C. Afterward, the fabric samples impregnated with nickel were calcinated in a pre-heated oven at 350 °C for 1.0 h using a quartz tube reactor where the samples were inserted and purged with argon gas at a volumetric flow rate of 100 cm^3 min^{-1} for 10 min. In the sequence, under reductive atmospheric conditions to induce the formation of NiO nanoparticles, using a hydrogen flow rate of 200 cm^3 min^{-1}, the temperature inside the quartz tube was increased by 10 °C min^{-1} until it reached 400 °C. After 1.0 h at this temperature, to foster the correct conditions for the growth of the carbon nanostructures (nanofibers) using an ethane flow rate of 50 cm^3 min^{-1} (e.g., the carbon source), the temperature inside the quartz tube was increased by 10 °C min^{-1} until it reached a final value of 700 °C, where it was held for 30 min. As a result, the nanofibers (e.g., CNFs) were grown on the surface of the carbon fabric substrate. After cooling the as-prepared material using an inert argon atmosphere, 14 mm diameter discs were cut from the modified carbon fabric and the samples were again impregnated with a 0.1 mol dm^{-3} Ni(NO$_3$)$_2$ alcoholic (e.g., 50% (*v/v*) ethanol–water) solution for 48 h. After immersion, samples were immersed in deionized water. After drying at 80 °C for 2 h, the discs were subjected to thermal treatment in a pre-heated oven at 350 °C for 2 h in an ambient atmosphere for the formation of NiO nanoparticles on the carbon nanofibers (e.g., NiO@CNFs). We will henceforward refer to porous carbon-based materials as CNFs and the composite electrode material as NiO@CNFs.

The overall masses of the CNF (model EDLC system) and NiO@CNF (model PC system) electrodes housed in the different symmetric coin cells were 12.3 and 12.6 mg, respectively. The specific capacitances reported in the electrochemical study were calculated using these masses.

2.2. Structural and Surface Morphology Characterization Studies

The surface morphology of the samples was examined using a FEI Inspect F-50 (Thermo Fisher Scientific, Hillsboro, USA) at 20 kV and with ETD detector. High-resolution images were obtained using a model 2100 MSC high-resolution transmission electron microscope (JEOL Inc., Peabody, USA). Samples were dispersed in isopropanol using an ultrasound bath and dropped on a TEM lacey carbon film fixed on the copper mesh.

Raman spectra of the samples were performed on a Renishaw inVia spectrometer (Michigan, USA) using a 488 nm (Argon ion) laser, with an integration time of 60 s and a 50× LWD objective lens in the range of 100 to 2500 cm^{-1}. The spectra analyses were accomplished by proper subtraction of the baseline signal. At the same time, the curve fitting procedure was performed in the region from 300 to 1750 cm^{-1} using the Lorentzian and Gaussians functions available in the software Fityk (Open Free).

The surface chemistry of the composite samples was analyzed using the K-alpha radiation with the aid of a Thermo Scientific (Massachusetts, USA) X-ray photoelectron spectrometer.

The structure of the composite material was characterized by X-ray diffraction analysis, performed with a model PAN analytical X'Pert PRO X-ray diffractometer (Malvern, UK) using Co-Kα radiation (λ = 0.178901 nm) in a Bragg–Brentano $\theta/2\theta$ configuration (Goniometer PW3050/65). The diffraction patterns were collected at steps of 0.04° and the accumulation time of 5 s per step within the 2θ-scale range from 20° to 80°.

The specific surface area (SSA/m^2 g^{-1}) obtained according to the BET method was measured using nitrogen at 77 K with a Micromeritics ASAP 2010 instrument (Norcross, USA). Before measuring, 100 mg of the active powder carbon fiber material was degassed at 100 °C for 12 h. Finally, the powder sample was conditioned at 200 °C to obtain a constant pressure of 0.02 μm Hg.

2.3. Electrochemical Characterization Studies

All electrochemical experiments were performed using a model CR2032 coin cell in the symmetric configuration containing a cellulosic filter paper soaked with a 1.0 mol dm^{-3} Li$_2$SO$_4$ aqueous solution to avoid short circuiting and to provide ionic conduction. A 302N potentiostat–galvanostat with an FRA module from AUTOLAB® (Utrecht, The Netherlands) was used throughout.

The study in the frequency domain was accomplished using the EIS technique, whereby a fixed cell potential corresponding to the open circuit cell potential (OCCP) was applied while the frequency of the superimposed alternated cell potential was swept from 100 kHz to 10 mHz using a low sinusoidal signal of 10 mV (peak-to-peak). The quantitative analysis of the impedance data was carried out based on the double-channel transmission line model denoted as Bisquert #2 using NOVA® software from AUTOLAB® (Utrecht, The Netherlands), where the fitting/simulation procedure was conducted using the complex nonlinear least squares (CNLS) method. Very good simulations were obtained in all cases ($r^2 \geq 0.998$), with a relative error for each model's parameter of less than 2%. Please see further details in the discussion section.

Cyclic voltammetry (CV) and galvanostatic charge–discharge (GCD) experiments were also performed using the symmetric coin cells. Voltammetric curves (VCs) were obtained at different scan rates (e.g., 5, 25, and 50 mV s^{-1}) for the pseudocapacitive voltage range of 1.0 V, while the GCD curves were measured at 4 A g^{-1}. The specific capacitance (C/F g^{-1}) was also determined from the galvanostatic charge–discharge using the equation $C = I/m(\Delta V/\Delta t)$, where I is the negative (cathodic) current, m is the overall electrode mass (cathode and anode), and $\Delta V/\Delta t$ is the negative slope of the discharge curve.

3. Results and Discussion

As already emphasized, our intention with this work is to obtain electrochemical information concerning the fundamental events during the charge storage process, i.e., charge transport anomalies involving the ionic and/or electronic charge carriers, which are affected by the disordered electrode materials used in EDLC and PC symmetric devices. However, to provide further information about the synthesized model materials, we present in this section an ex situ characterization.

3.1. Ex Situ Characterization Studies

3.1.1. Surface Morphology Analysis: SEM and TEM Studies

Figure 1 shows SEM and TEM micrographs of the CNF (Figure 1a–c) and NiO@CNF (Figure 1d–f) materials. Figure 1a,d presents SEM images of the carbon fabric macrostructure before (a) and after (d) the presence of the as-grown CNFs. Obviously, at this magnification, no significant changes in the surface morphology can be detected due to the presence of CNFs. Figure 1b shows an image with higher magnification, where we can verify the formation of CNFs with a spaghetti-like structure, i.e., CNFs were grown on fabric fibers in an entangled way. After immersion of the CNFs into the nickel nitrate aqueous solution, the fibers of the CNF tend to join together, forming a sponge-like electrode surface (see Figure 1e). Figure 1d–f shows SEM and TEM images of the CNFs' structures after decoration with NiO nanoparticles to obtain the composite electrode material (e.g., NiO@CNFs). As seen, TEM micrographs (Figure 1c,f) evidenced the presence of NiO on the CNF surface.

As verified from the TEM analysis, the modified CNFs are highly defective, with a nonlinear structure. The CNFs diameter range from 10 to 90 nm. At the same time, NiO exhibited quasispherical nanoparticles with diameters ranging from 1 to 5 nm.

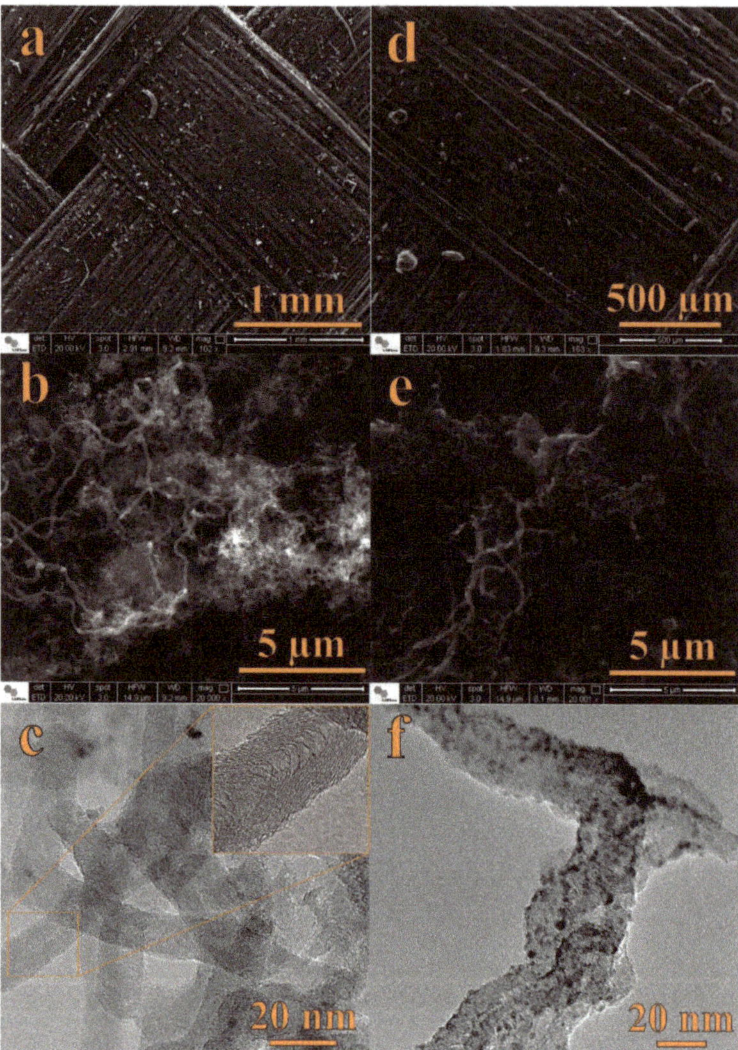

Figure 1. SEM and TEM data of CNFs (**a–c**) and NiO@CNFs (**d–f**).

3.1.2. Raman and XPS Studies

Raman spectra of CNFs and NiO@CNFs are presented in Figure 2. Raman spectra of CNFs (Figure 2a) were deconvoluted into four peaks referring to the G and D bands: G (~1600 cm^{-1}), D (~1360 cm^{-1}), D1 (~1270 cm^{-1}), and D2 (~1530 cm^{-1}). G and D bands were assigned to the sp^2 in-plane carbon vibration and out-of-plane vibrational modes, respectively [28]. D1 and D2 bands were ascribed to the C-C and C=C stretching modes (e.g., sp^3 and sp^2 bonds) and to the amorphous carbons containing different organic species, respectively [29]. Figure 2b shows the Raman spectrum of the NiO@CNFs composite, which was deconvoluted into seven peaks. The spectrum of NiO@CNFs also contains three additional characteristic bands due to the presence of NiO. The bands were located at ~370 cm^{-1}, ~498 cm^{-1}, and ~740 cm^{-1}. The 498 cm^{-1} peak is assigned to a lack of symmetry, i.e., defects due to high nickel vacancy concentration, around the atoms normally participating in the formation of phonons in a perfect crystal [30,31]. The 370 cm^{-1} peak is attributed to TO, and 740 cm^{-1} is harmonic 2TO modes [30–33]. From this analysis, we concluded that nickel oxide nanoparticles are highly defective due to the intensity of the 498 cm^{-1} peak.

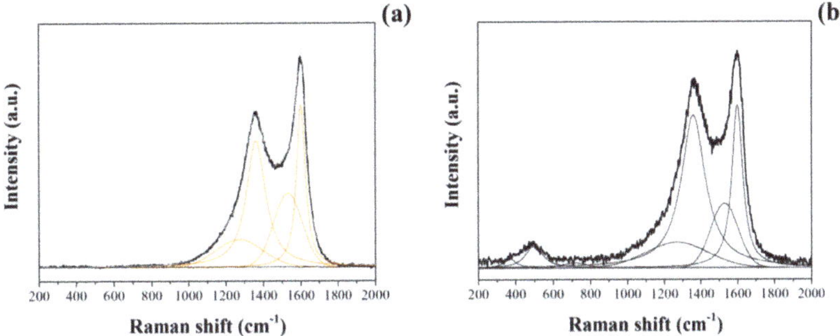

Figure 2. Raman spectra of CNFs (**a**) and NiO@CNFs (**b**) obtained at 488 nm.

A comparison of the XPS findings obtained for the two different samples was performed. In this sense, Figure 3 shows the long-range XPS spectra (Figure 3a,d), as well as the short-range spectra for the different chemical species: C1s (Figure 3b,e), O1s (Figure 3c,f), and Ni2p (Figure 3g).

Different deconvolutions were accomplished using Gaussian and Lorentzian functions with the Shirley baseline correction. Figure 3a,d shows the individual long-range region spectrum for the different materials. It is possible to verify the presence of the Ni2p peak for the NiO@CNFs, while it is absent for the CNFs, as expected. Although the CVD synthesis of CNFs uses nickel as the catalyst, its concentration in the sample is too low to be detected. This analysis is consistent with the Raman findings (see Figure 2). Figure 3b,c shows the main peak at ~284.8 eV, attributed to the C=C bond, which confirmed the presence of sigma and π bonds characteristic of the graphene structures present in the CNFs [34]. The C=O and C$-$C=O bonds, and $\pi-\pi^*$ transitions, were verified for the two distinct samples [35]. However, the C-OH bond was only verified for the CNFs and C-O-C only for NiO@CNFs.

The C1s region of the spectrum showed minor changes in the carbon structure due to the presence of nickel oxide nanoparticles, as previously observed from the TEM analysis (see Figure 1). On the contrary, the O1s region of the spectrum revealed a considerable increase in the XPS signal from 2 to 8 at. % after the decoration of CNFs with NiO. To identify the presence of Ni–O, the XPS spectra of the O1s and Ni2p regions were used. In the O1s region, the spectra were deconvoluted into two bands for the CNFs sample. The presence of C=O, C-O, and C-OH bonds was confirmed for the C1s region [36].

The formation of NiO nanoparticles occurred after the annealing process of CNFs, carried out at 350 °C in the presence of oxygen and Ni^{2+} species, as confirmed by the C$-$O and Ni$-$O bonds found in the XPS spectra. It is worth mentioning that the presence of the H$-$O$-$H bond in the XPS spectrum comes from air humidity. At the same time, the presence of the C=O bond was assigned to the carbonyl bonds, while the occurrence of the CO$_3^{2-}$ was ascribed to the carboxylic groups, and Ni–O is due to the oxide formation.

Figure 3g shows the Ni2p region of the XPS spectrum obtained for the NiO@CNFs composite. Even considering that the amount of nickel oxide nanoparticles present in the carbon structure is small, it was possible to obtain a high-resolution Ni2p spectrum to observe the Ni2p$_{(3/2)}$ and Ni2p$_{(1/2)}$ regions. The Ni2p$_{(3/2)}$ region was composed of two peaks and it was possible to observe two oxidation states for nickel (e.g., Ni^{2+} and Ni^{3+}), i.e., we observed the formation of NiO and Ni(OH)$_2$ species (e.g., Ni^{2+} comes from the multiplet splitting referring to NiO) [37]. The Ni2p$_{(1/2)}$ region is a doublet of the Ni2p$_{(3/2)}$ region, so we have the same peaks. These data are in agreement with the Raman findings already discussed in this work (see Figure 2b). All energies (B.E.) referring to different chemical bonds are shown in Table 1.

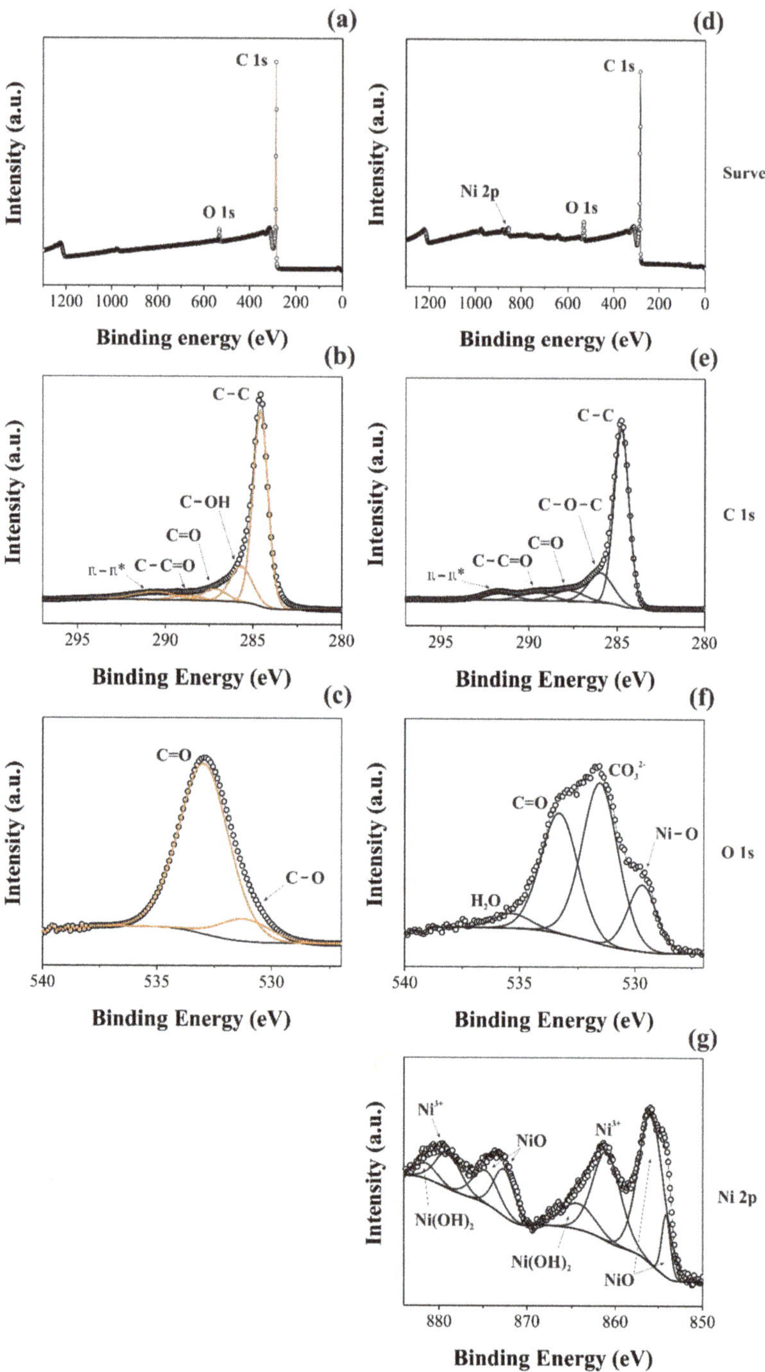

Figure 3. XPS spectra took for the CNFs (**a–c**) and NiO@CNFs (**d–g**) samples.

Table 1. XPS data obtained for the CNFs and NiO@CNFs samples.

Sample	Element	Functional Groups	B.E./eV
CNFs	C1s	C-C	284.6
		C-OH	285.6
		C=O	287.2
		O-C=O	288.8
		$\pi-\pi^*$	290.6
	O1s	C-O	531.3
		C=O	533.0
NiO@CNFs	Ni2p	NiO	854.2
		NiO	856.0
		Ni^{3+}	861.1
		$NiO(OH)_2$	864.6
		NiO	872.8
		NiO	875.0
		Ni^{3+}	879.2
		$NiO(OH)_2$	881.8
	C1s	C-C	284.8
		C-O-C	286.0
		C=O	287.8
		C-C=O	289.6
		$\pi-\pi^*$	291.8
	O1s	Ni-O	529.7
		CO_3^{2-}	531.6
		C=O	533.3
		H_2O	535.4

3.1.3. XRD and BET Studies

We performed X-ray diffraction (XRD) on CNFs and NiO@CNFs to characterize the crystalline structure. Figure 4 shows the XRD patterns obtained.

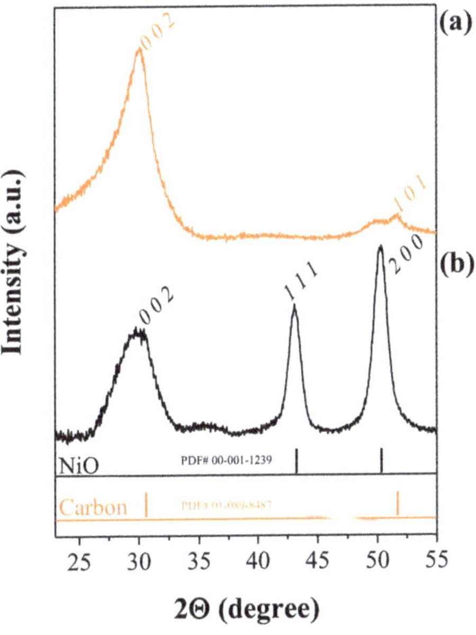

Figure 4. XRD patterns of (**a**) CNFs and (**b**) NiO@CNFs.

The analysis of Figure 4a confirms the existence of carbon (sp^2) structures (PDF# 01-089-8487), with the peaks corresponding to the (0 0 2) and (1 0 1) *hkl*-planes. In Figure 4b the peaks correspond to two different crystalline phases, i.e., the sp^2 carbon structure and NiO (cubic crystal system and the *Fm-3m* spatial group), in agreement with the (1 1 1) and (2 0 0) *hkl*-planes (PDF# 00-001-1239). These findings agree with the XPS, and Raman analyzes and confirm the presence of carbon and NiO phases. The presence of the (2 0 0) *hkl*-plane corroborates the interplanar spacing of 0.208 nm in the TEM study.

Figure 5a,c shows the volume of N_2 corresponding to the adsorption/desorption processes as a function of the relative pressure used to obtain the isotherms according to the BET analysis, while Figure 5b,d shows the incremental pore size distribution calculated using the BJH model.

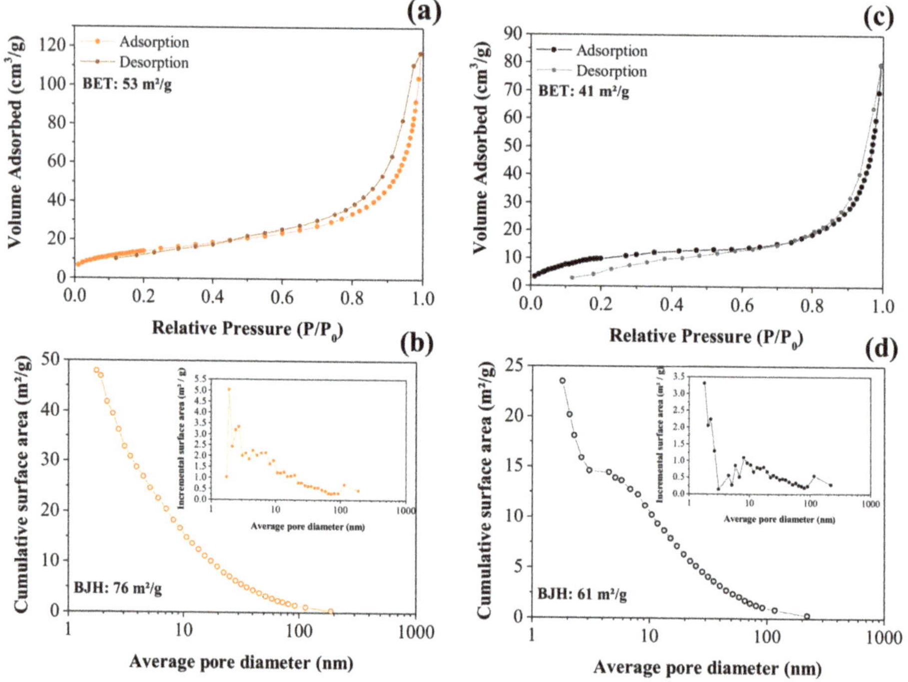

Figure 5. BET and BJH analyses of the adsorption/desorption nitrogen isotherm curves obtained for the CNFs (**a,b**) and NiO@CNFs (**c,d**).

The N_2 adsorption/desorption isotherms are shown in Figure 5a. The isotherm obtained for the CNFs exhibited an IV type according to the IUPAC classification; there is a region (e.g., ~0.6 to 1.0 P/P_0) where the relative pressure slightly varied when the adsorbed volume increased. These isotherms indicated the presence of slit-type pores. Due to the capillary condensation process, there was a hysteresis loop in the range of ~0.6 to 1.0 P/P_0 that can be classified as H3 type, i.e., in this case, we have complete filling of the mesopores at relative pressures lower than 1.0 P/P_0. The profile showed in Figure 5a was mainly characterized by two relatively vertical asymptotic branches at $P/P_0 = 1$, which are associated with a nonrigid aggregation of the plate-shaped particles, giving rise to slit pores, thus showing a higher specific surface area for CNFs of ~53 m^2 g^{-1} (see Figure 5a) [38]. The pore size distribution (see Figure 5b inset) revealed the presence of micropores ($d < 2.0$ nm), mesopores (2 nm < d < 50 nm), and macropores ($d > 50$ nm) [39]. Therefore, it can be concluded that the largest contribution to the total specific surface area is due to mesopores.

Accordingly, the corresponding value obtained from the NiO@CNF sample was ~41 m^2 g^{-1} (see Figure 5c). From these findings, we can affirm that some pores of the carbon structure were clogged during the oxide formation, thus reducing the specific surface area compared to the CNFs sample. As seen in the case of the NiO@CNF sample, the major contribution to the specific surface area is due to mesopores (Figure 5c). The isotherm obtained for the composite material exhibited an IV type with a characteristic hysteresis loop in the range of ~0.8 to 1.0 P/P_0 of the H3 type.

3.2. Frequency Domain Analysis Using the EIS Technique: Identification of Charge Transport Anomalies during the Charge Storage Process in EDLC and PC Devices

Figure 6 shows the complex plane (Nyquist) plots obtained for different symmetric coin cells containing the (a) CNF or (b) NiO@CNF electrodes, and the (c) generic double-channel transmission line model, where each impedance Z is composed of a circuit containing an ohmic resistor (R) in parallel to a constant phase element (CPE) representing the different dispersive effects. As can be seen, the impedance response was characterized by the following characteristics: (i) the presence of a resistive/capacitive arc in the high-frequency range; (ii) the occurrence of an inclined line with a phase angle close to $-45°$ at medium frequencies, and (iii) the presence of an almost vertical straight line in the low-frequency range with a phase angle close to $-90°$. According to [19], this type of impedance behavior, in the absence of irreversible Faradaic reactions (e.g., water splitting), is in agreement with the theoretical predictions of the porous electrode model, with the additional inclusion of the anomalous transport phenomenon for the ionic and/or electronic charge carriers. The anomalous transport effects occur from the medium- to the high-frequency interval of the impedance spectrum [21].

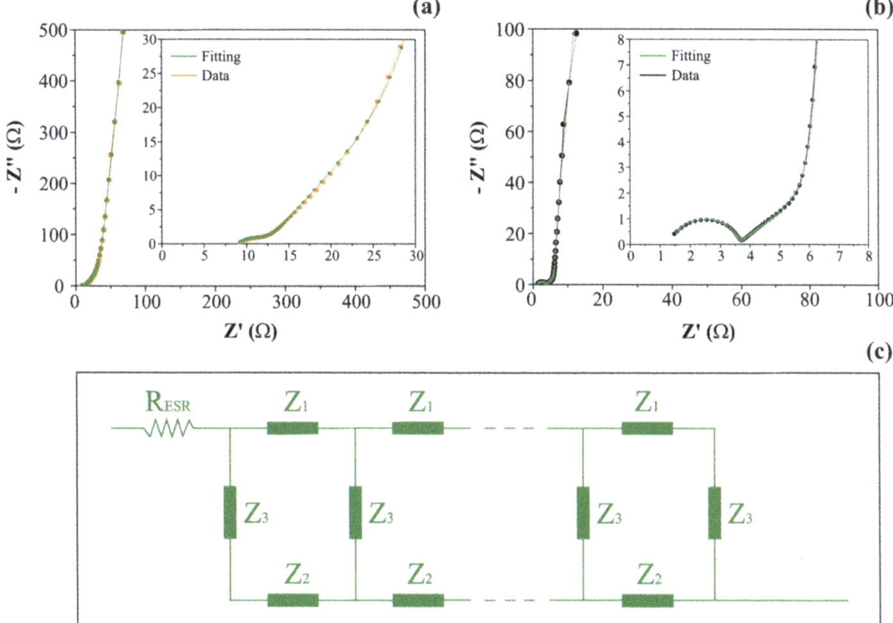

Figure 6. Complex plane plots (**a,b**) and the generic double-channel transmission line model (**c**), including the anomalous transport for porous/disordered electrodes. Plots (**a**) and (**b**) refer to CNF and NiO@CNF electrodes, respectively. Impedances Z_1 and Z_2 are composed of a circuit containing an ohmic resistor (R) parallel to a constant phase element (CPE). A CPE represents the interface (Z_3) impedance.

More specifically, when the intermixed solid (Z_1) and liquid (Z_2) phases have a similar *dc* resistance, the influence of the disordered solid phase on the electronic transport commonly appears as an arc in the high-frequency region of the impedance spectrum (see Figure 6a,b). However, it is worth mentioning that the *interfacial* (parallel) impedance (Z_3), including the electrical double-layer capacitance and pseudocapacitive effects, can also affect this region of the spectrum.

Inspired by the classical solid-state physics studies regarding the anomalous charge transport in disordered solids, Bisquert et al. [21] proposed a robust generic impedance model for the study of different types of electrochemical systems with disorder/dispersive characteristics (e.g., a power law behavior or dispersive effects). In addition, Bisquert [40] also discussed some particular cases of great interest for studying the different electrochemical systems used in technological applications. The total impedance (Z_{total}) for the porous or mixed-phase electrodes, considering the presence of anomalous transport and the additional influence of the uncompensated ohmic resistance (R_{ESR}) intrinsic to the supercapacitors, is given by the following transfer function [21]:

$$Z_{\text{total}} = R_{\text{ESR}} + \frac{Z_1 Z_2}{Z_1 + Z_2}\left[L + \frac{2\lambda}{\sin h\left(\frac{L}{\lambda}\right)}\right] + \lambda\left(\frac{Z_1^2 + Z_2^2}{Z_1 + Z_2}\right)\coth\left(\frac{L}{\lambda}\right), \tag{1}$$

where:

$$\lambda = \left(\frac{Z_3}{Z_1 + Z_2}\right)^{1/2} \tag{2}$$

$$Z_1 = \frac{r_1}{1 + r_1 q_1 (j\omega)^n} \tag{3}$$

$$Z_2 = \frac{r_2}{1 + r_2 q_2 (j\omega)^s} \tag{4}$$

$$Z_3 = \frac{1}{q_3 (j\omega)^\beta}. \tag{5}$$

The parameter L is the length of the intermixed (porous) phase, and is commonly unknown. From the point of view of the macro aspects of the impedance model (see further discussion in this section), the particular L-value is irrelevant for most applications. However, to obtain internal consistency between the unities of the transverse and parallel impedances, the apparent length of the porous electrode layer is given in the current work by the equation $L = m/\rho A$, where m is the mass of the active layer, ρ is the apparent density of the electrode layer, and A is the geometric surface area of the porous electrode.

The individual (macroscopic) parameters measured are $R_1 = Lr_1$ (e.g., the total *dc* electrolyte resistance inside the irregular ionic channels), $Q_1 = q_1/L$ (e.g., the information about the anomalous ionic transport mechanism or the transversal electrolyte capacitive-like effects), $R_2 = Lr_2$ (e.g., the total *dc* electrode resistance), $Q_2 = q_2/L$ (e.g., the anomalous electronic transport in the electrode material or the transverse electrode capacitance), and $Q_3 = q_3 L$ (e.g., the constant phase element coefficient (Q_{edl}*), which is representative of the nonideal overall electrical double layer, including pseudocapacitance). As emphasized by Bisquert et al. [21], impedances Z_1 and Z_2 represent "single transport mechanisms" rather than a conventional association of resistive and capacitive elements used in purely electrostatic processes.

In light of the theoretical analysis proposed by Paasch et al. [19], the impedance model represented by Equation (1) agrees with the effective macro homogeneous description of two closely mixed phases. The latter is more appropriate for practical applications than the traditional view, where the porous electrode model is derived based on the presence of a perfect cylinder geometry whose pore length is longer than its diameter. As it is a common practice in EIS studies to facilitate the numerical analysis of the experimental findings, the transfer function described by Equation (1) can be represented by the equivalent double-channel transmission line shown in Figure 6c. In this model, Z_1 and Z_2 are impedances per unit length (Ω m^{-1}) transverse to the macroscopic outer surfaces, while Z_3 is the impedance length (Ω m) parallel to the macroscopic surfaces. The impedance Z_3 represents the capacitance or pseudocapacitance of the electrode/solution interface, i.e., $Z_3 = 1/Q_3(j\omega)^\beta$. For convenience, the transverse and parallel impedances are represented using gravimetric quantities (e.g., Z_1/Ω g^{-1}, Z_2/Ω g^{-1}, and Z_3/Ω g), since, as discussed above, $L \propto m$.

The anomalous charge transport across narrow pores filled with the electrolyte can be understood considering the impedances Z_1 and/or Z_2 must be frequency-dependent, exhibiting a power law behavior (e.g., $n < 1$ and/or $s < 1$; see Equations (3) and (4)). These particular impedances must be lower at high frequencies than at lower frequencies due to the effect of narrow 'throats' and bottleneck structures that restrict the long-range (e.g., low-frequency) ionic motion, as well as the presence of disordered structures in the solid phase, which affects the electronic transport [21]. In general, the dispersive effects commonly found for semiconductors and conducting polymers and represented by the power law expressions (see Equations (3) and (4)) due to the anomalous charge transport in disordered phases being associated with discrete transitions between localized states that originated from the different types of structural disorder/defects present in porous electrode materials, which can be characterized by a characteristic time constant or relaxation time (τ_c) [41].

To overcome the difficulties involving the specification of a particular conduction mechanism, Bisquert et al. [21] considered the problem of *anomalous charge transport* using the concept of a model-independent macroscopic phenomenological theory based on a generalized constitutive equation and the general Einstein relationship for diffusional processes. As a result, different types of electrode materials that exhibit dispersive effects for charge transport can be studied using the proposed model. In this sense, the porous electrodes operate by simultaneous transport of electronic and ionic species occurring in the solid and liquid phases, respectively, to attain the principle of local electroneutrality. In this scenario, the solid phase provides a continuous path for the transport of electrons, but the dimensions of the structural elements in the disordered solid are quite small, especially in the presence of nano-sized domains. Accordingly, the electrolyte penetrates the accessible void regions present in the solid phase, resulting in very narrow liquid channels that exhibit a high degree of tortuosity. As a result, the electrode system is characterized by two closely mixed phases with a possible degree of disorder for the electronic and ionic charge carriers [21].

The results of the CNLS simulation are summarized in Table 2. As can be seen, the decoration of the CNFs with NiO caused strong changes in the electrochemical characteristics of the composite electrode. The major impedance parameters accounting for the performance of supercapacitors are R_{ESR} and Q_{edl}. As seen, the R_{ESR} value decreased after the decoration process, which is very good for the overall performance of the coin cell.

Table 2. Impedance parameters obtained from the CNLS simulation according to the effective macro homogeneous description of two closely mixed phases.

Electrodes	R_{ESR} (Ω g)	R_{ionic} (Ω g^{-1})	Q_{ionic} (F s^{n-1} g)	$R_{electronic}$ (Ω g^{-1})	$Q_{electronic}$ (F s^{s-1} g)	Q_{edl} or Q_{pc} * (F s$^{\beta-1}$ g^{-1})
CNFs	0.21	3.48×10^3	1.45×10^{-4} ($n = 0.42$)	2.16×10^2	4.92×10^{-4} ($s = 1.00$)	2.62 ($\beta = 0.95$)
NiO@CNFs	0.04	4.32×10^2	2.22×10^{-7} ($n = 0.92$)	1.11×10^2	3.02×10^{-3} ($s = 0.98$)	5.36×10^2 ($\beta = 0.96$)

* Q_{pc} is the pseudocapacitance for NiO@CNFs, while Q_{edl} is the electrical double-layer capacitance for CNFs.

In principle, these findings indicate that the spontaneous hydration of the nickel oxide (e.g., NiO + H$_2$O $\rightarrow$ Ni(OH)$_2$) promoted an increase of the wettability of the inner surface regions of the porous electrode, thus increasing the overall cell conductivity. As seen, the apparent (fractal) electrical double-layer capacitance verified for the carbon-based scaffold or the apparent (fractal) pseudocapacitance observed for the decorated electrode was characterized by a dispersive exponent very close to 1 (e.g., $\beta \geq 0.95$). This implies with great accuracy that $Q \approx C$. It was verified that the decoration process using NiO strongly increased the coin cell charge storage characteristics from 2.62 to ≈ 536 F g^{-1} (since $\beta \approx 1$), promoting an enormous improvement in the device's performance. These findings explicitly reveal the paramount importance of the reversible solid-state redox reactions (RSR) to the overall charge storage process.

Considering the lower specific surface area exhibited by the composite material compared to the carbon-based scaffold, one can propose that the main contribution to the overall specific capacitance is a bulk-like or near-surface pseudocapacitance instead of the purely surface electrostatic process. We can argue that the strong electrochemical activity exhibited by Ni(OH)$_2$ for the charge storage process is due to the presence of RSR involving the Ni^{2+}/Ni^{3+} redox couple [42]. According to the literature, the redox reaction involving Ni(OH)$_2$ is a solid-to-solid transformation [43]. We present the well-known Bode's reaction scheme to represent the electrochemical behavior of Ni(OH)$_2$ during the charging–discharging process [44]:

$$\alpha\text{-Ni(OH)}_2 \rightarrow \gamma\text{-NiOOH} + \text{H}^+ + \text{e}^- \tag{6}$$

$$\beta\text{-Ni(OH)}_2 \rightarrow \beta\text{-NiOOH} + \text{H}^+ + \text{e}^-$$

$$\alpha\text{-Ni(OH)}_2 \rightarrow \beta\text{-Ni(OH)}_2$$

$$\gamma\text{-NiOOH} \rightarrow \beta\text{-NiOOH}.$$

In short, the $\alpha \leftrightarrow \gamma$ and $\beta \leftrightarrow \beta$ pathways, involving the solid-state redox transitions of the type Ni^{2+}/Ni^{3+}, are of interest to the reversible charging–discharging process in supercapacitors. The $\alpha \rightarrow \beta$ phase change only occurs under potentially extended cycling, while the $\gamma \rightarrow \beta$ transformation occurs at the expense of excessive charge insertion.

For convenience, the gradual changes in the Ni(OH)$_2$ material occurring during proton intercalation/deintercalation can be simplified as follows [45]:

$$\text{Ni(OH)}_2 \leftrightarrow \text{NiO}_x\text{(OH)}_{(2-x)} + x\text{H}^+ + x\text{e}^-, \tag{7}$$

where it is commonly assumed that the $\beta \leftrightarrow \beta$ pathway of the Bode's scheme is dominant. It is worth mentioning that, due to the nature of amphoteric oxide, the issue of whether the species that diffuses through the Ni(OH)$_2$ structure is H$^+$ and/or OH$^-$ remains open to discussion [46].

Another possible origin for the pseudocapacitive behavior involving Ni(OH)$_2$ might be the intercalation/deintercalation of Li$^+$ ions into the hydrated oxide structure. According to [45], the intercalation/deintercalation of Li$^+$ in Ni(OH)$_2$ is more probable in a concentrated LiOH aqueous solution or in rigorously anhydrous electrolytes (e.g., LiClO$_4$ + PC (propylene carbonate)). According to Faria et al. [47], who proposed the occurrence of an exchange reaction, when different cations are present in the solution the proton intercalation can govern the overall charging–discharging processes comprising a mixed intercalation process, involving to a minor extent the intercalation/deintercalation of species like Li$^+$. Thus, it is plausible to consider for the hydrated oxide the following parallel process involving a substitutive solid-state redox reaction:

$$\text{Ni(OH)O}_x\text{H}_y + z\text{Li}^+ \leftrightarrow \text{Ni(OH)O}_x\text{Li}_{(y-g)} + g\text{H}^+ + \text{e}^-. \tag{8}$$

Therefore, it is prudent to consider for aqueous solutions that the overall pseudocapacitive process is a combined process given by the above solid-state reactions (Equations (7) and (8)) [46].

The other set of impedance parameters presented in Table 2 involves the ionic and electronic transport characteristics in the disordered phases. The ionic resistance inside the irregular pores decreased about 5-fold in the presence of Ni(OH)$_2$, while the exponent (n) representing the anomaly degree increased from 0.42 to 0.92, i.e., the anomalous ionic transport practically disappeared for the composite electrode. In addition, we found for the decorated electrode that $R_{ionic(CFs)} > R_{ionic(NiO@CNFs)}$. In principle, these findings suggest the occurrence of a Grotthuss-like mechanism for protons and/or Li^+ species inside the hydrated (gel layer) structure that formed during hydration of the nickel oxide. As a result, there is the formation of more regular paths for the ionic transport during the charge–discharge events and, therefore, the overall ionic transport in both liquid and solid (gel layer) phases behaves similarly to a normal (Fickian) process. On the contrary, for the carbon-based electrode, the transport of protons and/or Li^+ species is abruptly interrupted at the blocked electrode/solution interface, resulting in a severe anomaly during the fast charge–discharge process. Also, the more disordered structure of the carbon material creates zig-zag paths that decrease the mean free paths in narrow channels, thus reducing the overall ionic conductivity.

According to [48], the diffusion coefficients for protons ($D_H{}^+$) in the bulk liquid phase and the hydrated nickel oxide ($D_H{}^+{}_{(NiO)}$) are 9.32×10^{-5} cm^2 s^{-1} and $\approx 3 \times 10^{-10}$ cm^2 s^{-1}, respectively. Therefore, at least in principle, the Faradaic intercalation reaction during the charge storage process can be controlled by the slower ionic transport on the solid phase, which is sometimes indirectly verified in several *battery-like* systems by the irreversible peaked shape voltammograms obtained at low scan rates (e.g., $v \leq 10$ mV s^{-1}) and/or the pronounced voltage plateau verified in the GCD curves [49]. It was verified in the current work that $n_{(NiO)} = 0.92$ for ionic transport in the hydrated composite electrode and, therefore, we can consider that the overall proton diffusion in the two closely mixed phases is practically a nondispersive (Fickian) event. Thus, in the presence of a concentrated supporting electrolyte to sustain the migration current, there is the general phenomenological relationship $J = D(\Delta C_H{}^+ / \Delta x)$ for Nernst's layer, where $\Delta C_H{}^+ / \Delta x$ is the concentration gradient driving the flow (J), and $D/\Delta x = k_{mt}$ is the diffusion mass transport coefficient. In addition, from the continuity condition, we know that the three different coupled flows involved in the Faradaic (pseudocapacitive) process must be equal (e.g., $J_{(e^-)} = J_{(H^+)} = J_H{}^+{}_{(NiO)}$). Therefore, considering that $D_H{}^+ >> D_H{}^+{}_{(NiO)}$, we propose that $k_{(mt)\text{-}H}{}^+{}_{(NiO)}$ is not so different from $k_{(mt)\text{-}(H^+)}$, i.e., as already mentioned, the composite electrode material can provide many alternative routes for the ionic and electronic charges, thus resulting in short-range paths (Δx) for proton transport. As a result, the flow of ionic charge considerably increases in the hydrated oxide structure. The electrochemical system behaves like a real capacitive system instead of a battery-like one.

Sharma et al. [50] recently reported on tuning the nanoparticle interfacial properties and stability of the core shell structure in Zn-doped $NiMoO_4@AWO_4$ electrodes. They considered Zn-doped nickel molybdate ($NiMoO_4$) (ZNM) as a core crystal structure and AWO_4 (A = Co or Mg) as a shell surface. They verified the ability to tune the core shell nanocomposites with surface reconstruction as a source for surface energy (de)stabilization. It was verified that the performance of the core shell is significantly affected by the chosen intrinsic properties of metal oxides with high performance compared to a single-component system in supercapacitors. The constructed asymmetric device (e.g., Zn-doped $NiMoO_4@CoWO_4$ (ZNM@CW) | | activated carbon) exhibited superior pseudocapacitance, delivering a high areal capacitance of 892 mF cm^{-2} at 2 mA cm^{-2} and excellent cycling stability (i.e., 96% capacitance retention after 1000 charge–discharge cycles). Sharma et al. [50] presented theoretical and experimental insights into the extent of the surface reconstruction to explain the storage properties in SCs.

The diffuse or drift effects in a disordered solid phase containing many traps are correlated with the number of electrons effectively contributing to the charge flux, which in turn depends on the frequency. Thus, the presence of dispersive (anomalous) effects can be identified through the dispersive exponent (s) in Equation (4) [51]. Using the Nernst–Einstein relationship, we can verify that, for most crystalline electronic conductors, the diffusion coefficient for the electrons (D_e) is in the range of 7 to 241 cm^2 s^{-1} [52,53]. However, in some cases involving disordered electronic materials where $s << 1$, the D_e values can be drastically reduced by up to two orders of magnitude due to the pronounced multiple trapping events caused by the structural inhomogeneities present in the solid phase. On the contrary, we observed a nearly 2-fold improvement in the electronic transport process after the electrode decoration with NiO. Since $s \geq 0.98$, we verified that the anomalous transport in the solid electrode structure is practically absent for the different materials. These findings indicate that, in the nano-sized domains of the electrode material, the electronic transport behaves like a normal one. A comparison of the experimental findings revealed that $R_{ionic}/R_{electronic} = 16$. This small discrepancy in the resistance values is responsible for the presence of a well-defined straight line in the complex plane plot (see Figure 6b) in the medium-frequency range with a phase angle close to $-45°$, as is theoretically predicted when $Z_1 \approx Z_2$ [21]. By contrast, when this resistance ratio is very high (e.g., $R_{ionic}/R_{electronic} > 100$), the transmission line behavior is dictated only by the high impedance channel, i.e., the double-channel transmission line is converted to a single-channel one, and the complex plane plot exhibits a different profile to that shown in Figure 6b.

The overall DC resistance (e.g., the purely resistive impedance) incurred by the normal and/or anomalous transports of the electronic and ionic charge carriers in the two channels of the transmission line representation can be determined from the low-frequency limit ($\omega \to 0$) of Equation (1) (the physical model) [54]:

$$Z_{d.c.}(\omega \to 0) = \frac{\chi_1 \chi_2}{\chi_1 + \chi_2} L = \frac{R_{ionic} R_{electr.}}{R_{ionic} + R_{electr.}}. \tag{9}$$

Thus, the impedance of the transmission line is characterized by two ohmic resistances in parallel. It is predicted that the almost vertical capacitive straight line verified at very low frequencies for blocked electrodes, as is the case with supercapacitors, can be displaced more or less to the right-hand side of the complex plane plot, depending on the magnitude of the ohmic resistances imposed by the liquid and solid phases in intimate contact. Obviously, if $R_1 >> R_2$, $Z_{d.c.} \cong R_2$. On the other hand, $Z_{d.c.} \cong R_1$. These conditions imply that a single ohmic resistor describes the overall DC resistance. However, this is not the case in the present study since we verified that $R_1 \approx R_2$. We found that the $Z_{d.c.}$ values for the CNF and NiO@CNF electrodes were 203 Ω g^{-1} and 88 Ω g^{-1}, respectively. These findings reveal that the dissipative effects caused by ohmic losses are lower for the decorated electrode.

The crossover frequencies (ω_c) between DC and AC regimes for the transverse (e.g., Z_1 and Z_2) impedances of the two closely mixed phases are as follows [53]:

$$\omega_c(Z_1) = \frac{1}{(r_1 q_1)^{1/n}} = \frac{1}{(R_{ionic} Q_{ionic})^{1/n}} \tag{10}$$

$$\omega_c(Z_2) = \frac{1}{(r_2 q_2)^{1/s}} = \frac{1}{(R_{electr.} Q_{electr.})^{1/s}}. \tag{11}$$

Thus, considering the relationship between the time constant (e.g., $\tau_{c(1)} = (RQ)^{1/n}$ and $\tau_{c(2)} = (RQ)^{1/s}$), and the characteristic frequency (f_c) given by $f_c = 1/\tau_c$, one can evaluate these quantities for the ionic and electronic transport phenomena using Equations (10) and (11), respectively, as shown in Table 3.

Table 3. Characteristic frequencies and time constants for the ionic (Z_1) and electronic (Z_2) transports according to the theoretical impedance model represented by Equation (1). The exponents n and s are obtained from Equations (3) and (4), respectively.

Electrode	$f_c(Z_1)/s^{-1}$	$f_c(Z_2)/s^{-1}$	$\tau_c(Z_1)/s$	$\tau_c(Z_2)/s$
CNFs	0.81 ($n = 0.42$)	1.50 ($s = 1.00$)	1.25 ($n = 0.42$)	0.67 ($s = 1.00$)
NiO@CNFs	3.71×10^3 ($n = 0.92$)	0.49 ($s = 0.98$)	2.70×10^{-4} ($n = 0.92$)	2.06 ($s = 0.98$)

The analysis of the data in Table 3 revealed two distinct scenarios for the different electrode materials used in the symmetric coin cells. In the case of the CNF electrodes, the time constants (τ_c) were not so different for the distinct charge transport in the ionic ($\tau_{c(1)} = 1.25$ s) and electronic ($\tau_{c(2)} = 0.67$ s) phases. The very close characteristic frequencies of 0.81 s^{-1} and 1.50 s^{-1} revealed that the transition between DC and AC regimes for the ionic and electronic phases is coupled and occurs in the low to medium frequency range of the impedance spectrum. Therefore, the formation of a well-defined semicircle at the high frequencies characterized by a given time constant was not observed (see Figure 6a inset). For comparison, using a multiscale impedance model to study different supercapacitors using carbon-based porous electrodes, Huang et al. [14] recently reported $\tau_{c(1)}$ values in the range of 0.16 s to 2.35 s for their different electrodes. However, due to the limitations of the model, they did not evaluate the $\tau_{c(2)}$ values and the eventual presence of anomalous transport.

The analysis of the other case comprising the NiO@CNF composite electrodes revealed very different time constants of $\tau_{c(1)} = 2.70 \times 10^{-4}$ s and $\tau_{c(2)} = 2.06$ s for the ionic and electronic charge transports, respectively. Thus, we obtained different characteristic (crossover) frequencies of 3.71×10^{3} s^{-1} and 0.48 s^{-1} representing the transition regions in the complex plane plot for the ionic and electronic transports, respectively. As a result, three different regions can be clearly identified in the impedance spectrum (see Figure 6b): (i) the well-defined semicircle at high frequencies; (ii) the false Warburg-like straight line localized in the medium–low-frequency region, and (iii) the capacitive/pseudocapacitive straight line at very low frequencies. It is worth noting that the physicochemical origin of the high-frequency semicircle in the case of porous blocked electrodes is not due to a Faradaic (charge transfer) reaction. On the contrary, this behavior, which is predicted by the theory represented by Equation (1), is due to a combination of two factors: (i) the penetration depth dependency of the sinusoidal perturbation on applied frequency, and (ii) the presence of an "abnormal charge transport" phenomenon involving the electronic and/or ionic charge carriers in disordered media, i.e., the different phases being in intimate contact along the porous electrode surface. Unfortunately, this vital aspect, which has been known about for a long time, is ignored in most literature reports dealing with SCs. Commonly, authors not acquainted with the theoretical aspects of EIS misuse equivalent circuit analogs without a physicochemical meaning.

In fact, with rare exceptions, most of the circuit analogs used in EIS studies are merely statistical devices used as part of a trial and error method to obtain a good simulation of the impedance data using the different analog circuits present in commercial software packages. The impedance data are often simulated with good statistics. However, as expected, this nonphysical approach fails to provide a physicochemical meaning to the used circuit's parameters. For more details, please see the excellent books by Barsoukov and Macdonald [54], Orazem and Tribollet [55], and Lasia [18], which constitute a trustworthy source of knowledge about the impedance method of analysis. Unfortunately, as can be seen in several papers, the current literature using the EIS technique for dealing with energy storage devices is full of fundamental errors that are propagated in several important articles published by different research groups.

A possible explanation for the large difference in the time constants verified for the electron transport in the different electrode materials (e.g., $\tau_{c(\text{carbon material})} = 1.25$ s and $\tau_{c(\text{composite})} = 2.70 \times 10^{-4}$ s) is the pronounced occurrence of the RSR involving the Ni^{2+}/Ni^{3+} redox couple, i.e., due to the Faradaic nature of the charge storage process, a great fraction of the transported electrons taking part in the RSR process is subjected to an activation barrier, involving the presence of entropic (dissipative) effects, as predicted by the transition state theory (TST) [56]. As a result, the overall flux of electrons measured in the impedance experiments is partially suppressed by an energetic barrier in the case of the composite electrode, thus decreasing the time constant.

In general, the above discussion involving the EIS technique conveys the importance of using relevant physicochemical models represented by a transfer function (or the equivalent transmission line representation) for the detailed analysis of the significant events occurring during the charge storage process in SCs. Therefore, it becomes evident that the use of equivalent circuit analogs, commonly derived from modified versions of the well-known Randles–Ershler circuit, which was further improved by Grahame and Sluyters with the concept of Faradaic impedance for the study of different electrochemical reactions on the mercury electrode, must be used with great caution to avoid speculative discussions involving solid electrodes used in different energy storage devices that exhibit different dispersive effects.

3.3. CV and GCD Analyses

Obviously, there are several important parameters determined using EIS that are not available from the CV and GCD experiments. However, to verify the internal consistency of the specific capacitance experimental findings obtained using different electrochemical techniques, we also conducted studies using the CV and the GCD techniques. As will be seen, good agreement was found since the CV and GCD profiles are representative of true supercapacitors instead of undesirable battery-like systems. Also, the specific capacitance values determined from the EIS and GCD findings are similar.

Figure 7 contrasts the CV and GCD findings obtained for CNFs and NiO@CNFs in two distinct symmetric coin cells filled with a 1.0 M Li_2SO_4 aqueous solution. As seen in Figure 7a, we obtained a capacitive/pseudocapacitive voltage window of 1.0 V for both cells. Two important features ensured that our coin cells behaved as true supercapacitors: (i) the voltammetric curves were almost rectangular, with a "mirror-like" shape even at 50 mV s^{-1} (e.g., the absence of the peaked-shape voltammograms characteristic of "battery-like" systems), and (ii) the GCD profiles were almost triangular (e.g., the absence of the voltage plateau verified for "battery-like" systems). In addition, the retention of capacitance was excellent even after 30,000 cycles (see Figure 7e,f). The small oscillations verified for the capacitance values can be ascribed to the progressive activation of the inner surface regions by deeper penetration of the electrolyte ions [36]. In any case, the coin cell maintained high capacitance retention (e.g., >95%) during the long-term charge–discharge experiments, which is typical for well-behaved supercapacitors. These important findings revealed that the solid-state redox process involving the nickel species in the hydrated oxide (e.g., gel layer structure) is highly reversible.

A comparison of the VCs in Figure 7a,c,d revealed an enormous increase in the specific voltammetric current for the composite containing $Ni(OH)_2$. For the applied scan rates of 50, 25, and 5 mV s^{-1}, the specific capacitances obtained for CNF electrodes were 4.2, 5.0, and 5.6 F g^{-1}, respectively. At the same time, the corresponding values for the NiO@CNF electrodes were 500, 520, and 620 F g^{-1}, respectively. These findings are similar to those for Ni-based oxide electrode materials used in SCs [1,8–12]. As previously verified by Fantini and Gorenstein [57], the CV profiles for nickel hydroxide thin films are practically identical in neutral and alkaline solutions. Therefore, the absence in the present study of the pronounced peaks/bands commonly verified for battery-like $Ni(OH)_2$ composite materials in alkaline solutions can be understood considering the occurrence of a strong synergism in the composite, i.e., the pseudocapacitive process was spread over the entire voltage window where the electrolyte is stable due to the presence of a uniform distribution in the porous electrode structure of reactive sites with different activation energies for the charge transfer reaction [3,28,33]. As a result, the electrochemical response is quite similar to that commonly verified for EDLCs. These are very important findings since, in most studies, the authors are interested in fabricating a composite material that exhibits the intrinsic characteristics of well-behaved supercapacitors. This featureless voltammetric profile verified for a hydrated transition metal oxide (TMO) is not new. For example, similar findings are commonly verified for the well-known $RuO_2 \cdot xH_2O$ system in acidic and neutral solutions [58]. In addition, in the case of two-electrode cells, the faradaic current is distributed on a more flattened pattern in the voltammetric curves since the voltage for the working electrode (anode) is not measured against a true reference electrode having a potential benchmark that is constant during the experiments.

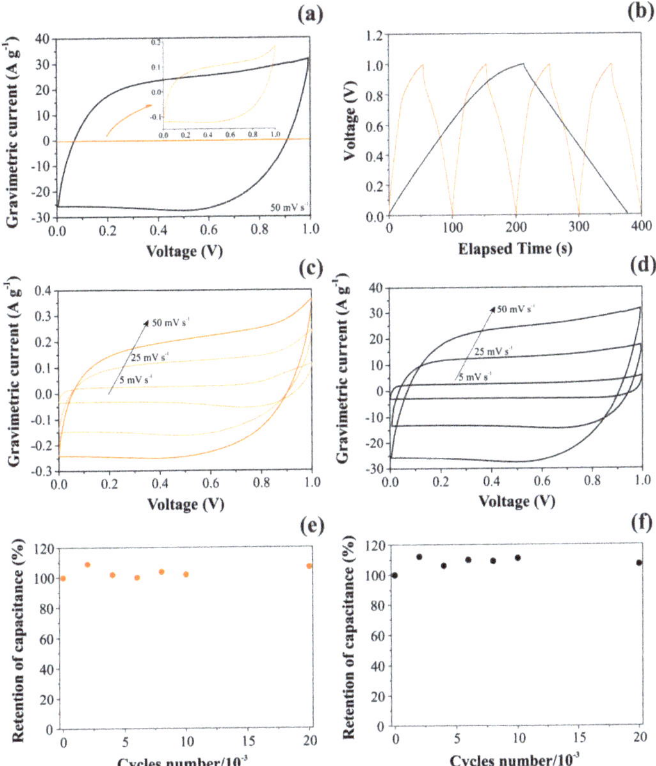

Figure 7. Electrochemical findings for CNFs (left) and NiO@CNFs (right) electrodes in symmetric coin cells filled with a 1.0 M Li_2SO_4 aqueous solution: (**a,c,d**) the scan rate is indicated in the figure; (**b**) GCD profiles obtained at 0.4 A g^{-1} for CNFs and 4 A g^{-1} for NiO@CNFs; (**e,f**) the cyclability test performed at 20 A g^{-1} for both cells. All experiments were carefully performed using the capacitive cell potential/voltage range where the electrolyte was stable (e.g., in the absence of water electrolysis).

The analysis of Figure 7b evidenced a huge increase in the discharge time when $Ni(OH)_2$ was incorporated in the carbon-based scaffold. As a result, the specific capacitance was strongly increased. Table 4 gathers the specific capacitances determined using the GCD findings for the different electrodes and normalizing factors. As seen, the overall specific capacitance for the two-electrode (coin cell) case is in good agreement with that verified in the EIS study (see Table 2). We chose to use the specific capacitance values corresponding to the individual (single) electrodes (e.g., the specific capacitances obtained in three-electrode cells) in addition to the two-electrode case obtained for the symmetric coin cell.

Table 4. Overall specific capacitances in the unities of F g^{-1} obtained from the GCD findings.

Conditions	NiO@ CNFs	CNFs
Single electrode	2548	16
Two electrodes	637	4

Obviously, the specific pseudocapacitance values of practical importance are those referring to the two-electrode case, as in the current EIS study. However, to facilitate a comparison with the literature regarding the use of traditional three-electrode cells, we calculated the capacitances obtained from GCDs for the individual electrodes. In this sense, using the experimental masses of 12.3 mg (CNFs) and 12.6 mg (composite), we verified a very small specific capacitance of 16 F g^{-1} for CNFs. On the contrary, we verified an enormous specific pseudocapacitance of 2548 F g^{-1} for NiO/Ni(OH)$_2$ that is very close to the predicted theoretical value of ~2600 F g^{-1} [59]. The maximum specific energy and power obtained for the NiO@CNF composite electrodes were 88.47 Wh kg^{-1} and 20,833 W kg^{-1}, respectively. The maximum specific energy and power obtained for the CNF electrodes were 0.56 Wh kg^{-1} and 96.78 W kg^{-1}, respectively. These GCD findings were obtained at 1 mA.

It is worth mentioning that it is not correct to normalize the capacitance using very small electrode masses for extrapolation purposes since the electrochemical data probably would not scale up with the larger masses used in practical electrodes [60]. Moreover, we would like to emphasize that, in several studies, the pseudocapacitance values reported for single- and two-electrode cases are illusory (incorrect), i.e., different battery-like electrochemical systems were erroneously characterized as true pseudocapacitors. As recently discussed by some of the present authors [1], this important issue arises from the incorrect distinction between the *capacity* (Ah g^{-1}) and *capacitance* (F g^{-1}) concepts [61].

4. Conclusions

Different symmetric supercapacitors (EDLC and PC) were used as "model systems" to apply a robust impedance model to understand the influence of disordered electrode materials on the transport anomalies occurring in the ionic and electronic conductors. For the first time, deviations from Fick's law were identified and quantified during the charge storage process in SCs using the electrochemical impedance spectroscopy (EIS) technique. The use of an impedance model containing two time constants was adequate to represent normal and anomalous charge transports in the different channels (phases) in intimate contact.

Abnormal charge transport in the ionic and electronic conductors was quantified by the dispersive parameters (n and s) extracted from the different time constants. The anomaly degree verified for the ionic transport inside the narrow pores was pronounced for the EDLC system ($n = 0.42$). In contrast, in the case of the NiO@CNF (composite) system, the ionic transport was practically regular ($n = 0.92$). At the same time, the electronic transport was nearly regular ($s \geq 0.98$) for the different solid-state conductors. The analysis of the exponent (β) representing the capacitance and pseudocapacitance dispersions revealed a low degree of deviation ($\beta \approx 0.95$) for the different electrode materials compared to the ideal case ($\beta = 1$).

It was verified that the specific capacitance increased from 2.62 to 536 F g^{-1} after decorating the carbon substrate (CNF—carbon nanofibers) using NiO nanoparticles. These findings support the occurrence of a strong synergism in the composite, where the porous electrode structure of CNFs propitiates a fast ionic transport towards the hydrated oxide structure (NiO·xH$_2$O) where the solid-state pseudocapacitance is localized. In addition, CNFs act as localized current collectors that promote a rapid capture of the electrons that originated from the solid-state redox reaction. Voltammetric and galvanostatic studies corroborated the very good capacitance and pseudocapacitance behaviors exhibited by the different symmetric coin cells, i.e., the presence of rectangular voltammetric profiles in conjunction with the triangular galvanostatic charge–discharge curves confirmed the strong capacitive behavior observed in the EIS study. Obviously, charge transport anomalies can only be identified using the impedance technique.

Author Contributions: Conceptualization, L.M.D.S., W.G.N. and H.Z.; data curation, A.M.P., L.G.D.S., D.V.F. and B.F.; methodology, W.G.N., H.Z. and L.M.D.S.; writing – original draft preparation, L.M.D.S., H.Z. and W.G.N.; review & editing, L.M.D.S. and W.G.N.; project administration, H.Z.; funding acquisition, H.Z. All authors have read and agreed to the published version of the manuscript.

Funding: This research was funded by Fundação de Amparo à Pesquisa do Estado de São Paulo grant number 2014/02163-7 and 2017/11958-1.

Institutional Review Board Statement: Not applicable.

Informed Consent Statement: Not applicable.

Data Availability Statement: The data is available on reasonable request from the corresponding author.

Acknowledgments: The authors are grateful to LNNano/CNPEM for SEM and XPS support and to the Brazilian funding agencies CNPq (301486/2016-6) and FAPESP (2014/02163-7, 2017/11958-1, 2018/20756-6) for financial support. L.M. Da Silva wishes to thank FAPEMIG (financial support for the LMMA/UFVJM Laboratory) and CNPq (PQ-2 grant: Process 301095/2018-3). The authors gratefully acknowledge support from Shell and the strategic importance of the support given by ANP (Brazil's National Oil, Natural Gas, and Biofuels Agency) through the R&D levy regulation.

Conflicts of Interest: The authors declare no conflict of interest.

References

1. Da Silva, L.M.; Cesar, R.; Moreira, C.M.; Santos, J.H.; De Souza, L.G.; Pires, B.M.; Vicentini, R.; Nunes, W.; Zanin, H. Reviewing the fundamentals of supercapacitors and the difficulties involving the analysis of the electrochemical findings obtained for porous electrode materials. *Energy Storage Mater.* **2019**, *27*, 555–590. [CrossRef]
2. Teles, J.J.; Faria, E.R.; Santos, J.H.; De Sousa, L.G.; Franco, D.V.; Nunes, W.G.; Zanin, H.; Da Silva, L.M. Supercapacitive properties, anomalous diffusion, and porous behavior of nanostructured mixed metal oxides containing Sn, Ru, and Ir. *Electrochim. Acta* **2018**, *295*, 302–315. [CrossRef]
3. De Levie, R. *Advances in Electrochemistry and Electrochemical Engineering*; Interscience: New York, NY, USA, 1967.
4. Randles, J.E.B. Kinetics of rapid electrode reactions. *Discuss. Faraday Soc.* **1947**, *1*, 11–19. [CrossRef]
5. Grahame, D.C. Mathematical Theory of the Faradaic Admittance. *J. Electrochem. Soc.* **1952**, *99*, 370C–385C. [CrossRef]
6. Sluyters, J.H.; Oomen, J.J.C. On the impedance of galvanic cells: II. Experimental verification. *Recl. des Trav. Chim. des Pays-bas* **1960**, *79*, 1101–1110. [CrossRef]
7. Delahay, P. *New Instrumental Methods in Electrochemistry*; Interscience: New York, NY, USA, 1954.
8. Nunes, W.G.; Da Silva, L.M.; Vicentini, R.; Freitas, B.G.; Costa, L.H.; Pascon, A.M.; Zanin, H. Nickel oxide nanoparticles supported onto oriented multi-walled carbon nanotube as electrodes for electrochemical capacitors. *Electrochim. Acta* **2018**, *298*, 468–483. [CrossRef]
9. Nunes, W.G.; Vicentini, R.; Freitas, B.G.; Oliveira, F.E.; Marque, A.M.P.; Filho, R.M.; Doubek, G.; Da Silva, L.M.; Zanin, H. Pseudo-capacitive behavior of multi-walled carbon nanotubes decorated with nickel and manganese (hydr)oxides nanoparticles. *J. Energy Storage* **2020**, *31*, 101583. [CrossRef]
10. Vicentini, R.; Nunes, W.; Freitas, B.G.; Da Silva, L.M.; Soares, D.M.; Cesar, R.; Rodella, C.B.; Zanin, H. Niobium pentoxide nanoparticles @ multi-walled carbon nanotubes and activated carbon composite material as electrodes for electrochemical capacitors. *Energy Storage Mater.* **2019**, *22*, 311–322. [CrossRef]
11. Pires, B.M.; Nunes, W.G.; Freitas, B.G.; Oliveira, F.E.R.; Katic, V.; Rodella, C.; Da Silva, L.M.; Zanin, H. Characterization of porous cobalt hexacyanoferrate and activated carbon electrodes under dynamic polarization conditions in a sodium-ion pseudocapacitor. *J. Energy Chem.* **2020**, *54*, 53–62. [CrossRef]
12. Nunes, W.G.; Miranda, A.N.; Freitas, B.; Vicentini, R.; Oliveira, A.C.; Doubek, G.; Freitas, R.G.; Da Silva, L.M.; Zanin, H. Charge-storage mechanism of highly defective NiO nanostructures on carbon nanofibers in electrochemical supercapacitors. *Nanoscale* **2021**, *13*, 9590–9605. [CrossRef]
13. Minakshi, M.; Mitchell, D.R.G.; Munnangi, A.R.; Barlow, A.J.; Fichtner, M. New insights into the electrochemistry of magnesium molybdate hierarchical architectures for high performance sodium devices. *Nanoscale* **2018**, *10*, 13277–13288. [CrossRef] [PubMed]
14. Huang, Q.-A.; Li, Y.; Tsay, K.-C.; Sun, C.; Yang, C.; Zhang, L.; Zhang, J. Multi-scale impedance model for supercapacitor porous electrodes: Theoretical prediction and experimental validation. *J. Power Sources* **2018**, *400*, 69–86. [CrossRef]
15. Hamann, C.H.; Hamnett, A.; Vielstich, W. *Electrochemistry*, 2nd ed.; Wiley-VCH: Weinheim, Germany, 2007.
16. Ates, M. Review study of electrochemical impedance spectroscopy and equivalent electrical circuits of conducting polymers on carbon surfaces. *Prog. Org. Coatings* **2011**, *71*, 1–10. [CrossRef]
17. Mei, B.-A.; Munteshari, O.; Lau, J.; Dunn, B.; Pilon, L. Physical Interpretations of Nyquist Plots for EDLC Electrodes and Devices. *J. Phys. Chem. C* **2017**, *122*, 194–206. [CrossRef]
18. Lasia, A. *Electrochemical Impedance Spectroscopy and Its Applications*; Springer: New York, NY, USA, 2014.

19. Paasch, G.; Micka, K.; Gersdorf, P. Theory of the electrochemical impedance of macrohomogeneous porous electrodes. *Electrochim. Acta* **1993**, *38*, 2653–2662. [CrossRef]

20. Srinivasan, V.; Weidner, J.W. Mathematical Modeling of Electrochemical Capacitors. *J. Electrochem. Soc.* **1999**, *146*, 1650–1658. [CrossRef]

21. Bisquert, J.; Garcia-Belmonte, G.; Fabregat-Santiago, F.; Compte, A. Anomalous transport effects in the impedance of porous film electrodes. *Electrochem. Commun.* **1999**, *1*, 429–435. [CrossRef]

22. De Levie, R. On porous electrodes in electrolyte solutions: I. Capacitance effects. *Electrochim. Acta* **1963**, *8*, 751–780. [CrossRef]

23. Eikerling, M.; Kornyshev, A.A.; Lust, E. Optimized Structure of Nanoporous Carbon-Based Double-Layer Capacitors. *J. Electrochem. Soc.* **2005**, *152*, E24–E33. [CrossRef]

24. Huang, J.; Zhang, J. Theory of Impedance Response of Porous Electrodes: Simplifications, Inhomogeneities, Non-Stationarities and Applications. *J. Electrochem. Soc.* **2016**, *163*, A1983–A2000. [CrossRef]

25. Itagaki, M.; Suzuki, S.; Shitanda, I.; Watanabe, K.; Nakazawa, H. Impedance analysis on electric double layer capacitor with transmission line model. *J. Power Sources* **2007**, *164*, 415–424. [CrossRef]

26. Huang, J.; Gao, Y.; Luo, J.; Wang, S.; Li, C.; Chen, S.; Zhang, J. Editors' Choice—Review—Impedance Response of Porous Electrodes: Theoretical Framework, Physical Models and Applications. *J. Electrochem. Soc.* **2020**, *167*, 166503. [CrossRef]

27. De Miranda, A.N.; Pardini, L.C.; Dos Santos, C.A.M.; Vieira, R. Evaluation of carbon fiber composites modified by in situ incorporation of carbon nanofibers. *Mater. Res.* **2011**, *14*, 560–563. [CrossRef]

28. Malard, L.M.; Pimenta, M.A.; Dresselhaus, G.; Dresselhaus, M.S. Raman spectroscopy in graphene. *Phys. Rep.* **2009**, *473*, 51–87. [CrossRef]

29. Dippel, B.; Jander, H.; Heintzenberg, J. NIR FT Raman spectroscopic study of flame soot. *Phys. Chem. Chem. Phys.* **1999**, *1*, 4707–4712. [CrossRef]

30. Dietz, R.E.; Parisot, G.I.; Meixner, A.E. Infrared Absorption and Raman Scattering by Two-Magnon Processes in NiO. *Phys. Rev. B* **1971**, *4*, 2302–2310. [CrossRef]

31. George, G.; Anandhan, S. Synthesis and characterisation of nickel oxide nanofibre webs with alcohol sensing characteristics. *RSC Adv.* **2014**, *4*, 62009–62020. [CrossRef]

32. Mironova-Ulmane, N.; Kuzmin, A.; Steins, I.; Grabis, J.; Sildos, I.; Pärs, M. Raman scattering in nanosized nickel oxide NiO. *J. Phys. Conf. Ser.* **2007**, *93*, 012039. [CrossRef]

33. Ramachandran, H.; Jahanara, M.M.; Nair, N.M.; Swaminathan, P. Metal oxide heterojunctions using a printable nickel oxide ink. *RSC Adv.* **2020**, *10*, 3951–3959. [CrossRef]

34. Silva, T.A.; Zanin, H.; Saito, E.; Medeiros, R.A.; Vicentini, F.C.; Corat, E.J.; Fatibello-Filho, O. Electrochemical behaviour of vertically aligned carbon nanotubes and graphene oxide nanocomposite as electrode material. *Electrochim. Acta* **2014**, *119*, 114–119. [CrossRef]

35. Upadhyay, G.; Devi, T.G. Raman spectroscopic study of polar aprotic molecule and its molecular associations with chemical and isotopic solvents: Comparative study with quantum-chemical calculations. *J. Mol. Liq.* **2014**, *197*, 263–271. [CrossRef]

36. Nunes, W.G.; Pires, B.M.; Oliveira, F.; de Marque, A.M.; Cremasco, L.F.; Vicentini, R.; Doubek, G.; Da Silva, L.M.; Zanin, H. Study of the aging process of nanostructured porous carbon-based electrodes in electrochemical capacitors filled with aqueous or organic electrolytes. *J. Energy Storage* **2020**, *28*, 101249. [CrossRef]

37. XPS Simplified—Nickel, Thermo Fish. Sci. (n.d.). Available online: https://xpssimplified.com/elements/nickel.php (accessed on 15 January 2021).

38. Khomenko, V.; Raymundo-Piñero, E.; Frackowiak, E.; Béguin, F. High-voltage asymmetric supercapacitors operating in aqueous electrolyte. *Appl. Phys. A* **2005**, *82*, 567–573. [CrossRef]

39. Dupuis, A. The catalyst in the CCVD of carbon nanotubes—A review. *Prog. Mater. Sci.* **2005**, *50*, 929–961. [CrossRef]

40. Bisquert, J. Influence of the boundaries in the impedance of porous film electrodes. *Phys. Chem. Chem. Phys.* **2000**, *2*, 4185–4192. [CrossRef]

41. Gharbage, B.; Mandier, F.; Lauret, H.; Roux, C.; Pagnier, T. Electrical properties of La0.5Sr0.5MnO3 thin films. *Solid State Ionics* **1995**, *82*, 85–94. [CrossRef]

42. Lokhande, C.D.; Dubal, D.P.; Joo, O.-S. Metal oxide thin film based supercapacitors. *Curr. Appl. Phys.* **2011**, *11*, 255–270. [CrossRef]

43. Pell, W.G.; E Conway, B. Analysis of power limitations at porous supercapacitor electrodes under cyclic voltammetry modulation and dc charge. *J. Power Sources* **2001**, *96*, 57–67. [CrossRef]

44. Granqvist, C. *Handbook of Inorganic Electrochromic Materials*; Elsevier BV: Amsterdam, The Netherlands, 1995.

45. Krishna, M.V.R.; Friesner, R.A. Quantum confinement effects in semiconductor clusters. *J. Chem. Phys.* **1991**, *95*, 8309–8322. [CrossRef]

46. Wehrens-Dijksma, M.; Notten, P. Electrochemical Quartz Microbalance characterization of $Ni(OH)_2$-based thin film electrodes. *Electrochim. Acta* **2006**, *51*, 3609–3621. [CrossRef]

47. Faria, I.; Torresi, R.M.; Gorenstein, A. Electrochemical intercalation in NiOx thin films. *Electrochim. Acta* **1993**, *38*, 2765–2771. [CrossRef]

48. MacArthur, D.M. The Proton Diffusion Coefficient for the Nickel Hydroxide Electrode. *J. Electrochem. Soc.* **1970**, *117*, 729–733. [CrossRef]

49. Decker, F.; Passerini, S.; Pileggi, R.; Scrosati, B. The electrochromic process in non-stoichiometric nickel oxide thin film electrodes. *Electrochim. Acta* **1992**, *37*, 1033–1038. [CrossRef]
50. Sharma, P.; Sundaram, M.M.; Watcharatharapong, T.; Jungthawan, S.; Ahuja, R. Tuning the Nanoparticle Interfacial Properties and Stability of the Core–Shell Structure in Zn-Doped NiMoO4@AWO4. *ACS Appl. Mater. Interfaces* **2021**, *13*, 56116–56130. [CrossRef] [PubMed]
51. Mott, N.F.; Davis, E.A.; Weiser, K. Electronic Processes in Non-Crystalline Materials. *Phys. Today* **1972**, *25*, 55. [CrossRef]
52. Palenskis, V. Drift Mobility, Diffusion Coefficient of Randomly Moving Charge Carriers in Metals and Other Materials with Degenerated Electron Gas. *World J. Condens. Matter Phys.* **2013**, *03*, 73–81. [CrossRef]
53. Garcia-Belmonte, G.; Bisquert, J.; Pereira, E.C.; Fabregat-Santiago, F. Switching behaviour in lightly doped polymeric porous film electrodes. Improving distributed impedance models for mixed conduction conditions. *J. Electroanal. Chem.* **2001**, *508*, 48–58. [CrossRef]
54. Barsoukov, E.; Macdonald, J.R. *Impedance Spectroscopy: Theory, Experiment and Applications*, 2nd ed.; Wiley-Interscience: Hoboken, New Jersey, USA, 2005.
55. Orazem, M.E.; Tribollet, B. *Electrochemical Impedance Spectroscopy*; Wiley: Hoboken, New Jersey, USA, 2008.
56. Bockris, J.O.M.; Reddy, A.K.N.; Gamboa-Aldeco, M. *Modern Electrochemistry 2A: Fundamentals of Electrodics*, 2nd ed.; Kluwer Academic/Plenum Publishers: New York, USA, 2000.
57. Fantini, M.; Gorenstein, A. Electrochromic nickel hydroxide films on transparent/conducting substrates. *Sol. Energy Mater.* **1987**, *16*, 487–500. [CrossRef]
58. Trasatti, S. *Electrodes of Conductive Metallic Oxides, Parts A and B*; Elsevier: Amsterdam, The Netherlands, 1980.
59. Brisse, A.-L.; Stevens, P.; Toussaint, G.; Crosnier, O.; Brousse, T. Ni(OH)$_2$ and NiO Based Composites: Battery Type Electrode Materials for Hybrid Supercapacitor Devices. *Materials* **2018**, *11*, 1178. [CrossRef]
60. Stoller, M.D.; Ruoff, R.S. Best practice methods for determining an electrode material's performance for ultracapacitors. *Energy Environ. Sci.* **2010**, *3*, 1294–1301. [CrossRef]
61. Deng, W.; Ji, X.; Chen, Q.; Banks, C.E. Electrochemical capacitors utilising transition metal oxides: An update of recent developments. *RSC Adv.* **2011**, *1*, 1171–1178. [CrossRef]

 *nanomaterials*

Article

Preparation and Bolometric Responses of MoS$_2$ Nanoflowers and Multi-Walled Carbon Nanotube Composite Network

Qin Wang, Yu Wu, Xin Deng, Liping Xiang, Ke Xu, Yongliang Li and Yangsu Xie *

College of Chemistry and Environmental Engineering, Shenzhen University, Shenzhen 518055, China; WQ1910223067@163.com (Q.W.); 2017145023@email.szu.edu.cn (Y.W.); dengxin2017@email.szu.edu.cn (X.D.); xlp727104513@163.com (L.X.); xkenergy@hotmail.com (K.X.); liyli@szu.edu.cn (Y.L.)
* Correspondence: ysxie@szu.edu.cn

Abstract: Due to their broadband optical absorption ability and fast response times, carbon nanotube (CNT)-based materials are considered promising alternatives to the toxic compounds used in commercial infrared sensors. However, the direct use of pure CNT networks as infrared sensors for simple resistance read-outs results in low sensitivity values. In this work, MoS$_2$ nanoflowers are composited with CNT networks via a facile hydrothermal process to increase the bolometric performance. The thermal diffusivity (α) against temperature (T) is measured using the transient electro-thermal (TET) technique in the range of 320 K to 296 K. The α-T curve demonstrates that the composite containing MoS$_2$ nanoflowers provides significant phonon scattering and affects the intertube interfaces, decreasing the α value by 51%. As the temperature increases from 296 K to 320 K, the relative temperature coefficient of resistance (TCR) increases from 0.04%/K to 0.25%/K. Combined with the enhanced light absorption and strong anisotropic structure, this CNT–MoS$_2$ composite network exhibits a more than 5-fold greater surface temperature increase under the same laser irradiation. It shows up to 18-fold enhancements in resistive responsivity (($R_{on} - R_{off})/R_{off}$) compared with the pure CNT network for a 1550 nm laser at room temperature (RT).

Keywords: CNT network; MoS$_2$ nanoflowers; bolometer; uncooled; photothermal performance

Citation: Wang, Q.; Wu, Y.; Deng, X.; Xiang, L.; Xu, K.; Li, Y.; Xie, Y. Preparation and Bolometric Responses of MoS$_2$ Nanoflowers and Multi-Walled Carbon Nanotube Composite Network. *Nanomaterials* **2022**, *12*, 495. https://doi.org/10.3390/nano12030495

Academic Editor: Antonio Di Bartolomeo

Received: 29 December 2021
Accepted: 26 January 2022
Published: 31 January 2022

Publisher's Note: MDPI stays neutral with regard to jurisdictional claims in published maps and institutional affiliations.

1. Introduction

Fast and sensitive infrared (IR) detectors operating at room temperature are of tremendous interest for industrial, scientific, and military applications, including in security, environmental monitoring, remote controls, optical communication, thermography, and astronomy, as well as for the latest technologies, such as in self-driving cars and for obstacle avoidance in robots [1–5]. Traditional bolometers consist of an absorber and a sensor. During detection, thermal radiation is absorbed by the absorber, leading to a temperature increase, subsequently resulting in a change in electrical resistance in the sensor, which can be measured using electrical circuits. Then, through electrical signal processing, the temperature of the target object is obtained. Nowadays, the main commercial uncooled thermistor materials are amorphous silicon (a-Si), vanadium oxide (VO$_2$), and germanium–silicon–oxide [6–8]. However, a-Si shows long response times of tens to hundreds of ms [9,10]. The production of VO$_2$ causes great environmental pollution [11,12]. Furthermore, the commercialized uncooled bolometers require sophisticated designs such as micro-bridges or thermal insulation layers to obtain good thermal insulation [13,14], as well as an extra IR absorption layer [15] to ensure good photon absorbance. Thus, although high performance can be achieved with the above complex designs, more accessible uncooled bolometric materials with self-absorbing, self-thermal-insulating, and self-sensing properties are in great demand to increase the application of bolometers in real life.

Due to their broadband IR absorption and fast responses of up to picoseconds resulting from the ultrahigh carrier mobility and weak electron–phonon scattering, carbon nanotubes (CNTs) and their composites have attracted wide attention as some of the most promising candidates for flexible IR detectors [16–20]. However, the TCR (temperature coefficient of resistance) of CNTs is low, which makes simple resistive read-outs difficult. Itkis et al. reported a large bolometric photoresponse of suspended single-walled CNT (SWCNT) films with TCR values of 1% at 330 K and 2.5% at 100 K [21], which were close to those of a VO_2 bolometer [22,23]. However, the large-scale production of single-walled carbon nanotubes (SWNTs) of high quality and purity is expensive and challenging, which limits their application [24,25]. The relatively cheaper price of MWCNTs and compromised but still excellent optical, electrical, and mechanical strength makes them a good candidate for bolometer applications. Randomly assembled MWCNT films synthesized by vacuum filtration is some of the most accessible forms of bulk CNT materials suitable for large-scale production and application. Nevertheless, for MWCNT films, the TCR was reported to be only 0.088%/K [26]. The high k and low TCR of pure MWCNT films result in weak temperature sensitivities and lead to poor bolometric performance. It would ideal if CNT bolometers could be used with simple resistive read-outs and could be manufactured without the use of high-quality CNTs or delicate microfabrication processes.

To improve the bolometric performance of CNTs, photothermal materials with high light absorption and TCR can be composited with CNTs such as graphene [17,18] and metal oxides (ZnO, VO_2) [20,27–29]. Lu et al. achieved novel exciton dissociation of a graphene–MWCNT hybrid film through heterojunctions self-assembled at the graphene–MWCNT interfaces. This method significantly improved the responsivity of the CNTs in the near-infrared region [18]. Nandi et al. used a spray coating method to prepare a suspended bolometer based on an MWCNT coated with vanadium oxide. The suspended bolometer showed a high TCR of ~−0.41%/K, which was ~4.86 times higher than that of the previously reported suspended MWCNT film [22]. Recently, it was reported that MoS_2 with a flower-like or spiral-like shape showed excellent light absorption performance [30–32]. Tahersima et al. reported on the rolling of Van der Waal heterostructures of molybdenum disulfide (MoS_2)–graphene (Gr)–hexagonal boron nitride (hBN) into a spiral solar cell, leading to strong light matter interactions and allowing for solar absorption up to 90% [31]. Yang et al. prepared an ultrathin 2D porous film for solar steam generation based on MoS_2 nanosheets and an SWCNT film. Even at an ultra-thin thickness of about 20 nm, its absorption rate across the entire solar spectrum range exceeded 82% [30]. Thus, it is advantageous for CNTs to be composited with flower-like or spiral-like MoS_2 to improve the bolometric performance.

In this work, MoS_2 nanoflowers are composited with a CNT network via a facile self-assembling strategy. The CNTs act as a thermally and electrically conductive network, while the MoS_2 nanoflowers not only enhance the broadband absorbance, but also influence the intertube coupling in the CNT network, resulting in an improved TCR value. The thermal and electrical transport properties over the temperature range of 296 K–320 K are investigated. The figures of merit of the free-standing composite network, including the photothermal performance, resistive responsivity [$(R_{on} - R_{off})/R_{off}$], detection sensitivity to a wide spectrum ranging from ultraviolet to near-infrared, and response times are studied and compared with the pure CNT network in detail.

2. Materials and Methods

2.1. Preparation of the CNT–MoS₂ Composite Network

The CNT network was purchased from XFNANO and was prepared from CNT powder by vacuum filtration. A piece of the CNT network with lateral dimensions of about 1 cm × 1 cm was cleaned with N_2 plasma (200 W, 120 s). Sodium molybdate (Na_2MoO_4) and thiourea (CH_4N_2S) were dissolved in deionized water with magnetic stirring for 30 min to form precursors with two different suspension concentrations (Table 1). The resulting solutions were denoted solution 1 and solution 2, respectively. Next, the CNT network and the prepared mixture were put into a 100 mL autoclave and reacted at 200 °C for 24 h. The samples were then removed and washed with deionized water and dried in an oven at 60 °C for 12 h. This hydrothermal process can be used to assemble MoS_2 flakes with flower-like or spiral-like nanostructures in the nm–um size range, which can significantly improve the light absorption performance [30,32–34]. Finally, the CNT–MoS$_2$ composite network was annealed in a tube furnace at 900 °C under Ar atmosphere for 2 h with a heating rate of 2 °C/min. The reaction routes can be expressed as follows [35]:

$$Na_2MoO_4\ 2H_2O + CH_4N_2S + H_2O \rightarrow MoS_2 + NH_3 + CH_3COOH + NaOH$$

Table 1. Different concentrations of precursors used for synthesizing the CNT–MoS$_2$ composite network.

Solution	Na$_2$MoO$_4$ 2H$_2$O (g)	CH$_4$N$_2$S (g)	DI Water (mL)
1	0.1210	0.1142	30
2	0.2420	0.2284	30

2.2. Structural Characterization Methods

In order to characterize the micro-structures of this composite network, we used X-ray diffraction (XRD), X-ray photoelectron spectroscopy (XPS), Raman spectroscopy, and scanning electron microscopy (SEM). The SEM images were taken using a JSM-7800F TEAM Octane Plus instrument with a voltage of 10 kV. The XRD spectroscopy was carried out by using an Empyrean diffractometer (PANalytical, the Netherlands) with Cu Kα radiation (λ = 1.54 Å) at a generator voltage of 45 kV and a generator current of 40 mA. The elemental composition and functional group analysis were tested using a Thermo Scientific K-Alpha XPS instrument. The Raman spectra were obtained using a Horiba LabRAM HR Evolution instrument. The UV–Vis–NIR spectrometer was used to characterize the absorbance of samples in the range of 300–2000 nm. The instrument was equipped with an integrating sphere to measure transmittance (T) and total reflectance (R), and finally to obtain the absorbance values ($A = 1 - T - R$).

2.3. Characterization of the Thermal Diffusivity and TCR

The transient electro-thermal (TET) technique was used to characterize the thermal diffusivity (α) of the samples. The CNT–MoS$_2$ composite network was cut into long rectangular strips, then suspended between two aluminium electrodes (the size of the measured samples in this work is presented in Table 2). A small amount of silver paste was used to fix the ends of the strip onto the electrodes and to reduce the contact resistance [1]. Before the measurement, the sample stage was installed on a cold head in a closed-cycle cryostat system (Janis, CCS) where the environmental temperature was controlled from 320 K to 296 K. The environment temperature, provided through the temperature of the cold head of the cryogenic system, was used to for the characterization of the electrical and thermal properties. At the same time a vacuum environment was provided, in which the air pressure was maintained below 10^{-2} Pa. The electrodes were connected in parallel with a current source (Keithley 6221) and an oscilloscope (Tektronix MDO 3054).

Table 2. Details of the samples measured in this study.

Sample	Length (mm)	Width (mm)	Thickness (μm)	Density (kg·m^{-3})
S1 (Low MoS$_2$ composite density)	5.74 ± 0.01	0.68 ± 0.01	33 ± 2	1470 ± 50
S2 (High MoS$_2$ composite density)	6.90 ± 0.01	0.76 ± 0.01	36 ± 2	1889 ± 50
Unannealed CNT Network	6.49 ± 0.01	0.73 ± 0.01	21 ± 2	702 ± 50
Annealed CNT Network	6.49 ± 0.01	0.45 ± 0.01	21 ± 2	365 ± 50

During the measurement, a step current was fed to the sample through a current source, causing a small and fast joule heating. Here, a one-dimensional heat transfer model can be assumed reasonably. Within a small temperature range, it can be assumed that the TCR of the sample is constant. Then, the normalized temperature can be obtained from the normalized voltage profile as: $T^* = V^* = (V_{sample} - V_0)/(V_\infty - V_0)$, where V_0 and V_∞ are the voltage of the sample before the joule heating and when it reaches steady state, respectively. Thus, the averaged normalized temperature $T^* = [T(t) - T_0]/[T(t \to \infty) - T_0]$ can be derived as [36,37]:

$$T^* = \frac{48}{\pi^4} \sum_{m=1}^{\infty} \frac{1 - (-1)^m}{m^2} \frac{1 - \exp\left[-m^2\pi^2\alpha_{measure}t/L^2\right]}{m^2} \tag{1}$$

where m is the normalized parameter, $\alpha_{measure}$ is the thermal diffusivity of sample, t is time, and L is the suspended length of the sample. Based on Equation (1), the $\alpha_{measure}$ can be obtained using MATLAB and via the least squares fitting of the V-t data. Different trial values of α are used for the fitting. The fitting errors were determined to be $\pm 10\%$ or better in our previous work based on the TET technique [36]. During the measurement, R is measured using the current source and the oscilloscope in 2-point configurations, with a small bias current (I) applied and voltage (V) probed. R is then calculated by $R = V/I$. TCR is then obtained by differentiating the R-T curve.

2.4. Test of Bolometric Response

In this process, the composite sample (S2, details shown in Table 2) is suspended between two silicon electrodes using the same method as that described in the TET characterization. Before the photodetection test, the whole sample is installed in a vacuum chamber, whose optical window is made of fused quartz. During the test, the suspended sample is fully covered by the laser spot. The laser power irradiated on the sample is adjusted using the laser output and an optical filter. The laser power is measured using an optical power meter (from Thorlabs company in this study). The power density is calculated by $P/(\pi d^2/4)$, where P is the laser power and d is the measured laser beam diameter, as illustrated in Figure S1 in the Supporting Information. The resistance response of the sample is collected using a $7\frac{1}{2}$ digital multimeter (KEITHLEY DMM7510). Upon laser irradiation, the resistances when the laser is turned on and off are denoted as R_{on} and R_{off}, respectively.

2.5. Measurement of the Response Time

To measure the transient resistive responses to the lasers, the 405 nm, 860 nm, 1064 nm, and 1550 nm laser outputs are used as the optical sources. The laser outputs are modulated to a 0.2 Hz square wave using a function generator. By applying a small DC current to the sample, with which no appreciable heating occurs, the two-point voltage profiles under the square-wave laser illumination can be recorded using the oscilloscope. In the comparative experiment, to measure the transient resistive response to the joule heating, a square-wave current of 16 mA in amplitude and 0.2 Hz in frequency is applied to the sample using the current source to check the response and to compare it with the response to the modulated laser. The transient resistive response (V-T profiles) is measured using the oscilloscope. Then, the normalized voltage can be obtained from $V^* = (V_{sample} - V_0)/(V_\infty - V_0)$, where V_0 and V_∞ are the voltages of the sample before the heating or illumination and when it reaches the steady state, respectively. From the V^*-t curve, the response time is identified when V^* is decreased by 0.95.

3. Results

3.1. Material Synthesis and Structural Characterization

Figure 1a shows the schematic of the synthesis process of the CNT–MoS$_2$ composite network. The details can be found in the experimental section. In this process, the N$_2$

plasma-cleaned CNT network is placed into the mixture of sodium molybdate and thiourea for hydrothermal treatment at 200 °C for 24 h, then it is thermally annealed at 900 °C in Ar atmosphere for 2 h. The hydrothermal method is chosen to synthesize MoS_2 because it can assemble the MoS_2 nanoflakes with different structures in the nm–μm size range. During the process of hydrothermal treatment, the amorphous MoS_2 nanoflakes grow on the surface and in the interlayer space of the CNT network. As the concentration of the mixture of sodium molybdate and thiourea increases, the shape of the MoS_2 changes from randomly arranged nanoflakes to a spherical assembly anchored at the surface and in the interlayer space of the CNT network (Figure S2). After the thermal annealing treatment, the amorphous MoS_2 is transformed into well-crystalized MoS_2 [30].

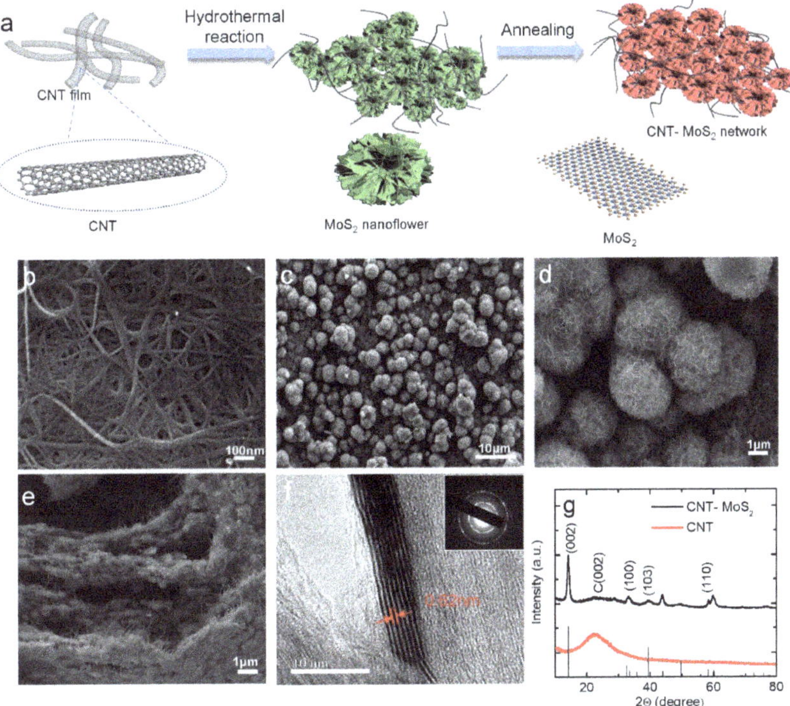

Figure 1. (**a**) Schematic illustration of the synthesis process of the CNT–MoS_2 composite network. (**b**) The SEM images of the unannealed CNT network. (**c,d**) The SEM images of the CNT–MoS_2 composite network with low to high magnification. (**e**) The SEM of the cross-section of the CNT–MoS_2 composite network. (**f**) HRTEM images of the CNT–MoS_2 composite network. The inset shows the SAED pattern. (**g**) XRD spectrum of the unannealed CNT network and CNT–MoS_2 composite network.

The SEM images of the unannealed CNT network and the CNT–MoS_2 composite network are shown in Figure 1b, c, respectively. From Figure 1b, it can be observed that the diameter of the CNTs ranges from 20 to 30 nm. These tubes are tightly entangled, displaying a randomly packed network [38]. Figure 1c shows the low-magnification SEM images of the CNT–MoS_2 composite network, where the 3D flower-like MoS_2 nanoflakes are grown on the surface and in the interlayer space of CNT network [39]. Under SEM at high magnification (Figure 1d), it can be clearly observed that the MoS_2 flowers with lateral sizes of 500 nm–3 μm assemble with each other [30]. Figure 1e shows a cross-section of the CNT–MoS_2 composite network, where it can be seen that the carbon nanotubes and MoS_2 spheres are well combined. The high-resolution transmission electron microscopy

(HRTEM) image of the CNT–MoS$_2$ composite network is shown in Figure 1f. The low-resolution TEM is shown in Figure S3. The TEM image shows a typical lattice spacing of 0.62 nm, corresponding to the (002) plane of MoS$_2$. Four peaks are shown in selected area electron diffraction (SAED) patterns (inset in Figure 1f), which correspond to the (002), (100), (103), and (110) crystal planes of MoS$_2$, respectively, indicating the high crystallinity of MoS$_2$ [30,40,41].

Figure 1g shows the XRD patterns of the unannealed CNT network and the CNT–MoS$_2$ composite network. The pure CNT network only displays a typical diffraction peak at 22.8°, which corresponds to the (002) crystal planes [30,42]. In comparison, the CNT–MoS$_2$ composite network shows five peaks at 14.4°, 22.8°, 32.7°, 39.5°, and 58.3°. The diffraction peak at 2θ = 22.8° corresponds to the CNTs [42] and the other peaks can be attributed to the (002), (100), (103), and (110) crystal planes of the hexagonal phase MoS$_2$, respectively [30,35,43]. The sharp peaks reveal that MoS$_2$ has a well-developed crystalline structure [41]. The (002) d-spacing of MoS$_2$ is calculated to be 0.62 nm according to the diffraction peak at 2θ = 14.4° using Bragg's equation, which agrees well with the TEM results [41]. These results demonstrate that the well-crystalized MoS$_2$ has been successfully composited within the CNT network.

The Raman spectra of the CNT network and the CNT–MoS$_2$ composite network are shown in Figure 2a, where the pure CNT network shows two pronounced peaks at 1341 cm^{-1} and 1588 cm^{-1}. The G mode originates from the stretching of the C-C bond, which is usually assigned to zone center phonons of E$_{2g}$ symmetry. The D peak characterizes the disordered degree of the sp^2 hybrid bond structure in the graphite structure [44–46]. The intensity of the D peak to that of the G peak (I_D/I_G) can be used to estimate the density of disorders of the carbon materials. The I_D/I_G of the original CNT network is 0.039, while the I_D/I_G is 0.028 after annealing treatment, which shows a small decrease, indicating that the structure of the CNTs is purified by the thermal annealing process. The full width at half maximum (FWHM) of the original CNT network is 27.2 cm^{-1}, which is larger than the CNT network after thermal annealing (22.3 cm^{-1}). The low I_D/I_G indicates that the defect density of the original CNT network is low. The thermal annealing treatment further reduces the defects density. After the MoS$_2$ deposition, two obvious peaks at 384 cm^{-1} and 409 cm^{-1} appear corresponding to the E$^1_{2g}$ and A$_{1g}$ modes of the hexagonal MoS$_2$, respectively. The E$^1_{2g}$ and A$_{1g}$ modes represent the molybdenum and sulphur atoms displaced in the layer, respectively. The frequency difference between A$_{1g}$ and E$^1_{2g}$ modes is 25 cm^{-1}, indicating that the MoS$_2$ in the CNT–MoS$_2$ composite network is multi-layered [47,48]. The D peak and G peak of the CNT network cannot be observed using Raman spectroscopy due to the MoS$_2$ composite layer covering the surface and the interlayer space of the CNT network.

The elemental composition and functional groups of the CNT–MoS$_2$ composite and CNT network are characterized and compared here using XPS. The XPS spectrum of the CNT–MoS$_2$ composite network reveals the existence of C, O, Mo, and S (Figure 2b). It can be observed that the intensity levels of O1s and C1s show an obvious weakening trend with the MoS$_2$ composite. The main reason for this phenomenon is the large amount of MoS$_2$ composite, which is consistent with the Raman spectra results [49]. Figure 2c shows the O1s spectrum, which can be deconvoluted into two peaks at 530.8 eV and 534.0 eV, corresponding to the C-O and O-C=O, respectively. As shown in Figure 2d, the peak of C1s can be deconvoluted into three peaks at 284.8 eV, 285.3 eV, and 286.9 eV, corresponding to C-C, C=C, and C-O, respectively. Figure 2e, f further proves the existence of the MoS$_2$. Figure 2e shows a high-resolution Mo3d spectrum with two peaks at 229.1 eV and 232.3 eV. These peaks correspond to the binding energies of Mo3d$_{5/2}$ and Mo3d$_{3/2}$, respectively, and confirm the presence of Mo^{4+} [50]. Furthermore, the weak peak at 226.3 eV is attributed to S2s. The peaks of S2p are located at 161.8 eV and 162.9 eV (Figure 2f), which are related to S2p$_{3/2}$ and S2p$_{1/2}$, respectively. These XPS data further confirm the formation of MoS$_2$.

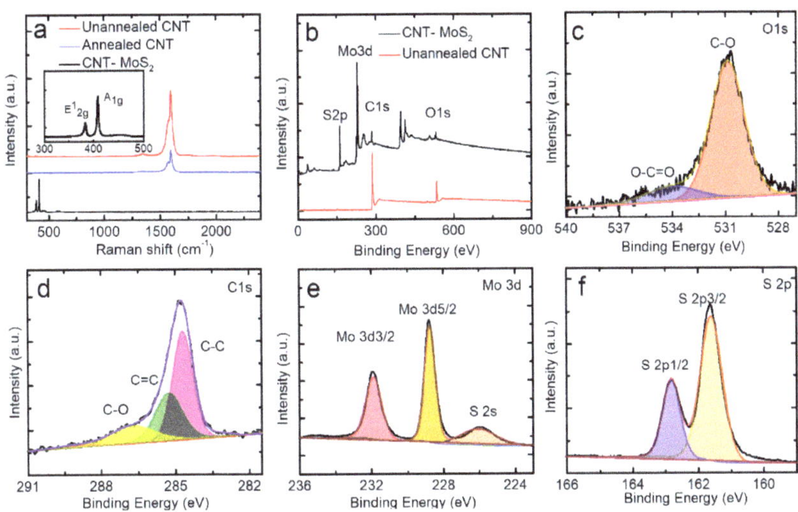

Figure 2. (**a**) Raman patterns of the unannealed and annealed CNT networks and CNT–MoS$_2$ composite network. (**b**) XPS survey of the unannealed CNT network and CNT–MoS$_2$ composite network, as well as the high-resolution deconvoluted (**c**) O1s, (**d**) C1s, (**e**) Mo3d, and (**f**) S2p spectra of the CNT–MoS$_2$ composite network.

3.2. Thermal Properties and Temperature Sensitivity

To study the effect of the MoS$_2$ composite concentration, we prepared samples with different composite concentrations. In this work, the transient electro-thermal (TET) technique was used to measure α values of the CNT–MoS$_2$ composite network [36,37,51,52]. For comparison, the pure CNT network after the thermal annealing was also studied. The details for the measured samples are presented in Table 2. Figure 3a shows a schematic of the experimental setup used for measuring the α and electrical resistance (R) values of the network using the TET technique. The details can be found in the experimental section.

To study the effect of the MoS$_2$ composite concentration, we prepared samples with different composite concentrations, as shown in Table 1, where S1 is the composite network with low MoS$_2$ composite density and S2 is the composite network with high MoS$_2$ composite density. Figure 3b shows the normalized voltage $V^* = [V(t)v - V_0]/[V_\infty - V_0]$ versus time for the unannealed CNT network and the CNT–MoS$_2$ composite network. According to Equation (1), when the suspended length is constant, the higher α, the shorter the time taken to reach the steady state. It can be seen that the characteristic time (the time when V^* reaches 0.8665) [36] of the CNT–MoS$_2$ composite network with the high composite density is much longer than that of the unannealed CNT network. The characteristic time of the unannealed CNT network is longer than the CNT–MoS$_2$ composite network with the low composite density [36,37,51,52]. As shown in Figure 3c, as the concentration of the MoS$_2$ composite increases, the α of the composite network first increases and then decreases. The α increases from $1.29 \pm 0.13 \times 10^{-5}$ m^2/s for pure CNTs to $1.50 \pm 0.15 \times 10^{-5}$ m^2/s for S1, which is a 1.2-fold increase. As the MoS$_2$ composite concentration further increases, the α decreases to $6.36 \pm 0.64 \times 10^{-6}$ m^2/s, which is a 51% reduction compared with the unannealed CNT network. Therefore, to ensure a good thermal insulation effect, S2 with the much higher MoS$_2$ composite and lower α was chosen for the bolometric performance study, which is denoted as the CNT–MoS$_2$ composite network in the following section. The fitting process for these TET signals was conducted using MATLAB. Different trial values of α were used for the fitting. The fitting errors were determined to be $\pm 10\%$ or better, as studied carefully in our previous work based on the TET technique [36].

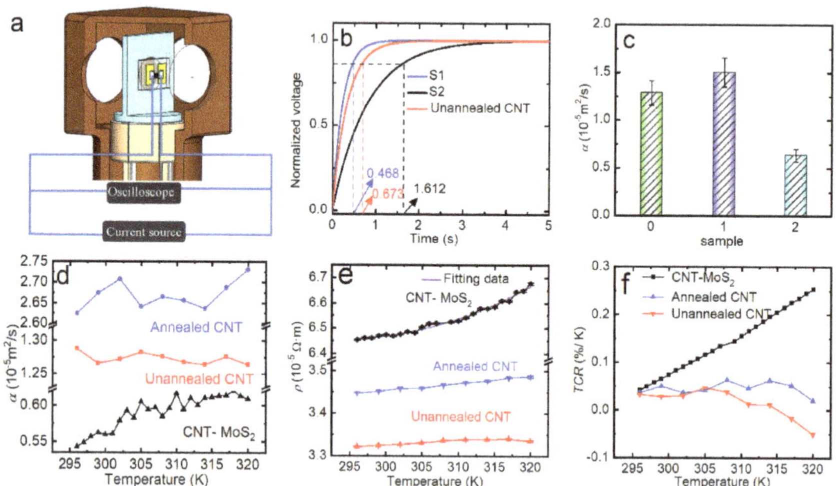

Figure 3. (**a**) Schematic of the experimental setup used for measuring the α and electrical resistance values from 296 K to 320 K. (**b**) The normalized voltage curves of TET signals and the characteristic times of the unannealed CNT network and the CNT–MoS$_2$ composite network with low and high MoS$_2$ composite density, respectively. (**c**) A comparison of the measured α value at RT against the MoS$_2$ composite density. (**d**) The measured α value. The measurement uncertainty of α based on the TET technique is ±10%, which is omitted in the figure for better comparison. (**e**) A comparison of the resistivity and (**f**) TCR values of the samples at different temperatures (296 K–320 K).

In order to study the underlying phonon propagation mechanisms, α values of the unannealed CNT network, annealed CNT network, and composite network (S2) were further measured in the temperature range of 320 K to 296 K (the details of the samples in this work are presented in Table 2). As shown in the Figure 3d, for the unannealed CNT network, α decreases from 1.29×10^{-5} m^2/s to 1.24×10^{-5} m^2/s when the temperature increases from 296 K to 320 K. This trend is similar to the previous reports for carbon-based materials [37]. However, the α of annealed CNT network increases from 2.62×10^{-5} m^2/s to 2.73×10^{-5} m^2/s when the temperature increases from 296 K to 320 K. For the CNT–MoS$_2$ composite network, as the environmental temperature increases from 296 K to 320 K, the α value of the CNT–MoS$_2$ composite network gradually increases from 5.43×10^{-6} m^2/s to 6.08×10^{-6} m^2/s. The unusual α-T behavior of the annealed CNT network and CNT–MoS$_2$ composite network indicates that the effect of phonon scattering at intertube interfaces dominates the thermal transport within them [51]. As the temperature goes down, the thermal expansion of the CNTs could deteriorate the contact among CNTs and contributes to the decreasing α. The detailed data for CNT–MoS$_2$ composite network can be found in Supporting Information in Figure S4.

Figure 3e and Figure S4 shows the measured ρ-T curves of the CNT network and the CNT–MoS$_2$ composite network. Since the maximum test temperature of the closed-cycle cryostat system (Janis, CCS) can only reach 320 K, we could not obtain data above 320 K. In the future, a new testing chamber will be required to measure the TCR at higher temperatures. As shown in the figures, the resistivity of the unannealed CNT network increases with the rising temperature from 296 K to 315 K, showing a metallic behavior [53]. As the temperature increases from 315 K to 320 K, the resistivity of the unannealed CNT network decreases a little. The resistivity of the annealed CNT network increases monotonously with the increasing temperature. For the CNT–MoS$_2$ composite network, the resistivity increases monotonously and nonlinearly with the increasing temperature across the whole temperature range from 295 K to 320 K. The ρ-T curve can be fitted well using a quadratic function (Figure 3e). The temperature coefficient of resistance (TCR) is the key characteristic used for evaluating the bolometric performance, which can be calculated using the formula $TCR = dR/(dT \cdot R_T)$, where R_T is the resistance at temperature T. To reduce the fluctuation of the TCR curve, the Savitzky–Golay function is used to smooth the resistance curves first. As shown in Figure 3f, the TCR of the CNT–MoS$_2$ composite network increases with the increasing temperature. At 296 K, the TCR is about 0.03–0.04%/K for both the pure CNT network and the composite network, which is consistent with the reported values in the literature [54]. The TCR for the pure CNT network stays around or below 0.05%/K in the temperature range of 296 K to 320 K. For the composite network, as the temperature increases from 296 K to 320 K, the TCR increases from 0.04%/K to 0.25%/K, which is 6 times higher.

Compared with the pure CNT network, the CNT–MoS$_2$ composite network shows a metallic electrical resistivity of stronger temperature dependence. As the temperature increases from 296 K to 320 K, the relative TCR of the CNT–MoS$_2$ composite network increases from 0.04%/K to 0.25%/K. From the XPS data, the CNTs are not chemically doped by S. Thus, the existence of the MoS$_2$ nanoflowers mainly affects the physical structure of CNT network. The 6-fold higher TCR at 320 K indicates that the thermal strain effect becomes more significant in the electron transport of CNTs due to the MoS$_2$ composite, leading to a much higher TCR. For CNT–MoS$_2$ composite network, the CNTs play the role of an electrical connecting network. When the temperature changes, the thermal expansion of the MoS$_2$ and CNTs is different, which leads to thermal strain on the CNTs. It has been reported that the electrical properties of CNTs are not only affected by intrinsic factors, but also extrinsic factors such as the thermal strain and the significant intertube contact resistance [55–59]. The positive TCR of graphene under strain has been illustrated in the literature [51,60,61]. For CNTs, first-principle calculations have shown that the electronic band structures and the electron–phonon scattering rates are strongly correlated with axial strain [62,63]. However, due to the much larger diameter, the intrinsic conductivity of MWCNTs is expected to be less affected by the strain. The strain can affect not only the intrinsic electrical transport of CNT, but also the intertube interface contact resistance, which could be the main reason for the nonlinear temperature dependence of the network resistance. Liu et al. reported an abnormal temperature coefficient of resistance for PMMA-supported graphene [61]. The combined effects, including the positive thermal expansion of the PMMA, negative thermal expansion coefficient of graphene, and intrinsic resistance change of relaxed graphene against temperature, determined the observed strong nonlinear R-T jointly. In our previous work, we found a very strong nonlinear temperature dependence of resistance for ultra-light graphene aerogels, where the interfaces played a dominating role in thermal transport. The strong nonlinear behavior resulted from the temperature-sensitive interconnection among graphene flakes [51]. In the literature, it was found that the temperature coefficient of resistance of graphene nanowall–polymer films changed from around 6%/K at 25 °C to 180%/K at 40 °C due the thermal strain effect [64]. Thus, the strain effect on CNTs is expected to contribute to the higher TCR of the CNT–MoS$_2$ composite network. For the carbon nanotube bolometer, the TCR values at room temperature were found to be about -0.07%/K and -0.03%/K for 90-nm-thick purified and 100-nm-thick COOH-functionalized SWCNT films, respectively [65]. Lu et al. prepared a SWCNT bolometer with a TCR of 0.17%/K and a MWCNT bolometer with a TCR of 0.07%/K [19]. Kumar et al. prepared a bolometer based on the MWCNT film with TCR of 0.088%/K at RT [26]. Although the TCR of the CNT–MoS$_2$ composite network was still lower than that of commercial thermistor materials, the TCR of the CNT–MoS$_2$ composite network at 320 K was improved significantly compared to the pure MWCNT films reported in the literature.

3.3. Photothermal Performance

The resistive bolometric responses to the laser illumination in ultraviolet to near-infrared wavelength ranges were measured in this work. Figure 4a shows the experimental setup. To compare the light absorbance of the CNT network, for the pure MoS$_2$ and the

CNT–MoS$_2$ composite network, the UV–Vis–NIR spectra characterization was conducted, where the absorption spectra from 300–2000 nm were measured. As shown in Figure 4b, the absorption of the composite network is higher than the CNT network and MoS$_2$ powders. The unannealed and annealed CNT networks show absorption in the ranges of 83–87% and 72–82%, respectively, while the MoS$_2$ exhibits an absorption range of 74–92%. The MoS$_2$ composite increases the absorbance of the CNT–MoS$_2$ composite network to 85%-94% over the whole range of 300–2000 nm. Yang et al. [30] also reported that in the wavelength range of 300 nm to 2500 nm, the photon absorption capability of a CNT–MoS$_2$ composite network was significantly higher than that of a CNT network, which increased from 40–88% to 90–95%. The main reason for this phenomenon can be attributed to the synergistic photon absorption effect of the MoS$_2$ and CNT, as well as the higher thickness of the samples after the MoS$_2$ composite.

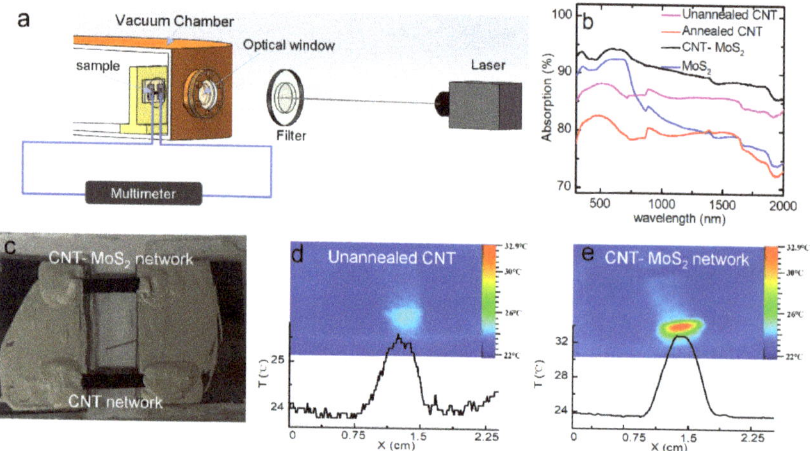

Figure 4. (**a**) Schematic of the experimental setup used for measuring the bolometric response at room temperature. (**b**) Comparison of UV–Vis–NIR absorption spectra for the CNT, MoS$_2$, and CNT–MoS$_2$ composite networks. (**c**) A photograph of the two suspended samples. Infrared images of the suspended (**d**) CNT network and (**e**) CNT–MoS$_2$ composite network under the same uniform laser irradiation. The coordinate axis shows the temperature distribution along the horizontal direction.

To investigate the photothermal performance of the composite network, the temperature increases of the CNT network and the CNT–MoS$_2$ composite network under the 36.8 mW uniform laser irradiation were measured using an infrared camera (Fotric 227s) in air. The CNT network and CNT–MoS$_2$ composite network were cut into rectangular shapes of the same length and width. Then, the two samples were suspended between two silicon electrodes. Silver paste was used to connect the samples with the electrodes. Figure 4c shows a digital photograph of the suspended samples. The infrared images of the samples under 36.8 mW uniform 405 nm laser irradiation as their temperature reached steady state are shown in Figure 4d, e, respectively. The inset figures show the temperature distributions along the horizontal direction for the two samples. It can be seen that at the steady state, the surface temperature of the pure CNT sample increases from 23.8 °C to 25.6 °C, while the surface temperature of the CNT–MoS$_2$ composite network increases from 23.8 °C to 32.9 °C. The surface temperature increase for the composite network (9.1 °C) is more than 5 times that of the CNT network (1.8 °C). This can be attributed to the higher photon absorbance and the stronger anisotropic structure of the composite network. According to Figure 4b, it can be seen that MoS$_2$ has strong light absorption in the ultraviolet wavelength and gradually weakens in the infrared wavelength, while CNTs can absorb the light in the infrared wavelength. The light is mainly absorbed by the top layer of the network.

When the temperature of the top layer is increased as a result of the absorbed light, the thermal energy is then conducted to the electrodes and the bottom layer. In addition, the thermal energy is dissipated through thermal radiation. As can be seen in Figure 1e, the MoS_2 is composited on the surface and in the interlayer space of the CNT network. As a result, along the thickness direction, the thermal conduction could be greatly impeded by the porous MoS_2 nanoflowers as well as the resulting interlayer voids. As a result, heat is localized significantly near the top layer of the CNT network. This means the temperature of the top layer is very high, resulting in higher thermal energy loss through thermal radiation. However, the bottom surface shows a smaller temperature rise. Therefore, the amount of thermal radiation from its lower surface is reduced compared to CNT network. It should be noted that since the infrared image was taken in air, the air convection effect was not avoided. For the bolometric sensing, the sensor was equipped in a vacuum, which further reduced the heat loss through air convection and led to much higher temperature increases.

3.4. Bolometer Performance

The resistive bolometric response to the laser illumination in ultraviolet to near-infrared wavelength ranges was measured. Figure 4a shows the experimental setup. The details of the experiment can be found in the experimental section. We chose 405 nm, 860 nm, 1064 nm, and 1550 nm lasers, which can represent the UV–Vis–NIR range. The resistances when the laser is turned on and off is denoted as R_{on} and R_{off}, respectively. The R_{on} and R_{off} results are summarized in Figure 5. Figure 5a shows the raw data for the resistance response of the CNT–MoS_2 composite network to the 405 nm laser. In the first round of testing, the laser power increased from 14 mW to 93 mW. The corresponding R_{on} and R_{off} are denoted as I-ON and I-OFF, respectively, in the figure. When the laser was turned on, R showed a liner increasing trend as the laser power increased (I-ON). To study the repeatability of the response, the resistance response was measured again as the laser power was reduced from 93 mW to 14 mW. The corresponding R_{on} and R_{off} are denoted as D-ON and D-OFF, respectively, in the figure. As is shown in Figure 5a, the data of the decreasing round shows good consistency with that of the increasing round. This proves that the bolometric response of the composite network has good repeatability. The relative resistive responsivity per mW of power $dR/(P{\cdot}R)$ is calculated using $(R_{on} - R_{off})/(R_{off}{\cdot}P)$, where P is the incident laser power [1]. As shown in Figure 5b, as the incident laser power increases from 14 mW to 93 mW, the corresponding responsivity changes from 0.114%/mW to 0.149%/mW.

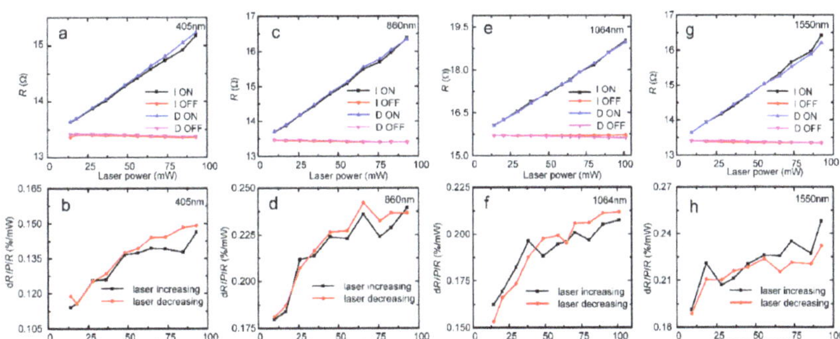

Figure 5. The *R-P* curves of the CNT–MoS_2 composite network under laser irradiation at different wavelengths: (**a**) 405 nm; (**c**) 860 nm; (**e**) 1064 nm; (**g**) 1550 nm. The relative resistive responsivity per mW of power $dR/(P{\cdot}R)$ curves under laser irradiation at different wavelength: (**b**) 405 nm; (**d**) 860 nm; (**f**) 1064 nm; (**h**) 1550 nm.

In addition, Figure 5c,e,g show the original data for the resistance responses to the 860 nm, 1064 nm, and 1550 nm lasers, respectively. All of the resistance responses show a similar trend, whereby the resistance increases linearly with the increasing laser power. The two rounds of data show good repeatability. Figure 5d,f,h show the relative resistive responses to the 860 nm, 1064 nm, and 1550 nm lasers, respectively. To check the bolometric response to lower laser power densities, the laser power was further reduced to 3 mW. Figure S5 shows that the CNT–MoS$_2$ composite network also exhibits good repeatability and high responsivity to low laser powers of 3–20 mW. It should be noted that the *R-P* curve appears to be linear in Figure 5. However, the *R-P* curves were measured under lower laser power. As can be seen in Figure S5, the dR/dP value under the lower laser power is lower than that under higher laser power. Under higher laser power, the dR/dP values of the 405 nm, 860 nm, 1064 nm, and 1550 nm lasers are 0.0192 Ω/mW, 0.0319 Ω/mW, 0.0335 Ω/mW, and 0.0321 Ω/mW, respectively. However, under the lower laser power, the dR/dP values of the 405 nm, 860 nm, 1064 nm, and 1550 nm lasers are 0.0150 Ω/mW, 0.0156 Ω/mW, 0.0208 Ω/mW, and 0.0178 Ω/mW, respectively. This indicates that the dependence of the network resistance on the laser power is nonlinear.

For better comparison of the CNT–MoS$_2$ composite network and the CNT network, the responsivity is calculated by dR/R = (R_{on} − R_{off})/R_{off}. For comparison, Figure S6 shows the *R-P* curves of the unannealed CNT network at different wavelengths. The annealed CNT network was also tested for comparison. However, the annealed CNT network showed very poor repeatability and responsivity, probably due to the unstable intertube connection. Thus, the unannealed CNT network was chosen for the bolometric performance study. Their responses for a laser power density of 2 mW/mm^2 are compared and summarized in Figure 6a (raw data presented in Figures S7 and S8). It can be seen that the responsivity of the CNT–MoS$_2$ composite network is much higher than that of the unannealed CNT network, which improves by 6.5-, 5.5-, 6.5-, and 18.5-fold under the 405 nm, 860 nm, 1064 nm, and 1550 nm laser irradiation, respectively.

In addition, it can be observed that when the laser is turned off, the variation of resistance (I-OFF and D-OFF) of the CNT–MoS$_2$ composite network is small (less than 0.147%). The noise of the resistance readout is calculated to be as low as R_N = 0.02 Ω (the standard deviation of the I-OFF and D-OFF). By taking the resistance stability into consideration, the minimum detectable laser power can be calculated by R_N/(dR/dP). Therefore, laser powers as low as 1.005 mW from the 405 nm laser, 0.592 mW from 860 nm, 1.040 mW from 1064 nm, and 0.616 mW from 1550 nm can be detected by the CNT–MoS$_2$ composite network-based bolometer. For comparison, for the unannealed CNT network bolometer, the minimum detectable laser power is 2.287 mW from the 405 nm laser, 1.100 mW from 860 nm, 1.645 mW from 1064 nm, and 0.894 mW from 1550 nm. As summarized in Figure 6b, the minimum detectable laser power of the CNT–MoS$_2$ composite network is lower than the unannealed CNT network, which indicates that the composite network-based bolometer shows higher detecting sensitivity.

Considering that the mechanism of the photoresponse could be photovoltaic or bolometric, to clarify the mechanism of the photoresponse, the resistance responses to the laser heating and the joule heating were compared. The experimental setup is shown in Figure 4a. To measure the transient resistive responses to the laser irradiation, the 405 nm, 860 nm, 1064 nm, and 1550 nm lasers were used as the optical sources. The laser output was modulated to a 0.2 Hz square wave using a function generator. In the comparative experiment, to measure the transient resistive response to the joule heating, a square-wave current of 16 mA in amplitude and 0.2 Hz in frequency was applied to the sample to check its response and to compare it with the response to the modulated laser. The transient voltage response (*V-t* profiles) was measured using the oscilloscope. The detailed raw data can be found in Figures S9 and S10 in the Supporting Information. All of the voltages of the CNT–MoS$_2$ composite network increase and reach the steady state under the three scenarios (Figure S11).

Figure 6c shows the normalized voltage−time profiles (*V**-*t*). Excellent agreement can be seen between the transient responses to the laser illumination and joule heating, where similar characteristic times of 469 ms for the joule heating, 446 ms for the 405 nm laser, and 460 ms for the 1550 nm laser heating can be seen. These results demonstrate that the photoresponse behavior of the CNT–MoS$_2$ composite network is bolometric [13]. Furthermore, the response time of the CNT–MoS$_2$ composite network and the CNT network under laser irradiation ay different wavelengths were compared. As shown in Figure 6d, the response time of the CNT–MoS$_2$ composite network is about twice of that of the CNT network. As discussed above, the α value of the CNT–MoS$_2$ composite network was measured to be about half of the α of the unannealed CNT network. Considering the similar suspended lengths of the samples, as demonstrated in Equation (1), the response time of the one-dimensional heat conduction under uniform heating was only determined by α. Thus, the response time results were consistent with the measured α results for the two samples discussed above.

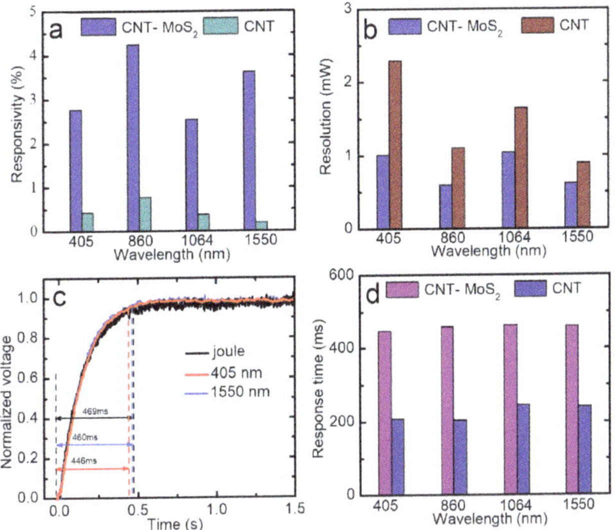

Figure 6. (**a**) A comparison of the reponsivity (dR/R) values of the unannealed CNT network and the CNT–MoS$_2$ composite network under the same 2 mW/mm^2 laser power density at different wavelengths. (**b**) A comparison of the sensitivity (the minimum detectable laser power) levels of the unannealed CNT network and the CNT–MoS$_2$ composite network to different laser wavelengths. (**c**) Comparison of normalized voltage–time profiles between the modulated laser heating and joule heating, showing the same response times and confirming that the photoresponse to the laser is a bolometric effect. (**d**) A comparison of the response times of the unannealed CNT network and the CNT–MoS$_2$ composite network to different laser wavelengths.

Therefore, the mechanism of the photoresponse for the CNT–MoS$_2$ composite network can be described as follows. Under laser illumination, the photons are absorbed by the sample, which produces photoexcited carriers (excitons) [1]. Subsequently, the electron–phonon interaction leads to a fast transfer of the energy into the CNT lattice. Then, the temperature increase provides more phonon scattering opportunities for electrons, thereby increasing the electrical resistance of the sample. Therefore, the resistance of the CNT–MoS$_2$ composite network increases with the laser power. According to the one-dimensional thermal conduction model shown in Equation (1), the decay time (the corresponding time when the normalized voltage reaches 0.95) can be derived as $\Delta t_c = 0.2026L^2/\alpha$. Thus, the response time is proportional to L^2 and inversely proportional to α [1]. In our work, the suspended length of the CNT–MoS$_2$ composite network was 2.15 mm. If the suspended length of the sample is reduced to 350 μm (the typical size of a pixel element of bolometric detector arrays) in the future, the response time of the CNT–MoS$_2$ composite network will be reduced to 1/36 of the original response time, corresponding to 11.76–12.25 ms and a frame rate of 4150–4000 Hz, meeting the requirements for real-time infrared imaging.

4. Conclusions

In summary, MoS$_2$ nanoflowers were composited with the MWCNT network via a facile self-assembling strategy to boost the bolometric performance. The α-T curve demonstrated that the MoS$_2$ nanoflowers provide significant phonon scattering and affect the intertube interfaces, decreasing α by 51%. As the temperature increased from 296 K to 320 K, the relative TCR increased from 0.04%/K to 0.25%/K. The detection experiment under low laser power proved that the CNT–MoS$_2$ composite network had strong sensitivity. It showed 5–18-fold enhancements in resistive responsivity compared with the pure CNT network to the 405–1550 nm laser irradiation at room temperature (RT). Under 2 mW/mm^2 power density for the 1550 nm laser, the responsivity reached 3.61%. The response time range of the 350-μm-long sample was about 11.76–12.25 ms, which was consistent with the joule heating result. This confirmed that the photoresponse of the CNT–MoS$_2$ composite network was bolometric. The simple device structure and the removal of the requirement for high-quality CNTs represent steps forward towards the wide application of CNT-based IR detectors.

Supplementary Materials: The following supporting information can be downloaded at: https://www.mdpi.com/article/10.3390/nano12030495/s1 Figure S1. Measure the diameter of (a) 405 nm, (b) 860 nm, (c) 1064 nm, and (d) 1550 nm laser through knife edge technique [66]; Figure S2. Low- and High- magnification of SEM images of the sample 1 with low MoS$_2$ decoration; Figure S3. Low resolution of SEM images of the CNT-MoS$_2$ composite network; Figure S4. The measured α and resistivity of the composite network at different temperatures (296 K-320 K). The measurement uncertainty of α based on the TET technique is ±10%, which is omitted in the figure for better comparison; Figure S5. the R-P curve comparison of the CNT-MoS$_2$ composite network under low laser power irradiation with different wavelength: (a) 405 nm, (b) 860 nm, (c) 1064 nm, (d) 1550 nm and (e) the comparison of the dR/R-PD (power density) curve; Figure S6. the R-P curve of the pure CNT network with different wavelength: (a) 405 nm, (b) 860 nm, (c) 1064 nm, and (d) 1550 nm; Figure S7. the dR/R-PD (power density) curve of the pure CNT network under laser irradiation with different wavelength: (a) 405 nm, (b) 860 nm, (c) 1064 nm, and (d) 1550 nm; Figure S8. the dR/R-PD curve of the CNT-MoS$_2$ composite network under laser irradiation with different wavelength: (a) 405 nm, (b) 860 nm, (c) 1064 nm, and (d) 1550 nm; Figure S9. The normalized voltage-time profiles of the pure CNT network under the laser irradiation of different wavelength: (a) 405 nm, (b) 860 nm, (c) 1064 nm, and (d) 1550 nm; Figure S10. The normalized voltage-time profiles of the CNT-MoS$_2$ composite network under the laser irradiation of different wavelength: (a) 405 nm, (b) 860 nm, (c) 1064 nm, and (d)1550 nm; Figure S11. the voltage-time profiles of the composite network under the modulated laser heating and the joule heating. (With offset for comparison)

Author Contributions: Conceptualization, Y.X.; methodology, Q.W., Y.X.; formal analysis, Q.W., L.X.; investigation, Q.W., Y.W., X.D.; data curation, Q.W., Y.W., X.D., K.X.; writing—original draft preparation, Q.W.; writing—review and editing, Y.X., Y.L., K.X. All authors have read and agreed to the published version of the manuscript.

Funding: National Natural Science Foundation of China (No. 51906161), Natural Science Foundation of Guangdong Province (No. 2020A1515011186), Educational Commission of Guangdong Province of China (No 2020ZDZX2011), the Start-Up Fund of Shenzhen University (QNJS0069), and the Scientific Research Foundation for Talented Scholars in Shenzhen (RC00052).

Institutional Review Board Statement: Not applicable.

Informed Consent Statement: Not applicable.

Data Availability Statement: Not applicable.

Conflicts of Interest: The authors declare no conflict of interest.

References

1. Xie, Y.; Han, M.; Wang, R.; Zobeiri, H.; Deng, X.; Zhang, P.; Wang, X. Graphene Aerogel Based Bolometer for Ultrasensitive Sensing from Ultraviolet to Far-Infrared. *ACS Nano* **2019**, *13*, 5385–5396. [CrossRef] [PubMed]
2. Lee, G.-H.; Efetov, D.K.; Jung, W.; Ranzani, L.; Walsh, E.D.; Ohki, T.A.; Taniguchi, T.; Watanabe, K.; Kim, P.; Englund, D.; et al. Graphene-based Josephson junction microwave bolometer. *Nature* **2020**, *586*, 42–46. [CrossRef] [PubMed]
3. Zhang, M.; Yeow, J.T.W. Flexible Polymer–Carbon Nanotube Composite with High-Response Stability for Wearable Thermal Imaging. *ACS Appl. Mater. Interfaces* **2018**, *10*, 26604–26609. [CrossRef] [PubMed]
4. Blaikie, A.; Miller, D.; Alemán, B.J. A fast and sensitive room-temperature graphene nanomechanical bolometer. *Nat. Commun.* **2019**, *10*, 4726. [CrossRef]
5. Tarasov, M.; Svensson, J.; Kuzmin, L.; Campbell, E.E.B. Carbon nanotube bolometers. *Appl. Phys. Lett.* **2007**, *90*, 163503. [CrossRef]
6. Weiler, D.; Hochschulz, F.; Würfel, D.; Lerch, R.; Geruschke, T.; Wall, S.; Heß, J.; Wang, Q.; Vogt, H. Uncooled digital IRFPA-family with 17μm pixel-pitch based on amorphous silicon with massively parallel Sigma-Delta-ADC readout. In Proceedings of the Infrared Technology and Applications XL, Baltimore, MD, USA, 5–9 May 2014; Volume 9070, p. 90701. [CrossRef]
7. Sumesh, M.A.; Thomas, B.; Vijesh, T.V.; Rao, G.M.; Viswanathan, M.; Karanth, S.P. Optically Immersed Bolometer IR Detectors Based on V_2O_5 Thin Films with Polyimide Thermal Impedance Control Layer for Space Applications. *J. Infrared Millim. Terahertz Waves* **2017**, *39*, 6–23. [CrossRef]
8. Sumesh, M.; Karanth, S.; Prakash, S.; Laxmiprasad, A.; Nagendra, C. Ion beam sputtered Ge-Si-O amorphous thin films for microbolometer infrared detectors and their application in earth sensors. *Sens. Actuators A Phys.* **2013**, *192*, 81–91. [CrossRef]
9. Syllaios, A.J.; Ha, M.J.; McCardel, W.L.; Schimert, T.R. Measurement of thermal time constant of microbolometer arrays. In Proceedings of the Infrared Technology and Applications XXXI, Orlando, FL, USA, 28 March–1 April 2005; Volume 5783, pp. 625–631. [CrossRef]
10. Esteves, B.; Pimenta, S.; Vieira, E.M.F.; Freitas, J.R.; Rodrigues, J.A.; Correia, J.H. SnO_X and a-Si thin-films based photodiode in a flexible substrate for visible spectral region. *Mater. Lett.* **2021**, *286*, 129251. [CrossRef]
11. Yang, J.; Teng, Y.; Wu, J.; Chen, H.; Wang, G.; Song, L.; Yue, W.; Zuo, R.; Zhai, Y. Current status and associated human health risk of vanadium in soil in China. *Chemosphere* **2017**, *171*, 635–643. [CrossRef]
12. Wang, S.; Zhang, B.; Li, T.; Li, Z.; Fu, J. Soil vanadium(V)-reducing related bacteria drive community response to vanadium pollution from a smelting plant over multiple gradients. *Environ. Int.* **2020**, *138*, 105630. [CrossRef]
13. Han, Q.; Gao, T.; Zhang, R.; Chen, Y.; Chen, J.; Liu, G.; Zhang, Y.; Liu, Z.; Wu, X.; Yu, D. Highly sensitive hot electron bolometer based on disordered graphene. *Sci. Rep.* **2013**, *3*, 3533. [CrossRef] [PubMed]
14. Zhang, Y.; Qiu, B.; Nagai, N.; Nomura, M.; Volz, S.; Hirakawa, K. Enhanced thermal sensitivity of MEMS bolometers integrated with nanometer-scale hole array structures. *AIP Adv.* **2019**, *9*, 085102. [CrossRef]
15. Evlashin, S.; Dyakonov, P.; Khmelnitsky, R.; Dagesyan, S.; Klokov, A.; Sharkov, A.; Timashev, P.; Minaeva, S.; Maslakov, K.; Svyakhovskiy, S.; et al. Controllable Laser Reduction of Graphene Oxide Films for Photoelectronic Applications. *ACS Appl. Mater. Interfaces* **2016**, *8*, 28880–28887. [CrossRef]
16. St-Antoine, B.C.; Menard, D.; Martel, R. Single-Walled Carbon Nanotube Thermopile For Broadband Light Detection. *Nano Lett.* **2011**, *11*, 609–613. [CrossRef]
17. Zhang, Y.; Deng, T.; Li, S.; Sun, J.; Yin, W.; Fang, Y.; Liu, Z. Highly sensitive ultraviolet photodetectors based on single wall carbon nanotube-graphene hybrid films. *Appl. Surf. Sci.* **2020**, *512*, 145651. [CrossRef]
18. Lu, R.; Christianson, C.; Weintrub, B.; Wu, J.Z. High Photoresponse in Hybrid Graphene–Carbon Nanotube Infrared Detectors. *ACS Appl. Mater. Interfaces* **2013**, *5*, 11703–11707. [CrossRef]
19. Lu, R.; Shi, J.J.; Baca, F.J.; Wu, J.Z. High performance multiwall carbon nanotube bolometers. *J. Appl. Phys.* **2010**, *108*, 084305. [CrossRef]
20. Pathak, P.; Park, S.; Cho, H.J. A Carbon Nanotube–Metal Oxide Hybrid Material for Visible-Blind Flexible UV-Sensor. *Micromachines* **2020**, *11*, 368. [CrossRef]
21. Itkis, M.E.; Borondics, F.; Yu, A.; Haddon, R.C. Bolometric Infrared Photoresponse of Suspended Single-Walled Carbon Nanotube Films. *Science* **2006**, *312*, 413–416. [CrossRef]
22. Nandi, S.; Misra, A. Spray Coating of Two-Dimensional Suspended Film of Vanadium Oxide-Coated Carbon Nanotubes for Fabrication of a Large Volume Infrared Bolometer. *ACS Appl. Mater. Interfaces* **2020**, *12*, 1315–1321. [CrossRef]
23. Hou, J.; Wang, Z.; Ding, Z.; Zhang, Z.; Zhang, J. Facile synthesize VO2 (M1) nanorods for a low-cost infrared photodetector application. *Sol. Energy Mater. Sol. Cells* **2018**, *176*, 142–149. [CrossRef]
24. Bertoni, G.; Cepek, C.; Romanato, F.; Casari, C.; Bassi, A.L.; Bottani, C.; Sancrotti, M. Growth of multi-wall and single-wall carbon nanotubes with in situ high vacuum catalyst deposition. *Carbon* **2004**, *42*, 440–443. [CrossRef]
25. Lin, D.; Zhang, S.; Liu, W.; Yu, Y.; Zhang, J. Carburization of Fe/Ni Catalyst for Efficient Growth of Single-Walled Carbon Nanotubes. *Small* **2019**, *15*, e1902240. [CrossRef] [PubMed]
26. Kumar, R.; Khan, M.A.; Anupama, A.; Krupanidhi, S.B.; Sahoo, B. Infrared photodetectors based on multiwalled carbon nanotubes: Insights into the effect of nitrogen doping. *Appl. Surf. Sci.* **2020**, *538*, 148187. [CrossRef]

27. Zhang, J.; Wei, Y.; Yao, F.; Li, D.; Ma, H.; Lei, P.; Fang, H.; Xiao, X.; Lu, Z.; Yang, J.; et al. SWCNT-MoS2-SWCNT Vertical Point Heterostructures. *Adv. Mater.* **2017**, *29*, 1604469. [CrossRef]

28. Wang, J.X.; Yang, J.F.; Yang, J.; Qiao, G.J.; Hang, W.; Rui, H. Superior MoS$_2$-decorated CNT composite materials for photoelectric detectors. *Opt. Mater.* **2018**, *86*, 113–118.

29. Fu, W.B.; Ma, H.; Wei, Y.; Jiang, K.; Fei, G.T.; De Zhang, L. Preparation and infrared response properties of vanadium dioxide nanowire/carbon nanotube composite film. *J. Mater. Sci.* **2017**, *52*, 7224–7231. [CrossRef]

30. Yang, X.; Yang, Y.; Fu, L.; Zou, M.; Li, Z.; Cao, A.; Yuan, Q. An Ultrathin Flexible 2D Membrane Based on Single-Walled Nanotube-MoS2 Hybrid Film for High-Performance Solar Steam Generation. *Adv. Funct. Mater.* **2017**, *28*, 1704505. [CrossRef]

31. Tahersima, M.H.; Sorger, V.J. Strong Photon Absorption in 2D Material-Based Spiral Photovoltaic Cells. *MRS Adv.* **2016**, *1*, 3915–3921. [CrossRef]

32. Feng, X.; Zhao, J.; Sun, D.; Shanmugam, L.; Kim, J.-K.; Yang, J. Novel onion-like graphene aerogel beads for efficient solar vapor generation under non-concentrated illumination. *J. Mater. Chem. A* **2019**, *7*, 4400–4407. [CrossRef]

33. Gao, C.; Han, Y.; Zhang, K.; Wei, T.; Jiang, Z.; Wei, Y.; Yin, L.; Piccinelli, F.; Yao, C.; Xie, X.; et al. Templated-Construction of Hollow MoS 2 Architectures with Improved Photoresponses. *Adv. Sci.* **2020**, *7*, 2002444. [CrossRef] [PubMed]

34. Ranganathan, K.; Fiegenbaum-Raz, M.; Ismach, A. Large-Scale and Robust Multifunctional Vertically Aligned MoS$_2$ Photo-Memristors. *Adv. Funct. Mater.* **2020**, *30*, 2005718. [CrossRef]

35. Chacko, L.; Swetha, A.K.; Anjana, R.; Aneesh, P.M. Structural and Optical Studies of Hydrothermally Synthesized MoS$_2$ Nanostructures. *Int. Conf. Condens. Matter Appl. Phys.* **2016**, *1728*, 20620.

36. Guo, J.; Wang, X.; Wang, T. Thermal characterization of microscale conductive and nonconductive wires using transient electrothermal technique. *J. Appl. Phys.* **2007**, *101*, 063537. [CrossRef]

37. Xie, Y.; Wang, T.; Zhu, B.; Yan, C.; Zhang, P.; Wang, X.; Eres, G. 19-Fold thermal conductivity increase of carbon nanotube bundles toward high-end thermal design applications. *Carbon* **2018**, *139*, 445–458. [CrossRef]

38. Liu, T.; Davijani, A.A.B.; Sun, J.; Chen, S.; Kumar, S.; Lee, S.W. Hydrothermally Oxidized Single-Walled Carbon Nanotube Networks for High Volumetric Electrochemical Energy Storage. *Small* **2016**, *12*, 3423–3431. [CrossRef]

39. Wang, S.; Zhu, J.; Shao, Y.; Li, W.; Wu, Y.; Zhang, L.; Hao, X. Three-Dimensional MoS2@CNT/RGO Network Composites for High-Performance Flexible Supercapacitors. *Chem. -A Eur. J.* **2017**, *23*, 3438–3446. [CrossRef]

40. Jiang, Y.; Li, X.; Yu, S.; Jia, L.; Zhao, X.; Wang, C. Reduced Graphene Oxide-Modified Carbon Nanotube/Polyimide Film Supported MoS2Nanoparticles for Electrocatalytic Hydrogen Evolution. *Adv. Funct. Mater.* **2015**, *25*, 2693–2700. [CrossRef]

41. Lei, Z.D.; Yu, X.; Zhang, Y.; Zhan, J. Thermally stable fishnet-like 1T-MoS$_2$/CNT heterostructures with improved electrode performance. *J. Mater. Chem. A* **2021**, *9*, 4707–4715. [CrossRef]

42. Jiab, C.; Yana, C.; Wang, Y.; Xiong, S.; Zhou, F.; Li, Y.; Suna, R.; Wong, C.-P. Thermal conductivity enhancement of CNT/MoS$_2$/graphene-epoxy nanocomposites based on structural synergistic effects and interpenetrating network. *Compos. Part B -Eng.* **2019**, *163*, 363–370.

43. Jiang, L.L.; Wang, Z.K.; Li, M.; Li, C.H.; Fang, P.-F.; Liao, L.-S. Flower-like MoS$_2$ nanocrystals: A powerful sorbent of Li+ in the Spiro-OMeTAD layer for highly efficient and stable perovskite solar cells. *J. Mater. Chem. A* **2019**, *7*, 3655–3663. [CrossRef]

44. Deng, X.; Nie, Q.; Wu, Y.; Fang, H.; Zhang, P.; Xie, Y. Nitrogen-Doped Unusually Superwetting, Thermally Insulating, and Elastic Graphene Aerogel for Efficient Solar Steam Generation. *ACS Appl. Mater. Interfaces* **2020**, *12*, 26200–26212. [CrossRef] [PubMed]

45. Ferrari, A.C. Raman spectroscopy of graphene and graphite: Disorder, electron–phonon coupling, doping and nonadiabatic effects. *Solid State Commun.* **2007**, *143*, 47–57. [CrossRef]

46. Ferrari, A.C.; Robertson, J. Interpretation of Raman spectra of disordered and amorphous carbon. *Phys. Rev. B* **2000**, *61*, 14095–14107. [CrossRef]

47. Lee, C.; Yan, H.; Brus, L.E.; Heinz, T.F.; Hone, J.; Ryu, S. Anomalous Lattice Vibrations of Single- and Few-Layer MoS$_2$. *ACS Nano* **2010**, *4*, 2695–2700. [CrossRef]

48. Chowdhury, T.; Kim, J.; Sadler, E.C.; Li, C.; Lee, S.W.; Jo, K.; Xu, W.; Gracias, D.H.; Drichko, N.V.; Jariwala, D.; et al. Substrate-directed synthesis of MoS$_2$ nanocrystals with tunable dimensionality and optical properties. *Nat. Nanotechnol.* **2019**, *15*, 29–34. [CrossRef]

49. Wu, T.; Jing, M.; Liu, Y.; Ji, X. Binding low crystalline MoS2 nanoflakes on nitrogen-doped carbon nanotube: Towards high-rate lithium and sodium storage. *J. Mater. Chem. A* **2019**, *7*, 6439–6449. [CrossRef]

50. Pan, F.; Wang, J.; Yang, Z.; Gu, L.; Yu, Y. MoS2–graphene nanosheet–CNT hybrids with excellent electrochemical performances for lithium-ion batteries. *RSC Adv.* **2015**, *5*, 77518–77526. [CrossRef]

51. Xie, Y.; Xu, S.; Xu, Z.; Wu, H.; Deng, C.; Wang, X. Interface-mediated extremely low thermal conductivity of graphene aerogel. *Carbon* **2016**, *98*, 381–390. [CrossRef]

52. Liu, J.; Xu, Z.; Cheng, Z.; Xu, S.; Wang, X. Thermal Conductivity of Ultrahigh Molecular Weight Polyethylene Crystal: Defect Effect Uncovered by 0 K Limit Phonon Diffusion. *ACS Appl. Mater. Interfaces* **2015**, *7*, 27279–27288. [CrossRef] [PubMed]

53. Liu, Y.; Yin, J.; Wang, P.; Hu, Q.; Wang, Y.; Xie, Y.; Zhao, Z.; Dong, Z.; Zhu, J.-L.; Chu, W.; et al. High-Performance, Ultra-Broadband, Ultraviolet to Terahertz Photodetectors Based on Suspended Carbon Nanotube Films. *ACS Appl. Mater. Interfaces* **2018**, *10*, 36304–36311. [CrossRef] [PubMed]

54. Nair, R.R.; Blake, P.; Grigorenko, A.N.; Novoselov, K.S.; Booth, T.J.; Stauber, T.; Peres, N.M.R.; Geim, A.K. Fine Structure Constant Defines Visual Transparency of Graphene. *Science* **2008**, *320*, 1308. [CrossRef] [PubMed]

55. Dużyńska, A.; Taube, A.; Korona, K.; Judek, J.; Zdrojek, M. Temperature-dependent thermal properties of single-walled carbon nanotube thin films. *Appl. Phys. Lett.* **2015**, *106*, 183108. [CrossRef]

56. Kumanek, B.; Janas, D. Thermal conductivity of carbon nanotube networks: A review. *J. Mater. Sci.* **2019**, *54*, 7397–7427. [CrossRef]

57. Yu, C.; Shi, L.; Yao, Z.; Li, D.; Majumdar, A. Thermal Conductance and Thermopower of an Individual Single-Wall Carbon Nanotube. *Nano Lett.* **2005**, *5*, 1842–1846. [CrossRef] [PubMed]

58. Li, Q.W.; Li, Y.; Zhang, X.F.; Chikkannanavar, S.B.; Zhao, Y.H.; Dangelewicz, A.M.; Zheng, L.; Doorn, S.K.; Jia, Q.; Peterson, D.E.; et al. Structure-Dependent Electrical Properties of Carbon Nanotube Fibers. *Adv. Mater.* **2007**, *19*, 3358–3363. [CrossRef]

59. Li, Q.-Y.; Katakami, K.; Ikuta, T.; Kohno, M.; Zhang, X.; Takahashi, K. Measurement of thermal contact resistance between individual carbon fibers using a laser-flash Raman mapping method. *Carbon* **2018**, *141*, 92–98. [CrossRef]

60. Kumar, N.; Sharma, J.D.; Kumar, A.; Ahluwalia, P.K. Band gap engineering in nano structured graphane by applying elastic strain. *Solid State Phys.* **2013**, *57*, 192–193. [CrossRef]

61. Liu, J.; Wang, T.; Xu, S.; Yuan, P.; Xu, X.; Wang, X. Thermal conductivity of giant mono- to few-layered CVD graphene supported on an organic substrate. *Nanoscale* **2016**, *8*, 10298–10309. [CrossRef]

62. Ito, T.; Nishidate, K.; Baba, M.; Hasegawa, M. First principles calculations for electronic band structure of single-walled carbon nanotube under uniaxial strain. *Surf. Sci.* **2002**, *514*, 222–226. [CrossRef]

63. Gautreau, P.; Ragab, T.; Chu, Y.; Basaran, C. Phonon dispersion and quantization tuning of strained carbon nanotubes for flexible electronics. *J. Appl. Phys.* **2014**, *115*, 243702. [CrossRef]

64. Zhang, H.; Zhao, K.; Cui, S.; Yang, J.; Zhou, D.; Tang, L.; Shen, J.; Feng, S.; Zhang, W.; Fu, Y. Anomalous temperature coefficient of resistance in graphene nanowalls/polymer films and applications in infrared photodetectors. *Nanophotonics* **2018**, *7*, 883–892. [CrossRef]

65. Lu, R.; Xu, G.; Wu, J.Z. Effects of thermal annealing on noise property and temperature coefficient of resistance of single-walled carbon nanotube films. *Appl. Phys. Lett.* **2008**, *93*, 213101. [CrossRef]

66. Khosrofian, J.M.; Garetz, B.A. Measurement of a Gaussian Laser-Beam Diameter through the Direct Inversion of Knife-Edge Data. *Appl. Opt.* **1983**, *22*, 3406–3410. [CrossRef] [PubMed]

nanomaterials

Article

Effects of Current Annealing on Thermal Conductivity of Carbon Nanotubes

Huan Lin [1,*], Jinbo Xu [1], Fuhua Shen [1], Lijun Zhang [1], Shen Xu [2], Hua Dong [1] and Siyi Luo [1]

[1] School of Environmental and Municipal Engineering, Qingdao University of Technology, Qingdao 266033, China; xujinbo0214@163.com (J.X.); Shenfh0126@163.com (F.S.); LJunZhang@outlook.com (L.Z.); dhua1959@hotmail.com (H.D.); luosiyi666@126.com (S.L.)

[2] School of Mechanical and Automotive Engineering, Shanghai University of Engineering Science, Shanghai 201620, China; shxu16@sues.edu.cn

* Correspondence: linhuan@qut.edu.cn

Abstract: This work documents the annealing effect on the thermal conductivity of nanotube film (CNTB) and carbon nanotube fiber (CNTF). The thermal properties of carbon nanotube samples are measured by using the transient electro-thermal (TET) technique, and the experimental phenomena are analyzed based on numerical simulation. During the current annealing treatment, CNTB1 always maintains the negative temperature coefficient of resistance (TCR), and its thermal diffusivity increases gradually. When the annealing current is 200 mA, it increases by 33.62%. However, with the increase of annealing current, the TCR of CNTB2 changes from positive to negative. The disparity between CNTB2 and CNTB1 suggests that they have different physical properties and even structures along their lengths. The high-level thermal diffusivity of CNTB2 and CNTF are 2.28–2.46 times and 1.65–3.85 times higher than the lower one. The results show that the decrease of the thermal diffusivity for CNTB2 and CNTF is mainly caused by enhanced Umklapp scattering, the high thermal resistance and torsional sliding during high temperature heating.

Keywords: carbon nanotubes; current annealing; thermal conductivity; graphitization

Citation: Lin, H.; Xu, J.; Shen, F.; Zhang, L.; Xu, S.; Dong, H.; Luo, S. Effects of Current Annealing on Thermal Conductivity of Carbon Nanotubes. *Nanomaterials* **2022**, *12*, 83. https://doi.org/10.3390/nano12010083

Academic Editor: Christophe Detavernier

Received: 1 December 2021
Accepted: 24 December 2021
Published: 29 December 2021

Publisher's Note: MDPI stays neutral with regard to jurisdictional claims in published maps and institutional affiliations.

1. Introduction

Carbon nanotubes (CNTs) have progressively attracted researchers' attention for their lightweight, small size and acceptable flexibility. Moreover, they have both excellent electrical and thermal conductivity, which determines that they have application value and development potential as a high-performance reinforcement material [1]. However, in practical applications, they have failed to reflect the excellent properties of CNTs because they are dispersed randomly and prone to agglomeration [2]. Previous studies on CNTs have concentrated on the preparation [3,4], the optimization of the mechanical properties of CNTs composites [5,6] and the enhancement of the effectiveness of CNTs as capacitor electrode materials [7]. In recent years, studies have shown that high temperature annealing is an effective approach to improve the structure and thermal conductivity of carbon materials [8,9]. Chen et al. [10] found that thermal treatment is capable of repairing the structure of graphene and making graphene sheets accumulate more regularly. Thereby, the thermal conductivity is increased. Mayhew et al. [11] found that the thermal conductivity of carbon nanofibers could be increased by nearly 40 times after annealing at 2800 °C for 20 h. However, the effect of high temperature annealing on the thermal conductivity of carbon materials is complicated, for which a mechanism has yet to be figured out.

The traditional method of annealing at present is indirect annealing in the furnace, and the current annealing in this experiment has the superiorities of straightforward and efficient in situ measurement compared with the traditional annealing. Current annealing can be accomplished in a few seconds for the sample annealing treatment. The sample is always in the invariable equipment before annealing until the sample is burned down after complete annealing to measure thermal conductivity, which reduces the measurement errors caused by factors such as the pollution of the area under measurement and the different qualities of the sample.

In this work, the focus is on the current annealing effect on CNTB and CNTF. The data is collected by using the TET technique, and the variation of thermal diffusivity with annealing current is analyzed. The evolution of material microstructures is studied based on the variation of their thermal properties.

2. Materials and Methods

2.1. Experimental Materials

The CNTB (Suzhou Tanfeng Graphene Technology Co., Ltd., Suzhou, China) was prepared from multi-walled carbon nanotubes (MWCNTs) by floating catalysis to pattern a film with the size of 10 cm × 10 cm (Figure 1a), with an electrical conductivity of $(0.8–3) \times 10^{-5}$ S/m, a strength of 60–100 MPa and a density of 400 kg/m^3. Figure 1b, the SEM image of CNTB, clearly shows that the film is made of innumerable carbon nanotubes arranged desultorily. Moreover, the carbon nanotubes have non-uniform diameters and randomly overlap with others, which makes the surface of the prepared film rough to a certain extent. The tested samples were prepared along the length direction of the square CNTB film (CNTB1) and along the other side of the CNTB film (CNTB2), as shown in Figure 1a.

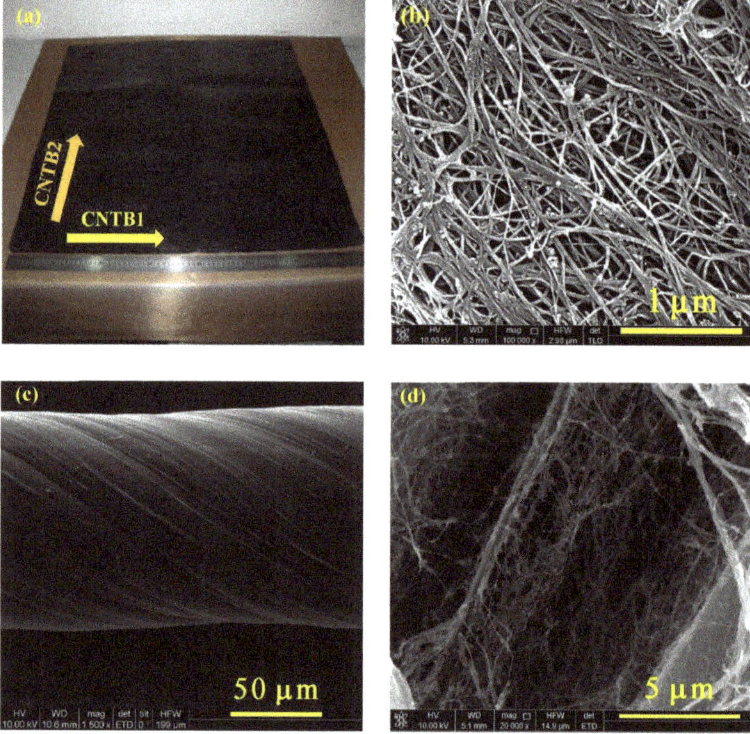

Figure 1. (a) The intact carbon nanotube film (CNTB) before the TET experiments. (b) The SEM image of the CNTB. The SEM images of CNTF under different magnifications of (c) 1500× and (d) 20,000×. These indicate CNTB and CNTF are made of innumerable carbon nanotube fibers arranged desultorily.

The carbon nanotube fiber (CNTF, Nanjing JCNANO Tech Co., Ltd., Nanjing, China) was also prepared from MWCNTs by using the floating catalyst method, with a density of 675.43 kg/m^3, the strength of 310–500 MPa, the modulus of 10 GPa and a tensile rate of 20–30%. From its SEM images (Figure 1c,d), the CNTF sample had a certain degree of twisted texture and roughness, and there is a cross-overlap as well.

2.2. Transient Electro-Thermal Technique

The thermal conductivities of carbon nanotube materials were measured by using TET. Figure 2 shows the schematic diagram of the TET experimental system. The samples were suspended on a sample holder with two separate electrodes. A small amount of silver paste was applied to stabilize both ends of the samples on the electrodes to reduce the contact resistance between the samples and electrodes. Then the sample holder was placed into a vacuum chamber to exclude heat convection. As the air pressure in the vacuum chamber during the measurement was maintained at 1×10^{-3} mbar, the heat convection effect on the measured thermal diffusivity was negligible. A step current supplied by a current source (KEITHLEY 2611A, Keithley Instruments Inc., Cleveland, OH, USA) was fed to the samples to generate Joule heating in the samples. The thermal diffusivity of the samples was obtained by analyzing the temperature rise curve with a physical model discussed below.

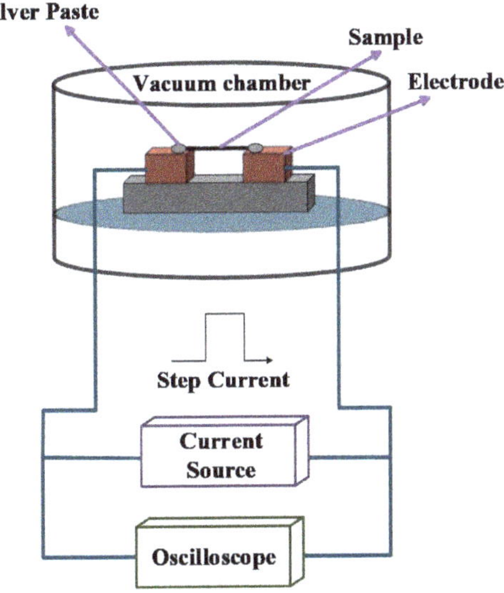

Figure 2. The schematic diagram of the TET experiment. TET is composed of a vacuum chamber, current source and oscilloscope. In the vacuum chamber, the air pressure is less than 1×10^{-3} mbar during the measurement. The sample is placed on the electrodes, and a silver paste is applied to the ends for reducing contact resistance.

As the CNTB and CNTF samples have a large aspect ratio, a one-dimensional heat transfer model was used for analysis [12]. The average temperature change of the sample directly affects the variation of the voltage over the sample as [13]:

$$V_{\text{sample}} = IR_0 + I\eta \frac{4q_0 L^2}{k\pi^2} \sum_{m=1}^{\infty} \frac{1 - \exp[(-(2m-1)^2 \pi^2 \alpha_{\text{eff}} t)/L^2]}{(2m-1)^4} \tag{1}$$

where η is the temperature coefficient of resistance, q_0 is the electrical heating power per unit of volume, k is the thermal conductivity, α_{eff} is the effective thermal diffusivity of the sample.

Defining a normalized average temperature rise as $T^* = (T_t - T_0)/(T_{t\to\infty} - T_0)$, it can be expressed as [13,14]:

$$T^* = \frac{48}{\pi^4} \prod_{m=1}^{\infty} \frac{1 - (-1)^m}{m^2} \frac{1 - \exp[-m^2\pi^2\alpha_{\text{eff}}t/L^2]}{m^2} \tag{2}$$

When a step current is applied to a sample, its resistance varies with the temperature, which leads to a change of voltage. Therefore, the experimental value of the normalized temperature rise T^*_{exp} can be calculated by the change of voltage as: $T^*_{\text{exp}} = V^* = (V_{\text{sample}} - V_0)/(V_\infty - V_0)$, where V_0 and V_∞ are the initial and steady-state voltages across the sample, respectively. The *V-t* curve of the sample was recorded by an oscilloscope (DSO-X3052A, Agilent Technologies Inc, Santa Clara, CA, USA); combined with Equation (1), the thermal diffusivity (α) of the sample was obtained, which was used to fit the normalized temperature curve. The α value with the best fitting was determined as α_{eff}, and associates with the density (ρ) and specific heat capacity (c_p) of the sample, its effective thermal conductivity (k_{eff}) can be obtained as calculated by: $k_{\text{eff}} = \rho c_p \alpha_{\text{eff}}$.

2.3. Experimental Procedure

The current annealing was applied to the sample in the same experimental setup as TET in this study. After the sample was laid in a vacuum chamber, the α_{eff} of the sample at room temperature was first measured using a step current with low intensity in order to raise the temperature as small as possible. Then a Direct Current (DC) with high intensity was applied to the same sample to generate large heat in the sample and complete the thermal annealing. The thermal annealing lasted for more than 120 s to ensure thermal equilibrium for one run. The second α_{eff} was measured after the sample finished the first annealing run. The annealing run and in-situ TET measurement were then performed alternatively by switching the form of the current between the large DC current (for annealing) and small step current (for TET measurement). The DC current increases a little at a time until the sample is burned down. This method can fully realize the effective monitoring of the structural variation in the annealing process. The error of transferring samples between the different annealing and measurement devices is successfully avoided. This is the whole current annealing procedure, in which the effects of current annealing on thermal conductivity are investigated.

3. Results and Discussions

3.1. Results

3.1.1. Positive Effect of Annealing on CNTB1

The annealing process and in-situ TET measurement are first applied to CNTB1 (length: 3620.71 μm; width: 288.42 μm; thickness: 25 μm). The decreasing voltage along with time demonstrate that the MWCNTs dominate the heat conduction in CNTB1 because most carbon materials have a negative temperature coefficient of resistance (TCR) [15]. The varying trend is fitted by Equation (2), and the best-fitted α is the effective thermal diffusivity α_{eff} of CNTB1. The detailed annealing current I_a and α_{eff} of CNTB1 are summarized in Table 1. With the increase in the annealing current, α_{eff} of CNTB1 increases likewise. When less heat is added, α_{eff} changes little. As the sample is heated in a vacuum chamber, the thermal reduction would occur in the sample to remove impurity induced in the sample production. With the increase of the current, the degree of reduction is enhanced, and the microstructure is optimized. Thus, the thermal conductivity and α_{eff} of CNTB1 rise. The annealing current of burning the sample is 210 mA, and when the annealing current is 200 mA, the thermal diffusivity increases by 33.62%.

Table 1. Partial experimental results of CNTB1 during current annealing.

Sample	I_a ($\times 10^{-3}$ A)	α_{eff} ($\times 10^{-5}$ m^2/s)
	0	6.52
	90	6.53
CNTB1	120	6.85
	150	7.34
	180	8.27
	200	8.71

3.1.2. Observation of Thermal Diffusivity Jump on CNTB2 and CNTF

In the process of current annealing experiments for CNTB2 (length: 3657.23 μm; width: 260.23 μm; thickness: 25 μm) and CNTF (length: 3429.35 μm; diameter: 135 μm), an unusual phenomenon appears where the thermal diffusivity of the sample has a "sudden jump". Figure 3a shows the voltage evolution of CNTB2 before annealing. It is obvious that the varying trend is different from that of CNTB1, though both of them are cut from the same carbon nanotube conductive film. The disparate phenomenon of CNTB2 and CNTB1 indicates that they have different physical properties and even structures along their length directions, which lead to the occurrence of different heat conduction mechanisms.

Figure 3b–f shows the *V-t* experimental data and the theoretical fitting curves of CNTB2 under different currents: 140 mA, 160 mA, 165 mA, 170 mA and 300 mA. It presents an interesting evolution of the voltage variations. When the annealing current varies from 0 to 140 mA, the voltage of CNTB2 increases gradually under Joule heating and then reaches the steady-state, which is a typical voltage evolution with a positive TCR. However, when the annealing current is above 150 mA, the TET signal for CNTB2 shows a small decrease at the beginning of Joule heating, and then it rises again until reaching the steady-state. With the increase in the annealing current, the descending part becomes noticeable and begins to dominate the TET signal. When the current passes 170 mA, the signal only has a decreasing trend until reaching the steady-state, and the rising portion completely disappears. The sample initiates to perform the normal signal which the carbon materials originally have when the sample has a negative TCR. The "sudden jump" of thermal diffusivity indicates that with the increase of the annealing current, the TCR of CNTB2 and CNTF turns from positive to negative.

CNTF has a similar behavior as CNTB2. Both samples are annealed with a higher and higher current until the sample is burned down. The thermal diffusivities of CNTB2 and CNTF against the annealing currents are shown in Figure 4a,b, respectively. The detailed annealing condition and determined thermal diffusivity are listed in Table 2. The measured thermal diffusivity is divided into two separate data groups. The lower thermal diffusivity group is denoted as α_1, and the higher thermal diffusivity group is denoted as α_2. The corresponding two states before and after switch-on are named State 1 and State 2, respectively. Combining Table 2 and Figure 4, it can be observed that when the annealing currents of CNTB2 and CNTF are 160 mA and 350 mA, the peak thermal diffusivity is 32.01×10^{-5} m^2/s and 19.63×10^{-5} m^2/s. α_1 is much lower than α_2. Wang et al. [16] found that high temperature induces C atoms to act in a thermal flutter in a large range at the structural equilibrium position, and this deformation increases the atomic energy in the local region of MWCNTs. When the threshold of the barrier constraint value is reached, the MWCNTs structure will produce irreversible deformation (the minimum distance between C atoms) and even collapse [17]. It can be further determined that the thermal diffusivity peaks in CNTB2 and CNTF occur at the threshold where instability is produced in MWCNTs' structures.

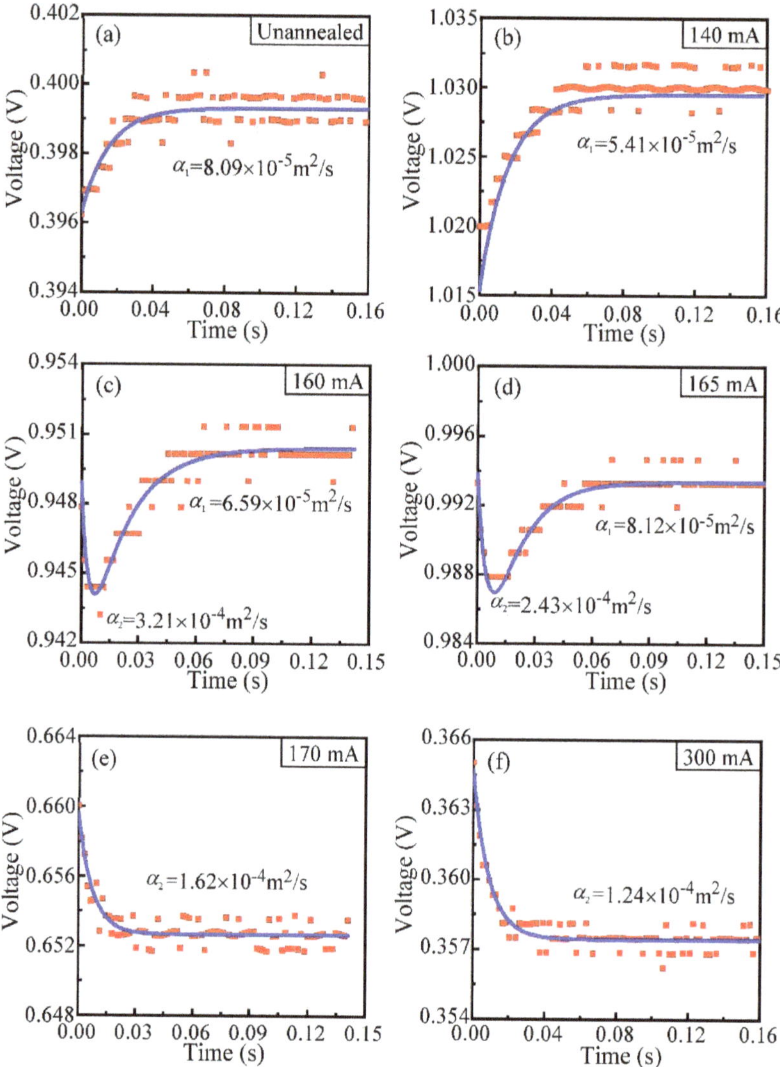

Figure 3. (**a–f**) Comparisons between the theoretical fitting and experimental data of CNTB2 for the voltage under different annealing currents. The red squares are experimental data, and the blue lines are the theoretical fitting. (**a**) Corresponding to the unannealed state and the variation of voltage is monotone increasing, which trend is similar to (**b**) under 140 mA. (**c**,**d**) are under 160 mA and 165 mA, respectively. The variations perform as decreasing firstly and then rising to the steady-state. (**e**,**f**) 170 mA and 300 mA, respectively, and the variations are monotone decreasing.

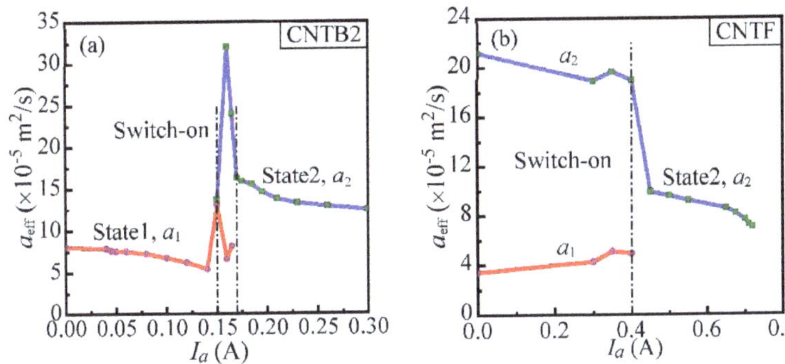

Figure 4. The curve of thermal diffusivity with an annealing current (I_a): (**a**) CNTB2; (**b**) CNTF.

Table 2. Partial experimental results of CNTB2 and CNTF during current annealing.

Sample	I_a $\times 10^{-3}$ A	Low-Level Thermal Diffusivity after Annealing ($\alpha_{\text{eff},1}$)	High-Level Thermal Diffusivity after Annealing ($\alpha_{\text{eff},2}$)	Low-Level Thermal Diffusivity before Annealing ($\alpha_{\text{eff},01}$)	High-Level Thermal Diffusivity before Annealing ($\alpha_{\text{eff},02}$)
		$\times 10^{-5}$ m^2/s		$\times 10^{-5}$ m^2/s	
CNTB2	40	7.89			
	100	6.79			
	140	5.41			
	150	13.02	13.72		
	160	6.59	32.01	8.09	
	165	8.12	24.02		
	170		16.25		
	210		13.72		
	300		12.38		
CNTF	300	4.27	18.90		
	350	5.10	19.63		
	400	4.94	18.95	3.45	21.19
	450		9.93		
	675		8.20		
	720		7.05		

3.1.3. Transient Annealing Behavior

The transient voltage variations of CNTB1, CNTB2 and CNTF under different annealing currents are shown in Figure 5. During the process of annealing, the time required by State 1 for CNTB and CNTF decreases. With the increase of the annealing current, State 2 presents complex and diverse changes, and when the annealing current approaches the maximum current that the sample can withstand, the voltage fluctuates greatly. It is clear in Figure 5 that transient voltage variations of CNTB and CNTF appear in a rising trend, suggesting that in the process of annealing, the resistance of the sample increases constantly with the heating temperature rising. This phenomenon is in conflict with the theory that carbon materials have negative TCR in themselves.

As shown in Figure 6a, the normalized resistance (R^*) of both samples has an upward trend with the rise of annealing power (P). After several times of annealing, the samples are burnt due to high-temperature heating eventually, and the final breakpoints of samples are shown in Figure 6b–d. CNTB1 is fractured at about 3/4 of the sample length, and CNTB2 and CNTF are both fractured at about 1/2 of their length, which indicates that during the annealing process, the temperature distribution along the length of the sample is non-uniform. The temperature at the breakpoint is the highest, and thus the fracture occurs first.

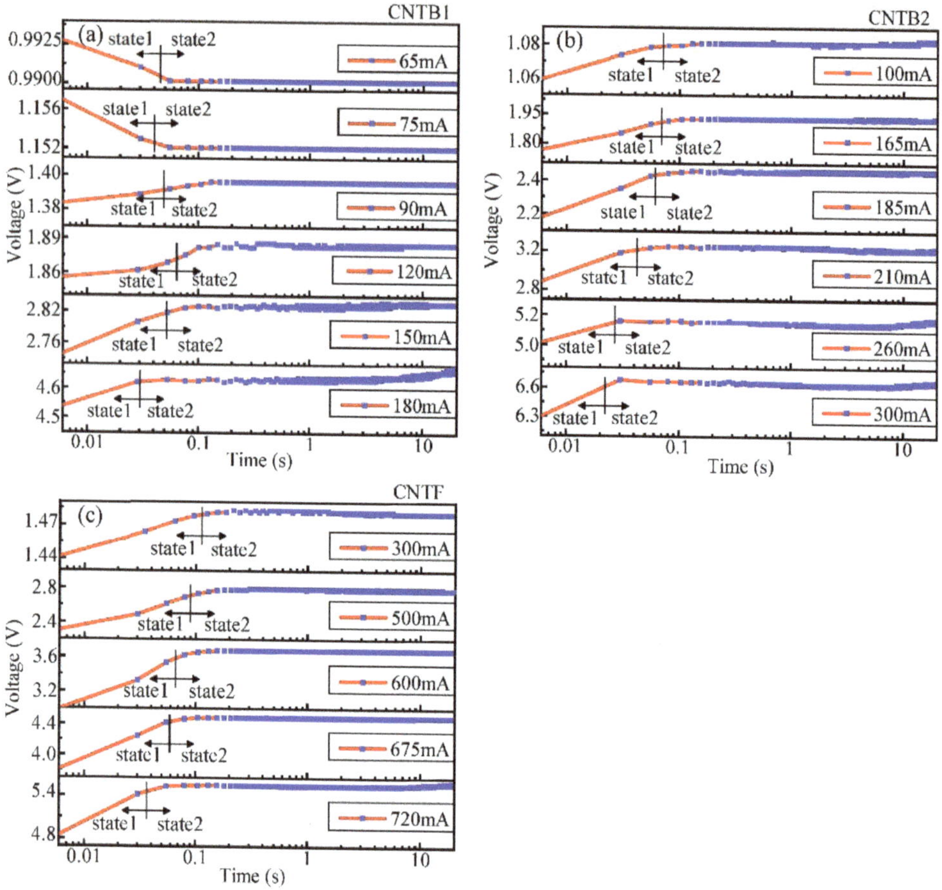

Figure 5. The transient voltage variations with time during annealing: (**a**) CNTB1; (**b**) CNTB2; (**c**) CNTF. The arrows indicate State 1 and State 2. During the current annealing, the time required for each sample in State 1 is reduced.

3.1.4. Temperature Distribution and Thermal Conductivity Change of CNTB

The temperature at different positions along the length of the sample is calculated by using a numerical method, and the results are shown in Figure 7a. The temperature distribution is non-uniform along the length of CNTB1 and CNTB2. The temperature at the middle point is the highest, and those further away from the middle point are lower in temperature. Moreover, the highest temperature of CNTB1 is lower than that of CNTB2, indicating that the thermal conductivity of CNTB1 is smaller than that of CNTB2, which is consistent with the experimental results that the thermal diffusivity of CNTB1 is smaller than that of CNTB2. In addition, the breakpoint of CNTB1 is further away from the middle point, and the inhomogeneity of temperature distribution will also cause the simulation temperature of CNTB1 to be at a low level.

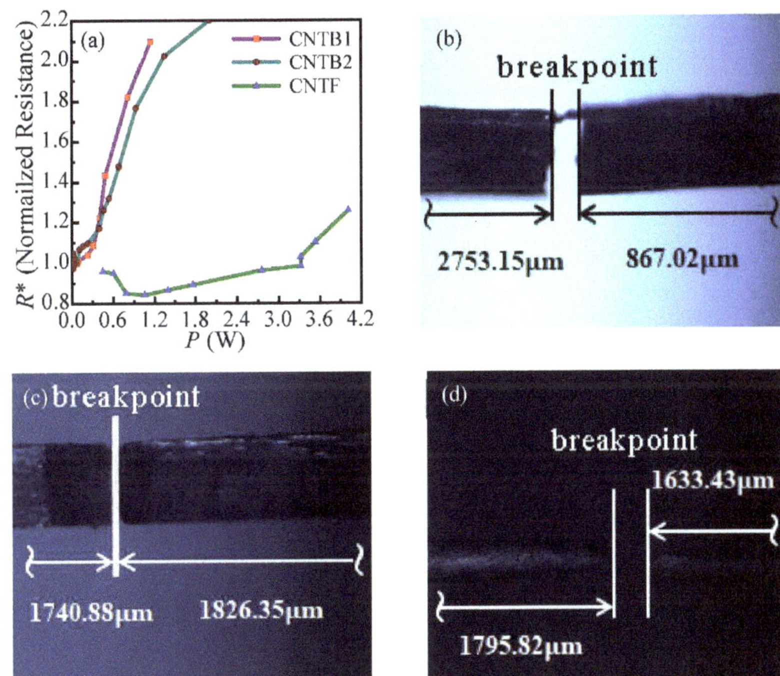

Figure 6. (**a**) Curves of sample-normalized resistance with annealing power. The R^* of samples has different degrees of increase with the increase of P. Diagram of burning down after annealing: (**b**) CNTB1; (**c**) CNTB2; (**d**) CNTF. The locations of breakpoints are shown in the figures.

Figure 7b indicates that the Joule heating generated by the current provides the high temperature environment required by the annealing process for CNTB. With the increase of heating energy, the average temperature of samples continues to rise, which makes the annealing process proceed in an orderly manner. The rising rate of the average temperature shows a trend of gradual decrease, which reveals that in the process of annealing, the graphitization levels increase. Nevertheless, the process of graphitization is slowing down, and the degree of graphitization is decreasing, indicating that the graphitizing level is close to the maximum degree of the sample.

Figure 7c shows the variation curves of the thermal conductivity of the middle point (k_m) with the annealing temperature of the middle point (T_{mid}) of CNTB1 and CNTB2, respectively. k_m of CNTB2 also appears to make a "sudden jump", as mentioned above. $k_{m,1}$ and $k_{m,2}$ correspond to the low thermal conductivity before switch-on and the high thermal conductivity after switch-on of CNTB2. As shown in this figure, with the increase of T_{mid}, the k_m of CNTB1 increases, while the k_m of CNTB2 decreases, which reveals that a single annealing treatment does not always have a positive effect on the thermal conductivity of carbon materials, and the analysis from the overall samples also shows this. α_{eff} and the average temperature (T_{ave}) reflect the average properties of the material. As shown in Figure 7d, with the increase of T_{ave}, α_{eff} of CNTB1 increases, the low $\alpha_{eff,1}$ and the high $\alpha_{eff,2}$ of CNTB2 decreases.

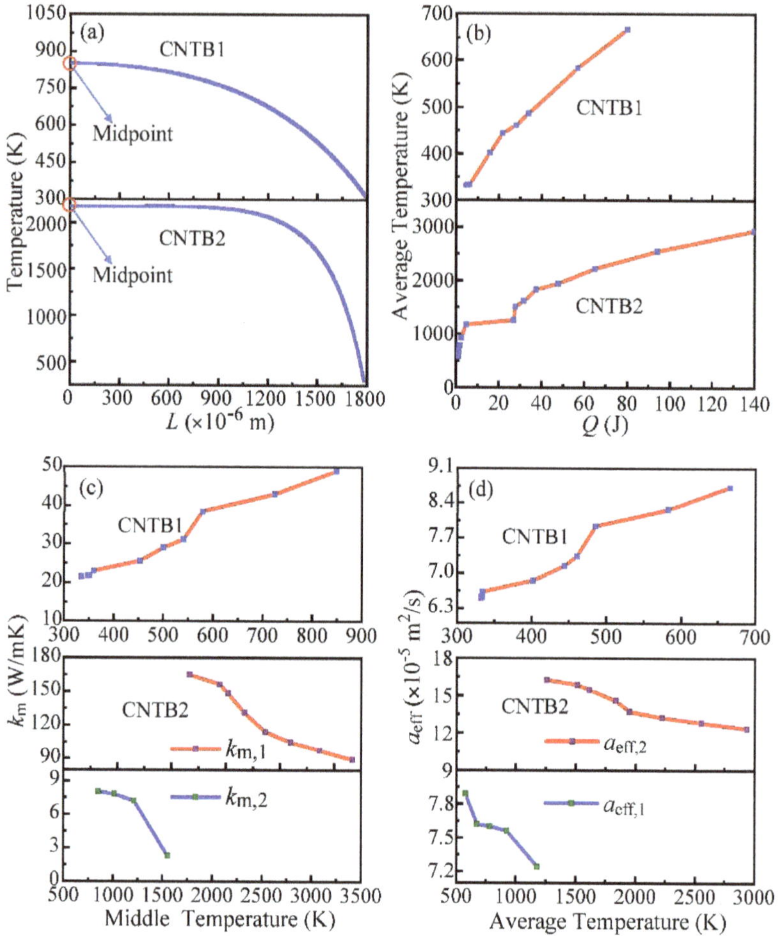

Figure 7. (**a**) Temperature distribution along the length of CNTB. The x-coordinate zero is the midpoint of the sample. (**b**) The average temperature of CNTB under different heating conditions. (**c**) Thermal conductivity of the midpoint varies with the annealing temperature of the midpoint. $k_{m,1}$ and $k_{m,2}$ correspond to the low thermal conductivity before switch-on and the high thermal conductivity after switch-on of CNTB2. (**d**) The thermal diffusivity varies with the average annealing temperature. $\alpha_{eff,1}$ and $\alpha_{eff,2}$ also correspond to the states before and after switch-on of CNTB2.

3.1.5. Temperature Distribution and Thermal Conductivity Change of CNTF

Unlike the "sudden jump" of CNTB2, CNTF does not have low-level thermal conductivity before switch-on. Therefore, the focus of CNTF is only the part with the high thermal conductivity after switch-on. As shown in Figure 8a, the temperature distribution along the length of CNTF is also non-uniform, and the temperature at the middle point is the highest.

Figure 8b shows the variation of the high k_m with T_{mid} after the switch-on of CNTF, indicating that k_m decreases continuously with the increase of T_{mid}. Figure 8c is the curve of T_{ave} under different heating conditions, and Figure 8d is the variation of α_{eff} against T_{ave}, which shows that the current annealing in this experiment has a certain degree of "negative" effect on the thermal conductivity of CNTF.

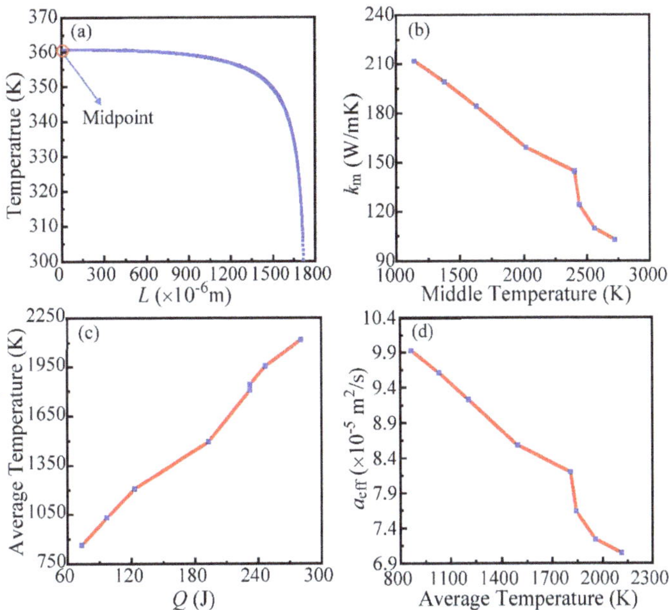

Figure 8. (**a**) Temperature distribution along the length of CNTF. The x-coordinate zero is the midpoint of the sample. (**b**) Thermal conductivity of the midpoint varies with the annealing temperature of the midpoint. (**c**) The average temperature of CNTF under different heating conditions after switch-on. (**d**) The thermal diffusivity varies with the average annealing temperature.

3.2. Discussions

3.2.1. Mechanism of Phonon Scattering

Heat conduction is normally dominated by phonons of carbon materials [18], whose heat transport is critical to the heat transport of materials. It is speculated that during the current annealing process of CNTB1, the size of graphite microcrystals increases, some of the impurity atoms are moved, and the order of the graphite microcrystalline structure is improved. These transformations reduce the probability of phonons colliding with other phonons, grain boundaries, impurities and edge boundaries in the process of heat transport, thus reducing the amount of phonon scattering and the scattering intensity. The integrity of phonon heat transport improves, and the phonon mean free path increases. Therefore, the thermal conductivity of CNTB1 increases.

The phonon scattering of CNTB2 and CNTF is determined by Umklapp scattering, normal scattering, impurity scattering, phonon-boundary scattering, phonon-defect scattering and thermal contact resistance. Normal scattering generally occurs at low temperatures, and Umklapp scattering is more likely to occur at higher temperatures. Combined with the previous analysis of the "sudden jump", in State 1, because of the interaction between adjacent pure carbon nanotube (P-CNT) and impurities-embedded carbon nanotube (I-CNT), the thermal diffusivity of material is restrained. Thermal expansion mismatch occurs between P-CNT and I-CNT due to thermal stress, which results in different degrees of stretching or contraction of carbon nanotubes. However, P-CNT is not separated from the surrounding I-CNT, and the restraint of boundary scattering on phonon heat transport is amplified to some extent, resulting in the thermal diffusivity decrease.

In the switch-on state, with the enhancement of annealing, the temperature increases gradually, and the elastic vibration of the lattice increases. Furthermore, more high-frequency phonons are excited, and the number of phonon groups increases, which promotes the heat transport of phonons. The thermal diffusivity of the material is ultimately improved. Because I-CNT is purified and the structure of CNT is optimized continuously, the effect of impurity and boundary scattering on heat conduction is weakened. Therefore, the thermal diffusivity peaks of CNTB2 and CNTF appear at this state.

In State 2, P-CNT and I-CNT are completely separated, and Umklapp scattering is more prevalent. Umklapp scattering is dominant in the phonon scattering mechanism [19], and the process of Umklapp scattering generally causes thermal resistance, which also affects the phonon mean free path. As the annealing temperature increases, the influence of thermal stress goes up. MWCNTs are continuously stretched or compressed, and the structure deforms to different degrees, which is irreversible due to excessive thermal stress [16]. The scattering produced by structural changes is classified as structure scattering. Because of the high thermal stress, the structure of MWCNTs collapses, and the structure scattering is enhanced, which impairs the original larger thermal conductivity of carbon nanotubes. In this state, MWCNT impurities are further removed, and the density of the defect is reduced, which results in the impurity scattering and defect scattering effects being weakened. The high temperature excites more high-frequency phonons to promote heat transport, but it also excites more scattering between phonons, which enhances Umklapp scattering and increases the thermal resistance. Combining with the above factors, the thermal diffusivity of CNTB2 and CNTF decreases.

3.2.2. Effects on Thermal Conductivity

MWCNT torsional sliding induced by high temperature is one of the reasons for the decrease of thermal conductivity. Wang et al. [20] showed that the external load causes the global buckling of carbon nanotubes and even the large torsion. Charlier et al. [21] found that Buckyball molecules rotate freely when it reaches the transition temperature (258 K), which can easily slide into or out of each other, and such movements are unhindered at room temperature. With the increase of annealing, the graphitization degree increases, the structure becomes ordered, and the density of the defect decreases. Chen [22] showed that structure defects limit rotation and sliding between MWCNTs layers. Therefore, the reduction of defect density promotes the rotational migration of CNT to some extent. With the increase of the annealing current, the effect of annealing on the structure gradually increases. When the current increases to a certain degree, the annealing will produce large thermal stress. The stress is equivalent to applying an external load on the material; the CNT rotates under the torque generated by the high temperature, resulting in the deviation of the MWCNTs distribution direction. The axial direction of the MWCNTs cylinder forms a certain angle with the length direction, and even the phenomenon that the MWCNTs is perpendicular to the axial direction appears. The more orderly structure also indicates that more CNT may rotate together along a certain angle and form an ordered arrangement with the axial direction [23]. Therefore, the thermal conductivity of CNTB2 and CNTF decreases.

On the other hand, high annealing temperature may result in greater thermal resistance between MWCNTs, which affects the thermal transport of materials. Gong [24] proved that 1800 °C is the appropriate annealing temperature to remove the impurities of MWCNTs. When the annealing temperature rises to 2100 °C, agglomeration occurs in MWCNTs, and aggregates are generated on the surface of the sample. This indicates that with the increase of annealing, the structure of MWCNTs deforms, becomes rough and even agglomerates, so the thermal resistance is increased, and the heat transport is inhibited. Feng et al. [25] showed that high temperature stimulates more phonon scattering, resulting in increased thermal resistance and reduced thermal conductivity. Kim et al. [26] reported that lattice defects of carbon tubes at high temperatures would motivate the Umklapp scattering, causing an increase in thermal resistance. Liu et al. [27] showed that in the graphitization process of carbon fiber, although the crystal size of material increases, the probability of the occurrence of maximum defects and large holes also increased. Therefore, it is speculated that during the annealing process, with the increasing of annealing temperature, the presence of thermal stress leads MWCNT to agglomerate. In the process of graphitization, larger vacancy and hole defects appear in the material, which causes greater thermal resistance, and hinders and inhibits the effective heat transport of phonons. At the beginning of annealing, the TCR of CNTB2 is positive, which means thermal resistance plays an important role in heat transfer. This also explains that the thermal conductivity decreases with the increase of annealing current.

3.2.3. Effects of Annealing on Structure

The Raman characterization of CNTB after burning off is shown in Figure 9. The positions of the measuring point are numbered as 1 to 9, which are closer and closer to the breakpoint from bottom to top. It can be seen that the effect of annealing is ununiformed along the length during the current annealing process, which appears as the effect of annealing is continuously enhanced from both ends to the breakpoint of the sample. Three prominent peaks are at around 1315 cm^{-1}, 1586 cm^{-1} and 2610 cm^{-1}, which correspond with D peak, G peak and 2G peak, respectively. Figure 10 shows the ratio of peak intensities I_D/I_G of different points of CNTB. From the endpoint to the breakpoint, the decreased I_D/I_G ratio means a lower defect. With the enhancement of annealing, the sample becomes orderly, the disorder of internal structure decreases and the defect density also decreases. Moreover, the closer to the breakpoint, the shape of the G peak and 2D peak in Raman become steeper with a narrower line width and stronger intensity, which also indicates the larger crystalline size and structure of the sample is improved gradually.

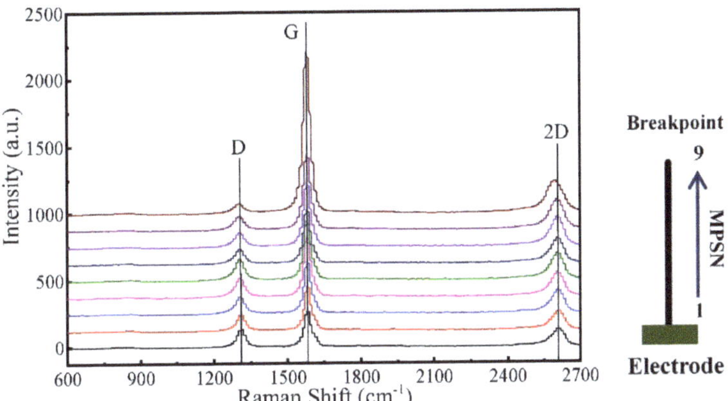

Figure 9. The Raman spectrum with measuring point positions 1–9 of the burned CNTB sample. Point 1 is the furthest from the breakpoint, and 9 is the closest.

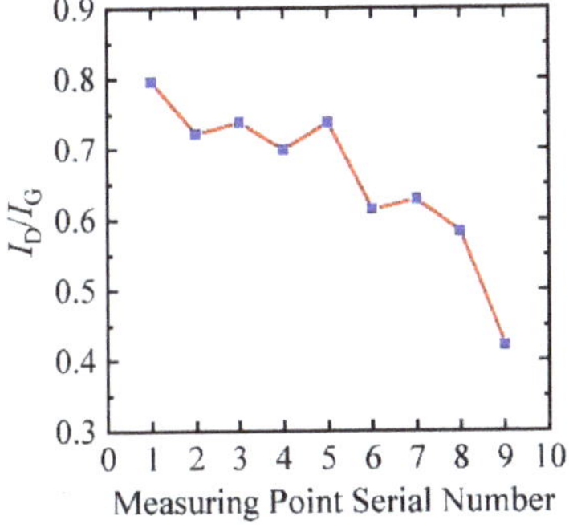

Figure 10. The I_D/I_G of CNTB varies with the position of measuring points 1–9.

4. Conclusions

This work shows the current annealing effect on the thermal conductivity of CNTB and CNTF. In the annealing process, the thermal diffusivity of CNTB1 increases gradually, and the highest thermal conductivity is 1.34 times the original thermal conductivity. Although both CNTB1 and CNTB2 are cut from the same carbon nanotube conductive film, the thermal diffusivity of CNTB2 has a "sudden jump", and the TCR of CNTB2 changes from positive to negative. The disparate phenomenon of CNTB2 and CNTB1 indicates that they have different physical properties and even structures along their length directions which lead to the occurrence of different heat conduction mechanisms. The results show that the high-level thermal diffusivity of CNTB2 is 2.28–2.46 times higher than the low one.

The high-level thermal diffusivity of CNTF is 1.65–3.85 times higher than the low one. The main reasons for the decrease of the thermal conductivity of CNTB2 and CNTF are as follows: enhanced Umklapp scattering; torsional sliding occurs in MWCNTs induced by high temperature; high thermal resistance between MWCNTs.

Author Contributions: H.L., J.X., F.S., L.Z., S.X., H.D. and S.L. wrote the main manuscript text. H.L. designed experiments. J.X., F.S., L.Z. carried out experiments. S.X. and H.D. analyzed experimental results. S.L. assisted with analyze the Raman result. All authors have read and agreed to the published version of the manuscript.

Funding: This work was supported by the National Key Research and Development Program (2019YFE0119900), Natural Science Foundation of Shandong Province (ZR2020ME183 and ZR2019MEE015) and China Postdoctoral Science Foundation (2017M612225).

Institutional Review Board Statement: Not applicable.

Informed Consent Statement: Not applicable.

Data Availability Statement: The data presented in this study are available on request from the corresponding author.

Acknowledgments: Huan Lin and Shen Xu are grateful to the China Scholarship Council. Shen Xu is grateful to the research supported by the Program for Professor of Special Appointment (Eastern Scholar) at Shanghai Institutions of Higher Learning.

Conflicts of Interest: The authors declare no conflict of interest.

References

1. Wu, Q.; Li, M.; Gu, Y.; Li, Y.; Zhang, Z. Nano-analysis on the structure and chemical composition of the interphase region in carbon fiber composite. *Compos. Part A Appl. Sci. Manuf.* **2014**, *56*, 143–149. [CrossRef]
2. Sun, X.M.; Sun, H.; Li, H.; Peng, H. Developing Polymer Composite Materials: Carbon Nanotubes or Graphene? *Adv. Mater.* **2013**, *25*, 5153–5176. [CrossRef]
3. Yamamoto, G.; Suk, J.W.; An, J.; Piner, R.D.; Hashida, T.; Takagi, T.; Ruoff, R.S. The influence of nanoscale defects on the fracture of multi-walled carbon nanotubes under tensile loading. *Diam. Relat. Mater.* **2010**, *19*, 748–751. [CrossRef]
4. Wei, R.Z.; Li, F.Y.; Yan, J. Preparation of Carbon Nanotubes from Methane on Ni/Cu/Al Catalyst. *J. Nat. Gas Chem.* **2005**, *14*, 173–176.
5. Xin, W.; Sarasini, F.; Tirillò, J.; Bavasso, I.; Sbardella, F.; Lampani, L.; De Rosa, I. Impact and post-impact properties of multiscale carbon fiber composites interleaved with carbon nanotube sheets. *Compos. Part B Eng.* **2019**, *183*, 107711. [CrossRef]
6. Hasan, M.; Zhao, J.; Jiang, Z. Micromanufacturing of composite materials: A review. *Int. J. Extreme Manuf.* **2019**, *1*, 012004. [CrossRef]
7. Futaba, D.; Hata, K.; Yamada, T.; Hiraoka, T.; Hayamizu, Y.; Kakudate, Y.; Tanaike, O.; Hatori, H.; Yumura, M.; Iijima, S. Shape-engineerable and highly densely packed single-walled carbon nanotubes and their application as super-capacitor electrodes. *Nat. Mater.* **2006**, *5*, 987–994. [CrossRef]
8. Feng, Z.-H.; Fan, Z.; Kong, Q.; Xiong, X.; Huang, B.-Y. Effect of high temperature treatment on the structure and thermal conductivity of 2D carbon/carbon composites with a high thermal conductivity. *Carbon* **2014**, *82*, 608. [CrossRef]
9. Silvain, J.-F.; Heintz, J.-M.; Veillere, A.; Constantin, L.; Lu, Y.F. A review of processing of Cu/C base plate composites for interfacial control and improved properties. *Int. J. Extrem. Manuf.* **2020**, *2*, 012002. [CrossRef]
10. Chen, C.-M.; Huang, J.-Q.; Zhang, Q.; Gong, W.-Z.; Yang, Q.-H.; Wang, M.-Z.; Yang, Y.-G. Annealing a graphene oxide film to produce a free standing high conductive graphene film. *Carbon* **2012**, *50*, 659–667. [CrossRef]
11. Mayhew, E.; Prakash, V. Thermal conductivity of individual carbon nanofibers. *Carbon* **2013**, *62*, 493–500. [CrossRef]

12. Lin, H.; Liu, X.; Kou, A.; Xu, S.; Dong, H. One-Dimensional Thermal Characterization at the Micro/Nanoscale: Review of the TET Technique. *Int. J. Thermophys.* **2019**, *40*, 108. [CrossRef]
13. Liu, G.; Xu, S.; Cao, T.-T.; Lin, H.; Tang, X.; Zhang, Y.-Q.; Wang, X. Thermally induced increase in energy transport capacity of silkworm silks. *Biopolymers* **2014**, *101*, 1029–1037. [CrossRef] [PubMed]
14. Xu, S.; Zobeiri, H.; Hunter, N.; Zhang, H.; Eres, G.; Wang, X. Photocurrent in carbon nanotube bundle: graded seebeck coefficient phenomenon. *Nano Energy* **2021**, *86*, 106054. [CrossRef]
15. Smith, K.M.; Holroyd, P. Engineering Principles for Electrical Technicians, Introduction to Electrical Units and Circuits—ScienceDirect. In *Engineering Principles for Electrical Technician*; Elsevier: Amsterdam, The Netherlands, 1968; pp. 175–195.
16. Wang, Y.; Ni, X.-G.; Wang, X.X.; Wu, H.-A. Effect of temperature on deformation of carbon nanotube under compression. *Chin. Phys.* **2003**, *12*, 1007–1010.
17. Balkanski, M. *Physical Properties of Carbon Nanotubes*; Saito, R., Dresselhaus, G., Dresselhaus, M.S., Eds.; Imperial College Press: London, UK, 1998.
18. Balandin, A.A. Thermal properties of graphene and nanostructured carbon materials. *Nat. Mater.* **2011**, *10*, 569–581. [CrossRef] [PubMed]
19. Liu, J.; Wang, T.; Xu, S.; Yuan, P.; Xu, X.; Wang, X. Thermal conductivity of giant mono- to few-layered CVD graphene supported on an organic substrate. *Nanoscale* **2016**, *8*, 10298–10309. [CrossRef] [PubMed]
20. Wang, Y.; Wang, X.-X.; Ni, X.-G.; Wu, H.-A. Simulation of the elastic response and the buckling modes of single-walled carbon nanotubes. *Comput. Mater. Sci.* **2005**, *32*, 141–146. [CrossRef]
21. Charlier, J.-C.; Michenaud, J.-P. Energetics of multilayered carbon tubules. *Phys. Rev. Lett.* **1993**, *70*, 1858–1861. [CrossRef]
22. Chen, Z.H. Overview of the structure of carbon nanotubes. *J. Fujian Inst. Educ.* **2003**, *4*, 76–83.
23. Kim, Y.A.; Hayashi, T.; Osawa, K.; Dresselhaus, M.; Endo, M. Annealing effect on disordered multi-wall carbon nanotubes. *Chem. Phys. Lett.* **2003**, *380*, 319–324. [CrossRef]
24. Gong, Q.J. Effect of Annealing on the Purity and Microstructure of Disorder Carbon Nanotubes. *Rare Met. Mater. Eng.* **2007**, *36*, 269–272.
25. Feng, D.L.; Feng, Y.H.; Chen, Y.; Li, W.; Zhang, X.-X. Effects of doping, Stone Wales and vacancy defects on thermal conductivity of single-wall carbon nanotubes. *Chin. Phys. B* **2013**, *22*, 016501. [CrossRef]
26. Kim, P.; Shi, L.; Majumdar, A.; McEuen, P.L. Thermal Transport Measurements of Individual Multiwalled Nanotubes. *Phys. Rev. Lett.* **2001**, *87*, 215502. [CrossRef] [PubMed]
27. Liu, F.-J.; Fan, L.-D.; Wang, H.-J.; Zhu, Z.-P. Study on the skin-core evolvement of carbon fibers as a function of heat treatment temperature by Raman spectroscopy. *Guang Pu* **2008**, *28*, 1819–1822.

Review

Thermal Transport in Extremely Confined Metallic Nanostructures: TET Characterization

Huan Lin [1,*], Fuhua Shen [1], Jinbo Xu [1], Lijun Zhang [1], Shen Xu [2], Na Liu [1] and Siyi Luo [1]

1   School of Environmental and Municipal Engineering, Qingdao University of Technology, Qingdao 266033, China
2   School of Mechanical and Automotive Engineering, Shanghai University of Engineering Science, Shanghai 201620, China
*   Correspondence: linhuan@qut.edu.cn

Abstract: In recent years, the continuous development of electronic chips and the increasing integration of devices have led to extensive research on the thermal properties of ultrathin metallic materials. In particular, accurate characterization of their thermal transport properties has become a research hotspot. In this paper, we review the characterization methods of metallic nanomaterials, focusing on the principles of the transient electrothermal (TET) technique and the differential TET technique. By using the differential TET technique, the thermal conductivity, electrical conductivity, and Lorenz number of extremely confined metallic nanostructures can be characterized with high measurement accuracy. At present, we are limited by the availability of existing coating machines that determine the thickness of the metal films, but this is not due to the measurement technology itself. If a material with a smaller diameter and lower thermal conductivity is used as the substrate, much thinner nanostructures can be characterized.

Keywords: ultra-thin metallic materials; thermal diffusivity; thermal conductivity; nanostructures; TET

Citation: Lin, H.; Shen, F.; Xu, J.; Zhang, L.; Xu, S.; Liu, N.; Luo, S. Thermal Transport in Extremely Confined Metallic Nanostructures: TET Characterization. *Nanomaterials* **2023**, *13*, 140. https://doi.org/10.3390/nano13010140

Academic Editors: Sergio Brutti and Jordi Sort

Received: 30 November 2022
Revised: 19 December 2022
Accepted: 21 December 2022
Published: 27 December 2022

1. Introduction

As an integral part of the semiconductor field, ultra-thin metallic materials are used in solar cells [1], communication [2], aerospace [3], and other applications [4–6]. As one of the important criteria for evaluating the performance of different nanomaterials and accurately characterizing the thermal diffusivity of ultrathin metallic materials, thermal transport properties have become an important research direction [7]. However, compared to the electrical transport properties, the characterization of thermal transport within nano-thick metal films is a challenge [8].

Wiedemann et al. [9] first discovered that at room temperature, the ratio of electrical conductivity to thermal conductivity was very close for most metals. Later, Lorenz [10] revealed that the ratio was positively correlated with temperature and related to the quantum of electrical charge and the Boltzmann constant. This is the famous Wiedemann–Franz (WF) law, but the WF law is not applicable to nanoscale metal film materials [11–16]. Based on the theoretical works related to the optimization of WF law and electrical conductivity [17–24], a series of methods have been developed to experimentally measure the thermal transport properties of metallic nanofilms and metallic nanowires. These methods include the 3ω method [25–28], the photothermal reflection technique [29,30], the femtosecond laser pumping detection method [31] and the non-stationary electrical heating method [32–35].

A distinctive feature of the 3ω method is that it is universally applicable to a variety of materials [36,37]. However, this method fails in the films thinner than 100 nm, mainly because the thermal contact resistance between the microsensor and the tested film is large and comparable or even larger than the equivalent thermal resistance of the film [38]. Nakamura et al. [39] first measured the thermal diffusivity of 90 nm-thick Pt films on glass substrates at low temperatures from 15 K to 273 K using a post-heating pre-detection type

(RF-type) femtosecond thermal reflectometry system. This RF-type system provided the thermal diffusivity of the films at low temperatures, and more information about non-thermal energy transfer processes. Wang et al. [40] studied the heat-transfer mechanism of metal nanofilms under ultrashort pulse laser heating, simultaneously establishing a femtosecond (fs) transient thermal reflection (TTR) technique to measure the transient electron temperature response induced by fs laser heating. They also used a pump-probe technique to ensure the fs time resolution of the experiment. Applying a back heating-front probing mode ensured the electron temperature response, which allowed the authors to determine the electron–phonon coupling coefficient and the propagation velocity of temperature oscillations. Finally, a non-equilibrium thermal diffusion model was employed to fit the temperature profiles of Au films with the thicknesses from 27.2 nm to 55.5 nm.

Laser-based ultrafast time-domain thermal reflection (TDTR) techniques are widely used to measure the thermal conductivity of bulk and thin-film materials [41]. As a pump measurement technique, TDTR requires neither the precisely designed electric heater nor temperature sensor, but only a small amount of sample, which enables one to operate under routine conditions. The frequency-dependent TDTR method is also applicable to thin-film materials. However, their thickness should be greater than the thermal penetration depth through the plane. Liu et al. [42] used this method to determine both the out-of-plane thermal conductivity and the bulk heat capacity for organic–inorganic Zn basin hybrid films with thickness in the range of 40–400 nm.

The photo-thermal technique usually deals with metal samples that act as both the heater and temperature sensor, making the equipment and electrode fabrication process difficult. On the contrary, the electrothermal route is faster and simpler compared with the above methods. Ma et al. [43] measured the in-plane thermal and electrical conductivity of metal nanofilms via direct current heating of suspended films. The advantage of the proposed approach is that contact resistance and thermal resistance can be completely eliminated by integrating the suspended Pt and Au nanofilms with the probe electrodes. Using this method, Boiko et al. [44] determined the thermal and electrical conductivities of 20–60 nm Pt and Au polycrystalline films in the temperature range of 80–300 K. Guo et al. first developed the TET technique to significantly improve the signal electrical frequency. To assess the accuracy of the method, they measured a 25 μm-diameter platinum wire. The thermal diffusivity of the three Pt wires is 2.53×10^{-5}, 2.54×10^{-5}, and 2.78×10^{-5} m^2 s^{-1}, respectively, which are close to the literature value of 2.51×10^{-5} m^2 s^{-1} (at 300 K). By means of gold coating, the technology can also measure non-conductive nanowires and tubes, but the gold coating needs to be as thin as possible.

The TET technique is an effective and accurate method (the total uncertainty for thermal diffusivity is 6%) for evaluating the thermal diffusivity of one-dimensional solid materials (including metals and dielectric materials), such as single-walled carbon nanotube bundles [45], graphene materials [46–49], silkworm silks, [50] silver nanowire network, [51] freestanding micrometer-thick poly films [52], carbon fibers [53,54], etc. In this review, we will focus primarily on the characterization of thermal transport in extremely confined metallic nanostructures using the TET and differential TET technique.

2. TET Technique

The typical experimental setup of the TET technique is shown in Figure 1. During the experiment, both ends of the specimen are suspended between two electrodes. The contact points between the end and the electrode are fixed with a conductive silver glue to increase the electrical and thermal contacts between the sample and the electrodes. The measurement is conducted in a vacuum chamber to eliminate the heat loss through thermal convection.

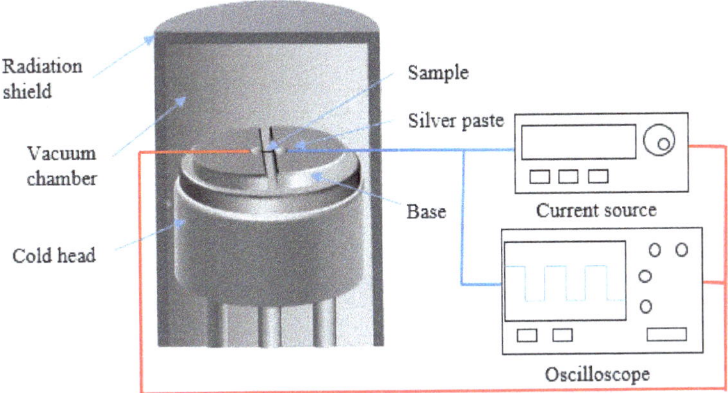

Figure 1. Schematic of the experimental principle and setup for the TET experiment.

In the process of the experiment, the step dc current is applied to the material to increase its temperature. The temperature rise in the sample causes the resistance to vary, consequently altering the voltage, which is recorded by an oscilloscope. Since the applied current and the resistance-temperature coefficient of the sample in a narrow temperature range are constant, the temperature change could be derived from the recorded voltage evolution. The thermal diffusivity of the sample is then determined based on the temperature/voltage changing rate.

It is noteworthy that direct measurement is possible only if the material is electrically conductive. Otherwise, the surface of the material is covered with a layer of metal to make it conductive, so the effect of the metallic film should be evaluated and removed.

The length of sample is much larger than its diameter or width and thickness. Therefore, the heat transfer in the samples can be simplified as one-dimensional heat conduction along the length direction. The heat transfer can be described using the equation below [55]:

$$\frac{1}{\alpha}\frac{\partial\theta(x,t)}{\partial t} = \frac{\partial^2\theta(x,t)}{\partial x^2} + \frac{I^2 R_0}{kLA} + \frac{Q}{kLA} \tag{1}$$

where $\theta = T - T_0$ T_0 is the room temperature, I is the constant current flowing through the sample, α is the thermal diffusivity, k is the thermal conductivity, and R_0 is the electrical resistance before electrical heating. L and A are the length and cross-sectional area of the sample, respectively, and Q is the thermal radiation rate. It can be assumed that the electrical heating power per unit volume of the sample is uniform. During Joule heating, the temperature in the sample rises sharply, while the temperature of the electrodes remains constant because of their relatively much larger volume and heat capacity. At the same time, heat flow is transferred from the sample to the electrodes and dissipates from the sample to the surroundings via thermal radiation. Therefore, the boundary conditions are $\theta(0,t) = \theta(L,t) = \theta(x,0)$. The solution to Equation (1) can be obtained by integrating Green's function.

The normalized temperature rise (T^*) is defined as $T^*(t) = [T(t) - T_0]/[T(t\to\infty) - T_0]$, which can be represented as:

$$T^* \cong \frac{48}{\pi^4}\sum_{m=1}^{\infty}\frac{1-(-1)^m}{m^2}\frac{1-\exp\left[-m^2\pi^2\alpha_{\text{eff}}t/L^2\right]}{m^2} \tag{2}$$

where α_{eff} is the measured thermal diffusivity. The relationship between the voltage variation recorded by the oscilloscope during the experiment and the mean temperature variation of the sample is as follows:

$$V_{\text{sample}} = IR_0 + I\eta \frac{4q_0 L^2}{k\pi^4} \times \sum_{m=1}^{\infty} \frac{1 - (-1)^m}{m^2} \frac{1 - \exp\left[-m^2\pi^2\alpha_{\text{eff}}t/L^2\right]}{m^2} \tag{3}$$

where η is the temperature resistivity coefficient and q_0 is the electrical power per unit volume.

The normalized temperature rise (T^*) is calculated from the experimental data as $T^* = \left(V_{\text{sample}} - V_0\right)/(V_1 - V_0)$, where V_0 and V_1 are the initial and steady-state voltages of the sample. After obtaining T^*, different values of α_{eff} are used to fit the experimental results T^* based on Equation (2). According to the least squares fitting technique, the value giving the best fit of T^* is used as the α_{eff} of the sample.

For the non-conductive materials, the value of α_{eff} includes thermal radiation and metal coating effects. Thus, it can be written as [56–58]:

$$\alpha_s = \alpha_{\text{eff}} - \frac{1}{\rho c_p} \frac{16\varepsilon_r \sigma T_0^3}{D} \frac{L^2}{\pi^2} - \frac{L_{\text{Lorenz}} T_{\text{ave}} L}{RA\rho c_p} \tag{4}$$

where α_s is the thermal diffusivity of the substrate, D is the diameter of the sample to be measured, ε_r is the surface emissivity, σ=5.67 $\times$ 10^{-8} W·m^{-2}·K^{-4} is the Stefan–Boltzmann constant, and ρc_p is the volumetric specific heat of the material. L_{Lorenz} is the Lorenz number, T_{ave} and R are the average temperature and resistance of the sample during the TET. The second term on the right side of the equation is the thermal radiation effect, and the third term refers to the coating effect. The radiation effect can be taken out by linearly fitting the α_{eff}–L^2/D curve to $L^2/D = 0$. The slope of the fitting line is $16\varepsilon_r\sigma T_0^3/(\pi^2\rho c_p)$. As the other parameters are all known, the emissivity of samples can be calculated from the slope of the curve. If the material is electrically conductive, it requires no metal coating; in this case, only the radiation impact should be considered.

3. Differential TET Technique

Since the independent structure of nanometer-thick materials is relatively weak to suspend, the differential TET technique [58–60] was developed to measure the in-plane thermal transport of metallic nanostructures so as to accurately represent their electrical conductivity, thermal conductivity, and Lorenz number.

Since the low-dimensional materials possess low thermal conductivity, they can be used as the substrates to brace the ultrathin films during testing. As shown in Figure 2a,b, a metallic layer is applied in the TET experiment to measure α_{eff}. It is clear from Equation (4) that α_{eff} is influenced by three factors, which are α_s, the thermal radiation effect, and the coating effect. Among them, α_s is a constant and the thermal radiation influence remains generally unchanged and can be neglected. If the coating is added, the value α_{eff} will be changed accordingly. Therefore, the relation between α_{eff} and the number of layers can be established. The effective thermal diffusivity of the sample has an expression as [56] $\alpha_{\text{eff}} = \alpha_s + \frac{4 \cdot n \cdot \delta_{\max}}{\pi D (\rho c_p)_s}\left[k_c - \alpha_s (\rho c_p)_c\right]$, where α_s is the thermal diffusivity of the substrate, being a constant value. The subscript c indicates the metallic structure. As shown in Figure 2c, α_{eff} changes with n conforming to a linear law, and its slope can be obtained from the fitting. Therefore, the inherent thermal conductivity of a thin coating structure can be accurately obtained according to the theoretical model. Using the same method, the electrical conductivity and Lorenz number can also be determined.

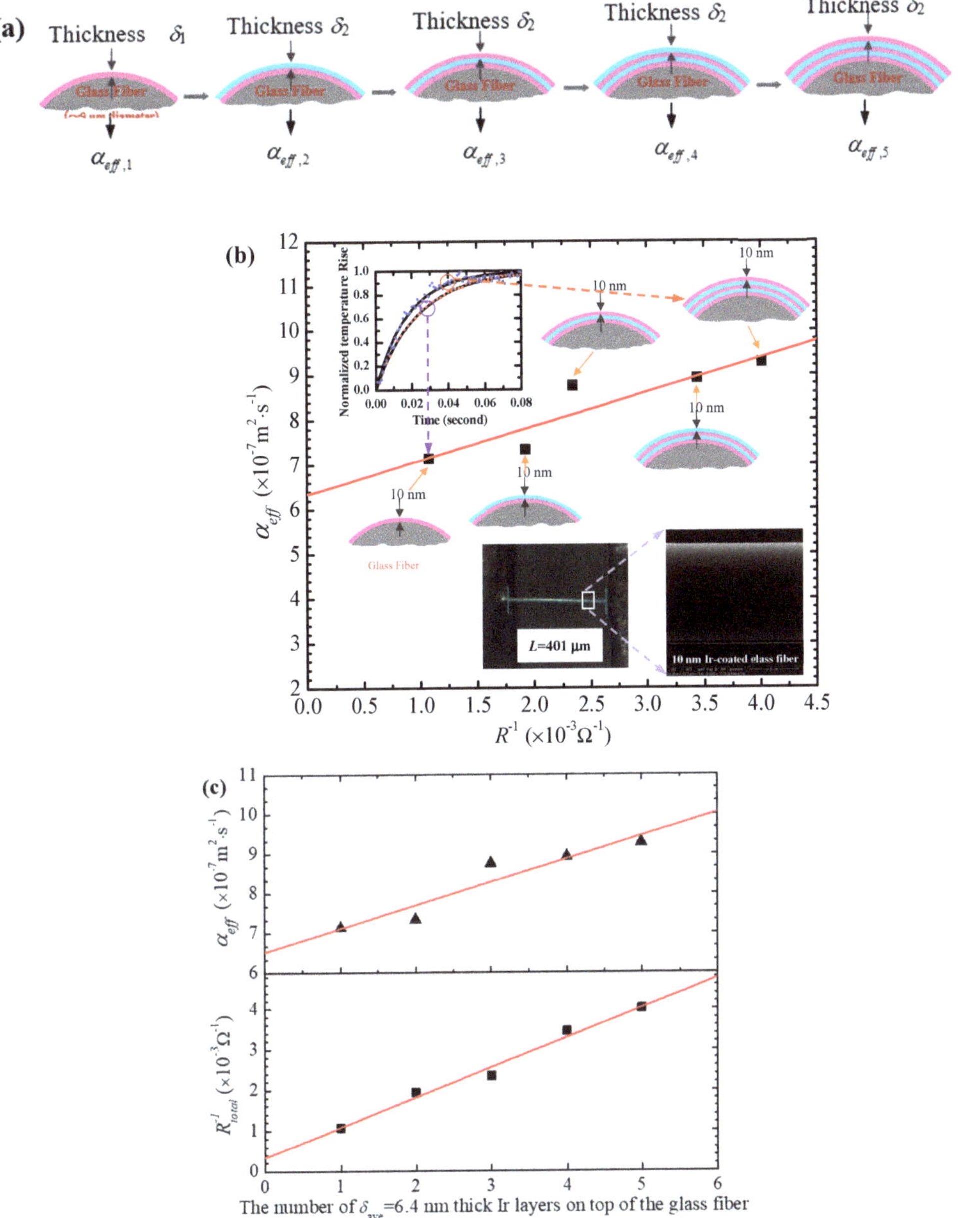

Figure 2. (a) Schematic cross-section of a substrate coated with different layers of nanofilms. The effective thermal diffusivity variation against the amount of metallic coating layers and electrical conductance (R^{-1}) used to obtain the Lorenz number, thermal conductivity, and electrical conductivity. (b) The effective thermal diffusivity versus the inverse electrical resistance of a substrate coated with 6.4 nm-thick Ir layers. (c) Linear fitting curves of the effective thermal diffusivity and resistance change with the number of Ir layers on the substrate. (Reprinted with permission from Ref. [56] Copyright John Wiley and Sons Small.).

Lin et al. measured k of 6.4 nm-thick gold films [61] and 7 nm-to-subnanometrically thick Ir films [56,60] by applying the differential TET technique. The average thermal conductivity of Ir films deposited on glass fibers was reduced by 51.2% compared with the bulk value (147 W·m^{-1}·K^{-1}) at 311 K. Moreover, the decrease in electrical conductivity was much faster than in thermal conductivity, which caused the Lorenz number to increase to 6–8 × 10^{-8} W Ω K^{-2}. It was noted that the thermal conductivity of the Au film on silkworm silks was 50% of that on glass fibers. However, the thermal conductivity of the 6.4 nm-thick Ir film on silkworm silks was only slightly higher than that on the glass fiber. These variations in thermal conductivity are probably caused by the difference between the film structures; that is, Ir film has a finer crystalline size than that of Au.

Dong et al. characterized the thermal and electronic transport properties of 3.2 nm gold films applied onto the alginate fibers via the differential TET technique [62]. It was concluded that the thermal and electrical conductivity were significantly reduced by 76.2% and 93.9%, respectively, compared to the corresponding values of the bulk material. Meanwhile, the calculated Lorenz number was almost three times higher than the Lorenz number of the bulk material.

The thermal and electrical conductivity of the metallic structures deposited on the substrates are lower than those of the bulk material. Additionally, the substrate structure exerts an important impact on the electrical and thermal properties of the metallic structure. For instance, the silkworm silk has lower thermal conductivity, and the electron tunneling along with hopping in this type of fiber can improve the electron conductivity of the metallic structure. Therefore, the silkworm silk is more suitable as a substrate material in flexible electronic devices.

Liu et al. [63] measured k of the chemical vapor deposited (CVD) graphene supported on poly(methyl methacrylate) (PMMA) using the differential TET technique shown in Figure 3. k of 1.33-layered, 1.53-layered, 2.74-layered, and 5.2-layered supported graphene were 365 W·m^{-1}·K^{-1}, 359 W·m^{-1}·K^{-1}, 273 W·m^{-1}·K^{-1}, and 33.5 W·m^{-1}·K^{-1}, respectively. These values were, on average, eight times lower than those reported for suspended graphene (k = 3000 W·m^{-1}·K^{-1}). The reduction in k was due to the suppression of ZA phonons by the substrate. The abundant C atoms in PMMA were more readily coupled with graphene than other atomic substrates. Hence, the differential TET technique is a fast and reliable method used to measure k of graphene. This work shows that the differential TET technique has great potential for future research on the thermal properties of graphene.

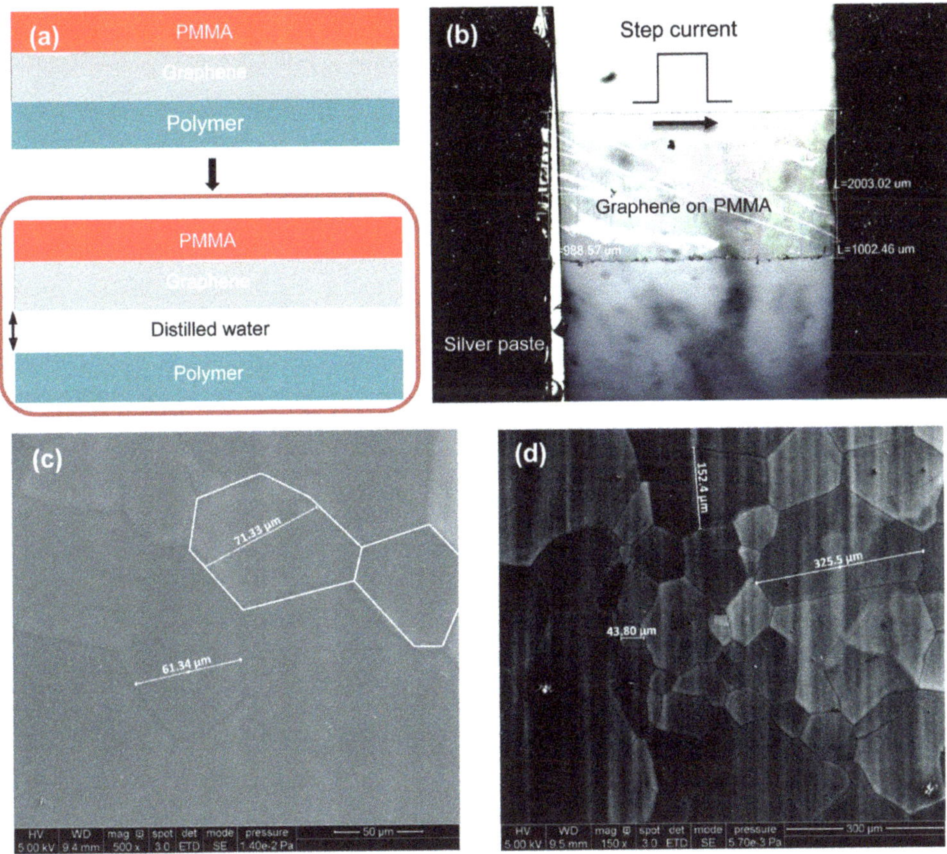

Figure 3. (**a**) Procedures for acquiring the sample of desired size from graphene. (**b**) Microscopic image of the graphene sample between the electrodes. (**c**,**d**) SEM images of the sample. The characteristic size of grains can be clearly seen in the range of tens to hundreds of microns. (Reproduced from Ref. [63] with permission from The Royal Society of Chemistry).

4. Summary and Prospects

In summary, the differential TET technique is one of the most optimal techniques for characterizing thermal transport properties in extremely confined metallic nanostructures, allowing one to precisely determine their thermal conductivity, electrical conductivity, and Lorenz number. Moreover, it possesses significant advantages over other widely used methods in terms of implementation simplicity, high signal-to-noise ratio, and high measurement accuracy. The disadvantages of the TET technique are that it cannot measure samples with extremely low resistance (less than 1 ohm) and measurement needs to be performed in a vacuum environment. The surface radiation effect cannot be ignored if the sample has a very large aspect ratio (L/D).

At present, the coating thickness can be explicitly controlled to the order of 0.1 nm. Additionally, we are limited by the availability of existing coating machines that determine the thickness of the metal films, but this is not due to the measurement technology itself. If the thermal conductivity of a substrate material is extremely low, the heat transfer between the substrate and the metal coating can be effectively reduced. Therefore, the substrates with low thermal conductivity and small diameter will soon make it possible to use very thin metallic structures. The TET technique will provide powerful aid in mastering the intrinsic heat transport properties of new materials, and it will be helpful for the development of new materials.

Author Contributions: Writing—original draft preparation, H.L., F.S., J.X. and L.Z.; writing—review and editing, S.X. and H.L.; supervision, N.L. and S.L. All authors have read and agreed to the published version of the manuscript.

Funding: This work was supported by the National Key Research and Development Program (2019YFE0119900), the Natural Science Foundation of Shandong Province (ZR2020ME183 and ZR2019MEE015), and the National Natural Science Foundation of China (52106220 and 51904325).

Institutional Review Board Statement: Not applicable.

Informed Consent Statement: Not applicable.

Data Availability Statement: The data presented in this study are available on request from the corresponding author.

Acknowledgments: Shen Xu is grateful to the research supported by the Program for Professor of Special Appointment (Eastern Scholar) at Shanghai Institutions of Higher Learning.

Conflicts of Interest: The authors declare no conflict of interest.

References

1. Tom, T.E.; Ros, N.; Lopez-Pinto, J.M.; Asensi, J.; Andreu, J.; Bertomeu, J.; Puigdollers, V.C. Influence of Co-Sputtered Ag:Al Ultra-Thin Layers in Transparent V2O5/Ag:Al/AZO Hole-Selective Electrodes for Silicon Solar Cells. *Materials* **2020**, *13*, 4905. [CrossRef]
2. Jilani, S.F.; Falade, O.; Wildsmith, T.; Reip, P.; Alomainy, A. A 60-GHz Ultra-Thin and Flexible Metasurface for Frequency-Selective Wireless Applications. *Appl. Sci. Basel* **2019**, *9*, 945. [CrossRef]
3. Liu, Z.Q.; Liu, G.; Huang, Z.; Liu, X.; Fu, G. Ultra-broadband perfect solar absorber by an ultra-thin refractory titanium nitride meta-surface. *Sol. Energy Mater. Sol. Cells* **2018**, *179*, 346–352. [CrossRef]
4. Wang, Y.H.; Qiu, Y.; Ameri, S.; Jang, H.; Dai, Z.; Huang, Y.; Lu, N.S. Low-cost, mu m-thick, tape-free electronic tattoo sensors with minimized motion and sweat artifacts. *NPJ Flex. Electron.* **2018**, *2*, 6. [CrossRef]
5. Pan, C.F.; Markvicka, E.; Malakooti, M.; Yan, J.; Hu, L.; Matyjaszewski, K.; Majidi, C. A Liquid-Metal-Elastomer Nanocomposite for Stretchable Dielectric Materials. *Adv. Mater.* **2019**, *31*, e1900663. [CrossRef] [PubMed]
6. Sun, Z.W.; Jin, S.; Jin, H.; Du, Z.; Zhu, Y.; Cao, A.; Ji, H.; Wan, L. Robust Expandable Carbon Nanotube Scaffold for Ultrahigh-Capacity Lithium-Metal Anodes. *Adv. Mater.* **2018**, *30*, e1800884. [CrossRef]
7. Guerin, H.; Yoshihira, M.; Kura, H.; Ogawa, T.; Sato, T.; Maki, H. Coulomb blockade phenomenon in ultra-thin gold nanowires. *J. Applied Physics* **2012**, *111*, 054304. [CrossRef]
8. Kim, Y.J.; Kumar, S.; Lee, C.; Koo, B.; Chung, J.; Kim, W. Influence of the thickness on structural, magnetic and electrical properties of La0. 7Ca0.3MnO3 thin film. *Curr. Appl. Phys.* **2010**, *10*, 821–824. [CrossRef]
9. Franz, R.; Wiedemann, G. Ueber die Wrme-Leitungsfhigkeit der Metalle. *Annalen Der Physik* **1853**.
10. Lorenz, L. Ueber das Leitungsvermögen der Metalle für Wärme und Electricität. *Ann. Der Phys.* **2010**, *249*, 422–447. [CrossRef]
11. Sondheimer, E.H. The Mean Free Path of Electrons in Metals. *Adv. Phys.* **2001**, *50*, 499–537. [CrossRef]
12. Zhang, X.; Xie, H.; Fujii, M.; Ago, H.; Takahashi, K.; Ikuta, T.; Abe, H.; Shimizu, T. Thermal and electrical conductivity of a suspended platinum nanofilm. *Appl. Phys. Lett.* **2005**, *86*, 1259. [CrossRef]
13. Beloborodov, I.; Lopatin, A.; Hekking, F. Thermal transport in granular metals. *Europhys. Lett.* **2005**, *69*, 435–441. [CrossRef]
14. Tripathi, V.; Loh, Y. Optical conductivity of a granular metal at not very low temperatures. *arXiv* **2006**, arXiv:cond-mat/0601138.
15. Fuchs, K. The conductivity of thin metallic films according to the electron theory of metals. *Math. Proc. Camb. Philos. Soc.* **2008**, *34*, 100–108. [CrossRef]
16. Stojanovic, N.D.; Maithripala, J.M.; Berg, M.; Holtz. Thermal conductivity in metallic nanostructures at high temperature: Electrons, phonons, the Wiedemann-Franz law. *Phys. Rev.* **2010**, *82*, 075418. [CrossRef]
17. Tzou, D.Y. A Unified Field Approach for Heat Conduction From Macro- to Micro-Scales. *Journal of Heat Transfer* **1995**, *117*, 8–16. [CrossRef]
18. Da, Y.T. The generalized lagging response in small-scale and high-rate heating. *Int. J. Heat Mass Transf.* **1995**, *38*, 3231–3240.
19. Duquesne, J.Y.; Fournier, D.; Fretigny, C. Analytical solutions of the heat diffusion equation for 3 omega method geometry. *J. Appl. Phys.* **2010**, *108*, 4067. [CrossRef]
20. Sheng, L.; Xing, D.; Wang, Z. Transport theory in metallic films: Crossover from the classical to the quantum regime. *Phys. Review. B Condens. Matter* **1995**, *51*, 7325–7328. [CrossRef]
21. Soffer, S.B. Statistical Model for the Size Effect in Electrical Conduction. *J. Appl. Phys.* **1967**, *38*, 1710–1715. [CrossRef]
22. Namba, Y. Resistivity and Temperature Coefficient of Thin Metal Films with Rough Surface. *Jpn. J. Appl. Phys.* **1970**, *9*, 1326–1329. [CrossRef]

23. Gurrum, S.P.; Joshi, Y.; King, W.; Ramakrishna, K.; Gall, M. A Compact Approach to On-Chip Interconnect Heat Conduction Modeling Using the Finite Element Method. *J. Electron. Packag.* **2008**, *130*, 031001. [CrossRef]

24. Gurrum, S.P.; Joshi, Y.; King, W.; Ramakrishna, K. Numerical simulation of electron transport through constriction in a metallic thin film. *Electron Device Lett. IEEE* **2015**, *25*, 696–698. [CrossRef]

25. Lu, L.; Yi, W.; Zhang, D. 3 omega method for specific heat and thermal conductivity measurements. *Rev. Sci. Instrum.* **2002**, *72*, 2996. [CrossRef]

26. Dames, C.; Chen, G. 1ω, 2ω, and 3ω methods for measurements of thermal properties. *Rev. Sci. Instrum.* **2005**, *76*, 124902. [CrossRef]

27. Choi, T.Y.; Poulikakos, D.; Tharian, J.; Sennhauser, U. Measurement of thermal conductivity of individual multiwalled carbon nanotubes by the 3-ω method. *Appl. Phys. Lett.* **2005**, *87*, 56. [CrossRef]

28. Hu, X.J.; Padilla, A.; Xu, J.; Fisher, T.; Goodson, K. 3-Omega Measurements of Vertically Oriented Carbon Nanotubes on Silicon. *J. Heat Transf.* **2006**, *128*, 1109–1113. [CrossRef]

29. Pezarini, R.R.; Bernabe, H.; Sato, F.; Malacarne, L.; Astrath, N.; Rohling, J.; Medina, A.; Reis, R.; Gandra, F. On the use of photothermal techniques to study NiTi phase transitions. *Mater. Res. Express* **2014**, *1*, 026502. [CrossRef]

30. Astrath, F.B.G.; Astrath, N.; Shen, J.; Zhou, J.; Baesso, M. A composite photothermal technique for the measurement of thermal properties of solids. *J. Applied Physics* **2008**, *104*. [CrossRef]

31. Bourgoin, J.P.; Allogho, G.; Hache, A. Thermal conduction in thin films measured by optical surface thermal lensing. *J. Appl. Phys.* **2010**, *108*, 223. [CrossRef]

32. Liu, J.; Wang, X. Characterization of thermal transport in one-dimensional microstructures using Johnson noise electro-thermal technique. *Appl. Phys. A Mater. Sci. Process.* **2015**, *119*, 871–879. [CrossRef]

33. Liu, G.Q.; Lin, H.; Tang, X.; Bergler, K.; Wang, X. Characterization of Thermal Transport in One-dimensional Solid Materials. *Jove-J. Vis. Exp.* **2014**, *83*, e51144. [CrossRef]

34. Deng, C.H.; Cong, T.; Xie, Y.; Wang, R.; Wang, T.; Pan, L.; Wang, X. In situ investigation of annealing effect on thermophysical properties of single carbon nanocoil. *Int. J. Heat Mass Transf.* **2020**, *151*, 119416. [CrossRef]

35. Guillou, J.; Lavadiya, D.; Munro, T.; Fronk, T.; Ban, H. From lignocellulose to biocomposite: Multi-level modelling and experimental investigation of the thermal properties of kenaf fiber reinforced composites based on constituent materials. *Appl. Therm. Eng.* **2018**, *128*, 1372–1381. [CrossRef]

36. Wang, H.; Sen, M. Analysis of the 3-omega method for thermal conductivity measurement. *Int. J. Heat and Mass Transf.* **2009**, *52*, 2102–2109. [CrossRef]

37. Ghukasyan, A.; Oliveira, P.; Goktas, N.; LaPierre, R. Thermal Conductivity of GaAs Nanowire Arrays Measured by the 3 omega Method. *Nanomaterials* **2022**, *12*, 1288. [CrossRef] [PubMed]

38. Qiu, L.; Zhu, N.; Zou, H.; Feng, Y.; Zhang, X.; Tang, D. Advances in thermal transport properties at nanoscale in China. *Int. J. Heat Mass Transf.* **2018**, *125*, 413–433. [CrossRef]

39. Nakamura, F.; Taketoshi, N.; Yagi, T.; Baba, T. Observation of thermal transfer across a Pt thin film at a low temperature using a femtosecond light pulse thermoreflectance method. *Meas. Sci. Technol.* **2011**, *22*, 500–502. [CrossRef]

40. Wang, H.-D.; Ma, W.-G.; Zhang, X.; Wang, W.; Guo, Z.-Y. Theoretical and experimental study on the heat transport in metallic nanofilms heated by ultra-short pulsed laser. *Int. J. Heat Mass Transf.* **2011**, *54*, 967–974. [CrossRef]

41. Jiang, P.Q.; Qian, X.; Yang, R. Tutorial: Time-domain thermoreflectance (TDTR) for thermal property characterization of bulk and thin film materials. *J. Appl. Phys.* **2018**, *124*, 161103. [CrossRef]

42. Liu, J.; Yoon, B.; Kuhlmann, E.; Tian, M.; Zhu, J.; George, S.; Lee, Y.; Yang, R. Ultralow Thermal Conductivity of Atomic/Molecular Layer-Deposited Hybrid Organic-Inorganic Zincone Thin Films. *Nano Lett.* **2013**, *13*, 5594–5599. [CrossRef]

43. Ma, W.G.; Zhang, X. Study of the thermal, electrical and thermoelectric properties of metallic nanofilms. *Int. J. Heat Mass Transf.* **2013**, *58*, 639–651. [CrossRef]

44. Boiko, B.T.; Pugachev, A.; Bratsychin, V. Method for the determination of the thermophysical properties of evaporated thin films. *Thin Solid Film.* **1973**, *17*, 157–161. [CrossRef]

45. Guo, J.Q.; Wang, X.; Wang, T. Thermal characterization of microscale conductive and nonconductive wires using transient electrothermal technique. *J. Appl. Phys.* **2007**, *101*, 063537. [CrossRef]

46. Lin, H.; Dong, H.; Xu, S.; Wang, X.; Zhang, J.; Wang, Y. Thermal transport in graphene fiber fabricated by wet-spinning method. *Mater. Lett.* **2016**, *183*, 147–150. [CrossRef]

47. Hunter, N.; Karamati, A.; Xie, Y.; Lin, H.; Wang, X. Laser Photoreduction of Graphene Aerogel Microfibers: Dynamic Electrical and Thermal Behaviors. *ChemPhysChem* **2022**, e202200417. [CrossRef] [PubMed]

48. Gao, J.; Zobeiri, H.; Lin, H.; Xie, D.; Yue, Y.; Wang, X. Coherency between thermal and electrical transport of partly reduced graphene paper. *Carbon.* **2021**, *178*, 92–102. [CrossRef]

49. Lin, H.; Hunter, N.; Zobeiri, H.; Yue, Y.; Wang, X. Ultra-high thermal sensitivity of graphene microfiber. *Carbon* **2023**, *203*, 620–629. [CrossRef]

50. Liu, G.Q.; Huang, X.; Wang, Y.; Zhang, Y.; Wang, X. Thermal transport in single silkworm silks and the behavior under stretching. *Soft Matter* **2012**, *8*, 9792–9799. [CrossRef]

51. Cheng, Z.; Han, M.; Yuan, P.; Xu, S.; Cola, B.; Wang, X. Strongly anisotropic thermal and electrical conductivities of a self-assembled silver nanowire network. *Rsc Adv.* **2016**, *6*, 90674–90681. [CrossRef]

52. Feng, X.; Wang, X. Thermophysical properties of free-standing micrometer-thick Poly(3-hexylthiophene) films. *Thin Solid Film.* **2011**, *519*, 5700–5705. [CrossRef]
53. Liu, X.; Dong, H.; Li, Y. Characterization of Thermal Conductivity of Carbon Fibers at Temperatures as Low as 10 K. *Int. J. Thermophys.* **2018**, *39*, 97. [CrossRef]
54. Liu, X.; Dong, H.; Li, Y.; Mei, N. Thermal Conductivity and Raman Spectra of Carbon Fibers. *Int. J. Thermophys.* **2017**, *38*, 1–9. [CrossRef]
55. Lin, H.; Liu, X.; Kou, A.; Xu, S.; Dong, H. 2019-One-Dimensional Thermal Characterization at the Micro Nanoscale Review of the TET Technique. *Int. J. Thermophys.* **2019**, *40*, 108. [CrossRef]
56. Lin, H.; Xu, S.; Wang, X.; Mei, N. Thermal and Electrical Conduction in Ultrathin Metallic Films: 7 nm down to Sub-Nanometer Thickness. *Small* **2013**, *9*, 2585–2594. [CrossRef] [PubMed]
57. Xie, Y.; Xu, Z.; Xu, S.; Cheng, Z.; Hashemi, N.; Deng, C.; Wang, X. The defect level and ideal thermal conductivity of graphene uncovered by residual thermal reffusivity at the 0 K limit. *Nanoscale* **2015**, *7*, 10101–10110. [CrossRef] [PubMed]
58. Xu, Z.; Wang, X.; Xie, H. Promoted electron transport and sustained phonon transport by DNA down to 10 K. *Polymer* **2014**, *55*, 6373–6380. [CrossRef]
59. Lin, H.; Xu, S.; Wang, X.; Mei, N. Significantly reduced thermal diffusivity of free-standing two-layer graphene in graphene foam. *Nanotechnology* **2013**, *24*, 415706. [CrossRef] [PubMed]
60. Lin, H.; Xu, S.; Zhang, Y.; Wang, X. Electron transport and bulk-like behavior of Wiedemann-Franz law for sub-7 nm-thin iridium films on silkworm silk. *Acs Appl. Mater Interfaces* **2014**, *6*, 11341–11347. [CrossRef]
61. Lin, H.; Xu, S.; Li, C.; Dong, H.; Wang, X. Thermal and electrical conduction in 6.4 nm thin gold films. *Nanoscale* **2013**, *5*, 4652–4656. [CrossRef] [PubMed]
62. Dong, H.; Chen, R.; Mu, Y.; Liu, S.; Zhang, J.; Lin, H. Thermal and Electrical Properties of 3.2 nm Thin Gold Films Coated on Alginate Fiber. *J. Therm. Sci. Eng. Appl.* **2017**, *10*, 011012. [CrossRef]
63. Liu, J.; Wang, T.; Xu, S.; Yuan, P.; Xu, X.; Wang, X. Thermal conductivity of giant mono- to few-layered CVD graphene supported on an organic substrate. *Nanoscale* **2016**, *8*, 10298–10309. [CrossRef] [PubMed]

 *nanomaterials*

Review

Thermal Transport in 2D Materials

Mohammad Hassan Kalantari and Xian Zhang *

Department of Mechanical Engineering, School of Engineering and Science, Stevens Institute of Technology, Hoboken, NJ 07030, USA
* Correspondence: xzhang4@stevens.edu

Abstract: In recent decades, two-dimensional materials (2D) such as graphene, black and blue phosphorenes, transition metal dichalcogenides (e.g., WS_2 and MoS_2), and h-BN have received illustrious consideration due to their promising properties. Increasingly, nanomaterial thermal properties have become a topic of research. Since nanodevices have to constantly be further miniaturized, thermal dissipation at the nanoscale has become one of the key issues in the nanotechnology field. Different techniques have been developed to measure the thermal conductivity of nanomaterials. A brief review of 2D material developments, thermal conductivity concepts, simulation methods, and recent research in heat conduction measurements is presented. Finally, recent research progress is summarized in this article.

Keywords: 2D materials; thermal conductivity; simulations; experimental measurements

Citation: Kalantari, M.H.; Zhang, X. Thermal Transport in 2D Materials. *Nanomaterials* **2023**, *13*, 117. https://doi.org/10.3390/nano13010117

Academic Editor: Gyaneshwar P. Srivastava

Received: 2 December 2022
Revised: 20 December 2022
Accepted: 22 December 2022
Published: 26 December 2022

1. Introduction

Two-dimensional materials are characterized by excellent structural, mechanical, and physical properties, making them suitable for basic science and engineering applications because of their superb properties [1]. Throughout recent years, 2D nanomaterials have been the subject of extensive studies, resulting in massive interest in their applications in novel nanodevices with unique functions. A growing interest in understanding the thermal properties of 2D materials has been observed over the last few years. In addition, in nanomaterials, thermal transport has revealed many unique phenomena, which, when understood, will open up new possibilities for the development of new nanotechnologies in thermal management. New technologies have become increasingly dependent on thermal conductivity as an essential parameter. Many benefits can be derived from nanoelectronic devices using 2D materials and they may potentially extend electronics into new fields of application.

A temperature increase occurs when advanced materials are used in some electronic applications. Increased thermal conductivity allows heat to diffuse faster and prevents large overheating, which can result in premature degradation. The majority of these unique phenomena are due to nanomaterials' notable properties. In fabrication and application, chemical functionalization, strain, and structural interruptions can alter their atomic structures, affecting their properties. Research on the micro/nano components of two-dimensional material has recently focused on their electrical, mechanical, and optical properties. It should be noted that for any micro/nano component, whether it is an electronic component or an optoelectronic component, the heat dissipation problem determines the device's performance and stability. High-density components will generate a lot of heat during high-speed operation. If the heat cannot be eliminated in time, it will cause the components to be too high in local and performance degradation, or even burnout. How to conduct immense heat away so that the components work in a relatively low-temperature environment becomes a common issue in the modern semiconductor industry [2–6].

Most microelectronic devices are combined with semiconductors and metals so the contact interface between semiconductors and metals can be seen everywhere. Microelectronic devices' heat dissipation problem involves the following physical issues: (1) How does heat transfer in micro/nano-scale materials? (2) How does heat pass through various interfaces? The most dominant heat carriers in semiconductor materials are phonons, which are found in micro/nano electronic devices. Consequently, the following questions arise: (1) How do phonons travel in micro/nano-scale semiconductor materials? (2) How do phonons pass through various interfaces? The study of these two problems enables us to solve heat dissipation problems related to micro/nano devices and thermal conductivity control.

An electronic device can generate heat in many different ways, such as by Joule heating, solar flux, or exothermic reactions. High-power density electronics such as integrated circuits, supercapacitors, LEDs, and lasers are notorious for localized Joule heating. Nanoscale devices have a higher power density, but a reduced amount of heat can be extracted as their dimensions decrease. Nanostructured solar cells and concentrated solar cells share a similar challenge of reducing efficiency with increased temperatures. For a final example, batteries can experience exothermic reactions and Joule heating, which may cause unwanted chemical reactions and device failure. Materials that must minimize heat transfer are at the other extreme. To reduce heat transfer across each leg, thermoelectric devices require materials with a low thermal conductivity. It creates a design conflict when thermoelectric materials must also be good electrical conductors. To prevent heat from reaching critical parts, thermal insulation is designed.

Advances in the electronics industry have fueled an enormous demand for pioneering thermal management strategies to enhance the performance and reliability of devices by controlling energy dissipation generated in the devices. In nanoelectronics, where heat dissipation is a vital factor in the performance of high-density nanoscale circuits, or in thermoelectric materials, where low thermal conductivity is desired, controlling heat diffusion by controlling the phononic properties of fundamental components is a major interest. For instance, among the promising candidates for field effect transistor applications with a high on/off ratio and high mobility, single-layer MoS_2 is a semiconductor with a large bandgap of ~1.1–2 eV [7–9]. Low-temperature carrier mobility can be significantly enhanced by improving sample quality and using appropriate electrode materials [10]. Following these recent breakthroughs, it is highly expected that 2D materials will be used in integrated circuits (ICs) in the near future. Another example is stanene, a single-layer buckled honeycomb structure of tin atoms that exhibits near-room temperature quantum anomalous Hall effects [11] and ultra-low thermal conductivity [12], which makes it ideal for thermoelectric applications. This article discusses in detail the thermal conductivity of 2D materials.

2. Two-Dimensional (2D) Materials

Understanding material systems is at the core of the technology. Each application requires specific material properties. For example, circuits are built with copper because of their electrical conductivity, skyscrapers are constructed with concrete because of their compressive strength, and car tires are constructed with vulcanized rubber, which is pliable and durable. Technology can advance further as we gain a deeper understanding of a material's properties. Nanomaterials refer to materials with a dimension of at least one nanometer in size. Qualitative changes in physicochemical properties and reactivity are related to the number of atoms or molecules determining the material in this scale. To illustrate, the surface plasmon resonance of metal nanoparticles and quantum confinement of semiconductor particles can be observed as size-effect properties. Recent years have seen an increased interest in two-dimensional (2D) nanomaterials due to their unique properties. Furthermore, two-dimensional nanomaterials bridge the gap between one-dimensional (1D) nanomaterials and three-dimensional (3D) bulk materials, raising new fundamental problems related to low-dimensional materials that can lead to a host of new applications. As these nanodevices become more widely available, the need to understand their thermal properties has increased. Two-dimensional nanomaterials are briefly introduced in this section.

Monolayer graphene flakes were isolated from bulk graphite by mechanical exfoliation, launching the field of two-dimensional (2D) materials [13]. There have also been numerous discoveries of 2D materials since then, including transition metal dichalcogenides (TMDs, e.g., MoS_2), hexagonal boron nitride (h-BN), and black phosphorus (BP) (or phosphorene). There is a wide range of physical properties available within the 2D materials family, from conducting graphene to semiconducting MoS_2 to insulating h-BN. As an added advantage, 2D crystal structures exhibit superior mechanical properties, exhibiting a high in-plane stiffness and strength, as well as an extremely low flexural rigidity. Together, the 2D materials have a wide range of potential applications [14,15].

Van der Waals forces or weak covalent bonds that hold together material layers can be mechanically or chemically exfoliated down to an in-plane, covalently bonded single layer. A 2D materials history dates back to the 1960s. As early as 1980, graphene, a one-atom thick graphite layer, was isolated and studied extensively as a monolayer. Novoselov and Geim introduced 2D materials by studying graphene under electric and magnetic fields [16]. Because of the high quality of the crystals and their ease of obtaining them, many researchers have developed more complicated 2D electron gas materials for graphene. A number of graphene effects were determined as a result. It has also been shown that other layered materials are known to mechanically exfoliate. Over a thousand materials have been identified by 2020 [17]. As layers often significantly influence the electrical, optical, and thermal properties of materials, this large number of materials can enable a plethora of novel physics. For example, by changing the gap energy, MoS_2 transitions from an indirect to a direct bandgap as the monolayer limit is reached.

Material properties are often thought to be determined solely by their material composition. Electricity is conducted by metals because they contain metallic bonds between their atoms, allowing electrons to drift freely throughout the material. The strength of concrete comes from the cement that rigidly locks incompressible sand and gravel together. Vulcanized rubber is made of flexible polymer chains that are firmly linked together, making it both pliable and durable. The size of a material, however, can influence its behavior. Materials with nanoscale dimensions (i.e., whose sizes can be expressed in nanometers) are particularly susceptible to this. The nanoscale can affect electrical conductivity, chemical reactivity, mechanical properties, and even how a material interacts with light. A fascinating and unexpected new property of nanomaterials is being revealed as we become more adept at creating and studying nanomaterials. With this advancement, future technologies that rely on both bulk properties and material size have opened up entirely new opportunities. A new era of nanotechnology has begun. Periodic tables of 2D materials are currently being worked on and may offer a new form of chemistry using layers rather than atoms (Figure 1). In this article, the thermal properties of 2D materials are discussed, following many excellent literature reviews on the subject.

The first novel 2D material introduced was graphene in 2004. Since then, many other 2D materials have been proposed [17] with an extensive range of properties. In this section, several of the researchers' materials of interest are presented briefly. The two types of 2D materials are single-element 2D materials (such as graphene, black phosphorus (BP), silicene, germanene, etc.) and compound 2D materials (such as TMDs, h-BN, TMCs, III–V group elements, compound semiconductors, etc.). Figure 2 below illustrates some of these types.

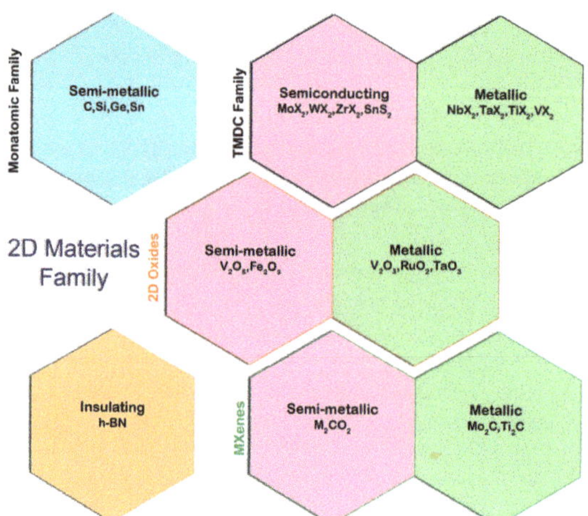

Figure 1. 2D materials family [18]. Reprinted with permission from ref. [18]. Springer Nature and Copyright Clearance Center.

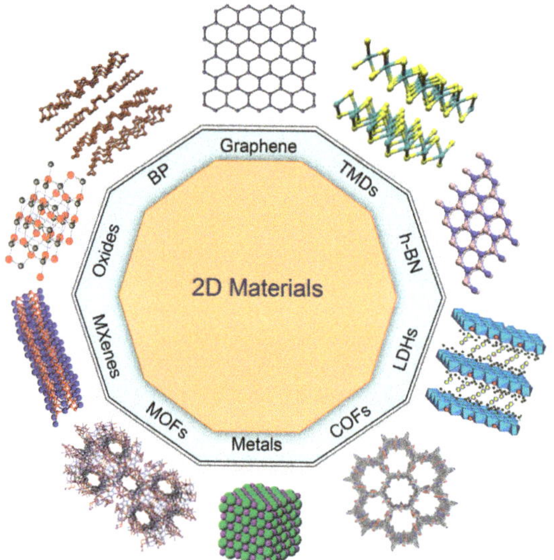

Figure 2. Some of the introduced 2D materials.

Graphene is a semimetal that consists of a covalently bonded hexagonal lattice of carbon atoms. In most cases, it is only one-atom thick (about 0.14 nm). The distinctive band structure of graphene enables electrons to move rapidly at speeds close to 1/300 the speed of light, resulting in its excellent thermal conductivity and high tensile strength. A single monolayer of graphene could support the weight of an entire football [19].

Hexagonal boron nitride (h-BN) is an isomorph of graphene (behaves similarly in terms of its crystallographic properties), except instead of carbon, boron and nitrogen atoms make up the structure. It is a wide-bandgap insulator, in contrast to graphene.

TMDCs are transition metal dichalcogenides with the chemical formula MX$_2$, where M is a transition metal (such as tungsten (W) or molybdenum (Mo)), and X represents a chalcogen (like selenium (Se), sulfur (S), or tellurium (Te)). A TMDC is made up of a metal layer sandwiched between two chalcogenide layers, with each layer being three atoms thick.

The crystal structure of TDMCs can vary. A 2H-phase with trigonal symmetry is the most common, resulting in semiconducting properties like MoS_2, WS_2, and $MoSe_2$. The bulk form of these semiconductors has an indirect bandgap. It is interesting for optoelectronics to use monolayers because their bandgap becomes direct and visible. The metallic 1T phase, the most stable polymorph of WTe_2, is another example of such structures.

A single layer of black phosphorus (BP) is called phosphorene, which is a stable allotrope of elemental phosphorus. This semiconductor has a puckered honeycomb structure with a direct bandgap. Layers can be stacked on top of each other to tune the bandgap throughout the visible region. Due to this, these materials are appropriate for transistors and optoelectronic devices. The corrugated structure of phosphorene causes its properties to vary noticeably depending on its measurement direction.

MXenes are monolayers of tin (stanene), germanium (germanene), and silicon (silicene). Similar 2D materials have also been developed, such as antimony [20] and bismuth [21]. Bismuth is found to have the potential for magneto-electronic applications [22].

3. Thermal Conductivity

A greater understanding of the thermal properties of 2D nanomaterials is required due to their rapid development. The main factors contributing to this demand are as follows. First, electronic devices are subjected to ever-increasing thermal loads due to continuous miniaturization and component density increases. Electronic device components are getting smaller and smaller every year, according to Moore's law. One of the crucial components of electronics is the field-effect transistor, which has now reached a channel length of 100 nm, and a 50 nm channel length is on the horizon. Thermal design has become an essential part of electronic device development at the nanoscale, as controlling heat is critical for reliability and performance.

Furthermore, at the nanoscale, electronic devices exhibit thermal transport characteristics that are dramatically different from those observed at the macroscale. The electrical−thermal design of the electronic device should also take these features into account. As the use and requirement of energy sources increases, practical and efficient solutions are required for energy generation, consumption, and recycling. Heat management can be improved by utilizing recently developed nanotechnologies and nanomaterials. In some cases, for efficient thermal dissipation, nanomaterials with high thermal conductivities are employed in nanoscale electronics. A low thermal conductivity is required to increase thermal conversion or preservation in other cases, such as in thermoelectric devices and thermal barrier coatings, nanomaterials, or nanoparticles.

Heat is carried primarily by phonons in the same way electricity is carried by electrons. A recent study demonstrated that phonons can carry and process information as well [23]. A variety of types of thermal logic devices have been developed theoretically and even experimentally, such as thermal rectifiers [24,25], thermal transistors [26], thermal logic gates [27], and thermal memory cells [28]. In a similar manner to electronic circuits, thermal circuits can be fabricated using these basic thermal components.

Two-dimensional nanomaterials have different thermal properties than bulk materials due to their atomic structures. For example, graphene as a 2D material has a thermal conductivity as high as ~2000 W/m·K [29], or even higher [30]. This is comparable to the highest thermal conductivity material found in nature, which is diamond. As a result, high-power electronics could potentially benefit from its use in thermal management. h-BN also has high mechanical strength and good thermal properties. High-quality bulk h-BN samples could reach a thermal conductivity of ~390 W/m·K, indicating its potential as a current generation dielectric material [31]. In a study by Joe et al., the thermal conductivity of an 11-layer sample was found to reach about ~360 W/m·K [32]. For silicene, different MD simulations calculated thermal conductivities ranging from 5 to 50 W/m·K [33,34]. TMDs show different thermal conductivity. As an illustration, it has been estimated that MoS_2 has a thermal conductivity of about 26 W/m·K, according to Wei et al. [35]. WS_2 CVD-grown monolayer and bilayer thermal conductivity was determined by Peimyoo et al. For monolayer and bilayer WS_2, the measured values are 32 and 53 W/m·K, respectively [36]. Theoretically, the thermal conductivity of phosphorene indicates low thermal conductivity. For instance, Qin et al. studied the simulated thermal conductivity along zigzag (ZZ) and armchair (AC) directions and found it to be 15.33 and 4.59 W/m·K, respectively [37]. However, during the manufacturing of 2D nanomaterials, structural defects such as voids, grain boundaries, and dislocations could be formed. A brief review of the thermal conductivity concept is provided in this section.

We review alternative approaches to determining temperatures and heat rates for a two-dimensional, steady-state conduction in the first step. A wide range of approaches are being used, which range from exact solutions that can be obtained for idealized conditions to approximate methods that vary in complexity and accuracy. In the following section, we consider some of the mathematical issues associated with obtaining an exact solution [38].

3.1. General Considerations and Solution Techniques

A heat flux equation, according to Fourier's law, can be expressed as follows [38]:

$$\frac{\partial}{\partial x}\left(k\frac{\partial T}{\partial x}\right) + \frac{\partial}{\partial y}\left(k\frac{\partial T}{\partial y}\right) + \frac{\partial}{\partial z}\left(k\frac{\partial T}{\partial z}\right) + \dot{q} = \rho c_p \frac{\partial T}{\partial t} \tag{1}$$

Here, $\dot{q}$ is the rate of energy generated per unit volume of the medium (W/m^3) and k is the thermal conductivity (W/m·K). In Cartesian coordinates, Equation (1) is the general form of heat diffusion. There are two primary objectives that are usually attached to any conduction analysis. Known as the heat equation, it provides the basic tool for analyzing heat conduction. T (x, y, z) can be calculated as a function of time from its solution. For the present problem, the first objective is to detect the distribution of temperature in the medium and in order to do so, it is necessary to determine T (x, y). Solving the heat equation in the appropriate form is the key to obtaining this objective. It is found that in two-dimensional steady-state conditions with no generation and constant thermal conductivity, this form can be calculated from Equation (1) as follows:

$$\frac{\partial^2 T}{\partial x^2} + \frac{\partial^2 T}{\partial y^2} = 0 \tag{2}$$

Equation (2) can be solved analytically by an exact mathematical solution. However, despite the fact that there are several techniques that can be used to solve these equations, the solutions usually involve complicated mathematical functions and series, and only a limited number of simple geometries and boundary conditions can be used. As a result of the dependent variable T being a continuous function of the independent variables (x, y), the solutions are valuable. Therefore, this solution can be used to calculate the temperature at any point within the medium.

A method of separation of variables is also used to compute an exact solution to Equation (2) in order to illustrate the nature and importance of analytical methods. For typical geometries that are usually existing in engineering practice, conduction shape factors and dimensionless conduction heat rates are sets of existing solutions. Graphical and numerical methods, on the other hand, can produce approximate results at discrete points, as opposed to analytical methods, which deliver exact results at any point. Although computer solutions based on numerical methods have replaced the graphical or flux-plotting methods, they can still be used to estimate temperature distribution quickly. Generally, it is used for two-dimensional problems with adiabatic and isothermal boundary conditions. A numerical method, on the other hand, can be used to obtain accurate results for complex, three-dimensional geometries involving an array of boundary conditions, in contrast to analytical or graphical approaches.

3.2. The Method of Separation of Variables

Two-dimensional conduction problems can be solved with the separation of variables method by applying the boundary conditions to a thin rectangular plate, a long rectangular rod, or any other shape that can be described by boundary conditions. By solving the heat equation, the temperature T corresponding value, heat flux, and heat flow lines can be determined, but this method is limited, complicated, and time-consuming [38]. For a variety of other geometries and boundary conditions, including cylindrical and spherical systems, exact solutions were obtained [39,40].

3.3. The Conduction Shape Factor

The process of finding an analytical solution to a two-dimensional or three-dimensional heat equation can be time-consuming and even impossible in some cases. This leads to the consideration of a different approach. For example, the heat diffusion equation can be quickly solved in many examples by employing existing solutions to it to solve two- or three-dimensional conduction problems. Shape factor S or steady-state dimensionless conduction heat rates q_{ss}^* are used to present these solutions [38].

In some cases, it may be possible to provide accurate mathematical solutions to steady, two-dimensional conduction problems by using analytical methods, as outlined above. For a variety of simple geometry and boundary conditions, these solutions have been generated [41–43]. In spite of this, there are many two-dimensional problems that do not involve simple geometries and boundary conditions that would allow them to be solved with such solutions. A numerical approach such as finite-difference, finite-element, or boundary element may be the best choice in these cases in order to solve the problem.

Although the corresponding κ may differ significantly between 2D materials (such as graphene, molybdenum sulfide, and black phosphorus) and their bulk counterparts, taking advantage of these differences can lead to new possibilities in a variety of applications, such as thermal management and energy conversion. It is necessary to study the microscopic picture of two-dimensional materials in order to understand the heat transfer properties of these materials. This section will discuss some general fundamentals and concepts of phonon thermal transport before discussing details of 2D materials.

3.4. Thermal Transport at the Nanoscale

A brief description of thermal transport at the microscale is necessary before discussing different effects in 2D materials. In order to transfer energy from one region of space to another region of space, the transportation or conduction of thermal energy requires the use of carriers, such as particles or waves. Except for alloys with extremely low electrical conductivity, metals conduct thermal energy mainly through electrons [44]. As shown in Figure 3, from a microscopic perspective, in dielectrics and semiconductors, it can be seen that heat is primarily carried by phonons or quantized vibrations of atoms in the lattice that can function as a particle to represent the phonon wave packets, according to the quantum state during their production. A phonon, when viewed from the angle of energy, will behave as a particle and collide with other phonon particles, as well as impurities and boundaries around it.

Firstly, before starting the detailed analysis, it is crucial that the length scales be clarified in advance. The figure shows a structure with a size of L (in 2D materials, L can be considered as the material's thickness) and a wavelength of λ for phonon wave packets. It is noted that the phonon is considered to be a particle in the spherical regime (gray regime). Phonons collide with other phonons, impurities, and boundaries when they move within solids. A phonon mean free path Λ is a distance between two collisions, which is an incredibly significant concept in the field of thermal transport. At room temperature, the mean free path Λ typically ranges from nanometers to tens of micrometers. It can be much longer at low temperatures. Generally, transport properties are discussed primarily on length scales larger than phonon wavelengths λ and comparable to or smaller than mean free paths Λ. When size L exceeds the mean free path Λ, the size effect will not be taken into consideration, which echoes the bulk of classical Fourier's law. A smaller size L than the mean free path Λ will result in phonons scattering on the boundaries before further phonon-to-phonon scattering. Due to these extra scatterings on the boundary, heat transfer will then be constrained by the boundaries. A primary cause of the reduction in thermal conductivity of 2D materials can be attributed to this phenomenon. It is known as the classical size effect when this type of effect occurs. In cases where the size L is smaller than the wavelength λ, we will encounter a quantum size effect as a result. A 2D material with a thickness of L usually exceeds the wavelength of the phonons unless the temperature is very low [44].

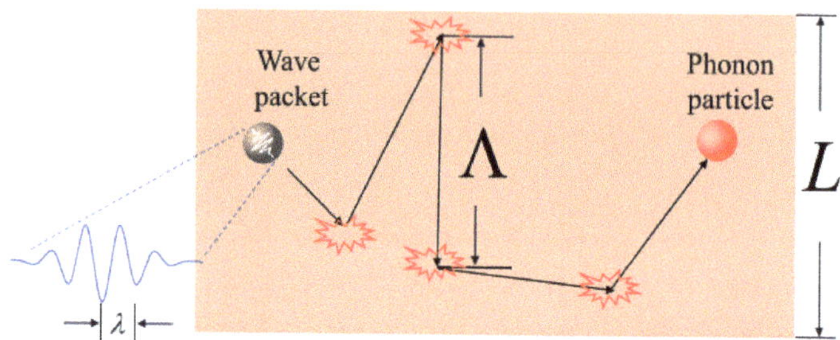

Figure 3. The schematic for the phonon particle picture [44]. Reprinted with permission from ref. [44]. Elsevier and Copyright Clearance Center.

Materials, even crystals, do not have infinite thermal conductivity because phonons are scattered with one another. As result of this scattering, it is known as phonon−phonon scattering. High temperatures lead to stronger scattering and shorter mean free paths Λ. There is a great deal of complexity involved when it comes to phonon–phonon scattering, and it can also be very challenging to determine the phonon–phonon scattering time. As a result of the advancement of computation algorithms and the availability of more powerful computation capabilities, there have been noticeable advances in the calculation of the phonon–phonon scattering rate through the first principle. The following section provides an overview of some of these methods.

4. Simulation Methods

Advancement of computers and technology resulted in the development of atomistic models that have become so precise that they can typically be compared with experimental results. The use of atomic simulations has therefore become more common in nanomaterials research in the past few decades.

4.1. Atomistic Simulations of Thermal Transport

The thermal transport properties of a material can be predicted using atomic simulations by understanding its atomic structure and interatomic interactions. A variety of atomistic simulation approaches have been developed to study nanomaterial thermal transport properties.

To study the thermal transport properties of 2D materials, various theoretical methods have been introduced, including molecular dynamics simulations (MD), Boltzmann transport equations (BTE), and atomistic Green's functions (AGF).

4.2. Introduction to Simulation Approaches

In Figure 4, a variety of simulation techniques are presented for the study of material thermal properties [45]. The Boltzmann transport equation and the non-equilibrium Green's function are examples of first-class approaches. In each of these methods, the thermal properties are predicted by solving the lattice dynamics equations based on understanding the fundamentals of phonon properties. Direct MD simulation is used in the second class for calculating thermal properties, such as the equilibrium Green–Kubo approach and the non-equilibrium MD method (also called the direct approach).

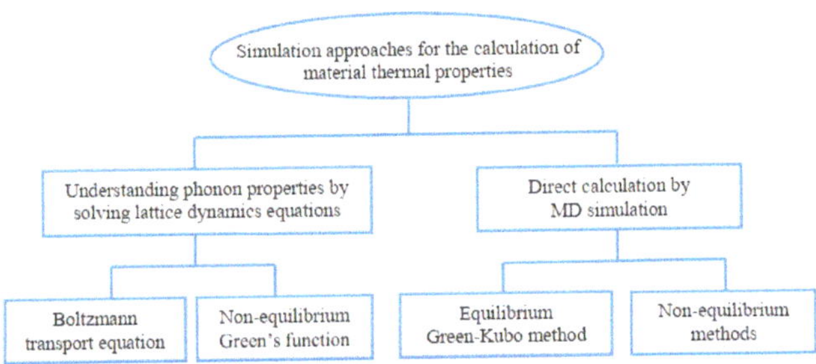

Figure 4. Materials thermal property classifications based on atomistic simulations [45]. Reprinted with permission from ref. [45]. Taylor & Francis Group LLC—Books.

In the case of first-class methods, such as Monte Carlo (MC), during the calculation, phonon transport and scattering are taken into consideration. As a result, prior knowledge of phonon transport is needed. Obtaining such a requirement is easy if the material has a simple lattice structure. On the other hand, phonon transport is usually difficult to predict when there are structural disruptions, such as sharp interfaces. Contrary to the first-class approaches, the MD simulation in the second class uses Newton's equations of motion in terms of time for a group of atoms interacting with each other via potential empirical functions. Furthermore, MD simulations are capable of modeling both small and large systems to calculate material thermal properties using phonon properties and solving lattice dynamics equation simulations, while a system's size can be modeled. The following brief overview presents three of the more commonly used simulation methods for predicting the thermal conductivity of nanostructured materials.

4.3. A Mento Carlo Simulation Method

Boltzmann's equation for the transport of phonons usually forms the basis of a theoretical analysis of phonon transport [46]. To solve this equation in a closed-form manner, many critical assumptions and simplifications must be made, which can cause huge deviations from experimental observations, especially for materials whose geometrical and lattice structure are relatively complicated and whose defects are multiple types. The MC approach was originally developed as a numerical solution to the Boltzmann equation in the context of electron transport [46]. The method has been widely applied since then to manage the transport problems of particles. In bulk materials [47], thin films [48,49], nanowires [50], and nanocomposites [51], the MC simulation has been successfully applied to determine thermal transport properties.

In the MC method, phonons are treated as random particles drifting in space when solving the transport problem. While MC simulations are typically used to predict thermal properties using lattice dynamics, i.e., phonons, this approach lacks the disadvantage that a numerical expression of the phonon dispersion is required to obtain reasonable phonon numbers and distributions in both the spatial and spectral spaces. A clear understanding of the scattering rate $\tau^{-1}(\omega)$ resulting from different scattering mechanisms should also be provided in order to address scattering events. For GE-based nanomaterials, these two requirements necessitate a lot of considerations, including strain, chemical functionalization, interface, and defects.

4.4. First Principles Method

Using the Boltzmann transport equation (BTE) in conjunction with the Schrödinger equation, first principles calculations can be performed on thermal transport. For the first principles calculation, no fitting parameters are required, as opposed to the traditional method of extracting phonon scattering times. The following steps are involved in the first principles of the thermal transport-based method. As a first step, first principles simulation refers to solving the Schrödinger equation numerically. Numerical computation is performed to calculate the atomic potential force constant. Based on these force constants, the anharmonic lattice dynamics will be used to extract the phonon dispersion relation and scattering rate. Then, the Boltzmann transport equation (BTE) can be linearized and solved numerically as well. As a result of this process, both the dispersion relation and the phonon scattering rate (or the relaxation time) for each phonon mode are calculated. Lastly, in order to calculate thermal conductivity, the lattice thermal connectivity can be extracted.

A wide range of 2D materials have been studied by using the first principles method since its development, including graphene [52,53], phosphorene [54,55], molybdenum disulfide (MoS_2) [56,57], and silicene [34,58]. More detailed explanations of this method can be found in a number of outstanding review papers [59,60] or books [61].

4.5. Molecular Dynamics Simulations Method

There is also another widely accepted method for thermal transport in 2D materials known as Molecular Dynamics (MD), which relies on Newton's law of motion as its physical foundation. Starting with the atomic potential between atoms, the process begins. As a result, the force acting on each atom can be calculated, as well as its velocity at any given moment. In the modern era of supercomputers, it is possible to determine the location of every atom at any time. Then, based on statistical mechanics principles, it is possible to study the expected macroscale properties.

To calculate the material's thermal conductivity directly during MD simulation, non-equilibrium MD and equilibrium Green–Kubo approaches are most commonly used. A non-equilibrium MD approach is similar to the experimental measurement of thermal conductivity. As a result of this method, one region of the simulation cell is heated up, and another region that is situated at a distance is cooled down. As soon as the system reaches a stable state, it is possible to extract the temperature profile between the hot and cold regions, from which the temperature gradient between the two regions can be determined. It is a direct approach that can be easily implemented in MD simulation since it relies only on classical quantities such as force, velocity, and position to compute the temperature and heat flux. Furthermore, the calculation of the thermal properties does not require any significant assumptions to be made.

A note should be made here that the accuracy of classical MD calculations is highly dependent on the quality of the interatomic potentials. Recent studies have focused on constructing a reliable potential function from first principles calculations [62]. To obtain the thermal properties of 2D materials, equilibrium MD (EMD) and non-equilibrium MD (NEMD) simulations are modified. The Green–Kubo formula or the Einstein Relation ratio is used to calculate thermal conductivity in EMD [63,64]. The hot and cold reservoirs are connected to each side of a sample for NEMD simulations. To calculate thermal conductivity, the stationary-state heat flux and temperature are extracted after sufficient run-time in terms of Fourier's law of heat conduction.

A major advantage of MD is that it is of atomic scale, yet it can be applied to large structures. Moreover, the computational cost can be significantly reduced when compared to the first principles approach. Therefore, the MD method is able to simulate systems that are several orders of magnitude larger than a first principle. The simulation can include millions, or even billions, of atoms. A 2D material can benefit from this since one direction is isolated. For example, recent research has modeled the thermal rectification device employing different graphene geometries [65]. This method can only be applied to systems with well-known potentials, such as carbon-based materials, due to the limited number of potentials identified and verified. Machine learning algorithms have become extremely useful methods of calculating atomic potentials over the past few decades [59]. We can expect more reliable potentials as these algorithms develop and computational power increases.

The simulation of nanoscale objects, such as GE, is usually carried out by either first principles simulations or molecular dynamics simulations (MD). MD simulations are a suitable alternative to first principles simulations because they allow the system size to get relatively large compared to first principles simulations. A study of nanomaterials' thermal properties can thus be facilitated by this method.

4.6. Equilibrium Green–Kubo Approach

According to the equilibrium Green–Kubo approach, thermal conductivity is calculated by monitoring the dissipation time of these fluctuations. The Green–Kubo approach calculates the thermal conductivity of an isotropic material as follows [60]:

$$\lambda = \frac{1}{3k_B V T^2} \int_0^{\infty} \langle \vec{J}(0) \vec{J}(t) \rangle dt \tag{3}$$

where $\langle \vec{J}(0) \vec{J}(t) \rangle$ is the autocorrelation function for heat flux and the angular brackets demonstrate ensemble averages. Here, T is the temperature, k_B is the Boltzmann constant, and V is the system volume.

The benefit of this method is that it requires significantly fewer simulation cells than non-equilibrium MD. It is also suitable for perfect crystals like Si and diamond with long phonons. However, when complex potential functions are employed, this approach lacks convergence and makes it difficult to calculate the heat flux. Furthermore, when dealing with inhomogeneous systems, this approach computes a thermal conductivity average over all the systems, i.e., an interface. As a result, the detailed behavior of phonons at the interface cannot be studied. Based on these facts, it seems that this approach cannot be used to investigate the thermal properties of 2D nanomaterials containing impurities and interfaces.

4.7. Atomistic Green's Functions

Since it is evident, phonons are wave-like particles. Wave effects on a discrete atomic lattice can be accurately modeled using Atomistic Green's Functions (AGF). Initially, this method was introduced to deal with quantum electron transport in nanostructures [61,66–71]. The approach can be applied to a variety of nanostructures by making a few careful substitutions [72–75]. It is particularly suitable for low-dimensional heterostructures such as Si/Ge [76], graphene/h-BN [77], MoS_2/metal [78] interfaces, and others [79].

5. Experimental Measurement

Due to the difficulty of extracting precise temperature gradients and heat fluxes, measuring the thermal conductivity of 2D materials is challenging. These nanostructures cannot be measured with traditional tools for temperature and heat flux measurements since most nanostructures are orders of magnitude smaller than the finest thermocouples. Therefore, a variety of optical and electrical tools have been utilized to measure the thermal properties of 2D materials.

There are two experimental method types in the micro/nano-scale thermal conductivity measurements: steady-state measurement (i.e., suspended thermal bridge method, Raman method, etc.) and transient measurement (i.e., 3ω method, time-domain thermal reflection technique, shock optical pulse thermal measurement method, etc.). Some 2D measurement producers are briefly discussed in the following sections.

5.1. Suspended Thermal Bridge Method

The invention of the suspended thermal bridge method benefits from the advancement of micro/nano processing technology development. For the first time, the suspended thermal bridge method was used in micro/nano-scale thermal conductivity measurements in 2001. The sample measured in this experiment was a single root of multi-walled carbon nanotubes [80]. Previously, traditional methods could only measure the overall thermal conductivity of a bundle of nanowires. The phonon scattering between nanowires (or nanotubes) makes it impossible to accurately determine the thermal conductivity of a single sample [81]. The suspended thermal bridge method is more useful for the study of low-dimensional thermoelectric materials [82,83]. A thermal bridge microdevice is made of two suspended silicon nitride membranes (SiN$_x$) that are patterned with thin metal lines (Pt resistors). Figure 5 illustrates how the resistors are electrically connected to contact pads via four Pt leads and used as microheaters and thermometers, providing Joule heating and four-probe resistance measurements, respectively. The heat transfer in the suspended sample is extracted by considering the generated Joule heating on the heated membrane and the temperature change on the sensing membrane while the sample is held between the two membranes and bonded to Pt electrodes. As a result of the high accuracy of Pt thermometers and direct temperature calibration, this method can provide a high temperature resolution of ~0.05 K in a range from 4 to 400 K [80,84]. The experimentally measured thermal conductance G and thermal conductivity k are calculated from the equations $G = 1/R_{tot}$ and $K = L/(AR_{tot})$, respectively. Here, R_{tot} is the total measured thermal resistance, L is known as the length of the sample, and A is the cross-sectional area of the sample. As mentioned, R_{tot} is the total thermal resistance of the entire system, including the thermal resistance of the suspended sample, the thermal resistance contribution from the membrane-connected parts of the sample, the internal thermal resistances of the two membranes, and the additional thermal resistance contribution from the part of the membranes which are linked with the heaters/thermometers.

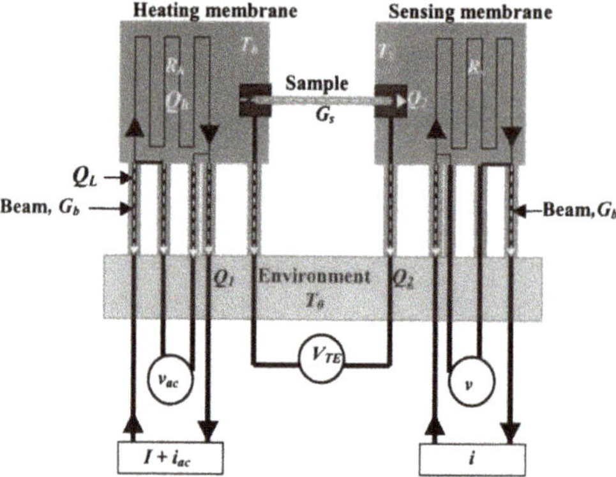

Figure 5. Thermal bridge method [84]. Reprinted with permission from ref. [84]. American Society of Mechanical Engineers ASME.

In recent years, there has been a massive demand for measurement of the thermal conductivity of low thermal conductivity micro/nano-scale materials. Therefore, the Wheatstone bridge method [85] and the comparator method [86] were developed to improve the measurement. Xu Xiangfan et al. [86] used the comparator method to measure the thermal conductivity of a single polyimide nanofiber. In this experiment, the thermal conductivity of the sample is about 1.0×10^{-10} W/K, which is an order of magnitude lower than the lower limit that can be measured by the ordinary thermal bridge method. It can be seen that the use of this method greatly broadens the application range of the thermal bridge method. Zheng et al. [87] used AC heating to eliminate white noise, which can further increase the measurement accuracy to about 0.25 W/K.

In spite of this, some technical challenges still need to be considered. In order to measure R_{tot} accurately, it is necessary to account for the thermal contact resistance components that unavoidably contribute to them. The first component that needs to be mentioned is thermal contact resistance ($R_{c,f}$) between the two ends of the suspended sample and the SiN$_x$ membranes [88,89]. Various studies have shown the need for a fin resistance model to estimate this resistance [90,91]. The thermal contact resistance between the sample−membrane interface and the thermometer $R_{c,m}$ is another component of R_{tot}, as it results from a non-uniform temperature distribution on the heating membrane. The $R_{c,m}$ factor can be ignored if the membrane has a uniform temperature distribution, i.e., when the thermal resistance of the suspended sample is greater than the internal thermal resistance of the membrane. A high thermal conductivity material, such as graphene or carbon nanotubes, however, is not the case. By re-analyzing heat transport results in CVD single-layer graphene samples, Jo et al. concluded that these extrinsic thermal contact resistances contribute up to 20% of the measured thermal resistance [91]. Recently, several studies found that resistance line thermometers can be employed as a replacement for serpentine Pt thermometers to reduce the size of the temperature measurement resistance (between heater/sensor and contact point) [92,93]. It has been determined that by employing numerical heat conduction calculations, the contribution of $R_{c,m}$ decreases to about 30–40% compared to the values that correspond to the serpentine resistance thermometer [91]. The device fabrication and sample transfer are also time-consuming and complex with this technique. In most cases, exfoliated 2D materials are transferred to the thermal bridge structure using a dry transfer method, causing polymer residues, defects, and rough edges on the sample surface that greatly affect the measured total thermal resistance [32,94]. Within the temperature range of 4 to 400 K, the suspended thermal bridge method can be applied. An advanced method based on the tunnel current in a metal−insulator−superconductor junction has been proposed for sub-Kelvin measurements [95]. This allows measurements to be made down to 1 m·K

Additionally, various materials, such as nanofilms [88,89] and 2D materials, including graphene [91,96–99], boron nitride [100], and TMDC materials [101,102], have also been measured using the thermal bridge method.

5.2. Electron Beam Self-Heating Method

In the above-mentioned suspended thermal bridge method, the thermal contact resistance between the sample and the suspended platform is one of the main faults of this process. Although there are already some methods to improve it, the effect of this defect cannot be eliminated from the experimental principle. Researchers at Li Baowen's lab developed the electron beam self-heating method based on the suspended thermal bridge method in 2010 [103,104]. This method omits the influence of the contact thermal resistance between the sample and the suspended platform on the experimental results in principle and measures the spatial distribution of the thermal resistance of the micro/nano-scale materials. A scanning electron microscope (SEM) is used to measure the electron beam self-heating method. As demonstrated in Figure 6, heat is generated by the interaction between the high-energy electron beam in the SEM and the sample. It is possible to scan (move on) the sample continuously.

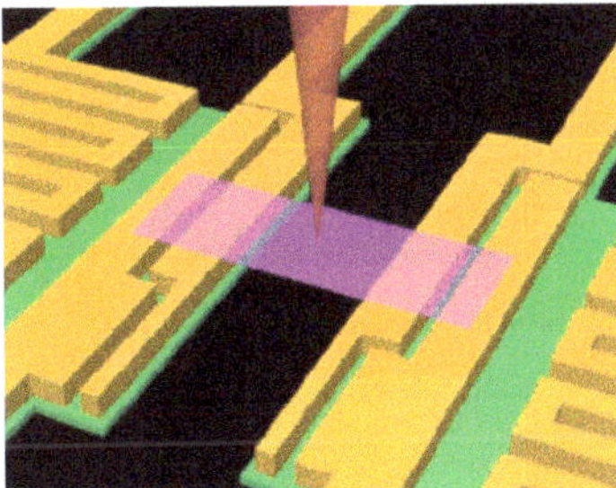

Figure 6. Electron beam self-heating method [104]. Reprinted with permission from ref. [104]. Elsevier and Copyright Clearance Center.

A scanning electron beam is used as a heating source, while the two suspended membranes behave as temperature sensors in the electron beam self-heating method. Hot spots emerged as a result of the electrons' energy absorption along the length of the sample during the scanning of the focused electron. As heat is generated from the local spots, it flows to the two membranes where it increases their temperature. The thermal conductivity of the sample can be obtained by:

$$k = A/(dR/dx) \tag{4}$$

Here, A is the cross-sectional area of the sample, x represents the distance between the membrane and the heating spot, and R is the calculated thermal resistance from one membrane to the heating spot.

This method has the advantage of measuring R by combining the diffusive thermal resistance of the suspended part (R_d) and the thermal contact resistance between the suspended sample and contact electrodes (R_c), as shown by Equation (5):

$$R = R_d + R_c \tag{5}$$

In this equation, (R_d) and (R_c) can be calculated by solving the following equations:

$$R_d = L/ktW \tag{6}$$

$$RW = L/kt + R_cW \tag{7}$$

The thermal conductivity, length, thickness, and width of the suspended sample are represented by k, L, t, and W, respectively. According to the R_d formulation, it is evident that its value decreases as t increases and L decreases. Also, taking the limit $L/t \rightarrow 0$ will give R_c. However, generally in laser-based methods, the spatial resolution is restricted by the heating volume within the sample rather than the spot size. It follows that the spatial resolution of this technique is dependent on the properties of the studied materials [105]. Recent studies have used electron beam self-heating to determine the thermal conductivity and thermal resistance of suspended Si and SiGe nanowires and MoS_2 ribbons [105–107]. Also, this method has been employed to measure the interfacial thermal resistance between few-layer MoS_2 and Pt electrodes [102].

Although the advantages of the electron beam self-heating technique are evident, its drawback cannot be ignored, such as the fact that it cannot apply variable temperature measurement, cannot measure materials that are sensitive to electron beams, and is susceptible to impurities on the sample surface (organic matter, etc.).

5.3. Raman Method

In 2008, the first experimental measurement of the thermal conductivity of two-dimensional material, single-layer graphene in the suspended plane was the Raman method [84]. In two-dimensional materials, the Raman method has become one of the most important experimental methods for measuring thermal conduction. Several two-dimensional materials have been measured successfully using this method, including boron nitride [108,109], black phosphorus [110], and molybdenum sulfide [56,111,112]. The Raman method can be used to measure the thermal conductivity of two-dimensional materials by taking into account the following two factors: (1) Raman lasers can be used as heat sources because 2D materials have an absorption effect on them; (2) The Raman spectrum absorption peak positions of two-dimensional materials and a certain linear relationship between temperature [110,112,113]; in this way, the surface temperature of the material can be determined by the Raman spectrum of the material. The thermal conductivity of a two-dimensional material can be calculated by combining the two principles mentioned above through the heat conduction model. A schematic of Raman spectroscopy is shown in Figure 7. Using Raman peaking shifting, the temperature is measured for the sample [30,114]. Obtaining the temperature can be achieved since the Raman peak is a linear function of the temperature. Thermal conductivity can be measured based on the absorbed power and temperature.

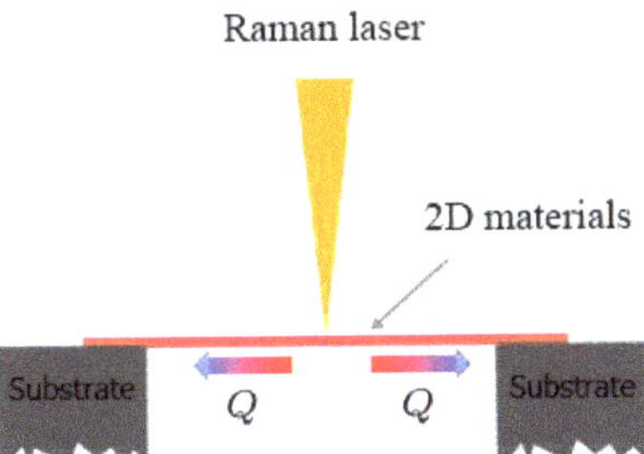

Figure 7. Raman spectroscopy schematic.

As an optical method, Raman studies the phonons and vibrational modes of molecular vibrations in solids. In this method, the inelastically scattered light of a monochromatic laser beam that interacts with a material is studied. An oscillating dipole moment is generated as a result of the oscillating electromagnetic field of the incident light which acts as a radiation source causing Raman scattering. Based on the nature of the chemical bonds and the crystal structure, each material or solid crystal has a characteristic set of molecular vibrations and phonons. Materials can be characterized in an elementary and structural manner using this technique. In addition, this method can be used to determine small changes in the crystal structure resulting from embedded strain, thermal expansion, sample composition, and structural disorder, impurities, and contamination, as well as pseudo-phases and deformation of the material [115–118].

With the continuous development and improvement of the Raman method, it has become one of the most accepted methods of micro/nano scale heat conduction measurement. In a recent review article, Malekpour and Balandin provide a detailed description of Raman-based techniques to measure the thermal properties of graphene and related materials [114].

There is, however, considerable uncertainty associated with this method due to the uncertainty of absorptivity. By using a method known as energy transfer state-resolved Raman (ET-Raman), the accuracy of this method can be improved in order to overcome this issue [119]. To achieve this, two steady-state lasers with different sizes are used to heat the sample and measure the temperature shifts as a result. The absorptivity term in this method will be canceled and the signal-to-noise ratio will be improved significantly with this method. In this way, the measurements made with this method are more accurate than those performed using the original optothermal Raman method.

5.4. Time-Domain Thermoreflectance Method

In 1983, Eesley applied the picosecond pulsed laser to detect the non-equilibrium heat transport process in metallic copper [120] since the time-domain thermoreflectance (TDTR) method has been formally applied to the measurement of material thermal properties. The TDTR method has been developed over a period of thirty years. It has now become one of the most widely used methods for measuring the thermal properties of materials in an unsteady state. This method is usually employed to measure the thermal conductivity and interfacial thermal resistance of materials [92,93,121]. Its basic principle is that a beam of a femtosecond pulsed laser is divided into a pump light and a probe light through a beam splitter. In this system, the pump light is used as a heat source for heating the surface of the material, and the probe light measures the change in the surface temperature of the material (the reflectivity of the material surface to the laser is related to the temperature). The displacement platform can accurately control the optical path difference between the two beams and then control the time interval between them to reach the surface of the material, resulting in a certain time delay (t_d). A schematic is illustrated in Figure 8. The temperature change process is related to the thermophysical properties of the material.

The measurement system of the TDTR includes a femtosecond laser generator, beam splitter, displacement platform, electro-optic (acousto-optic) modulator, photodiode detector, lock-in amplifier, etc. [122]. Before measurement, generally, it is necessary to coat a metal film on the sample surface to be tested as the sensing layer because the reflectivity of the metal surface to the laser is approximately linear with the temperature under the condition of a small temperature rise, and the surface temperature can be calibrated more accurately through the above measurement process. The lock-in amplifier will output the in-phase signal (V_{in}) and the inverted signal (V_{out}) based on the modulation frequency, which contains the information of the temperature change of the sample surface, and then the in-phase signal and the inverted signal can be obtained. Finally, the thermal conductivity model is derived and the experimental data is fitted to extract the correlation of the thermal properties of the sample data. Measurements of the thermophysical properties of 2D materials, such as graphene [123], black phosphorus [55], molybdenum sulfide [92,93], and tungsten selenide [124], including thermal interface resistance between the graphene and SiO_2 [125], have been conducted using the TDTR method.

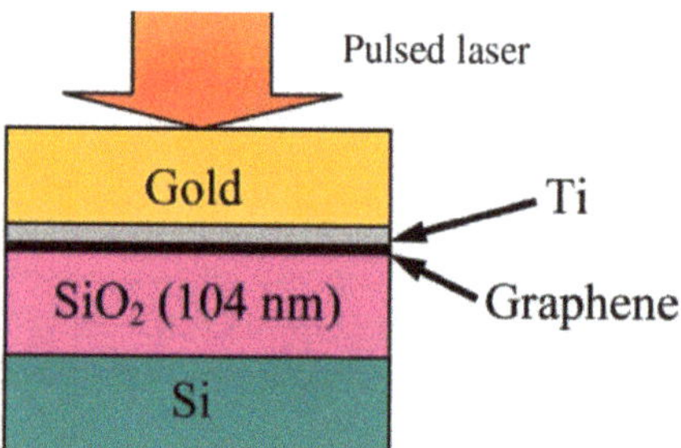

Figure 8. Time-domain thermoreflectance diagram (TDTR) [125]. Reprinted with permission from ref. [125]. Copyright 2003 American Chemical Society.

Compared with the steady-state thermal measurement method, TDTR does not require measurement in a vacuum chamber. Secondly, it can be applied for ultra-fast thermal transport mechanism research (i.e., electro-acoustic interaction, etc.). Some 2D materials, especially single-layer and multi-layer materials, adsorb impurities or deposits on their surfaces in order to suppress acoustic phonons out of plane, so this method cannot accurately measure the intrinsic heat of these materials [126].

5.5. Micro-Suspended-Pad Method

The suspended-pad method, first used to measure carbon nanotubes [80] and silicon nanowires [126,127], is another method frequently used for nanostructures, nanoribbons, and 2D materials. The micro-pad devices are manufactured in batches as part of this method. A device consists of two adjacent silicon nitride membranes suspended by a silicon nitride long beam [127]. The patterned platinum heaters are manufactured on both the pads and long beams. Normally, samples are transferred using a nanomanipulator. Utilizing focused ion-beam deposition, the thermal contacts can be increased by Pt deposition, making the contacts electrically and thermally ohmic. It is, therefore, possible to ignore the thermal resistance of the junction. Various 2D materials have been measured using the suspended-pad method, such as h-BN [32], black phosphorus [128], and MoS$_2$ [129]. Due to the accuracy of this method, the electrical signal can be very precisely derived. In addition, the interpretation of the data is very clear. The input current can accurately control the heat flux, and the temperature can be precisely measured via temperature-dependent electrical resistance. Thermal conductivity can therefore be accurately measured with the heat flux across the pads and the temperature on both pads (usually the uncertainty level is under 5%). A few factors limit its application, despite its effectiveness in measuring the thermal transport properties of nanostructures. First, it is heavily dependent on intricate manufacturing. There is also the possibility of defects arising from sample preparation as a second factor. This includes the polymer residues on BN samples [43] or the defects in black phosphorus [128]. Before using this method, it is important to take into account these factors.

6. Research Progress on 2D Thermal Conductivity

The thermal conductivity of various two-dimensional materials has been studied, and research progress on the thermal conductivity of the most regular 2D materials is summarized here.

6.1. Graphene

As the first 2D material successfully prepared, graphene became the favorite of scientific research once discovered. It has a series of excellent physical properties including ultra-high conductivity, ultra-high carrier mobility, etc. [16,130,131]. In terms of thermal conductivity, graphene also performs well, and its intrinsic thermal conductivity at room temperature can reach 2000–3000 W/m·K, which is the highest thermal conductivity material found so far. In 2008, for the first time, Balandin et al. [40] measured the thermal conductivity of suspended single-layer graphene at room temperature using the Raman method and graphite bulk materials reaching 4840–5300 W/m·K; however, upon further study by scientists, it was discovered that the experiment may have had an excessive estimate of the Raman laser absorption power of graphene, resulting in a result 4–6 times larger [30,132]. In 2010, Wei et al. [133] used the same method to measure the thermal conductivity of suspended single-layer graphene and, by employing a laser power meter, measured the Raman laser absorption rate of graphene simultaneously.

The results illustrate that the thermal conductivity of single-layer graphene grown by chemical vapor deposition (CVD) is around 2500–3100 W/m·K (T = 350 K) and 1200–1400 W/m·K (T = 500 K). It has also been found that the shape, size, and measurement environment of the suspended part of the graphene will affect the final result. In addition to the dispute about the laser absorption rate, it caused the difference between different experimental results. Another major reason for the large difference is that the preparation methods of graphene are different (mechanical exfoliation or chemical vapor deposition), resulting in certain differences in its quality (impurities, grain boundaries, organic residues, etc.). These factors will affect the phonon and generate additional scattering. Table 1 lists the thermal conductivity of suspended single-layer/multi-layer graphene measured by different experimental methods, including the Raman method.

Table 1. Experimental detail of thermal conductivity in suspended single-/few-layer graphene from different studies.

Preparation Method	Graphene Layers	Thermal Conductivity k/W (m·K)$^{-1}$
	Raman Method	
Mechanical exfoliation [30]	1	~4840–5300 (Room temperature)
Mechanical exfoliation [132]	1	~3080–5150 (Room temperature)
CVD [133]	1	~2500 +1100/−1050 (T = 350 K)
CVD [133]	1	~1400 +500/−480 (T = 500 K)
CVD [134]	1	~2600–3100 (T = 350 K)
Mechanical exfoliation [135]	1	~630 (T = 660 K)
Mechanical exfoliation [136]	1	~1800 (T = 325 K)
Mechanical exfoliation [136]	1	~710 (T = 500 K)

Table 1. *Cont.*

Preparation Method	Graphene Layers	Thermal Conductivity k/W $(m \cdot K)^{-1}$
CVD [137]	1	~850–1100 (T = 303–644 K)
Mechanical exfoliation [137]	1	~1500 (T = 330–445 K)
Mechanical exfoliation [137]	2	~970 (T = 303–630 K)
Suspended thermal bridge method		
CVD [138]	1	~190 (T = 280 K, L = 0.5 μm)
CVD [98]	2	~560–620 (Room temperature, L = 5 μm)
CVD [97]	1	~1689–1831 (T = 300 K, L = 9 μm)
Scanning thermal microscopy (SThM)		
CVD [139]	1	~2100–2430 (T = 335 K)

In order to understand graphene's ultra-high thermal conductivity, it is important to know how different phonon modes contribute to it. In graphene, heat is mainly transmitted through acoustic phonons, and its acoustic phonon modes include in-plane acoustic longitudinal wave (LA), in-plane acoustic transverse wave (TA), and out-of-plane acoustic shear wave (ZA). Nika et al. [140] believe that the heat transport process in single-layer graphene is almost entirely carried by the LA/TA phonon mode, while the contribution of the ZA phonon mode to the thermal conductivity is negligible. However, according to Lindsay et al. [52,53], the ZA phonon mode has a relatively high density of low-frequency phonons, so its contribution to the thermal conductivity will be relatively large, and it is predicted that the contribution of the ZA phonon mode to the thermal conductivity of single-layer graphene can reach about 70% at room temperature. In addition to ultra-high thermal conductivity, graphene is also an excellent platform for studying phonon ballistic transport. Because the mean free path of phonons in graphene is very long, it can reach the order of micrometers at room temperature, so the (quasi) ballistic transport properties of phonons can be studied by adjusting the length and width of the graphene band [141]. In 2010, Xu Xiangfan et al. used the suspended thermal bridge technique to measure the monolayer for the first time. The thermal conductivity of CVD graphene nanoribbons (width of about 3 μm, length of about 500 nm) is found to have a certain exponential relationship between thermal conductivity and temperature in the low-temperature region (T < 140 K), which can be explained by the thermal transport in single-layer suspended graphene, mainly depends on the ZA phonon mode, and experimental evidence of phonon quasi-ballistic transport has been found [97,138]. Although Petters et al. [98] object to the low thermal conductivity (about 225 W/m·K) measured in the above experiment, it is believed that the observed k~1.53 ± 0.18 is not from ZA phonons but due to impurities on the surface of the sample.

The thermal conductivity theory discussed above is calculated based on the three-phonon scattering model. Four-phonon scattering is often directly ignored because it is a type of phonon scattering behavior that only appears in high-temperature regions [142]. However, recent studies found that even at room temperature, the four-phonon scattering process caused by a large number of low-energy ZA mode phonons in single-layer graphene cannot be ignored. Therefore, the thermal conductivity of single-layer graphene, calculated using only the three-phonon scattering model, may be relatively high [142,143]. By solving the Boltzmann equation and introducing four-phonon scattering, Feng et al. [142] found that the thermal conductivity of single-layer graphene at room temperature is only 810 W/m·K; this value is much lower than the calculation result including only three-phonon scattering (about 3383 W/m·K), and the result shows that under the influence of four-phonon scattering, the contribution of the ZA phonon mode to the thermal conductivity is only 31%. The atomic force constant used in this work to calculate the thermal conductivity of single-layer graphene at room temperature is 0 K. Subsequently, Gu Xiaokun et al. [143]

corrected the above results, and the result value obtained was slightly larger than that in the above literature, further confirming the severe impact of four-phonon scattering on the thermal conductivity of single-layer graphene at room temperature. It can be seen that the thermal conductivity of single-layer-suspended graphene is still inconclusive. There is a certain controversy about this problem, whether in theory or in experiments. In practical applications, graphene is more likely to be attached to a certain substrate.

Therefore, in addition to floating graphene, the in-plane heat conduction of graphene on substrate performance is also necessary to study. Seol et al. [52] measured the in-plane thermal conductivity of a single layer of graphene on a silicon oxide substrate (about 600 W/m·K, 300 K). When the graphene is attached to the substrate, the ZA phonon mode will be suppressed, so its in-plane thermal conductivity is lower than that of suspended graphene. As shown in the above theoretical calculation results, the contribution of the ZA phonon to the thermal conductivity can reach about 70% at room temperature, but when there is a lining at the end, the contribution of the ZA phonon mode will be severely suppressed or even disappear, and the thermal conductivity value will be reduced from ~3000 W/m·K to ~600 W/m·K. This experiment effectively verifies that the graphene ZA phonons make a significant contribution to its thermal conductivity. In addition to silicon oxide, silicon nitride is also a common substrate material. Thong et al. [103] measured the in-plane thermal conductivity of multi-layer graphene on a silicon nitride substrate. The value is ~150–1250 W/m·K (room temperature). In order to further verify the contribution of ZA phonons to thermal conductivity, Wang et al. [99] deposited gold atoms on the surface of three-layer suspended graphene. It was found that its thermal conductivity decreased from about 1500 W/m·K to about 270 W/m·K (a decrease of 82%) and Seol et al. came to the same conclusion. Jang et al. [144] studied the heat transport properties of the SiO_2−graphene−SiO_2 sandwich structure and found that the thermal conductivity will be further reduced, especially the single-layer sandwich graphene structure. Iits room temperature thermal conductivity is far below 160 W/m·K (the specific value in this article is too low to be measured and only an upper limit is given), indicating that the substrate has a very significant inhibitory effect on the thermal conductivity of graphene.

6.2. Boron Nitride

Due to the large bandgap and the very smooth surface, boron nitride (h-BN) is an ideal type of dielectric material. At the same time, the thermal conductivity of boron nitride bulk materials (about 400 W/m·K, room temperature) is very close to copper, and its mass is much lower than copper under the same volume, so it has broad application prospects in terms of the heat dissipation of electronic devices [145,146]. Boron nitride is called white graphene. The crystal structure is similar to graphene. Nitrogen atoms and boron atoms in the plane are interlaced to form a honeycomb structure, and the layers are combined with each other by van der Waals forces. It is one of the two-dimensional materials discovered earlier [147]. The physical properties of boron nitride and graphene also have certain similarities. Lindsay et al. [148] predicted the room temperature in-plane thermal conductivity of single-layer boron nitride through theoretical research by solving the Boltzmann equation. The rate is 600 W/m·K, which is higher than that of the boron nitride bulk material. At the same time, it is also found that the contribution of the out-of-plane ZA phonon mode to the thermal conductivity can reach ~60%. In 2013, Jo et al. [32] adopted a microbridge resistance thermometer method to measure the in-plane thermal conductivity of multi-layer boron nitride (250 W/m·K, five layers; 360 W/m·K, 11 layers; T = 300 K). They believe that the reason why the measured data is lower than the theoretical prediction and even lower than the thermal conductivity of the boron nitride bulk material is mainly due to a large amount of organic residue on the surface of the boron nitride during the experiment, which causes serious phonon scattering. In the subsequent experiments of the thermal conductivity of the multi-layer boron nitride floating plane, it was not observed that the thermal conductivity exceeds the bulk material, and the quality of the sample is the key factor [108,113,149]. Wang et al. [100] improved the sample transfer method (PDMS-assisted dry transfer), which greatly reduced the organic residues on the surface of the boron nitride film. At the same time, they used high-quality bulk materials to mechanically peel off the multi-layer boron nitride and for the first time, measured the thermal conductivity of the suspended double-layer boron nitride as being greater than that of the bulk material, reaching 460–625 W/m·K at room temperature. Subsequently, Cai et al. [109] used the Raman method to measure the thermal conductivity of single-layer/double-layer and three-layer floating boron nitride near room temperature. The thermal conductivity value decreases as the thickness increases, but it is still higher than bulk boron nitride. The thermal conductivity of single-layer boron nitride reaches ~751 W/m·K. The highest value of the thermal conductivity of single-layer/multi-layer boron nitride was obtained in previous experiments. Table 2 lists the in-plane thermal conductivity of floating boron nitride measured in different documents. According to the data in the table, the thermal conductivity of multi-layer boron nitride prepared by the mechanical exfoliation method is generally higher than that prepared by the CVD method. The reason is that the chemical vapor deposition method often introduces more in the sample. However, the mechanical exfoliation method performs better at controlling the sample quality.

Table 2. Experimental results of thermal conductivity of suspended single-/few-layer h-BN in different kinds of studies.

Number of Boron Nitride Film Layers	Preparation Method	Measurement Methods	Thermal Conductivity (Room Temperature/300 K) $k/(W(m·K)^{-1})$
5	Mechanical exfoliation [32]	Microbridge thermometer	~250
11	Mechanical exfoliation [32]	Microbridge thermometer	~360
9	CVD [113]	Raman method	~227–280
2.1 nm	CVD [108]	Raman method	~223
10 nm/20 nm	CVD [149]	Steady/transient state	~100
2	Mechanical exfoliation [100]	Thermal bridge method	~484 +141/−24
4	Mechanical exfoliation [44]	Thermal bridge method	~286
1	Mechanical exfoliation [109]	Raman method	751 ± 340
2	Mechanical exfoliation [109]	Raman method	646 ± 242
3	Mechanical exfoliation [109]	Raman method	602 ± 247

6.3. Molybdenum Sulfide and Other Transition Metal Sulfides

Transition metal sulfides (MX_2, where M is transition metal elements such as Mo, W, Ti, and X represents chalcogen elements, including S, Se, and Te) are a very important group of two-dimensional materials and their crystal structure is a "sandwich"-like layered structure [150]. Unlike single-layer graphene, single-layer boron nitride, and other two-dimensional materials that only contain one atomic layer, a single-layer transition metal sulfide contains three atomic layers (the transition metal atomic layer is sulfurized). The atomic layer of group elements is "sandwiched" in the middle, as shown in Figure 9.

Molybdenum sulfide is the most widely studied transition metal sulfide. Because of its controllable bandgap and excellent electrical properties, it can also exist stably in the air. It is considered a material for the next generation of microelectronic devices with great potential. Optics, thermoelectrics, and other fields also have certain application prospects [151–153]. Sahoo et al. [112] used the Raman method to measure the in-plane thermal conductivity of 11 layers of molybdenum sulfide (about 52 W/m·K, room temperature). Later, Yan et al. [56] and Jo et al. [129] measured the in-plane thermal conductivity of single-layer and multi-layer molybdenum sulfide at room temperature and the values were 35–52 W/m·K. However, Zhang et al. [154] also used the Raman method to measure the in-plane thermal conductivity of single-layer/double-layer molybdenum sulfide, and the result (77–84 W/m·K) was much larger than the previous experimental data. It is because the critical data, such as the relationship between the Raman peak frequency change and temperature of molybdenum sulfide, the absorption power of the Raman laser, and the contact thermal resistance obtained in the experiment are quite different from the previous literature. Aiyiti et al. [104] used the electron beam self-heating method to measure the in-plane thermal conductivity of the multi-layer molybdenum sulfide. This is the first time this method has been applied to the experimental measurement of the thermal conductivity of two-dimensional materials. The experimental results also confirm the feasibility of this method. The results of the experimental measurements of the in-plane thermal conductivity of molybdenum sulfide are summarized in Table 3.

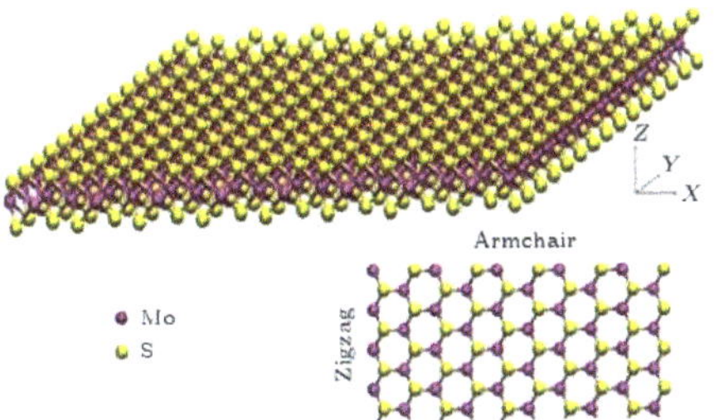

Figure 9. Molybdenum sulfide [151]. Reprinted with permission from ref. [10]. AIP Publishing and Copyright Clearance Center.

Table 3. Experimental results of thermal conductivity of single-/few-layer MoS$_2$ in different kinds of studies.

Preparation Method	Molybdenum Sulfide Film Layers	Measurement Methods	Thermal Conductivity (Room Temperature/300 K) k/(W(m·K)$^{-1}$)
CVD [112]	11	Raman method	~52
Mechanical exfoliation [56]	1	Raman method	34.5 ± 4
Mechanical exfoliation [129]	4	Thermal bridge method	~44–45
Mechanical exfoliation [129]	7	Thermal bridge method	~48–52
Mechanical exfoliation [154]	1	Raman method	84 ± 17
Mechanical exfoliation [154]	2	Raman method	77 ± 25
Mechanical exfoliation [104]	4	Electron beam self-heating	34 ± 6
Mechanical exfoliation [104]	5	Electron beam self-heating	30 ± 3
CVD [155]	1	Raman method	13.3 ± 1.4
CVD [155]	2	Raman method	15.6 ± 1.5
CVD [156]	1	Thermal bridge method	~21–24
CVD [111]	1	Raman method	60.3 ± 5.2
CVD [111]	2	Raman method	38.4 ± 3.1
CVD [111]	3	Raman method	44.8 ± 5.9
CVD [111]	4	Raman method	36.9 ± 4.9
Mechanical exfoliation [157]	1	Raman method	~62.2
Mechanical exfoliation [158]	4	Raman method	60.3 ± 5

Compared with graphene and boron nitride, the crystal structure of molybdenum sulfide has certain differences, so its thermal conductivity properties will also be different, mainly as follows: First, the thermal conductivity of single-layer molybdenum sulfide is higher than that of single-layer graphene and single-layer nitrogen. The boron sulfide is 1-2 orders of magnitude lower. Wei et al. [35] found through theoretical calculations that the low thermal conductivity of single-layer molybdenum sulfide is due to the lower phonon group velocity and the larger Grüneisen constant. As a result, the mean free path of phonons is only 14.6 nm. Secondly, in single-layer graphene and single-layer boron nitride, the contribution of the out-of-plane ZA phonon mode to the thermal conductivity is more than 50%, but in a single layer of molybdenum sulfide, the contribution of the in-plane phonon mode to the thermal conductivity exceeds the out-of-plane phonon mode. Finally, unlike graphene and boron nitride, single-/multi-layer molybdenum sulfide has been experimentally measured. The in-plane thermal conductivity is lower than the in-plane thermal conductivity of molybdenum sulfide block (85–110 W/m·K, room temperature). This phenomenon is inconsistent with the theoretical prediction. Gu et al. [57] predicted that the room temperature in-plane thermal conductivity of a single layer of molybdenum sulfide could reach 138 W/m·K. The reason may be that the quality of molybdenum sulfide in these experiments has not reached a good condition, or the deeper reasons need to be further studied. In addition to the in-plane thermal conductivity, the inter-plane thermal conductivity of molybdenum sulfide is also one of the issues worthy of study, but there are relatively few studies in this direction. Initially, Muratore et al. [159] and Cahill et al. [160] measured the room temperature interfacial thermal conductivity of bulk molybdenum sulfide, which was only 2–3 W/m·K. However, Jiang et al. [93] showed a higher numerical result (about 4.75 W/m·K) experimentally, and the result is closer to the theoretical prediction. The difference between the above experimental results is in the follow-up Sood et al. [92] explained in the experiment. They measured the room-temperature inter-plane thermal conductivity of different thicknesses of molybdenum sulfide by the TDTR method, and the results showed that the room-temperature inter-plane thermal conductivity of samples with a thickness of 240 nm and 20 nm were 2.0 ± 0.3 W/m·K, 0.9 ± 0.2 W/m·K. Through comparison with the above experimental data, it is found that as the thickness increases, the inter-face thermal conductivity of molybdenum sulfide increases, and when the thickness reaches about 1 μm, the inter-face thermal conductivity value gradually approaches the saturation threshold (about 5 W/m·K). Theoretical calculation results show that the mean free path of phonons between the molybdenum sulfide surfaces far exceeds the previously estimated value (1.5–4 nm), and more than 80% of the heat transport is contributed by phonons with a mean free path of 10–500 nm.

With the continuous development of the preparation technology of two-dimensional materials, more and more multi-layer transition metal sulfides have been discovered, so their thermal conductivity is gradually being studied. Table 4 lists other transitions in different literatures except for molybdenum sulfide. Experimental measurement of the thermal conductivity of metal sulfides in the suspended plane. From the data in the table, it can be seen that although the crystal structures of these materials are very similar, their thermal conductivity properties are significantly different.

Table 4. Experimental detail of thermal conductivity of single-/few-layer transition metal dichalcogenides in different literatures.

Preparation Method	Number of Film Layers	Measurement Methods	Thermal Conductivity (Room Temperature/300 K) $k/(W(m \cdot K)^{-1})$
Molybdenum Selenide ($MoSe_2$)			
Mechanical exfoliation [154]	1	Raman method	59 ± 18
Mechanical exfoliation [154]	2	Raman method	42 ± 13
Mechanical exfoliation [161]	45 nm	Raman method	11.1 ± 0.4
Mechanical exfoliation [161]	140 nm	Raman method	20.3 ± 0.9
Mechanical exfoliation [162]	5 nm	Raman method	6.2 ± 0.9
Mechanical exfoliation [162]	36 nm	Raman method	10.8 ± 1.7
Tantalum Selenide ($TaSe_2$)			
Mechanical exfoliation [163]	45 nm	Raman method	~9
Mechanical exfoliation [163]	55 nm	Raman method	~11
Tungsten Sulfide (WS_2)			
CVD [36]	1	Raman method	~32
CVD [36]	2	Raman method	~53
CVD [111]	1	Raman method	74.8 ± 17.2
Tungsten Selenide (WSe_2)			
CVD [111]	1	Raman method	66 ± 20.9
Mechanical exfoliation [164]	1	Raman method	36 ± 12
Tungsten Telluride (WTe_2)			
Mechanical exfoliation [165]	220 nm	TDTR	~2
Mechanical exfoliation [166]	11.2 nm	Raman method	~0.639–0.743
Rhenium sulfide (ReS_2)			
Mechanical exfoliation [167]	150 nm	TDTR	~50–70

6.4. Black Phosphorus, Black Arsenic

Due to the advantages of the controllable bandgap and relatively high switching, black phosphorous (BP) is one of the first materials for the next generation of microelectronic devices to be studied [168–170]. However, initially, researchers were interested in the thermal conductivity of black phosphorous. This is mainly because of its in-plane anisotropic "Great Wall"-like structure [128], which may lead to the anisotropy of thermal conductivity [171]. It is worth noting that the black phosphorous pole is easy to oxidize, so in experiments with black phosphorus, the exposure time of the sample in the air needs to be strictly controlled. Qin et al. [172] predicted the room temperature surface of the single-layer black phosphorus along the Zigzag (ZZ) direction and the (Armchair) AC direction through theoretical research. The internal thermal conductivity ratio can reach 30.15 W/m·K in the ZZ direction and 13.65 W/m·K in the AC direction, and due to its "Great Wall"-like structure, the out-of-plane phonon mode has a positive effect on the thermal conductivity. The contribution of efficiency is very low (about 5%). Lou et al. [110] experimentally measured the in-plane thermal conductivity of the multi-layer black phosphorus with different thicknesses at room temperature and the smallest thickness was ~10 nm. The thermal conductivity in the ZZ direction is 20 W/m·K, while the thermal conductivity in the AC direction is only ~10 W/m·K, which confirms the above theoretical prediction. As the same main group element of phosphorus, arsenic, i.e., black arsenic (Bas), has a crystal structure similar to black phosphorus and also has a significant in-plane thermal conductivity anisotropy effect. Chen et al. [173] first experimentally measured the in-plane thermal conductivity of black arsenic with a thickness of 124 nm along with the ZZ and AC directions (5 W/m·K, ZZ direction; 3 W/m·K, AC direction, 350 K). In subsequent experiments, researchers measured the in-plane thermal conductivity of multi-layer black phosphorus with different thicknesses using the Raman method, thermal bridge method, etc. They found the anisotropy of in-plane thermal conductivity. In these experiments, the thickness of the multi-layer black phosphorus was above 10 nm. This is because the chemical properties of black phosphorus are too active and it is challenging to prepare single-layer black phosphorus in heat conduction experiments. Therefore, the heat conduction properties of single-layer or few-layer black phosphorus need to be further studied.

6.5. Telluride

Bulk tellurium (Te) is a new and high-quality thermoelectric material [174]. At the same time, due to its two-dimensional structure, telluride can be used as an effective means to further improve its thermoelectric properties [175]. In the bulk material, the tellurium atom is combined with a neighboring atom through a covalent bond and extends [illegible] a spiral shape. Adjacent spiral chains are then combined by van der Waals forces [illegible] a spiral tellurium belongs to a quasi-one-dimensional chain structure. However [illegible] [176], so bulk that the structure of monolayer telluride is different from that [illegible] the theory predicts [illegible] of bulk tellurium. There are three possible crystal structures (α-Te, β-Te, γ-Te) [177]. Gao et al. [178,179], through first principles calculations, studie[illegible] the thermal conductivity and thermoelectric properties of single-layer telluride with different structures, and they have been found to have low thermal conductivity and excellent thermoelectric properties. But only b-type telluride has been synthesized in experiments and the synthesis conditions are relatively harsh, so there is no experimental study on the physical properties of monolayer telluride [180,181]. Wang et al. developed a liquid-phase synthesis method [182], which can be used to prepare multi-layer telluride with the same bulk structure in large quantities. In further research, the research group and its collaborators used the Raman method to measure the room temperature suspended thermal conductivity of telluride with a thickness of 35 nm in the intra-chain direction (about 1.5 W/m·K) and compared with the bulk material (about 3 W/m·K, 300 K), there is a certain degree of reduction. They believe that the main reason for this is that the surface of the multi-layer telluride will interact with the phonons. Because the structure of this type of telluride is the same as that of the bulk material, its in-plane thermal conductivity will be different along the in-chain direction and the inter-chain direction.

6.6. Silicene

After the discovery of graphene, as an element of the same family of carbon, silicene was naturally noticed. However, it was not until 2012 that silicene was synthesized, and the growth conditions were too harsh [183,184]. Therefore, the thermal conductivity of silicene is still in theoretical research and there has been no progress in experimental research. In addition to the intrinsic thermal conductivity, theoretically, the use of stress, electric fields, defects, isotopes, and other methods to control the thermal conductivity of silicene has been studied in theory, which will provide guidance for future experimental research of silicene.

6.7. Other 2D Materials

With the continuous development of nanomaterial preparation technology and computational simulation technology, the family of two-dimensional materials is becoming larger and larger. Not only can a new type of two-dimensional material be synthesized experimentally, but it is also possible to predict some unknown two-dimensional materials through theoretical simulation. In addition to the above-mentioned materials, there are many other two-dimensional materials whose thermal conductivity properties have also been studied. In terms of experiments, researchers have used different methods to measure multi-layer bismuth telluride [185], multi-layer indium selenide [186], and the in-plane thermal conductivity of two-dimensional materials such as multi-layer tin sulfide [187], zirconium telluride [83], and multi-layer bismuth selenium oxide [188]. Thermal conductivity and related properties of two-dimensional materials such as gallium nitride [189], boronene [190], single-layer carbon nitride [191], and single-layer nitrogen boron carbide [192] have also been studied.

7. Summary

To sum up, this article uses the thermal conductivity of 2D materials as a research platform to discuss the most basic physical issues of heat conduction at the micro/nano scale. Compared with ten years ago, we have a certain understanding of the thermal conduction mechanism of two-dimensional materials. However, there is a long way to go, and there are still many problems in the study of the heat conduction of two-dimensional materials, but this can also point out the need for further research related to the heat conduction of two-dimensional materials.

Here are some issues that need to be considered: (1) There is no rigorous analytical solution for abnormal heat conduction in two-dimensional materials. Existing models for abnormal heat conduction are limited to two-dimensional lattices; (2) What is the thermal conductivity of graphene? There are significant differences between different experiments, and the calculation results of three-phonon scattering and four-phonon scattering are not self-consistent. With the current experimental measurement technology, the measurement of the intrinsic thermal conductivity of single-layer floating graphene seems to be an impossible task; (3) In the current theoretical framework, four-phonon scattering is often directly ignored because it is a type of phonon scattering behavior that only gradually appears in high-temperature regions. However, some theoretical studies have found that even at room temperature, the four-phonon dispersion process is caused by a large number of low-energy ZA mode phonons in single-layer graphene, and this cannot be ignored. Therefore, it is necessary to re-examine the thermal conduction behavior of two-dimensional materials with four-phonon scattering theory; (4) Although theoretical work has shown that even when the scale of the sample reaches the order of millimeters or even centimeters, there is still a scale effect of thermal conductivity; (5) Thermal conductivity measurements, such as the Raman method and thermal bridge method, inevitably have contact thermal resistance problems, which will greatly affect the experimental results. Although some research groups use the dual Raman laser method and electronic beam self-heating method to eliminate the influence of contact thermal resistance, harsh experimental conditions and expensive experimental equipment make it impossible for most research groups to carry out related experiments; (6) The commonly used interfacial thermal conductivity measurements, such as the TDTR and 3w methods, can provide micron-scale spatial resolution, but they can only be used to measure the interfacial thermal resistance of thin-film materials, and their in-plane spatial resolution is also limited to the spot size of the heating laser (usually ~micrometers). Therefore, it is necessary to develop a new measurement method, which needs a spatial resolution that can reach the nanometer scale and detect the interfacial thermal resistance information of two-dimensional materials.

Author Contributions: Writing—original draft preparation, M.H.K.; writing—review and editing, X.Z.; supervision, X.Z.; project administration, X.Z.; funding acquisition, X.Z. All authors have read and agreed to the published version of the manuscript.

Funding: This research was funded by the National Science Foundation CAREER Award, CBET-2145417, and National Science Foundation LEAPS Award, DMR-2137883.

Data Availability Statement: Not applicable.

Conflicts of Interest: The authors declare no conflict of interest.

References

1. Fiori, G.; Bonaccorso, F.; Iannaccone, G.; Palacios, T.; Neumaier, D.; Seabaugh, A.; Banerjee, S.K.; Colombo, L. Electronics Based on Two-Dimensional Materials. *Nat. Nanotechnol.* **2014**, *9*, 768–779. [CrossRef] [PubMed]
2. Kobayashi, M. More than Moore. *Kyokai Joho Imeji Zasshi/J. Inst. Image Inf. Telev. Eng.* **2016**, *70*, 324–327. [CrossRef]
3. Russ, B.; Glaudell, A.; Urban, J.J.; Chabinyc, M.L.; Segalman, R.A. Organic Thermoelectric Materials for Energy Harvesting and Temperature Control. *Nat. Rev. Mater.* **2016**, *1*, 16050. [CrossRef]
4. Saraiva, E.F.; Milan, L.A. Clustering Gene Expression Data Using a Posterior Split-Merge-Birth Procedure. *Scand. J. Stat.* **2012**, *39*, 399–415. [CrossRef]
5. Xu, X.; Zhou, J.; Chen, J. Thermal Transport in Conductive Polymer–Based Materials. *Adv. Funct. Mater.* **2020**, *30*, 1904704. [CrossRef]
6. Moore, A.L.; Shi, L. Emerging Challenges and Materials for Thermal Management of Electronics. *Mater. Today* **2014**, *17*, 163–174. [CrossRef]
7. Qiu, H.; Xu, T.; Wang, Z.; Ren, W.; Nan, H.; Ni, Z.; Chen, Q.; Yuan, S.; Miao, F.; Song, F.; et al. Hopping Transport through Defect-Induced Localized States in Molybdenum Disulphide. *Nat. Commun.* **2013**, *4*, 2642. [CrossRef]
8. Qiu, H.; Pan, L.; Yao, Z.; Li, J.; Shi, Y.; Wang, X. Electrical Characterization of Back-Gated Bi-Layer MoS_2 Field-Effect Transistors and the Effect of Ambient on Their Performances. *Appl. Phys. Lett.* **2012**, *100*, 67–70. [CrossRef]
9. Yu, Z.; Pan, Y.; Shen, Y.; Wang, Z.; Ong, Z.Y.; Xu, T.; Xin, R.; Pan, L.; Wang, B.; Sun, L.; et al. Towards Intrinsic Charge Transport in Monolayer Molybdenum Disulfide by Defect and Interface Engineering. *Nat. Commun.* **2014**, *5*, 5290. [CrossRef]
10. Liu, Y.; Wu, H.; Cheng, H.C.; Yang, S.; Zhu, E.; He, Q.; Ding, M.; Li, D.; Guo, J.; Weiss, N.O.; et al. Toward Barrier Free Contact to Molybdenum Disulfide Using Graphene Electrodes. *Nano Lett.* **2015**, *15*, 3030–3034. [CrossRef]
11. Wu, S.C.; Shan, G.; Yan, B. Prediction of Near-Room-Temperature Quantum Anomalous Hall Effect on Honeycomb Materials. *Phys. Rev. Lett.* **2014**, *113*, 256401. [CrossRef] [PubMed]
12. Cherukara, M.J.; Narayanan, B.; Kinaci, A.; Sasikumar, K.; Gray, S.K.; Chan, M.K.Y.; Sankaranarayanan, S.K.R.S. Ab Initio-Based Bond Order Potential to Investigate Low Thermal Conductivity of Stanene Nanostructures. *J. Phys. Chem. Lett.* **2016**, *7*, 3752–3759. [CrossRef] [PubMed]
13. Novoselov, K.S.; Jiang, D.; Schedin, F.; Booth, T.J.; Khotkevich, V.V.; Morozov, S.V.; Geim, A.K. Two-Dimensional Atomic Crystals. *Proc. Natl. Acad. Sci. USA* **2005**, *102*, 10451–10453. [CrossRef]
14. Butler, S.Z.; Hollen, S.M.; Cao, L.; Cui, Y.; Gupta, J.A.; Gutiérrez, H.R.; Heinz, T.F.; Hong, S.S.; Huang, J.; Ismach, A.F.; et al. Progress, Challenges, and Opportunities in Two-Dimensional Materials Beyond Graphene. *ACS Nano* **2013**, *7*, 2898–2926. [CrossRef]
15. Bhimanapati, G.R.; Lin, Z.; Meunier, V.; Jung, Y.; Cha, J.; Das, S.; Xiao, D.; Son, Y.; Strano, M.S.; Cooper, V.R.; et al. Recent Advances in Two-Dimensional Materials beyond Graphene. *ACS Nano* **2015**, *9*, 11509–11539. [CrossRef] [PubMed]
16. Novoselov, K.S.; Geim, A.K.; Morozov, S.V.; Jiang, D.; Zhang, Y.; Dubonos, S.V.; Grigorieva, I.V.; Firsov, A.A. Electric Field Effect in Atomically Thin Carbon Films. *Science* **2004**, *306*, 666–669. [CrossRef] [PubMed]
17. Mounet, N.; Gibertini, M.; Schwaller, P.; Campi, D.; Merkys, A.; Marrazzo, A.; Sohier, T.; Castelli, I.E.; Cepellotti, A.; Pizzi, G.; et al. Two-Dimensional Materials from High-Throughput Computational Exfoliation of Experimentally Known Compounds. *Nat. Nanotechnol.* **2018**, *13*, 246–252. [CrossRef]
18. Kasirga, T.S. *Thermal Conductivity Measurements in Atomically Thin Materials and Devices*; Springer Nature: Gateway East, Singapore, 2020; ISBN 9811553483.
19. Lee, C.; Wei, X.; Kysar, J.W.; Hone, J. Measurement of the Elastic Properties and Intrinsic Strength of Monolayer Graphene. *Science* **2008**, *321*, 385–388. [CrossRef]
20. Wu, X.; Shao, Y.; Liu, H.; Feng, Z.; Wang, Y.-L.; Sun, J.-T.; Liu, C.; Wang, J.-O.; Liu, Z.-L.; Zhu, S.-Y.; et al. Epitaxial Growth and Air-Stability of Monolayer Antimonene on PdTe2. *Adv. Mater.* **2017**, *29*, 1605407. [CrossRef]
21. Reis, F.; Li, G.; Dudy, L.; Bauernfeind, M.; Glass, S.; Hanke, W.; Thomale, R.; Schäfer, J.; Claessen, R. Bismuthene on a SiC Substrate: A Candidate for a High-Temperature Quantum Spin Hall Material. *Science* **2017**, *357*, 287–290. [CrossRef]
22. Chen, S.C.; Wu, J.Y.; Lin, M.F. Feature-Rich Magneto-Electronic Properties of Bismuthene. *New J. Phys.* **2018**, *20*, 062001. [CrossRef]
23. Wang, L.; Li, B. Phononics Gets Hot. *Phys. World* **2008**, *21*, 27–29. [CrossRef]
24. Hu, B.; Yang, L.; Zhang, Y. Asymmetric Heat Conduction in Nonlinear Lattices. *Phys. Rev. Lett.* **2006**, *97*, 2–5. [CrossRef] [PubMed]
25. Xie, Z.X.; Li, K.M.; Tang, L.M.; Pan, C.N.; Chen, K.Q. Nonlinear Phonon Transport and Ballistic Thermal Rectification in Asymmetric Graphene-Based Three Terminal Junctions. *Appl. Phys. Lett.* **2012**, *100*, 183110. [CrossRef]
26. Lo, W.C.; Wang, L.; Li, B. Thermal Transistor: Heat Flux Switching and Modulating. *J. Phys. Soc. Jpn.* **2008**, *77*, 54402.
27. Wang, L.; Li, B. Thermal Logic Gates: Computation with Phonons. *Phys. Rev. Lett.* **2007**, *99*, 177208. [CrossRef]
28. Wang, L.; Li, B. Thermal Memory: A Storage of Phononic Information. *Phys. Rev. Lett.* **2008**, *101*, 267203. [CrossRef]
29. Madelung, O.; Klemens, P.G.; Neuer, G.; White, G.K.; Sundqvist, B.; Uher, C. *Thermal Conductivity of Pure Metals and Alloys/Wärmeleitfähigkeit von Reinen Metallen Und Legierungen*; Springer: Berlin/Heidelberg, Germany, 1991; Volume 3.
30. Balandin, A.A.; Ghosh, S.; Bao, W.; Calizo, I.; Teweldebrhan, D.; Miao, F.; Lau, C.N. Superior Thermal Conductivity of Single-Layer Graphene. *Nano Lett.* **2008**, *8*, 902–907. [CrossRef]
31. Geick, R.; Perry, C.H.; Rupprecht, G. Normal Modes in Hexagonal Boron Nitride. *Phys. Rev.* **1966**, *146*, 543–547. [CrossRef]

32. Jo, I.; Pettes, M.T.; Kim, J.; Watanabe, K.; Taniguchi, T.; Yao, Z.; Shi, L. Thermal Conductivity and Phonon Transport in Suspended Few-Layer Hexagonal Boron Nitride. *Nano Lett.* **2013**, *13*, 550–554. [CrossRef]
33. Liu, B.; Reddy, C.D.; Jiang, J.; Zhu, H.; Baimova, J.A.; Dmitriev, S.V.; Zhou, K. Thermal Conductivity of Silicene Nanosheets and the Effect of Isotopic Doping. *J. Phys. D Appl. Phys.* **2014**, *47*, 165301. [CrossRef]
34. Zhang, X.; Xie, H.; Hu, M.; Bao, H.; Yue, S.; Qin, G.; Su, G. Thermal Conductivity of Silicene Calculated Using an Optimized Stillinger-Weber Potential. *Phys. Rev. B Condens. Matter Mater. Phys.* **2014**, *89*, 054310. [CrossRef]
35. Wei, X.; Wang, Y.; Shen, Y.; Xie, G.; Xiao, H.; Zhong, J.; Zhang, G. Phonon Thermal Conductivity of Monolayer MoS_2: A Comparison with Single Layer Graphene. *Appl. Phys. Lett.* **2014**, *105*, 2–7. [CrossRef]
36. Peimyoo, N.; Shang, J.; Yang, W.; Wang, Y.; Cong, C.; Yu, T. Thermal Conductivity Determination of Suspended Mono- and Bilayer WS_2 by Raman Spectroscopy. *Nano Res.* **2015**, *8*, 1210–1221. [CrossRef]
37. Qin, G.; Zhang, X.; Yue, S.-Y.; Qin, Z.; Wang, H.; Han, Y.; Hu, M. Resonant Bonding Driven Giant Phonon Anharmonicity and Low Thermal Conductivity of Phosphorene. *Phys. Rev. B* **2016**, *94*, 165445. [CrossRef]
38. Bergman, T.L.; Incropera, F.P.; DeWitt, D.P.; Lavine, A.S. *Fundamentals of Heat and Mass Transfer*; John Wiley & Sons: New York, NY, USA, 2011; ISBN 0470501979.
39. Poulikakos, D. *Conduction Heat Transfer*; Prentice Hall: Englewood Cliffs, NJ, USA, 1994.
40. Carslaw, H.S.; Jaeger, J.C. *Conduction of Heat in Solids*; Oxford University Press: London, UK, 1959.
41. Kutateladze, S.S. *Fundamentals of Heat Transfer*; Edward Arnold: London, UK, 1964; p. 294.
42. Hahne, E.; Grigull, U. Formfaktor Und Formwiderstand Der Stationären Mehrdimensionalen Wärmeleitung. *Int. J. Heat Mass Transf.* **1975**, *18*, 751–767. [CrossRef]
43. General Electric Company. *Research and Development Center. Heat Transfer Data Book*; Heat Transfer and Fluid Flow Data Books; General Electric Company: New York, NY, USA, 1980.
44. Chen, X.K.; Zeng, Y.J.; Chen, K.Q. Thermal Transport in Two-Dimensional Heterostructures. *Front. Mater.* **2020**, *7*, 578791. [CrossRef]
45. Goddard, W.A., III; Brenner, D.; Lyshevski, S.E.; Iafrate, G.J. *Handbook of Nanoscience, Engineering, and Technology*, 1st ed.; CRC Press: Boca Raton, FL, USA, 2002. [CrossRef]
46. Chen, Y.; Li, D.; Lukes, J.R.; Majumdar, A. Monte Carlo Simulation of Silicon Nanowire Thermal Conductivity. *J. Heat Transf.* **2005**, *127*, 1129–1137. [CrossRef]
47. Lacroix, D.; Joulain, K.; Lemonnier, D. Monte Carlo Transient Phonon Transport in Silicon and Germanium at Nanoscales. *Phys. Rev. B Condens. Matter Mater. Phys.* **2005**, *72*, 064305. [CrossRef]
48. Mazumder, S.; Majumdar, A. Monte Carlo Study of Phonon Transport in Solid Thin Films Including Dispersion and Polarization. *J. Heat Transf.* **2001**, *123*, 749–759. [CrossRef]
49. Aksamija, Z.; Knezevic, I. Anisotropy and Boundary Scattering in the Lattice Thermal Conductivity of Silicon Nanomembranes. *Phys. Rev. B Condens. Matter Mater. Phys.* **2010**, *82*, 045319. [CrossRef]
50. Ramayya, E.B.; Maurer, L.N.; Davoody, A.H.; Knezevic, I. Thermoelectric Properties of Ultrathin Silicon Nanowires. *Phys. Rev. B Condens. Matter Mater. Phys.* **2012**, *86*, 115328. [CrossRef]
51. Jeng, M.-S.; Yang, R.; Song, D.; Chen, G. Modeling the Thermal Conductivity and Phonon Transport in Nanoparticle Composites Using Monte Carlo Simulation. *J. Heat Transf.* **2008**, *130*, 042410. [CrossRef]
52. Seol, J.H.; Jo, I.; Moore, A.L.; Lindsay, L.; Aitken, Z.H.; Pettes, M.T.; Li, X.; Yao, Z.; Huang, R.; Broido, D.; et al. Two-Dimensional Phonon Transport in Supported Graphene. *Science* **2010**, *328*, 213–216. [CrossRef] [PubMed]
53. Lindsay, L.; Broido, D.A.; Mingo, N. Flexural Phonons and Thermal Transport in Graphene. *Phys. Rev. B Condens. Matter Mater. Phys.* **2010**, *82*, 2–7. [CrossRef]
54. Zhu, J.; Park, H.; Chen, J.Y.; Gu, X.; Zhang, H.; Karthikeyan, S.; Wendel, N.; Campbell, S.A.; Dawber, M.; Du, X.; et al. Revealing the Origins of 3D Anisotropic Thermal Conductivities of Black Phosphorus. *Adv. Electron. Mater.* **2016**, *2*, 1600040. [CrossRef]
55. Jang, H.; Wood, J.D.; Ryder, C.R.; Hersam, M.C.; Cahill, D.G. Anisotropic Thermal Conductivity of Exfoliated Black Phosphorus. *Adv. Mater.* **2015**, *27*, 8017–8022. [CrossRef] [PubMed]
56. Yan, R.; Simpson, J.R.; Bertolazzi, S.; Brivio, J.; Watson, M.; Wu, X.; Kis, A.; Luo, T.; Hight Walker, A.R.; Xing, H.G. Thermal Conductivity of Monolayer Molybdenum Disulfide Obtained from Temperature-Dependent Raman Spectroscopy. *ACS Nano* **2014**, *8*, 986–993. [CrossRef]
57. Gu, X.; Li, B.; Yang, R. Layer Thickness-Dependent Phonon Properties and Thermal Conductivity of MoS_2. *J. Appl. Phys.* **2016**, *119*, 085106. [CrossRef]
58. Xie, H.; Hu, M.; Bao, H. Thermal Conductivity of Silicene from First-Principles. *Appl. Phys. Lett.* **2014**, *104*, 131906. [CrossRef]
59. Narayanan, B.; Kinaci, A.; Sen, F.G.; Davis, M.J.; Gray, S.K.; Chan, M.K.Y.; Sankaranarayanan, S.K.R.S. Describing the Diverse Geometries of Gold from Nanoclusters to Bulk—A First-Principles-Based Hybrid Bond-Order Potential. *J. Phys. Chem. C* **2016**, *120*, 13787–13800. [CrossRef]
60. Schelling, P.K.; Phillpot, S.R.; Keblinski, P. Comparison of Atomic-Level Simulation Methods for Computing Thermal Conductivity. *Phys. Rev. B Condens. Matter Mater. Phys.* **2002**, *65*, 144306. [CrossRef]
61. Deng, Y.X.; Chen, S.Z.; Zeng, Y.; Feng, Y.; Zhou, W.X.; Tang, L.M.; Chen, K.Q. Spin Gapless Semiconductor and Half-Metal Properties in Magnetic Penta-Hexa-Graphene Nanotubes. *Org. Electron.* **2018**, *63*, 310–317. [CrossRef]

62. Rowe, P.; Csányi, G.; Alfè, D.; Michaelides, A. Development of a Machine Learning Potential for Graphene. *Phys. Rev. B* **2018**, *97*, 054303. [CrossRef]
63. Sellan, D.P.; Landry, E.S.; Turney, J.E.; McGaughey, A.J.H.; Amon, C.H. Size Effects in Molecular Dynamics Thermal Conductivity Predictions. *Phys. Rev. B Condens. Matter Mater. Phys.* **2010**, *81*, 214305. [CrossRef]
64. Sevik, C.; Kinaci, A.; Haskins, J.B.; Çağın, T. Characterization of Thermal Transport in Low-Dimensional Boron Nitride Nanostructures. *Phys. Rev. B Condens. Matter Mater. Phys.* **2011**, *84*, 085409. [CrossRef]
65. Wang, Y.; Vallabhaneni, A.; Hu, J.; Qiu, B.; Chen, Y.P.; Ruan, X. Phonon Lateral Confinement Enables Thermal Rectification in Asymmetric Single-Material Nanostructures. *Nano Lett.* **2014**, *14*, 592–596. [CrossRef]
66. Zeng, J.; Chen, K.Q.; Tong, Y.X. Covalent Coupling of Porphines to Graphene Edges: Quantum Transport Properties and Their Applications in Electronics. *Carbon* **2018**, *127*, 611–617. [CrossRef]
67. Chen, T.; Xu, L.; Li, Q.; Li, X.; Long, M. Direction and Strain Controlled Anisotropic Transport Behaviors of 2D GeSe-Phosphorene VdW Heterojunctions. *Nanotechnology* **2019**, *30*, 445703. [CrossRef]
68. Zhou, Y.; Zheng, X.; Cheng, Z.Q.; Chen, K.Q. Current Superposition Law Realized in Molecular Devices Connected in Parallel. *J. Phys. Chem. C* **2019**, *123*, 10462–10468. [CrossRef]
69. Fan, Z.Q.; Zhang, Z.H.; Yang, S.Y. High-Performance 5.1 Nm in-Plane Janus WSeTe Schottky Barrier Field Effect Transistors. *Nanoscale* **2020**, *12*, 21750–21756. [CrossRef] [PubMed]
70. Fan, Z.Q.; Chen, K.Q. Negative Differential Resistance and Rectifying Behaviors in Phenalenyl Molecular Device with Different Contact Geometries. *Appl. Phys. Lett.* **2010**, *96*, 23–26. [CrossRef]
71. Chen, T.; Guo, C.; Xu, L.; Li, Q.; Luo, K.; Liu, D.; Wang, L.; Long, M. Modulating the Properties of Multi-Functional Molecular Devices Consisting of Zigzag Gallium Nitride Nanoribbons by Different Magnetic Orderings: A First-Principles Study. *Phys. Chem. Chem. Phys.* **2018**, *20*, 5726–5733. [CrossRef] [PubMed]
72. Xu, Y.; Chen, X.; Gu, B.L.; Duan, W. Intrinsic Anisotropy of Thermal Conductance in Graphene Nanoribbons. *Appl. Phys. Lett.* **2009**, *95*, 10–13. [CrossRef]
73. He, J.; Li, D.; Ying, Y.; Feng, C.; He, J.; Zhong, C.; Zhou, H.; Zhou, P.; Zhang, G. Orbitally Driven Giant Thermal Conductance Associated with Abnormal Strain Dependence in Hydrogenated Graphene-like Borophene. *NPJ Comput. Mater.* **2019**, *5*, 47. [CrossRef]
74. Zhou, Y.H.; Zhang, X.; Ji, C.; Liu, Z.M.; Chen, K.Q. The Length and Hydrogenation Effects on Electronic Transport Properties of Carbon-Based Molecular Wires. *Org. Electron.* **2017**, *51*, 332–340. [CrossRef]
75. Peng, X.F.; Chen, K.Q. Thermal Transport for Flexural and In-Plane Phonons in Graphene Nanoribbons. *Carbon* **2014**, *77*, 360–365. [CrossRef]
76. Tian, Z.; Esfarjani, K.; Chen, G. Enhancing Phonon Transmission across a Si/Ge Interface by Atomic Roughness: First-Principles Study with the Green's Function Method. *Phys. Rev. B Condens. Matter Mater. Phys.* **2012**, *86*, 235304. [CrossRef]
77. Peng, X.F.; Zhou, X.; Tan, S.H.; Wang, X.J.; Chen, L.Q.; Chen, K.Q. Thermal Conductance in Graphene Nanoribbons Modulated by Defects and Alternating Boron-Nitride Structures. *Carbon* **2017**, *113*, 334–339. [CrossRef]
78. Yan, Z.; Chen, L.; Yoon, M.; Kumar, S. The Role of Interfacial Electronic Properties on Phonon Transport in Two-Dimensional MoS_2 on Metal Substrates. *ACS Appl. Mater. Interfaces* **2016**, *8*, 33299–33306. [CrossRef]
79. Ma, D.; Ding, H.; Meng, H.; Feng, L.; Wu, Y.; Shiomi, J.; Yang, N. Nano-Cross-Junction Effect on Phonon Transport in Silicon Nanowire Cages. *Phys. Rev. B* **2016**, *94*, 165434. [CrossRef]
80. Kim, P.; Shi, L.; Majumdar, A.; McEuen, P.L. Thermal Transport Measurements of Individual Multiwalled Nanotubes. *Phys. Rev. Lett.* **2001**, *87*, 215502. [CrossRef]
81. Hone, J.; Whitney, M.; Piskoti, C.; Zettl, A. Thermal Conductivity of Single-Walled Carbon Nanotubes. *Phys. Rev. B* **1999**, *59*, R2514–R2516. [CrossRef]
82. Hochbaum, A.I.; Chen, R.; Delgado, R.D.; Liang, W.; Garnett, E.C.; Najarian, M.; Majumdar, A.; Yang, P. Enhanced Thermoelectric Performance of Rough Silicon Nanowires. *Nature* **2008**, *451*, 163–167. [CrossRef] [PubMed]
83. Guo, J.; Huang, Y.; Wu, X.; Wang, Q.; Zhou, X.; Xu, X.; Li, B. Thickness-Dependent In-Plane Thermal Conductivity and Enhanced Thermoelectric Performance in p-Type $ZrTe_5$ Nanoribbons. *Phys. Status Solidi RRL* **2019**, *13*, 1800529. [CrossRef]
84. Shi, L.; Li, D.; Yu, C.; Jang, W.; Kim, D.; Yao, Z.; Kim, P.; Majumdar, A. Measuring Thermal and Thermoelectric Properties of One-Dimensional Nanostructures Using a Microfabricated Device. *J. Heat Transf.* **2003**, *125*, 881–888. [CrossRef]
85. Wingert, M.C.; Chen, Z.C.Y.; Kwon, S.; Xiang, J.; Chen, R. Ultra-Sensitive Thermal Conductance Measurement of One-Dimensional Nanostructures Enhanced by Differential Bridge. *Rev. Sci. Instrum.* **2012**, *83*, 24901. [CrossRef]
86. Dong, L.; Xi, Q.; Chen, D.; Guo, J.; Nakayama, T.; Li, Y.; Liang, Z.; Zhou, J.; Xu, X.; Li, B. Dimensional Crossover of Heat Conduction in Amorphous Polyimide Nanofibers. *Natl. Sci. Rev.* **2018**, *5*, 500–506. [CrossRef]
87. Zheng, J.; Wingert, M.C.; Dechaumphai, E.; Chen, R. Sub-Picowatt/Kelvin Resistive Thermometry for Probing Nanoscale Thermal Transport. *Rev. Sci. Instrum.* **2013**, *84*, 114901. [CrossRef]
88. Mavrokefalos, A.; Pettes, M.T.; Zhou, F.; Shi, L. Four-Probe Measurements of the in-Plane Thermoelectric Properties of Nanofilms. *Rev. Sci. Instrum.* **2007**, *78*, 34901. [CrossRef]
89. Alaie, S.; Goettler, D.F.; Abbas, K.; Su, M.F.; Reinke, C.M.; El-Kady, I.; Leseman, Z.C. Microfabricated Suspended Island Platform for the Measurement of In-Plane Thermal Conductivity of Thin Films and Nanostructured Materials with Consideration of Contact Resistance. *Rev. Sci. Instrum.* **2013**, *84*, 105003. [CrossRef] [PubMed]

90. Yu, C.; Saha, S.; Zhou, J.; Shi, L.; Cassell, A.M.; Cruden, B.A.; Ngo, Q.; Li, J. Thermal Contact Resistance and Thermal Conductivity of a Carbon Nanofiber. *J. Heat Transf.* **2005**, *128*, 234–239. [CrossRef]

91. Jo, I.; Pettes, M.T.; Lindsay, L.; Ou, E.; Weathers, A.; Moore, A.L.; Yao, Z.; Shi, L. Reexamination of Basal Plane Thermal Conductivity of Suspended Graphene Samples Measured by Electro-Thermal Micro-Bridge Methods. *AIP Adv.* **2015**, *5*, 53206. [CrossRef]

92. Sood, A.; Xiong, F.; Chen, S.; Cheaito, R.; Lian, F.; Asheghi, M.; Cui, Y.; Donadio, D.; Goodson, K.E.; Pop, E. Quasi-Ballistic Thermal Transport Across MoS$_2$ Thin Films. *Nano Lett.* **2019**, *19*, 2434–2442. [CrossRef] [PubMed]

93. Jiang, P.; Qian, X.; Gu, X.; Yang, R. Probing Anisotropic Thermal Conductivity of Transition Metal Dichalcogenides MX$_2$ (M = Mo, W and X = S, Se) Using Time-Domain Thermoreflectance. *Adv. Mater.* **2017**, *29*, 1701068. [CrossRef]

94. Sadeghi, M.M.; Jo, I.; Shi, L. Phonon-Interface Scattering in Multilayer Graphene on an Amorphous Support. *Proc. Natl. Acad. Sci. USA* **2013**, *110*, 16321–16326. [CrossRef]

95. Feshchenko, A.V.; Casparis, L.; Khaymovich, I.M.; Maradan, D.; Saira, O.-P.; Palma, M.; Meschke, M.; Pekola, J.P.; Zumbühl, D.M. Tunnel-Junction Thermometry Down to Millikelvin Temperatures. *Phys. Rev. Appl.* **2015**, *4*, 34001. [CrossRef]

96. Cahill, D.G.; Braun, P.V.; Chen, G.; Clarke, D.R.; Fan, S.; Goodson, K.E.; Keblinski, P.; King, W.P.; Mahan, G.D.; Majumdar, A.; et al. Nanoscale Thermal Transport. II. 2003–2012. *Appl. Phys. Rev.* **2014**, *1*, 11305. [CrossRef]

97. Xu, X.; Pereira, L.F.C.; Wang, Y.; Wu, J.; Zhang, K.; Zhao, X.; Bae, S.; Tinh Bui, C.; Xie, R.; Thong, J.T.L.; et al. Length-Dependent Thermal Conductivity in Suspended Single-Layer Graphene. *Nat. Commun.* **2014**, *5*, 3689. [CrossRef]

98. Pettes, M.T.; Jo, I.; Yao, Z.; Shi, L. Influence of Polymeric Residue on the Thermal Conductivity of Suspended Bilayer Graphene. *Nano Lett.* **2011**, *11*, 1195–1200. [CrossRef]

99. Wang, J.; Zhu, L.; Chen, J.; Li, B.; Thong, J.T.L. Suppressing Thermal Conductivity of Suspended Tri-Layer Graphene by Gold Deposition. *Adv. Mater.* **2013**, *25*, 6884–6888. [CrossRef]

100. Wang, C.; Guo, J.; Dong, L.; Aiyiti, A.; Xu, X.; Li, B. Superior Thermal Conductivity in Suspended Bilayer Hexagonal Boron Nitride. *Sci. Rep.* **2016**, *6*, 25334. [CrossRef] [PubMed]

101. Yarali, M.; Wu, X.; Gupta, T.; Ghoshal, D.; Xie, L.; Zhu, Z.; Brahmi, H.; Bao, J.; Chen, S.; Luo, T.; et al. Effects of Defects on the Temperature-Dependent Thermal Conductivity of Suspended Monolayer Molybdenum Disulfide Grown by Chemical Vapor Deposition. *Adv. Funct. Mater.* **2017**, *27*, 1704357. [CrossRef]

102. Aiyiti, A.; Hu, S.; Wang, C.; Xi, Q.; Cheng, Z.; Xia, M.; Ma, Y.; Wu, J.; Guo, J.; Wang, Q.; et al. Thermal Conductivity of Suspended Few-Layer MoS$_2$. *Nanoscale* **2018**, *10*, 2727–2734. [CrossRef] [PubMed]

103. Wang, Z.; Xie, R.; Bui, C.T.; Liu, D.; Ni, X.; Li, B.; Thong, J.T.L. Thermal Transport in Suspended and Supported Few-Layer Graphene. *Nano Lett.* **2011**, *11*, 113–118. [CrossRef]

104. Aiyiti, A.; Bai, X.; Wu, J.; Xu, X.; Li, B. Measuring the Thermal Conductivity and Interfacial Thermal Resistance of Suspended MoS2 Using Electron Beam Self-Heating Technique. *Sci. Bull.* **2018**, *63*, 452–458. [CrossRef]

105. Liu, D.; Xie, R.; Yang, N.; Li, B.; Thong, J.T.L. Profiling Nanowire Thermal Resistance with a Spatial Resolution of Nanometers. *Nano Lett.* **2014**, *14*, 806–812. [CrossRef] [PubMed]

106. Zhao, Y.; Liu, X.; Rath, A.; Wu, J.; Li, B.; Zhou, W.X.; Xie, G.; Zhang, G.; Thong, J.T.L. Probing Thermal Transport across Amorphous Region Embedded in a Single Crystalline Silicon Nanowire. *Sci. Rep.* **2020**, *10*, 821. [CrossRef] [PubMed]

107. Zhao, Y.; Liu, D.; Chen, J.; Zhu, L.; Belianinov, A.; Ovchinnikova, O.S.; Unocic, R.R.; Burch, M.J.; Kim, S.; Hao, H.; et al. Engineering the Thermal Conductivity along an Individual Silicon Nanowire by Selective Helium Ion Irradiation. *Nat. Commun.* **2017**, *8*, 15919. [CrossRef]

108. Lin, Z.; Liu, C.; Chai, Y. High Thermally Conductive and Electrically Insulating 2D Boron Nitride Nanosheet for Efficient Heat Dissipation of High-Power Transistors. *2D Mater.* **2016**, *3*, 041009. [CrossRef]

109. Cai, Q.; Scullion, D.; Gan, W.; Falin, A.; Zhang, S.; Watanabe, K.; Taniguchi, T.; Chen, Y.; Santos, E.J.G.; Li, L.H. High Thermal Conductivity of High-Quality Monolayer Boron Nitride and Its Thermal Expansion. *Sci. Adv.* **2022**, *5*, eaav0129. [CrossRef] [PubMed]

110. Luo, Z.; Maassen, J.; Deng, Y.; Du, Y.; Garrelts, R.P.; Lundstrom, M.S.; Ye, P.D.; Xu, X. Anisotropic In-Plane Thermal Conductivity Observed in Few-Layer Black Phosphorus. *Nat. Commun.* **2015**, *6*, 8572. [CrossRef] [PubMed]

111. Yu, Y.; Minhaj, T.; Huang, L.; Yu, Y.; Cao, L. In-Plane and Interfacial Thermal Conduction of Two-Dimensional Transition-Metal Dichalcogenides. *Phys. Rev. Appl.* **2020**, *13*, 034059. [CrossRef]

112. Sahoo, S.; Gaur, A.P.S.; Ahmadi, M.; Guinel, M.J.F.; Katiyar, R.S. Temperature-Dependent Raman Studies and Thermal Conductivity of Few-Layer MoS$_2$. *J. Phys. Chem. C* **2013**, *117*, 9042–9047. [CrossRef]

113. Zhou, H.; Zhu, J.; Liu, Z.; Yan, Z.; Fan, X.; Lin, J.; Wang, G.; Yan, Q.; Yu, T.; Ajayan, P.M.; et al. High Thermal Conductivity of Suspended Few-Layer Hexagonal Boron Nitride Sheets. *Nano Res.* **2014**, *7*, 1232–1240. [CrossRef]

114. Balandin, A.A. Thermal Properties of Graphene and Nanostructured Carbon Materials. *Nat. Mater.* **2011**, *10*, 569–581. [CrossRef]

115. Camassel, J.; Falkovsky, L.A.; Planes, N. Strain Effect in Silicon-on-Insulator Materials: Investigation with Optical Phonons. *Phys. Rev. B Condens. Matter Mater. Phys.* **2001**, *63*, 353091–3530911. [CrossRef]

116. Campbell, I.H.; Fauchet, P.M. The Effects of Microcrystal Size and Shape on the One Phonon Raman Spectra of Crystalline Semiconductors. *Solid State Commun.* **1986**, *58*, 739–741. [CrossRef]

117. Chávez, E.; Fuentes, S.; Zarate, R.A.; Padilla-Campos, L. Structural Analysis of Nanocrystalline BaTiO$_3$. *J. Mol. Struct.* **2010**, *984*, 131–136. [CrossRef]

118. Mishra, P.; Jain, K.P. Temperature-Dependent Raman Scattering Studies in Nanocrystalline Silicon and Finite-Size Effects. *Phys. Rev. B Condens. Matter Mater. Phys.* **2000**, *62*, 14790–14795. [CrossRef]

119. Yuan, P.; Wang, R.; Tan, H.; Wang, T.; Wang, X. Energy Transport State Resolved Raman for Probing Interface Energy Transport and Hot Carrier Diffusion in Few-Layered MoS$_2$. *ACS Photonics* **2017**, *4*, 3115–3129. [CrossRef]

120. Tripp, R.; Ferro-Luzzi, M.; Glashow, S.; Rosenfeld, A. Physical Review Letters. *Nature* **1958**, *182*, 227–228. [CrossRef]

121. Islam, A.; Van Den Akker, A.; Feng, P.X.L. Anisotropic Thermal Conductivity of Suspended Black Phosphorus Probed by Opto-Thermomechanical Resonance Spectromicroscopy. *Nano Lett.* **2018**, *18*, 7683–7691. [CrossRef] [PubMed]

122. Jiang, P.; Qian, X.; Yang, R. Tutorial: Time-Domain Thermoreflectance (TDTR) for Thermal Property Characterization of Bulk and Thin Film Materials. *J. Appl. Phys.* **2018**, *124*, 161103. [CrossRef]

123. Schmidt, A.J.; Collins, K.C.; Minnich, A.J.; Chen, G. Thermal Conductance and Phonon Transmissivity of Metal-Graphite Interfaces. *J. Appl. Phys.* **2010**, *107*, 104907. [CrossRef]

124. Costescu, R.M.; Cahill, D.G.; Fabreguette, F.H.; Sechrist, Z.A.; George, S.M. Ultra-Low Thermal Conductivity in W/Al$_2$O$_3$ Nanolaminates. *Science* **2004**, *303*, 989–990. [CrossRef]

125. Koh, Y.K.; Bae, M.H.; Cahill, D.G.; Pop, E. Heat Conduction across Monolayer and Few-Layer Graphenes. *Nano Lett.* **2010**, *10*, 4363–4368. [CrossRef]

126. Cahill, D.G. Thermal-Conductivity Measurement by Time-Domain Thermoreflectance. *MRS Bull.* **2018**, *43*, 768–774. [CrossRef]

127. Li, D.; Wu, Y.; Kim, P.; Shi, L.; Yang, P.; Majumdar, A. Thermal Conductivity of Individual Silicon Nanowires. *Appl. Phys. Lett.* **2003**, *83*, 2934–2936. [CrossRef]

128. Lee, S.; Yang, F.; Suh, J.; Yang, S.; Lee, Y.; Li, G.; Choe, H.S.; Suslu, A.; Chen, Y.; Ko, C.; et al. Anisotropic In-Plane Thermal Conductivity of Black Phosphorus Nanoribbons at Temperatures Higher than 100 K. *Nat. Commun.* **2015**, *6*, 8573. [CrossRef]

129. Jo, I.; Pettes, M.T.; Ou, E.; Wu, W.; Shi, L. Basal-Plane Thermal Conductivity of Few-Layer Molybdenum Disulfide. *Appl. Phys. Lett.* **2014**, *104*, 201902. [CrossRef]

130. Zhang, Y.; Tan, Y.W.; Stormer, H.L.; Kim, P. Experimental Observation of the Quantum Hall Effect and Berry's Phase in Graphene. *Nature* **2005**, *438*, 201–204. [CrossRef] [PubMed]

131. Novoselov, K.S.; Geim, A.K.; Morozov, S.V.; Jiang, D.; Katsnelson, M.I.; Grigorieva, I.V.; Dubonos, S.V.; Firsov, A.A. Two-Dimensional Gas of Massless Dirac Fermions in Graphene. *Nature* **2005**, *438*, 197–200. [CrossRef] [PubMed]

132. Ghosh, S.; Calizo, I.; Teweldebrhan, D.; Pokatilov, E.P.; Nika, D.L.; Balandin, A.A.; Bao, W.; Miao, F.; Lau, C.N. Extremely High Thermal Conductivity of Graphene: Prospects for Thermal Management Applications in Nanoelectronic Circuits. *Appl. Phys. Lett.* **2008**, *92*, 151911. [CrossRef]

133. Cai, W.; Moore, A.L.; Zhu, Y.; Li, X.; Chen, S.; Shi, L.; Ruoff, R.S. Thermal Transport in Suspended and Supported Monolayer Graphene Grown by Chemical Vapor Deposition. *Nano Lett.* **2010**, *10*, 1645–1651. [CrossRef]

134. Chen, S.; Moore, A.L.; Cai, W.; Suk, J.W.; An, J.; Mishra, C.; Amos, C.; Magnuson, C.W.; Kang, J.; Shi, L.; et al. Raman Measurements of Thermal Transport in Suspended Monolayer Graphene of Variable Sizes in Vacuum and Gaseous Environments. *ACS Nano* **2011**, *5*, 321–328. [CrossRef]

135. Faugeras, C.; Faugeras, B.; Orlita, M.; Potemski, M.; Nair, R.R.; Geim, A.K. Thermal Conductivity of Graphene in Corbino Membrane Geometry. *ACS Nano* **2010**, *4*, 1889–1892. [CrossRef]

136. Lee, J.U.; Yoon, D.; Kim, H.; Lee, S.W.; Cheong, H. Thermal Conductivity of Suspended Pristine Graphene Measured by Raman Spectroscopy. *Phys. Rev. B Condens. Matter Mater. Phys.* **2011**, *83*, 081419. [CrossRef]

137. Li, Q.Y.; Xia, K.; Zhang, J.; Zhang, Y.; Li, Q.; Takahashi, K.; Zhang, X. Measurement of Specific Heat and Thermal Conductivity of Supported and Suspended Graphene by a Comprehensive Raman Optothermal Method. *Nanoscale* **2017**, *9*, 10784–10793. [CrossRef]

138. Xu, X.; Wang, Y.; Zhang, K.; Zhao, X.; Bae, S.; Heinrich, M.; Bui, C.T.; Xie, R.; Thong, J.T.L.; Hong, B.H. Phonon Transport in Suspended Single Layer Graphene. *arXiv* **2010**, arXiv:1012.2937.

139. Yoon, K.; Hwang, G.; Chung, J.; Kim, H.G.; Kwon, O.; Kihm, K.D.; Lee, J.S. Measuring the Thermal Conductivity of Residue-Free Suspended Graphene Bridge Using Null Point Scanning Thermal Microscopy. *Carbon* **2014**, *76*, 77–83. [CrossRef]

140. Nika, D.L.; Ghosh, S.; Pokatilov, E.P.; Balandin, A.A. Lattice Thermal Conductivity of Graphene Flakes: Comparison with Bulk Graphite. *Appl. Phys. Lett.* **2009**, *94*, 203103. [CrossRef]

141. Mei, S.; Maurer, L.N.; Aksamija, Z.; Knezevic, I. Full-Dispersion Monte Carlo Simulation of Phonon Transport in Micron-Sized Graphene Nanoribbons. *J. Appl. Phys.* **2014**, *116*, 164307. [CrossRef]

142. Feng, T.; Lindsay, L.; Ruan, X. Four-Phonon Scattering Significantly Reduces Intrinsic Thermal Conductivity of Solids. *Phys. Rev. B* **2017**, *96*, 161201. [CrossRef]

143. Gu, X.; Fan, Z.; Bao, H.; Zhao, C.Y. Revisiting Phonon-Phonon Scattering in Single-Layer Graphene. *Phys. Rev. B* **2019**, *100*, 64306. [CrossRef]

144. Jang, W.; Chen, Z.; Bao, W.; Lau, C.N.; Dames, C. Thickness-Dependent Thermal Conductivity of Encased Graphene and Ultrathin Graphite. *Nano Lett.* **2010**, *10*, 3909–3913. [CrossRef]

145. Duclaux, L.; Nysten, B.; Issi, J.-P.; Moore, A.W. Structure and Low-Temperature Thermal Conductivity of Pyrolytic Boron Nitride. *Phys. Rev. B* **1992**, *46*, 3362–3367. [CrossRef]

146. Simpson, A.; Stuckes, A.D. The Thermal Conductivity of Highly Oriented Pyrolytic Boron Nitride. *J. Phys. C Solid State Phys.* **1971**, *4*, 1710–1718. [CrossRef]

147. Alem, N.; Erni, R.; Kisielowski, C.; Rossell, M.D.; Gannett, W.; Zettl, A. Atomically Thin Hexagonal Boron Nitride Probed by Ultrahigh-Resolution Transmission Electron Microscopy. *Phys. Rev. B* **2009**, *80*, 155425. [CrossRef]

148. Lindsay, L.; Broido, D.A. Theory of Thermal Transport in Multilayer Hexagonal Boron Nitride and Nanotubes. *Phys. Rev. B* **2012**, *85*, 35436. [CrossRef]

149. Alam, M.T.; Bresnehan, M.S.; Robinson, J.A.; Haque, M.A. Thermal Conductivity of Ultra-Thin Chemical Vapor Deposited Hexagonal Boron Nitride Films. *Appl. Phys. Lett.* **2014**, *104*, 13113. [CrossRef]

150. Mak, K.F.; Lee, C.; Hone, J.; Shan, J.; Heinz, T.F. Atomically Thin MoS_2: A New Direct-Gap Semiconductor. *Phys. Rev. Lett.* **2010**, *105*, 2–5. [CrossRef] [PubMed]

151. Liu, X.; Zhang, G.; Pei, Q.X.; Zhang, Y.W. Phonon Thermal Conductivity of Monolayer MoS_2 Sheet and Nanoribbons. *Appl. Phys. Lett.* **2013**, *103*, 133113. [CrossRef]

152. Radisavljevic, B.; Radenovic, A.; Brivio, J.; Giacometti, V.; Kis, A. Single-Layer MoS_2 Transistors. *Nat. Nanotechnol.* **2011**, *6*, 147–150. [CrossRef] [PubMed]

153. Liu, X.; Zhang, Y.W. Thermal Properties of Transition-Metal Dichalcogenide. *Chin. Phys. B* **2018**, *27*, 034402. [CrossRef]

154. Zhang, X.; Sun, D.; Li, Y.; Lee, G.H.; Cui, X.; Chenet, D.; You, Y.; Heinz, T.F.; Hone, J.C. Measurement of Lateral and Interfacial Thermal Conductivity of Single- and Bilayer MoS_2 and $MoSe_2$ Using Refined Optothermal Raman Technique. *ACS Appl. Mater. Interfaces* **2015**, *7*, 25923–25929. [CrossRef]

155. Bae, J.J.; Jeong, H.Y.; Han, G.H.; Kim, J.; Kim, H.; Kim, M.S.; Moon, B.H.; Lim, S.C.; Lee, Y.H. Thickness-Dependent in-Plane Thermal Conductivity of Suspended MoS_2 Grown by Chemical Vapor Deposition. *Nanoscale* **2017**, *9*, 2541–2547. [CrossRef]

156. Zhao, Y.; Zheng, M.; Wu, J.; Huang, B.; Thong, J.T.L. Studying Thermal Transport in Suspended Monolayer Molybdenum Disulfide Prepared by a Nano-Manipulator-Assisted Transfer Method. *Nanotechnology* **2020**, *31*, 225702. [CrossRef]

157. Taube, A.; Judek, J.; Łapińska, A.; Zdrojek, M. Temperature-Dependent Thermal Properties of Supported MoS_2 Monolayers. *ACS Appl. Mater. Interfaces* **2015**, *7*, 5061–5065. [CrossRef]

158. Yuan, P.; Wang, R.; Wang, T.; Wang, X.; Xie, Y. Nonmonotonic Thickness-Dependence of in-Plane Thermal Conductivity of Few-Layered MoS_2: 2.4 to 37.8 Nm. *Phys. Chem. Chem. Phys.* **2018**, *20*, 25752–25761. [CrossRef]

159. Muratore, C.; Varshney, V.; Gengler, J.J.; Hu, J.J.; Bultman, J.E.; Smith, T.M.; Shamberger, P.J.; Qiu, B.; Ruan, X.; Roy, A.K.; et al. Cross-Plane Thermal Properties of Transition Metal Dichalcogenides. *Appl. Phys. Lett.* **2013**, *102*, 5–9. [CrossRef]

160. Liu, J.; Choi, G.M.; Cahill, D.G. Measurement of the Anisotropic Thermal Conductivity of Molybdenum Disulfide by the Time-Resolved Magneto-Optic Kerr Effect. *J. Appl. Phys.* **2014**, *116*, 233107. [CrossRef]

161. Wang, R.; Wang, T.; Zobeiri, H.; Yuan, P.; Deng, C.; Yue, Y.; Xu, S.; Wang, X. Measurement of the Thermal Conductivities of Suspended MoS_2 and $MoSe_2$ by Nanosecond ET-Raman without Temperature Calibration and Laser Absorption Evaluation. *Nanoscale* **2018**, *10*, 23087–23102. [CrossRef] [PubMed]

162. Zobeiri, H.; Wang, R.; Wang, T.; Lin, H.; Deng, C.; Wang, X. Frequency-Domain Energy Transport State-Resolved Raman for Measuring the Thermal Conductivity of Suspended Nm-Thick $MoSe_2$. *Int. J. Heat Mass Transf.* **2019**, *133*, 1074–1085. [CrossRef]

163. Yan, Z.; Jiang, C.; Pope, T.R.; Tsang, C.F.; Stickney, J.L.; Goli, P.; Renteria, J.; Salguero, T.T.; Balandin, A.A. Phonon and Thermal Properties of Exfoliated $TaSe_2$ Thin Films. *J. Appl. Phys.* **2013**, *114*, 204301. [CrossRef]

164. Wang, Y.; Gao, Y.; Easy, E.; Yang, E.H.; Xu, B.; Zhang, X. Thermal Conductivities and Interfacial Thermal Conductance of 2D WSe_2. In Proceedings of the 15th IEEE International Conference on Nano/Micro Engineered and Molecular System, NEMS 2020, San Diego, CA, USA, 27–30 September 2020; pp. 575–579. [CrossRef]

165. Zhou, Y.; Jang, H.; Woods, J.M.; Xie, Y.; Kumaravadivel, P.; Pan, G.A.; Liu, J.; Liu, Y.; Cahill, D.G.; Cha, J.J. Direct Synthesis of Large-Scale WTe_2 Thin Films with Low Thermal Conductivity. *Adv. Funct. Mater.* **2017**, *27*, 1605928. [CrossRef]

166. Chen, Y.; Peng, B.; Cong, C.; Shang, J.; Wu, L.; Yang, W.; Zhou, J.; Yu, P.; Zhang, H.; Wang, Y.; et al. In-Plane Anisotropic Thermal Conductivity of Few-Layered Transition Metal Dichalcogenide Td-WTe_2. *Adv. Mater.* **2019**, *31*, 1804979. [CrossRef]

167. Jang, H.; Ryder, C.R.; Wood, J.D.; Hersam, M.C.; Cahill, D.G. 3D Anisotropic Thermal Conductivity of Exfoliated Rhenium Disulfide. *Adv. Mater.* **2017**, *29*, 1700650. [CrossRef] [PubMed]

168. Villegas, C.E.P.; Rocha, A.R.; Marini, A. Anomalous Temperature Dependence of the Band Gap in Black Phosphorus. *Nano Lett.* **2016**, *16*, 5095–5101. [CrossRef]

169. Zhang, Y.; Zheng, Y.; Rui, K.; Hng, H.H.; Hippalgaonkar, K.; Xu, J.; Sun, W.; Zhu, J.; Yan, Q.; Huang, W. 2D Black Phosphorus for Energy Storage and Thermoelectric Applications. *Small* **2017**, *13*, 1700661. [CrossRef]

170. Li, L.; Yu, Y.; Ye, G.J.; Ge, Q.; Ou, X.; Wu, H.; Feng, D.; Chen, X.H.; Zhang, Y. Black Phosphorus Field-Effect Transistors. *Nat. Nanotechnol.* **2014**, *9*, 372–377. [CrossRef] [PubMed]

171. Hong, Y.; Zhang, J.; Cheng Zeng, X. Thermal Transport in Phosphorene and Phosphorene-Based Materials: A Review on Numerical Studies. *Chin. Phys. B* **2018**, *27*, 36501. [CrossRef]

172. Qin, G.; Yan, Q.-B.; Qin, Z.; Yue, S.-Y.; Hu, M.; Su, G. Anisotropic Intrinsic Lattice Thermal Conductivity of Phosphorene from First Principles. *Phys. Chem. Chem. Phys.* **2015**, *17*, 4854–4858. [CrossRef]

173. Chen, Y.; Chen, C.; Kealhofer, R.; Liu, H.; Yuan, Z.; Jiang, L.; Suh, J.; Park, J.; Ko, C.; Choe, H.S.; et al. Black Arsenic: A Layered Semiconductor with Extreme In-Plane Anisotropy. *Adv. Mater.* **2018**, *30*, 1800754. [CrossRef] [PubMed]

174. Lin, S.; Li, W.; Chen, Z.; Shen, J.; Ge, B.; Pei, Y. Tellurium as a High-Performance Elemental Thermoelectric. *Nat. Commun.* **2016**, *7*, 10287. [CrossRef] [PubMed]

175. Reed, E.J. Two-Dimensional Tellurium. *Nature* **2017**, *552*, 40–41. [CrossRef]

176. Du, Y.; Qiu, G.; Wang, Y.; Si, M.; Xu, X.; Wu, W.; Ye, P.D. One-Dimensional van Der Waals Material Tellurium: Raman Spectroscopy under Strain and Magneto-Transport. *Nano Lett.* **2017**, *17*, 3965–3973. [CrossRef]

177. Qiao, J.; Pan, Y.; Yang, F.; Wang, C.; Chai, Y.; Ji, W. Few-Layer Tellurium: One-Dimensional-like Layered Elementary Semiconductor with Striking Physical Properties. *Sci. Bull.* **2018**, *63*, 159–168. [CrossRef]

178. Gao, Z.; Tao, F.; Ren, J. Unusually Low Thermal Conductivity of Atomically Thin 2D Tellurium. *Nanoscale* **2018**, *10*, 12997–13003. [CrossRef]

179. Gao, Z.; Liu, G.; Ren, J. High Thermoelectric Performance in Two-Dimensional Tellurium: An Ab Initio Study. *ACS Appl. Mater. Interfaces* **2018**, *10*, 40702–40709. [CrossRef]

180. Chen, J.; Dai, Y.; Ma, Y.; Dai, X.; Ho, W.; Xie, M. Ultrathin β-Tellurium Layers Grown on Highly Oriented Pyrolytic Graphite by Molecular-Beam Epitaxy. *Nanoscale* **2017**, *9*, 15945–15948. [CrossRef] [PubMed]

181. Zhu, Z.; Cai, X.; Yi, S.; Chen, J.; Dai, Y.; Niu, C.; Guo, Z.; Xie, M.; Liu, F.; Cho, J.-H.; et al. Multivalency-Driven Formation of Te-Based Monolayer Materials: A Combined First-Principles and Experimental Study. *Phys. Rev. Lett.* **2017**, *119*, 106101. [CrossRef] [PubMed]

182. Wang, Y.; Qiu, G.; Wang, R.; Huang, S.; Wang, Q.; Liu, Y.; Du, Y.; Goddard, W.A.; Kim, M.J.; Xu, X. Field-Effect Transistors Made from Solution-Grown Two-Dimensional Tellurene. *Nat. Electron.* **2018**, *1*, 228–236. [CrossRef]

183. Fleurence, A.; Friedlein, R.; Ozaki, T.; Kawai, H.; Wang, Y.; Yamada-Takamura, Y. Experimental Evidence for Epitaxial Silicene on Diboride Thin Films. *Phys. Rev. Lett.* **2012**, *108*, 245501. [CrossRef] [PubMed]

184. Vogt, P.; De Padova, P.; Quaresima, C.; Avila, J.; Frantzeskakis, E.; Asensio, M.C.; Resta, A.; Ealet, B.; Le Lay, G. Silicene: Compelling Experimental Evidence for Graphenelike Two-Dimensional Silicon. *Phys. Rev. Lett.* **2012**, *108*, 155501. [CrossRef] [PubMed]

185. Pettes, M.T.; Maassen, J.; Jo, I.; Lundstrom, M.S.; Shi, L. Effects of Surface Band Bending and Scattering on Thermoelectric Transport in Suspended Bismuth Telluride Nanoplates. *Nano Lett.* **2013**, *13*, 5316–5322. [CrossRef] [PubMed]

186. Zhou, S.; Tao, X.; Gu, Y. Thickness-Dependent Thermal Conductivity of Suspended Two-Dimensional Single-Crystal In_2Se_3 Layers Grown by Chemical Vapor Deposition. *J. Phys. Chem. C* **2016**, *120*, 4753–4758. [CrossRef]

187. Lee, M.-J.; Ahn, J.-H.; Sung, J.H.; Heo, H.; Jeon, S.G.; Lee, W.; Song, J.Y.; Hong, K.-H.; Choi, B.; Lee, S.-H.; et al. Thermoelectric Materials by Using Two-Dimensional Materials with Negative Correlation between Electrical and Thermal Conductivity. *Nat. Commun.* **2016**, *7*, 12011. [CrossRef]

188. Yang, F.; Wang, R.; Zhao, W.; Jiang, J.; Wei, X.; Zheng, T.; Yang, Y.; Wang, X.; Lu, J.; Ni, Z. Thermal Transport and Energy Dissipation in Two-Dimensional Bi_2O_2Se. *Appl. Phys. Lett.* **2019**, *115*, 193103. [CrossRef]

189. Qin, Z.; Qin, G.; Zuo, X.; Xiong, Z.; Hu, M. Orbitally Driven Low Thermal Conductivity of Monolayer Gallium Nitride (GaN) with Planar Honeycomb Structure: A Comparative Study. *Nanoscale* **2017**, *9*, 4295–4309. [CrossRef]

190. Li, D.; Gao, J.; Cheng, P.; He, J.; Yin, Y.; Hu, Y.; Chen, L.; Cheng, Y.; Zhao, J. 2D Boron Sheets: Structure, Growth, and Electronic and Thermal Transport Properties. *Adv. Funct. Mater.* **2020**, *30*, 1904349. [CrossRef]

191. Mortazavi, B.; Shahrokhi, M.; Raeisi, M.; Zhuang, X.; Pereira, L.F.C.; Rabczuk, T. Outstanding Strength, Optical Characteristics and Thermal Conductivity of Graphene-like BC_3 and BC_6N Semiconductors. *Carbon* **2019**, *149*, 733–742. [CrossRef]

192. Zhang, Y.-Y.; Pei, Q.-X.; Liu, H.-Y.; Wei, N. Thermal Conductivity of a H-BCN Monolayer. *Phys. Chem. Chem. Phys.* **2017**, *19*, 27326–27331. [CrossRef] [PubMed]

Review

Review of Photothermal Technique for Thermal Measurement of Micro-/Nanomaterials

Jianjun Zhou [1], Shen Xu [1,*] and Jing Liu [2]

1   School of Mechanical and Automotive Engineering, Shanghai University of Engineering Science, Shanghai 201620, China; jjzhousues@163.com
2   College of New Materials and New Energies, Shenzhen Technology University, Shenzhen 518116, China; liujing@sztu.edu.cn
*   Correspondence: shxu16@sues.edu.cn

Abstract: The extremely small size of micro-/nanomaterials limits the application of conventional thermal measurement methods using a contact heating source or probing sensor. Therefore, non-contact thermal measurement methods are preferable in micro-/nanoscale thermal characterization. In this review, one of the non-contact thermal measurement methods, photothermal (PT) technique based on thermal radiation, is introduced. When subjected to laser heating with controllable modulation frequencies, surface thermal radiation carries fruitful information for thermal property determination. As thermal properties are closely related to the internal structure of materials, for micro-/nanomaterials, PT technique can measure not only thermal properties but also features in the micro-/nanostructure. Practical applications of PT technique in the thermal measurement of micro-/nanomaterials are then reviewed, including special wall-structure investigation in multiwall carbon nanotubes, porosity determination in nanomaterial assemblies, and the observation of amorphous/crystalline structure transformation in proteins in heat treatment. Furthermore, the limitations and future application extensions are discussed.

Keywords: photothermal technique; thermal properties; nanostructure characterization; thermal conductivity; specific heat; thermal effusivity

Citation: Zhou, J.; Xu, S.; Liu, J. Review of Photothermal Technique for Thermal Measurement of Micro-/Nanomaterials. *Nanomaterials* **2022**, *12*, 1884. https://doi.org/10.3390/nano12111884

Academic Editor: Enyi Ye

Received: 8 May 2022
Accepted: 30 May 2022
Published: 31 May 2022

1. Introduction

With reductions in size to the micro-/nanometer level, temperature probing and thermal measurement have become difficult to conduct using traditional contact-based methods and equipment (thermal couples and thermistor, etc.). Non-contact thermal measurement methods have thus become prevalent for the thermal characterization of micro-/nanomaterials [1,2]. Non-contact methods mainly benefit from the laser heating source and thermally induced phenomena, which can be detected from a distance [3–11]. Based on the features of the phenomena, the widely adopted non-contact thermal methods are typically divided into three types: time-domain techniques, frequency-domain techniques, and spectroscopy [1].

Among these techniques, time-domain thermoreflectance (TDTR) [7,12,13] and frequency-domain thermoreflectance (FDTR) [14,15] detect the temperature rise by sensing changes in the surface optical properties in the time and frequency domains. They utilize an ultrafast heating pulse to generate a nanometer-level thermal penetration depth and thus have a good ability to measure the in-plane and out-of-plane thermal conductivity for thin films and bulks. The obvious drawbacks of these two methods are that they require smooth surfaces and post-processing. The photoacoustic (PA) method is a frequency-domain method that measures the surface temperature by detecting the sound waves produced by the work done by the periodical thermal expansion of the heated surface [3]. Avoiding the mechanical piston effect induced by the thermal expansion of the heated surface, the modulation frequency of the heating laser is limited so that it is lower than the order of

10 kHz [9,11,16]. The PA method can work well with micrometer-thick films and bulks due to the long thermal penetration depth at a lower frequency [9]. Furthermore, as it is limited by the microphone, the PA method is usually deployed at room temperature [3,9,11]. The laser flash method [17,18] involves heating a suspended material on the front side and analyzing the transient temperature rise in the time domain from the back based on the thermal radiation. Compared with the PA method, the laser flash method can be used with a wide temperature range from -125 to 2800 °C [1]. However, this method has thickness limitations with regard to samples [19,20]. More recently, Raman-based thermal methods have become popular due to its feature of being material-specific. The steady-state Raman method has a simple physical mechanism for thermal characterization [21,22], while the transient Raman method offers high accuracy in measurement results [8,23–31]. It is notable that the temperature probing depth with the Raman method is usually tens of nanometers. It is less often used to measure the thermal properties of thick films or bulks. More comprehensive reviews of general photothermal technologies can be found in [1,2].

In this paper, a short review is provided for the photothermal (PT) technique based on thermal radiation established in Wang's lab [32,33]. This PT technique stems from PA technology. However, in contrast to PA technology, PT technique acquires the frequency-domain thermal radiation instead of sound waves, which can reduce the complexity of the measurement setup and widen the temperature range for thermal measurement, as the microphone is no longer necessary. Furthermore, it has no frequency limitation and, thus, can theoretically measure samples with thicknesses ranging from nanoscale to bulk. The PT method also has a low requirement for smooth surfaces when compared to thermoreflectance methods because it detects thermal radiation rather than reflections. In Sections 2 and 3, the theory and a typical experimental setup for PT technique are introduced. Section 4 discusses the application of PT technique in the thermal characterization of micro-/nanomaterials, especially the measurement of thermophysical properties and structure probing. Furthermore, considerations for the thermal measurement of micro-/nanomaterials using PT technique are also discussed.

2. PT Theory for Thermal Property Measurements

The PT technique developed in Wang's lab employs a periodically modulated laser source to heat a solid surface. In each period, the surface temperature immediately rises after heating is applied. The speed and intensity of the thermal response of the surface are strongly dependent on the thermal properties of the materials under the surface. Thermal radiation due to surface temperature rise carries important information regarding the thermal properties of the materials and structures beneath, both for homogeneous and multilayered structures.

2.1. Physical Model Derivation

PT technique stems from the physical model of PA technology proposed by Rosencwaig et al. [3], which is a one-dimensional cross-plane heat conduction model in a multilayered structure, as shown in Figure 1a. The model requires that the size of the heating source be much larger than heat diffusion length in each layer, so that the in-plane heat conduction can be safely neglected and the generated heat conducts one-dimensionally along the cross-plane direction. Furthermore, the surface temperature rise should be moderate, and the heat loss through thermal convection and radiation is reasonably negligible. Hence, the governing equation of 1D cross-plane heat conduction under periodical heating is

$$\frac{\partial^2 \theta_i}{\partial x^2} = \frac{1}{\alpha_i}\frac{\partial \theta_i}{\partial t} - \frac{\beta_i I_0}{2\kappa_i}\exp\left(\sum_{m=i+1}^{N} -\beta_m L_m\right) \times e^{\beta_i(x-l_i)}(1 + e^{j\omega t}), \tag{1}$$

The subscript i means that the physical properties are for a certain layer i; therefore, $\theta_i = T_i - T_{amb}$ is the temperature rise of layer i and T_{amb} is the ambient temperature. I_0 is the incident laser power and ω is the angular frequency ($2\pi f$) corresponding to the modulation frequency f. α_i, κ_i, and β_i are the thermal diffusivity, thermal conductivity, and optical absorption coefficient for layer i. $L_i = l_i - l_{i-1}$ is the thickness of layer i, where l_i is the surface location of layer i on the x axis in Figure 1. j is $\sqrt{-1}$. A detailed derivation of Equation (1) is provided in [9].

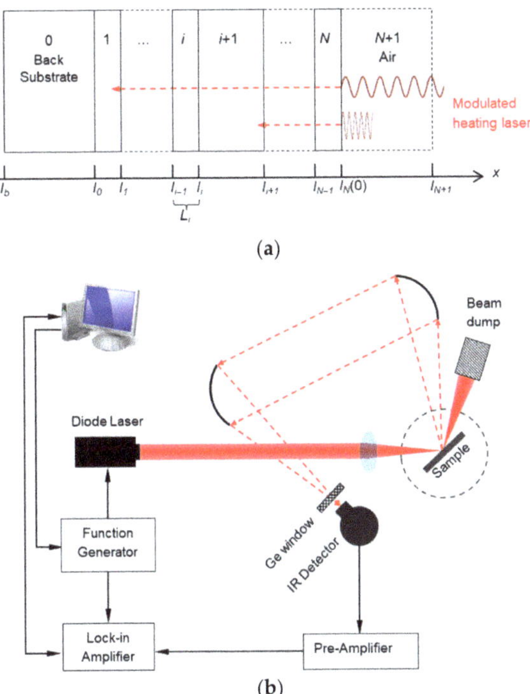

Figure 1. Physical schematics of PT technique: (**a**) mechanism of modulated heating and 1D heat conduction across the multilayered structure; (**b**) a typical experimental setup for PT technique.

The resultant surface temperature rise θ_i for layer i gradually increases from zero to a new steady state with fluctuations. Thus, θ_i can be divided into three components: the transient component, $\theta_{i,t}$; the steady DC component, $\overline{\theta}_{i,s}$; and the steady AC component, $\widetilde{\theta}_{i,s}$. $\theta_{i,t}$ represents the initial temperature rise immediately after the laser heating is applied. When the sample reaches the steady state, $\overline{\theta}_{i,s}$ indicates the steady state temperature, while $\widetilde{\theta}_{i,s}$ is the fluctuation in temperature due to the modulated heating source. $\widetilde{\theta}_{i,s}$ is easily determined by a lock-in amplifier at a set modulation frequency. It has an explicit expression as follows:

$$\widetilde{\theta}_{i,s} = [A_i e^{\sigma_i(x-l_i)} + B_i e^{-\sigma_i(x-l_i)} - E_i e^{\beta_i(x-l_i)}]e^{j\omega t}, \tag{2}$$

where $E_i = G_i/(\beta_i^2 - \sigma_i^2)$ with $G_i = \beta_i I_0/(2k_i)\exp\left(-\sum_{m=i+1}^{N}\beta_m L_m\right)$, and for $I < N$, $G_N = \beta_N I_0/2k_N$, and $G_{N+1} = 0$. σ_I is $(1+j)\cdot a_i$, where $a_i = 1/\mu_i$ is the thermal diffusion coefficient and $\mu_i = \sqrt{\alpha_i/\pi f}$ is the thermal diffusion length.

A_i and B_i are important coefficients derived from the interfacial transmission matrix of heating U and the absorption matrix of light V:

$$\begin{bmatrix} A_i \\ B_i \end{bmatrix} = U_i \begin{bmatrix} A_{i+1} \\ B_{i+1} \end{bmatrix} + V_i \begin{bmatrix} E_i \\ E_{i+1} \end{bmatrix}, \tag{3}$$

where U_i and V_i from layer $i + 1$ to I are

$$U_i = \frac{1}{2}\begin{bmatrix} u_{11,i} & u_{12,i} \\ u_{21,i} & u_{22,i} \end{bmatrix}; \ V_i = \frac{1}{2}\begin{bmatrix} v_{11,i} & v_{12,i} \\ v_{21,i} & v_{22,i} \end{bmatrix}, \tag{4}$$

where

$$u_{1n,i} = (1 \pm k_{i+1}\sigma_{i+1}/k_i\sigma_i \mp k_{i+1}\sigma_{i+1}R_{i,i+1}) \times \exp(\mp\sigma_{i+1}L_{i+1}), \ n = 1,\ 2, \tag{5}$$

$$u_{2n,i} = (1 \pm k_{i+1}\sigma_{i+1}/k_i\sigma_i \mp k_{i+1}\sigma_{i+1}R_{i,i+1}) \times \exp(\mp\sigma_{i+1}L_{i+1}), \ n = 1,\ 2, \tag{6}$$

$$v_{n1,i} = 1 \mp \beta_i/\sigma_i, \ n = 1,\ 2, \tag{7}$$

and

$$v_{n2,i} = (-1 \mp k_{i+1}\beta_{i+1}/k_i\sigma_i \mp k_{i+1}\beta_{i+1}R_{i,i+1}) \times \exp(-\beta_{i+1}L_{i+1}), \ n = 1,\ 2. \tag{8}$$

$R_{i,i+1}$ is the thermal contact resistance between layer i and $(i + 1)$. It is noticeable that the thermal and optical properties of the materials in the multilayered structure are all included in Equations (5)–(8). Thus, the thermal properties are closely related to the temperature rise $\widetilde{\theta}_{i,s}$ of the layer i.

Under the assumption that the front air layer and back substrate are thermally thick—that is, $|\sigma_0 L_0| \gg 1$ and $|\sigma_{N+1}L_{N+1}| \gg 1$—$A_{N+1}$ and B_0 are equal to zero. Then, applying the interfacial condition between layer i and $(i + 1)$,

$$k_i\frac{\partial\widetilde{\theta}_{i,s}}{\partial x} - k_{i+1}\frac{\partial\widetilde{\theta}_{i+1,s}}{\partial x} = 0 \tag{9}$$

$$\text{and } k_i\frac{\partial\widetilde{\theta}_{i,s}}{\partial x} + \frac{1}{R_{i,i+1}}\left(\widetilde{\theta}_{i,s} - \widetilde{\theta}_{i+1,s}\right) = 0, \tag{10}$$

the solved A_i and B_i are

$$\begin{bmatrix} A_i \\ B_i \end{bmatrix} = \left(\prod_{m=i}^{N} U_m\right)\begin{bmatrix} 0 \\ B_{N+1} \end{bmatrix} + \sum_{m=i}^{N} \left(\prod_{k=i}^{m-1} U_k\right)V_m\begin{bmatrix} E_m \\ E_{m+1} \end{bmatrix} \tag{11}$$

$$B_{N+1} = -\frac{[0 \ \ 1]\sum_{m=0}^{N}\left(\prod_{i=0}^{m-1} U_i\right)V_m\begin{bmatrix} E_m \\ E_{m+1} \end{bmatrix}}{[0 \ \ 1]\left(\prod_{i=0}^{m-1} U_i\right)\begin{bmatrix} 0 \\ 1 \end{bmatrix}} \tag{12}$$

By substituting A_i, B_i, and E_i into Equation (2), we can obtain the temperature distribution in any layer of interest. This greatly increases the flexibility of the PT method. For the purpose of non-contact measurement, an infrared detector is usually employed to gather the surface radiation from either the front or back.

2.2. Phase Shift and Amplitude

The AC temperature rise component $\widetilde{\theta}_{i,s}$ has two critical properties, amplitude and phase. Compared with the original periodical heating source, the occurrence of temperature rises and thermal radiation is delayed by the heat conduction inside the multilayered structure. Correspondingly, the phase of the radiation is slower than the phase of the heating source, and the difference (phase shift) between these two can be deducted to be $Arg(B_{N+1}) - \pi/4$. According to Equation (12), the thermal properties are included in B_{N+1}. Measurement based on the phase shift—the phase shift method—can be used to accurately evaluate the thermal properties of a specific layer and the interfacial thermal conductance in the multilayered structure due to the high sensitivity of ~0.1° [32]. However, for bulk materials with a smooth surface, it becomes a constant of $-45°$ [16]. In contrast, the amplitude of thermal radiation is proportional to the temperature rise. Since the thermal diffusion depth is different with different modulation frequencies, the amplitude of the thermal radiation changes against the frequency. Alternatively to the phase shift method, measurement based on the amplitude is able to determine the thermal properties of the bulk materials.

3. Experimental Implementation of PT Method for Thermal Property Measurements

3.1. Experimental Setup

A typical measurement setup using the PT technique developed in Wang's lab [11] is shown in Figure 1b. The function generator-modulated diode laser (at a visible wavelength) is focused on a sample surface by using a focal lens to heat the sample. Then, a pair of off-axis parabolic mirrors collect the raised thermal radiation resulting from the temperature rise and send it to an infrared (IR) detector. Along with the radiation collection, the diffuse reflection of the incident laser from the surface is also gathered. Though the IR detector is much less sensitive to the visible wavelength, the reflection is still much stronger than the radiation. Thus, an IR window (germanium (Ge) window in Figure 1b) is placed in front of the detector to eliminate the visible diffuse reflection and let only the thermal radiation enter into the detector. The radiation-converted voltage signal is then intensified in a preamplifier and finally analyzed in a lock-in amplifier to extract the phase shift and the amplitude when compared with the reference signal from the function generator.

When using PT technique, given that the unexpected, complex photon–electron–phonon process may occur under laser irradiation in the sample, especially for semiconductors, a metal coating (usually gold, aluminum, etc.) is applied to the sample surface to act as a well-defined energy absorber and heater. The coating is optically thick and can totally absorb the incidence. At the same time, it is thermally thin and has a negligible effect on heat conduction (phase shift). It is physically understandable that the heat diffusion length/depth in the multilayered structure should be controllable by changing the modulating frequency. The selection of the modulating frequency of the heating laser needs to be evaluated in advance because the sample layer in the multilayered structure should be involved in the heat conduction.

3.2. System Calibration

The raw data recorded by the lock-in amplifier—the phase shift ϕ_{raw} and amplitude A_{raw}—are not available for direct analysis because the measurement system induces additional errors in the raw data (the phase shift and amplitude). For example, the optical path and electric devices involved raise an additional time delay in the phase shift, and the fluctuations in the laser power, as well as the optical path, cause unexpected variations in amplitude. Thus, calibration of the measurement system is necessary to exclude these effects from the raw data. The diffuse reflection of the incident laser is measured to calibrate the measurement system, since it passes through the same path as the thermal radiation does. The calibrated phase shift ϕ_{cal} and amplitude A_{cal} are shown in Figure 2. To calibrate ϕ_{raw}, the absolute phase shift due to heat conduction is quickly determined as $\phi_{nor} = \phi_{raw} - \phi_{cal}$. For the amplitude, it is more complicated. The amplitude is affected by not only the laser power and attenuation in the optical path but also the modulation frequency f. Xu et al. proposed the equation $A_{nor} = A_{raw} \cdot \sqrt{f} / A_{cal}$ to normalize A_{raw} and exclude all the possible errors induced by the system, detailed in [33]. The calibrated A_{nor} is approximated to ζ / e_t, where ζ is a system-related constant and the effusivity $e_t = \sqrt{\kappa \rho c_p}$. It directly correlates A_{nor} with the thermal properties. After calibration, ϕ_{nor} and A_{nor} can be used to determine the thermal properties of the materials of interest.

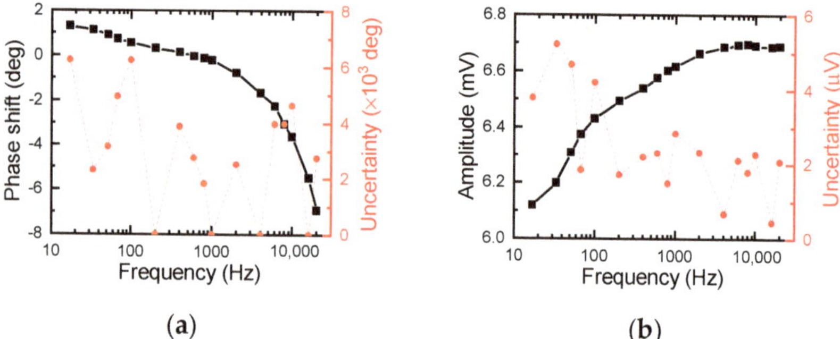

Figure 2. The calibration of a typical experimental setup for PT technique: (**a**) phase shift and (**b**) amplitude. The black square is the measured phase shift and amplitude, and the red dot denotes the measurement uncertainty of the phase shift and amplitude.

3.3. Uncertainty

During the data measurement, different heat conduction processes occur when the modulation frequency is changed. Then, the thermal properties can be determined by fitting the temperature variation against the frequencies. Wang et al. found that the uncertainty is related to the ratio of the thermal diffusion length μ_i to the layer thickness L_i [11]. Based on their SiO_2/Si sample, the numerical uncertainty for the phase shift method was around $\pm5\%$ when μ_i and L_i were in the same order, and it increased to $\pm15\%$ when μ_i/L_i was around 100. For the case in which μ_i/L_i was less than 0.15, the thermal energy would not diffuse across the SiO_2 layer. The phase shift method would not be suitable for this case, while the amplitude method showed a $\pm10\%$ uncertainty. Xu et al. studied a similar SiO_2/Si sample and achieved an experimental uncertainty of 5% based on the phase shift method and 10% with the amplitude method [33]. For thermal contact resistance measurement, the experimental sensitivity and uncertainty were limited by the uncertainty in the thermal conductivity discussed above. The sensible limit was reported to be 10^{-8} m^2K/W [11] for the phase shift method and 10^{-7} m^2K/W [33] for the amplitude method. Since the thermal contact resistance fell in the range of 10^{-9}–10^{-7} m^2K/W, the amplitude method was not sensitive to the thermal contact resistance. It could thus accurately measure the thermal conductivity without knowledge of the interface.

4. PT Measurement of Nanomaterials

When the characteristic lengths of materials are reduced to the micro-/nanoscale, the thermal properties also significantly decrease due to the size effect. Based on this fact, investigation of thermal properties can be an efficient supplementary way to characterize the micro-/nanostructure in addition to the most commonly used micro-/nanoscale imaging.

4.1. Nanostructure Analysis through Thermal Characterization

Wang et al. [32,34] adopted the PT method and studied the axial thermal conductivity of multiwall carbon nanotubes (CNTs) prepared using plasma-enhanced chemical vapor deposition (PECVD). The CNT sample for PT measurement was composed of three layers. As in Figure 3a, the layers from top to bottom were a thin silicon wafer (14 μm thick), a layer of chromium (Cr, 70 nm thick), and the layer of vertically aligned CNTs. Between the Cr layer and CNTs, there was a thin nickel (Ni) film of a negligible thickness, which offered seeds for CNTs' growth. The Si wafer was transparent to the incident laser wavelength (1064 nm) and thermal radiation. Therefore, the incident laser heated the Cr film, the partial generated heat was conducted along the axial direction of the CNTs, and the radiation from the Cr surface was analyzed to obtain the axial thermal conductivity of the CNTs. The resultant thermal conductivity of 27.3 W/m·K was dramatically lower than the theoretical thermal conductivity of 1600–6600 W/m·K for single-wall CNTs, where phonons can conduct heat in a perfect wall plane. Combined with the TEM result for the CNTs, it was found that the special structure of the Ni seeds led to the CNTs' walls being tilted with respect to the tube axis, as shown in Figure 3b. This unexpected structure raised a large number of boundaries along the axial direction and thus reduced the axial thermal conductivity of the CNTs. Here, though the PT method measured the CNTs' axial thermal conductivity as a bulk, the result greatly helped interpret the special growth mechanism of the CNTs.

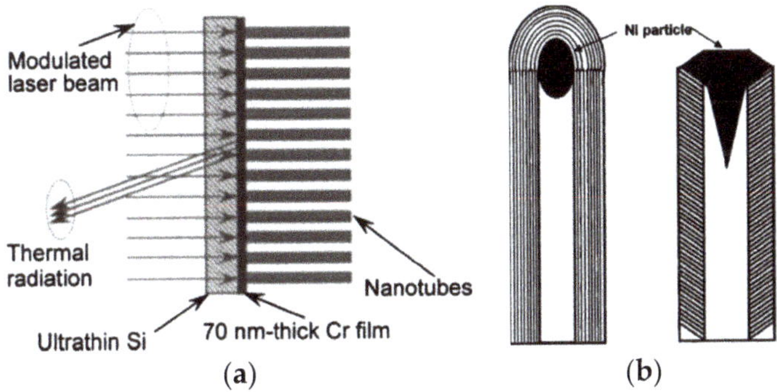

Figure 3. Thermal and structural characterization of CNTs: (a) multilayered structure of CNTs; (b) schematics of CNTs' wall growth on a Ni particle with a special structure. Reprinted with permission from Ref. [32], Copyright (2022), AIP Publishing.

4.2. Porosity Determination in Nanostructures

For loosely assembled nanoparticles, porosity is an important parameter demonstrating the quality of the assembly, but it is hard to measure by mapping only the surface. Pores and cavities in the nanostructure generate additional defects and boundaries and then reduce the thermal properties of the assembled nanostructure. Based on this mechanism, Chen et al. [35] measured the effective thermal conductivity and volumetric heat capacity of a hydrogenated vanadium-doped magnesium (V-doped Mg) porous nanostructure using PT technique. Under the effect of cavities on the V-doped Mg composite (MgH_2 was the main component), the effective volumetric heat capacity was apparently lower than that of the MgH_2 bulk counterpart. The volumetric heat capacity ratio of nanostructure to bulk helped further reveal the porosity level φ of the nanostructure. The determined porosity level was validated through SEM observation. The porosity level φ was estimated to be 25–42% from SEM, and the φ calculated from the PT results was 9.0–39.4%, with an upper limit falling into the range of the SEM observation. It should be noted that the SEM observation scale (microscale) was much smaller than that probed with PT technique (~millimeter scale). Thus, the PT-determined porosity level is more applicable when the size of nanostructured assemblies reaches the macroscale. The intrinsic thermal conductivity of the solid part of the porous nanostructure was then determined to be ~3.5 W/m·K, while it had been ~1.9 W/m·K before excluding the effect of the cavities. PT technique provides a new and convenient way to characterize the porosity level of porous nanostructures, as well as intrinsic thermal conductivity.

4.3. Nano-Crystalline Structure Evolution under Heating

Heat treatment facilitates the transformation between amorphous and crystalline structures. It is hard to observe this kind of structural transformation with conventional imaging methods. Thermal properties can again be a good indicator showing the variation in the state of the crystalline structure because the amorphous and crystalline structures of the same material have differences in their thermal conductivities. Xu et al. [36] applied the PT method to study internal structure transformations of spider silk proteins under heat treatment based on thermal effusivity. Two spider silk protein films prepared from two different types of spiders, *N. clavipes* and *L. Hesperus*, were studied, as shown in Figure 4. When elevating the heating temperature, the thermal effusivity of the protein films significantly increased because of the transformation from random coils (amorphous structure) to α-helices and antiparallel β-sheets (crystalline structure). Supplementary Raman studies of the films showed that the characteristic peak of protein started to shift when the heating temperature reached 60 °C. In the heating process in this low temperature range (lower than 60 °C), the increase in crystallinity was the main reason accounting for the increase in the thermal effusivity. As the temperature increased to more than 80 °C, the Raman characteristic peaks disappeared because the crystalline structures were destroyed due to H-bond breaking among molecular chains. Increases in both thermal conductivity (fewer boundaries) and volumetric heat capacity quickened the increasing rate of the thermal effusivity from 100 to 120 °C. In this work, the Raman spectra of the protein films were strongly affected by fluorescence induced by surface carbonization, especially in the high temperature range, while the thermal effusivity from the PT technique continuously responded well to the structure variation across the whole temperature range. Thus, PT technique could be a good candidate for nanostructure investigation when conventional methods are not applicable.

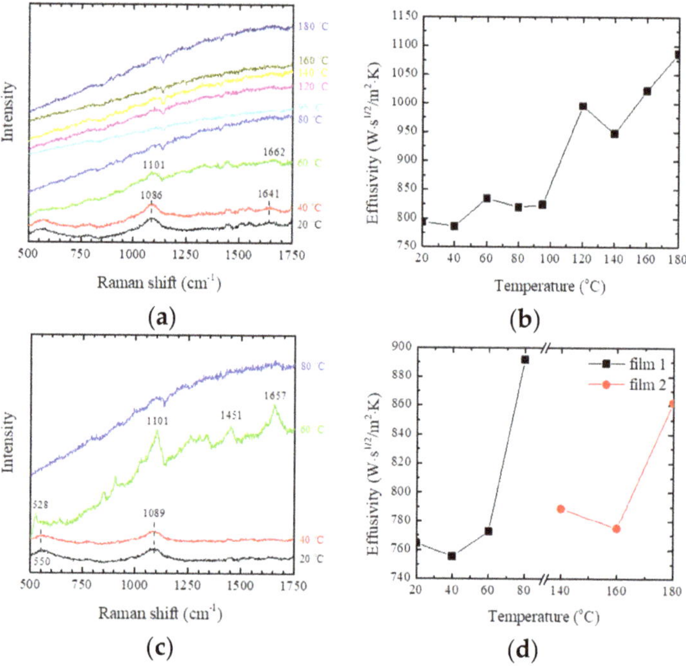

Figure 4. Thermal and structural characterization of spider silk protein film: (**a**) Raman spectra and (**b**) PT determined thermal effusivity of *N. clavipes* spider silk protein film; (**c**) Raman spectra and (**d**) PT determined thermal effusivity of *L. Hesperus* spider silk protein film. Reprinted with permission from Ref. [36], Copyright (2022), Elsevier.

4.4. Considerations in the Measurement of Micro-/Nanomaterials

The abovementioned PT technique is able to measure the cross-plane thermal conductivity, heat capacity (ρc_p), and thermal contact resistance for a multilayered sample under the assumption of 1D heat conductance along the thickness direction. From Equations (5)–(8), it can be seen that the method determines the absolute value of thermal resistance for conductance (the sum of L/κ and R) and heat capacitance ($L\rho c_p$). For a certain layer i with a thin thickness L_i, when its thermal resistance (L_i/κ_i) is much smaller than the uncertainty ΔR of R, R will dominate the variation in the PT signal and the change in L_i/κ_i will not be sensed. The minimum thickness in the PT method should thus be larger than $\Delta R \cdot \kappa_i$. As alternatives, the TDTR and FDTR methods employ an ultrafast pulsed laser (femtosecond to nanosecond) to realize a nanometer-level thermal penetration depth and, thus, the thermal measurement of nanometer-thick coatings [14]. Raman-based thermal methods measure temperature according to the variation in the materials' characteristic peaks in the Raman spectrum. They are available for both suspended and supported films and need no metal coating on the top of samples [24,26,30,37,38].

Another concern about the PT method is the in-plane thermal conductivity. As described in the physical model, the heating laser spot size should be larger than the in-plane thermal diffusion length in each layer so that the 1D model is valid. However, if the sample has a high in-plane thermal conductivity (such as graphene, etc.), the 1D model is violated. A direct solution is to build a 3D heat conduction model and also consider the spatial distribution of the heating laser [39,40]. For suspended samples, the evaluation of the transient term in Equation (2) in the time domain and the steady-state temperature field mapping can be used achieve in-plane thermal conductivity measurement using the current experimental setup. Moreover, other methods, such as the TDTR [41], FDTR [14], and Raman-based thermal methods [25,42,43], can achieve both kinds of in-plane thermal conductivity measurement.

Furthermore, infrared thermal radiation is not material-specific. When measuring an individual nanostructure, such as a single nanoparticle, an IR detector may gather the thermal radiation from the nanoparticle and its surroundings/supporting materials. The determined thermal properties are thus averages one rather than the properties for a specific nanostructure. In contrast, Raman spectroscopy has a fingerprint feature and can respond to temperature changes and detect the temperature rise for individual micro-/nanostructures [24,38,44–47].

5. Conclusions

In this paper, we reviewed the physical mechanism of PT technique for thermal property measurement and its practical application in the thermal characterization of nanomaterials. With PT technique, the phase shift method provides a high sensitivity to the thermal properties while the amplitude method can measure thermal conductivity without considering interfacial contact. Utilizing the dependency of thermal properties on the internal structure of materials, PT technique has shown its unique capabilities for nanostructure investigation where commonly used micro-/nanoscale imaging technologies might not be applicable. Though limitations exist, PT technique is quite mature. Future application of PT technique can be extended to thermal property and structure detection beneath the surface.

Author Contributions: Conceptualization, S.X.; writing—original draft preparation, J.Z.; writing—review and editing, S.X. and J.L.; supervision, S.X.; funding acquisition, S.X. All authors have read and agreed to the published version of the manuscript.

Funding: This review work was funded by National Natural Science Foundation of China, grant number 52106220 (for S.X.), and the Program for Professor of Special Appointment (Eastern Scholar) at Shanghai Institutions of Higher Learning (for S.X.).

Institutional Review Board Statement: Not applicable.

Informed Consent Statement: Not applicable.

Data Availability Statement: Not applicable.

Conflicts of Interest: The authors declare no conflict of interest.

References

1. Abad, B.; Borca-Tasciuc, D.A.; Martin-Gonzalez, M.S. Non-contact methods for thermal properties measurement. *Renew. Sustain. Energy Rev.* **2017**, *76*, 1348–1370. [CrossRef]
2. Liu, J.; Han, M.; Wang, R.; Xu, S.; Wang, X. Photothermal phenomenon: Extended ideas for thermophysical properties characterization. *J. Appl. Phys.* **2022**, *131*, 065107. [CrossRef]
3. Rosencwaig, A.; Gersho, A. Theory of the photoacoustic effect with solids. *J. Appl. Phys.* **1976**, *47*, 64–69. [CrossRef]
4. Campbell, S.D.; Yee, S.S.; Afromowitz, M.A. Applications of Photoacoustic-Spectroscopy to Problems in Dermatology Research. *IEEE Trans. Biomed. Eng.* **1979**, *26*, 220–227. [CrossRef]
5. Bennett, C.A.; Patty, R.R. Thermal Wave Interferometry—A Potential Application of the Photo-Acoustic Effect. *Appl. Opt.* **1982**, *21*, 49–54. [CrossRef]
6. Lin, H.; Wang, R.; Zobeiri, H.; Wang, T.; Xu, S.; Wang, X. The in-plane structure domain size of nm-thick MoSe$_2$ uncovered by low-momentum phonon scattering. *Nanoscale* **2021**, *13*, 7723–7734. [CrossRef]
7. Zhu, J.; Tang, D.; Wang, W.; Liu, J.; Holub, K.W.; Yang, R. Ultrafast thermoreflectance techniques for measuring thermal conductivity and interface thermal conductance of thin films. *J. Appl. Phys.* **2010**, *108*, 094315. [CrossRef]
8. Zobeiri, H.; Wang, R.; Wang, T.; Lin, H.; Deng, C.; Wang, X. Frequency-domain energy transport state-resolved Raman for measuring the thermal conductivity of suspended nm-thick MoSe$_2$. *Int. J. Heat Mass Transf.* **2019**, *133*, 1074–1085. [CrossRef]
9. Hu, H.; Wang, X.; Xu, X. Generalized theory of the photoacoustic effect in a multilayer material. *J. Appl. Phys.* **1999**, *86*, 3953–3958. [CrossRef]
10. Hu, H.; Zhang, W.; Xu, J.; Dong, Y. General analytical solution for photoacoustic effect with multilayers. *Appl. Phys. Lett.* **2008**, *92*, 014103. [CrossRef]
11. Wang, X.; Hu, H.; Xu, X. Photo-Acoustic Measurement of Thermal Conductivity of Thin Films and Bulk Materials. *J. Heat Trans.* **2001**, *123*, 138–144. [CrossRef]
12. Cahill, D.G. Analysis of heat flow in layered structures for time-domain thermoreflectance. *Rev. Sci. Instrum.* **2004**, *75*, 5119–5122. [CrossRef]
13. Capinski, W.S.; Maris, H.J.; Ruf, T.; Cardona, M.; Ploog, K.; Katzer, D.S. Thermal-conductivity measurements of GaAs/AlAs superlattices using a picosecond optical pump-and-probe technique. *Phys. Rev. B* **1999**, *59*, 8105–8113. [CrossRef]
14. Schmidt, A.J.; Cheaito, R.; Chiesa, M. A frequency-domain thermoreflectance method for the characterization of thermal properties. *Rev. Sci. Instrum.* **2009**, *80*, 094901. [CrossRef]
15. Regner, K.T.; Sellan, D.P.; Su, Z.; Amon, C.H.; McGaughey, A.J.H.; Malen, J.A. Broadband phonon mean free path contributions to thermal conductivity measured using frequency domain thermoreflectance. *Nat. Commun.* **2013**, *4*, 1640. [CrossRef]
16. Wang, X.; Cola, B.A.; Bougher, T.; Hodson, S.L.; Fisher, T.S.; Xu, X. Photoacoustic technique for thermal conductivity and thermal interface measurements. *Annu. Rev. Heat Trans.* **2013**, *16*, 135–157. [CrossRef]
17. Parker, W.J.; Jenkins, R.J.; Butler, C.P.; Abbott, G.L. Flash Method of Determining Thermal Diffusivity, Heat Capacity, and Thermal Conductivity. *J. Appl. Phys.* **1961**, *32*, 1679–1684. [CrossRef]
18. Ohta, H.; Shibata, H.; Suzuki, A.; Waseda, Y. Novel laser flash technique to measure thermal effusivity of highly viscous liquids at high temperature. *Rev. Sci. Instrum.* **2001**, *72*, 1899–1903. [CrossRef]
19. Lindemann, A.; Blumm, J.; Brunner, M. Current limitations of commercial laser flash techniques for highly conducting materials and thin films. *High Temp. High Press.* **2014**, *43*, 243–252.
20. Larson, K.B.; Koyama, K. Correction for finite-pulse-time effects in very thin samples using the flash method of measuring thermal diffusivity. *J. Appl. Phys.* **1967**, *38*, 465–474. [CrossRef]
21. Tang, X.; Xu, S.; Zhang, J.; Wang, X. Five orders of magnitude reduction in energy coupling across corrugated graphene/substrate interfaces. *ACS Appl. Mater. Interfaces* **2014**, *6*, 2809–2818. [CrossRef] [PubMed]
22. Yue, Y.; Zhang, J.; Wang, X. Micro/nanoscale spatial resolution temperature probing for the interfacial thermal characterization of epitaxial graphene on 4H-SiC. *Small* **2011**, *7*, 3324–3333. [CrossRef] [PubMed]
23. Xu, S.; Fan, A.; Wang, H.; Zhang, X.; Wang, X. Raman-based Nanoscale Thermal Transport Characterization: A Critical Review. *Int. J. Heat Mass Transf.* **2020**, *154*, 119751. [CrossRef]
24. Xu, S.; Wang, T.; Hurley, D.; Yue, Y.; Wang, X. Development of time-domain differential Raman for transient thermal probing of materials. *Opt. Express* **2015**, *23*, 10040–10056. [CrossRef] [PubMed]
25. Yuan, P.; Wang, R.; Wang, T.; Wang, X.; Xie, Y. Nonmonotonic thickness-dependence of in-plane thermal conductivity of few-layered MoS$_2$: 2.4 to 37.8 nm. *Phys. Chem. Chem. Phys.* **2018**, *20*, 25752–25761. [CrossRef] [PubMed]
26. Yue, X.F.; Wang, Y.Y.; Zhao, Y.; Jiang, J.; Yu, K.; Liang, Y.; Zhong, B.; Ren, S.T.; Gao, R.X.; Zou, M.Q. Measurement of interfacial thermal conductance of few-layer MoS$_2$ supported on different substrates using Raman spectroscopy. *J. Appl. Phys.* **2020**, *127*, 104301. [CrossRef]
27. Zhang, X.; Sun, D.; Li, Y.; Lee, G.H.; Cui, X.; Chenet, D.; You, Y.; Heinz, T.F.; Hone, J.C. Measurement of Lateral and Interfacial Thermal Conductivity of Single- and Bilayer MoS$_2$ and MoSe$_2$ Using Refined Optothermal Raman Technique. *ACS Appl. Mater. Inter.* **2015**, *7*, 25923–25929. [CrossRef]
28. Zobeiri, H.; Hunter, N.; Van Velson, N.; Deng, C.; Zhang, Q.; Wang, X. Interfacial thermal resistance between nm-thick MoS$_2$ and quartz substrate: A critical revisit under phonon mode-wide thermal non-equilibrium. *Nano Energy* **2021**, *89*, 106364. [CrossRef]

29. Zobeiri, H.; Hunter, N.; Wang, R.; Wang, T.; Wang, X. Direct Characterization of Thermal Nonequilibrium between Optical and Acoustic Phonons in Graphene Paper under Photon Excitation. *Adv. Sci.* **2021**, *8*, 2004712. [CrossRef]

30. Zobeiri, H.; Wang, R.; Zhang, Q.; Zhu, G.; Wang, X. Hot carrier transfer and phonon transport in suspended nm WS_2 films. *Acta Mater.* **2019**, *175*, 222–237. [CrossRef]

31. Zobeiri, H.; Xu, S.; Yue, Y.; Zhang, Q.; Xie, Y.; Wang, X. Effect of temperature on Raman intensity of nm-thick WS_2: Combined effects of resonance Raman, optical properties, and interface optical interference. *Nanoscale* **2020**, *12*, 6064–6078. [CrossRef] [PubMed]

32. Wang, X.; Zhong, Z.; Xu, J. Noncontact thermal characterization of multiwall carbon nanotubes. *J. Appl. Phys.* **2005**, *97*, 064302. [CrossRef]

33. Xu, S.; Wang, X. Across-plane thermal characterization of films based on amplitude-frequency profile in photothermal technique. *AIP Adv.* **2014**, *4*, 107122. [CrossRef]

34. Xu, Y.; Zhang, Y.; Suhir, E.; Wang, X. Thermal properties of carbon nanotube array used for integrated circuit cooling. *J. Appl. Phys.* **2006**, *100*, 074302. [CrossRef]

35. Chen, X.; He, Y.; Zhao, Y.; Wang, X. Thermophysical properties of hydrogenated vanadium-doped magnesium porous nanostructures. *Nanotechnology* **2009**, *21*, 055707. [CrossRef]

36. Xu, S.; Xu, Z.; Starrett, J.; Hayashi, C.; Wang, X. Cross-plane thermal transport in micrometer-thick spider silk films. *Polymer* **2014**, *55*, 1845–1853. [CrossRef]

37. Yuan, P.; Tan, H.; Wang, R.; Wang, T.; Wang, X. Very fast hot carrier diffusion in unconstrained MoS_2 on a glass substrate: Discovered by picosecond ET-Raman. *RSC Adv.* **2018**, *8*, 12767–12778. [CrossRef]

38. Yuan, P.; Wang, R.; Tan, H.; Wang, T.; Wang, X. Energy Transport State Resolved Raman for Probing Interface Energy Transport and Hot Carrier Diffusion in Few-Layered MoS_2. *ACS Photonics* **2017**, *4*, 3115–3129. [CrossRef]

39. Cole, K.D.; McGahan, W.A. Theory of Multilayers Heated by Laser Absorption. *J. Heat Trans.* **1993**, *115*, 767–771. [CrossRef]

40. Machlab, H.; McGahan, W.A.; Woollam, J.A.; Cole, K. Thermal characterization of thin films by photothermally induced laser beam deflection. *Thin Solid Films.* **1993**, *224*, 22–27. [CrossRef]

41. Koh, Y.K.; Bae, M.-H.; Cahill, D.G.; Pop, E. Heat conduction across monolayer and few layer graphenes. *Nano Lett.* **2010**, *10*, 4363–4368. [CrossRef] [PubMed]

42. Wang, T.; Han, M.; Wang, R.; Yuan, P.; Xu, S.; Wang, X. Characterization of anisotropic thermal conductivity of suspended nm-thick black phosphorus with frequency-resolved Raman spectroscopy. *J. Appl. Phys.* **2018**, *123*, 145104. [CrossRef]

43. Wang, R.; Zobeiri, H.; Lin, H.; Qu, W.; Bai, X.; Deng, C.; Wang, X. Anisotropic thermal conductivities and structure in lignin-based microscale carbon fibers. *Carbon* **2019**, *147*, 58–69. [CrossRef]

44. Li, C.; Xu, S.; Yue, Y.; Yang, B.; Wang, X. Thermal characterization of carbon nanotube fiber by time-domain differential Raman. *Carbon* **2016**, *103*, 101–108. [CrossRef]

45. Wang, T.; Xu, S.; Hurley, D.H.; Yue, Y.; Wang, X. Frequency-resolved Raman for transient thermal probing and thermal diffusivity measurement. *Opt. Lett.* **2016**, *41*, 80–83. [CrossRef]

46. Yuan, P.; Liu, J.; Wang, R.; Wang, X. The hot carrier diffusion coefficient of sub-10 nm virgin MoS_2: Uncovered by non-contact optical probing. *Nanoscale* **2017**, *9*, 6808–6820. [CrossRef]

47. Wang, R.; Wang, T.; Zobeiri, H.; Yuan, P.; Deng, C.; Yue, Y.; Xu, S.; Wang, X. Measurement of the thermal conductivities of suspended MoS_2 and $MoSe_2$ by nanosecond ET-Raman without temperature calibration and laser absorption evaluation. *Nanoscale* **2018**, *10*, 23087–23102. [CrossRef]

 *nanomaterials*

Review

Methods for Measuring Thermal Conductivity of Two-Dimensional Materials: A Review

Huanyu Dai and Ridong Wang *

State Key Laboratory of Precision Measuring Technology and Instruments, Tianjin University, Tianjin 300072, China; huanyu_dai2266@tju.edu.cn
* Correspondence: rdwang@tju.edu.cn

Abstract: Two-dimensional (2D) materials are widely used in microelectronic devices due to their excellent optical, electrical, and mechanical properties. The performance and reliability of microelectronic devices based 2D materials are affected by heat dissipation performance, which can be evaluated by studying the thermal conductivity of 2D materials. Currently, many theoretical and experimental methods have been developed to characterize the thermal conductivity of 2D materials. In this paper, firstly, typical theoretical methods, such as molecular dynamics, phonon Boltzmann transport equation, and atomic Green's function method, are introduced and compared. Then, experimental methods, such as suspended micro-bridge, 3ω, time-domain thermal reflectance and Raman methods, are systematically and critically reviewed. In addition, the physical factors affecting the thermal conductivity of 2D materials are discussed. At last, future prospects for both theoretical and experimental thermal conductivity characterization of 2D materials is given. This paper provides an in-depth understanding of the existing thermal conductivity measurement methods of 2D materials, which has guiding significance for the application of 2D materials in micro/nanodevices.

Keywords: 2D materials; thermal conductivity; molecular dynamics; Raman spectroscopy

Citation: Dai, H.; Wang, R. Methods for Measuring Thermal Conductivity of Two-Dimensional Materials: A Review. *Nanomaterials* **2022**, *12*, 589. https://doi.org/10.3390/nano12040589

Academic Editor: Gyaneshwar P. Srivastava

Received: 31 December 2021
Accepted: 28 January 2022
Published: 9 February 2022

Publisher's Note: MDPI stays neutral with regard to jurisdictional claims in published maps and institutional affiliations.

1. Introduction

The thermal conductivity of 2D materials is of great significance for both basic research [1–10] and practical application [11–13]. In basic research, Fourier's law has been successful in studying heat conduction in macroscopic systems. However, when down to micro or nanoscale, due to the existence of size effect [1], thermal rectification [2], and ballistic transport [3], this law is no longer usable. In addition, with the advent of new materials such as newly discovered borophene [4,5], MXene [6,7], and various heterostructures [8–10], it is also crucial to determine the thermal conductivity of these new materials. From a practical perspective, 2D materials are widely used in optoelectronic devices [11], biological monitoring [12], and energy storage [13] due to their excellent optical, electrical, and mechanical properties. It is necessary to explore the thermal conductivities of these 2D materials to optimize heat dissipation in optoelectronic devices.

Various theoretical calculation methods such as molecular dynamics simulation [14–17], phonon Boltzmann transport equation [18–23], and atomistic Green's functions [24–26] have been developed to study the underlying physical mechanism of heat transfer in 2D materials. Yet, due to the ignorance of surface defects, the accuracy of these methods is limited. Experimental methods, such as the suspended micro-bridge method [27–32], 3ω method [33–36], time-domain thermoreflectance method [37–46], and Raman method [47–53], have been developed to study the thermal conductivity of 2D materials. Bao et al. [54] introduced heat transfer research methods in micro-nano structures from the perspective of theoretical calculation. Experimental-based thermal characterization techniques for low-dimensional materials were also reviewed [55,56]. Considering all these different techniques, however, there is still a lack of comprehensive review on the thermal conductivity measurement methods of 2D materials. In this paper, both theoretical and experimental methods for studying the thermal conductivity of 2D materials are reviewed. In addition, the factors affecting the thermal conductivity of 2D materials are also discussed.

2. Theoretical Methods

The theoretical calculation is an effective way to deeply understand the potential mechanism of phonon transport in 2D materials. Currently, the molecular dynamics (MD) simulation, phonon Boltzmann transport equation (PBTE), and atomistic Green's functions (AGF) were the 3 mainstream theoretical methods.

2.1. MD Simulation

In MD simulation, the motion of each particle in the dynamic process was described based on Newton's second law, and the position, velocity, and force of each atom were calculated at each step. The interatomic forces were derived from the potential function, and the commonly used empirical potential functions were Lennard–Jones (LJ) potential for interlayer van der Waals (vdW) interaction, Stillinger–Weber (SW) [15] potential for atomic interaction, and REBO potential [16] for the covalent bonding of the carbon atoms in diamond and graphite. Two common methods were used to calculate the thermal conductivity of 2D materials: the equilibrium MD (EMD) method based on the Green–Kubo formalism and the nonequilibrium MD (NEMD) method based on Fourier's law.

In EMD method, the thermal conductivity is expressed as the integration of the heat current autocorrelation function (HCACF) with respect to a given correlation time t,

$$\kappa_{\mu v}(t) = \frac{1}{\kappa_B T^2 V} \int_0^t \langle J_\mu(0) J_v(t') \rangle dt' \tag{1}$$

where κ_B is Boltzmann's constant, T is the absolute temperature of the system, V is the volume and J_μ is the μth component of the full heat current vector J. The heat current at a given time depends on the positions and velocities of the particles in the system. The key point of EMD based thermal conductivity calculation is to calculate the time integral with the upper limit of infinity in Equation (1) and ensure its convergence. In addition, the size effect of thermal conductivity is also difficult to be studied in EMD, which can be solved in NEMD. The NEMD technique can be employed to characterize the in-plane thermal conductivity of a sample with finite length L by driving the system out of equilibrium. When steady state is achieved after sufficient time, the heat current (flux) Q and temperature gradient ∇T are obtained to calculate thermal conductivity $\kappa(L)$ according to Fourier's law:

$$\kappa(L) = -\frac{Q}{\nabla T} \tag{2}$$

For the MD method, one advantage is that the simulation is based on a real physical model in space, which makes it convenient to study the effects of physical parameters, such as strain, defect, doping, etc. However, the accuracy of MD simulation is highly dependent on the potential empirical function used, which is usually developed by fitting the existing material properties. Moreover, as the MD method is modeled in real space, the calculation range is limited due to the simulation time, which makes the calculation of thermal conductivity not very accurate. In addition, the phonon scattering rate in MD is related to the Maxwell Boltzmann distribution while ignoring the quantum effect below the Debye temperature. Thus, erroneous results were obtained for the calculated thermal conductivity below the Debye temperature [17].

2.2. PBTE Method

Recently, PBTE, combined with first principles, was used much more frequently to explore the thermal conductivity of non-metallic materials, such as 2D selinene [18], phosphorene [19], borophane [20], and transition metal dichalcogenide (TMDC) MX_2 [21].

Under the effect of temperature gradient (∇T), the phonon distribution f_λ deviates from the Bose–Einstein distribution in equilibrium f_λ^0, which can be obtained by solving PBTE:

$$\left.\frac{\partial f_\lambda}{\partial t}\right|_{\text{diff}} + \left.\frac{\partial f_\lambda}{\partial t}\right|_{\text{scatt}} = 0 \tag{3}$$

where the diffusion term ($\left.\frac{\partial f_\lambda}{\partial t}\right|_{\text{diff}}$) is caused by the temperature gradient ∇T and given by:

$$\left.\frac{\partial f_\lambda}{\partial t}\right|_{\text{diff}} = -v_\lambda \nabla T \frac{\partial f_\lambda^0}{\partial T} \tag{4}$$

where v_λ is the group velocity of phonon mode λ. The scattering term ($\left.\frac{\partial f_\lambda}{\partial t}\right|_{\text{scatt}}$) in Equation (5) is determined by the scattering process in the system. Under the relaxation time approximation (RTA), the scattering term can be written as:

$$\left.\frac{\partial f_\lambda}{\partial t}\right|_{\text{scatt}} = \frac{f_\lambda - f_\lambda^0}{\tau_\lambda} \tag{5}$$

where τ_λ is the relaxation time. Considering anharmonic phonon–phonon interactions τ_λ can be obtained by perturbation theory. The heat flow J^α in α direction can be written as:

$$J^\alpha = \sum_\lambda \int \hbar \omega_\lambda f_\lambda v_\lambda^\alpha \frac{dk}{2\pi^3} \tag{6}$$

where k denotes the phonon wave vector, ω_λ is the frequency of phonon mode. According to Fourier's law $J^\alpha = -\sum_\beta \kappa^{\alpha\beta}(\nabla T)^\beta$, the lattice thermal conductivity tensor $\kappa^{\alpha\beta}$ under the RTA can be written as:

$$\kappa^{\alpha\beta} = \frac{1}{k_B T^2 N V}\sum_\lambda (\hbar \omega_\lambda)^2 f_\lambda^0 (1 + f_\lambda^0) v_\lambda^\alpha v_\lambda^\beta \tau_\lambda \tag{7}$$

where N is the total number of phonon wave vectors included in the summation, V is the volume of the unit cell, v_λ^α and v_λ^β are the group velocity of phonon mode λ with Cartesian coordinates indexed by α and β, respectively. In the actual simulation, the parameters v_λ^α and v_λ^β were obtained from the interatomic force constants (IFCs), which can be extracted from DFT packages such as VASP. Some open-source software packages such as ShengBTE [22] were available to predict the lattice thermal conductivity of solid materials with the input files of these IFCs.

In PBTE, the calculation accuracy depends on the accuracy of the scattering mechanism in the 2D material. Anharmonicity causes inelastic scattering of phonons. Meanwhile, many factors such as isotopes, holes, and interfaces may disturb the lattice vibration. At present, PBTE lacks the description of some scattering mechanisms, such as holes [23].

2.3. AGF Method

The AGF method, which is based on a dynamical equation and the quantum mechanical phonon energy distribution, is an effective tool to simulate ballistic transport in nanoscale devices. As shown in Figure 1, the quantum thermal transport system can be divided into 3 parts: central scattering region (abbreviated as C), left and right lead (abbreviated as L, R). Under the harmonic approximation, the phonon waves in the system can be described as:

$$(\omega^2 I - H)\Phi(\omega) = 0 \tag{8}$$

where ω is the angular frequency of lattice vibration, I is the identity matrix, H is the harmonic matrix, and $\Phi(\omega)$ is the eigenvector of H. The response of the system under small disturbance can be obtained by Green's function:

$$(\omega^2 I - H)G = 0 \tag{9}$$

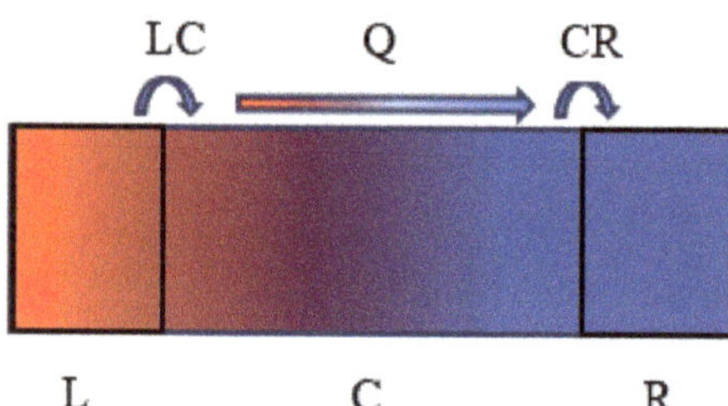

Figure 1. Schematic diagram of heat transport model for low dimensional system. (The L, C and R in the figure represents three parts of the system: central scattering region, left and right lead, and Q indicates the direction of heat flow).

The atomic interactions in each region are described by constructing a harmonic matrix for AGF calculation [24]. The phonon transmission function $\Xi(\omega)$ is calculated by:

$$\Xi(\omega) \ = \ Tr[\Gamma_L G_C^r \Gamma_R G_C^{r*}] \tag{10}$$

where G_C^r and G_C^{r*} are the Green's function of the central region and its complex conjugate [25], Γ_L and Γ_R are phonon escape rates from left contact and right contact, and Tr represents the trace of the matrix.

According to the Landauer formula and the phonon transmission function, the thermal conductivity κ of the system can be calculated as:

$$\kappa \ = \ \frac{\hbar}{2\pi} \int_0^\infty \frac{\partial f(\omega, T)}{\partial T} \Xi(\omega) \omega d\omega \tag{11}$$

where $f(\omega, T)$ is the Bose–Einstein distribution and $\hbar$ is the Planck's constant. AGF studies the thermal conductivity based on the harmonic approximation condition and does not consider the anharmonic interaction, that is, phonon–phonon scattering. Therefore, AGF, which studies the structure dominated by elastic scattering, is mainly used in nanostructures dominated by harmonic scatterings, such as defects, interfaces, lattice mismatch [26].

3. Experimental Methods

The theoretical simulation methods, including MD, PBTE, and AGF, have become effective tools for calculating the thermal conductivity of 2D materials. However, it is challenging to ensure the accuracy when considering the impurities, defects, and rough surface of real samples. That is, it is of great significance to developing experimental methods to improve the measuring accuracy. The measuring accuracy can also be further improved by combining the experimental methods with the theoretical calculation. At present, experimental measurement methods mainly include electro-thermal and optothermal methods.

3.1. Electro-Thermal Techniques

Electro-thermal techniques, which include the suspended micro-bridge method, 3ω method, electron beam self-heating, T-bridge, four-probe transport measurements techniques, characterize the thermal conductivities of materials based on the temperature dependence of thermal resistance. The suspended micro-bridge method and 3ω method are two typical techniques and are introduced in detail.

3.1.1. Suspended Micro-Bridge Method

The suspended micro-bridge method was first used by Majumdar et al. [27,28] in 2001 to measure the thermal conductivity of a single multi-walled nanotube. Since then, the suspended micro-bridge method has been applied to measure the thermal conductivities of graphene [29], hexagonal boron nitride [30], MoS$_2$ [31] and other 2D materials. As shown in Figure 2, the suspended device is composed of 2 adjacent silicon nitride (SiNx) membranes suspended by 5 SiNx beams. The platinum resistance thermometer coil designed on each membrane is connected to the substrate through a platinum (Pt) leads on the long SiNx beam. A mixed current of DC (microampere level) and AC (nano ampere level) is introduced to the heating membrane.

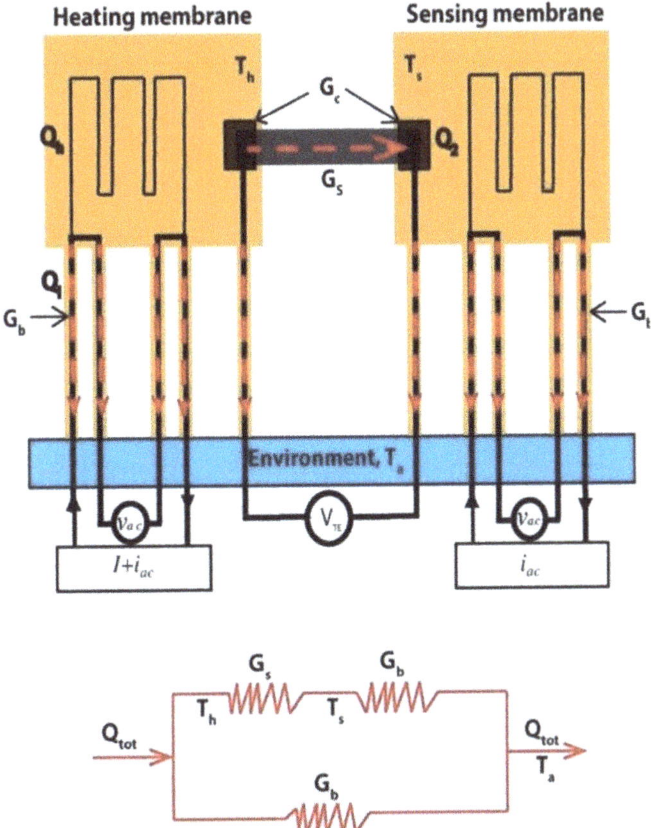

Figure 2. Schematic diagram of microbridge measurement. Reprinted with permission from Ref. [32]. Copyright 2017, John Wiley and Sons.

The DC current is used to generate Joule heat (Q_{tot}) on one side, and the Pt resistance is measured by AC to characterize the temperature change (ΔT_h, ΔT_s) of heating and sensing membrane caused by Q_{tot}. Heat is transferred between the heating membrane and the sensing membrane only through the sample. Since the Q_{tot} is transferred only from the heating membrane to the substrate with an environment temperature T_a and sample, we can express the heat flux distribution on the whole device and sample as follows:

$$Q_{tot} = Q_1 + Q_2 \tag{12}$$

$$Q_1 = G_b \times \Delta T_h \tag{13}$$

$$Q_2 = G_s(\Delta T_h - \Delta T_s) = G_b \times \Delta T_s \tag{14}$$

where Q_{tot} is the total heat on the heating membrane, Q_1 and Q_2 are the heat transferred from the heating membrane to the substrate and the sample, G_s and G_b are the conductance of the sample and SiNx beams, respectively. The thermal conductivity (κ) of the sample can be written as:

$$\kappa = G_s \frac{L}{S} \tag{15}$$

where L and S are the length and sectional area of the sample, respectively. In practice, there is thermal resistance (R_c) at the interface between the sample and the heating/sensing membrane. The measured total thermal resistance is $R = R_G + 2R_C$, where R_G is the actual thermal resistance of the sample. Some methods have been designed to reduce the effect of R_C. One is to calculate the temperature rise between the sample and membrane through numerical simulation [30]. In addition, it can be considered to add high thermal conductivity materials to the membrane to reduce R_C and improve the uniformity of membrane temperature [29].

3.1.2. 3ω Method

The 3ω method is based on the frequency-domain feedback characteristic that the temperature of the heating resistor varies with the frequency of the applied AC electrical current. As shown in Figure 3a, a metal electrode such as Pt with a certain shape and thickness (the yellow part) was prepared on the surface of the thin film sample (the blue part) by photolithography and thermal evaporation, which was used both as a heater and a thermometer. Thin-film samples are usually deposited on the substrate (the bottom gray part) by chemical vapor deposition (CVD) and high-temperature oxidation. When an AC power supply with a frequency of 1ω is connected to the metal electrode, the internal resistance of the metal electrode changes approximately at a frequency of 2ω due to the linear relationship with the temperature change. Finally, the voltage signal with 3ω frequency variation can be extracted by the lock-in amplifier (shown in Figure 3b).

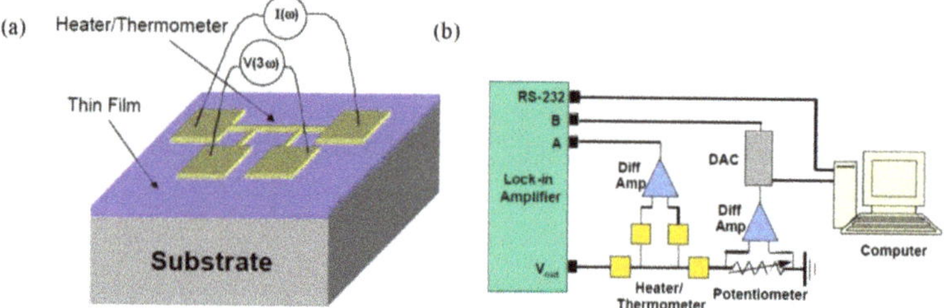

Figure 3. Schematic diagram of (**a**) 3ω method. (**b**) experimental circuit. Reprinted with permission from Ref. [33]. Copyright 2008, AIP Publishing.

In this technique, 2 structures were prepared: substrate and film-substrate structure. Metal electrodes were deposited on the 2 structures to measure the corresponding temperature changes (ΔT_s, ΔT_{s+f}). Then, temperature change caused by the film can be written as $\Delta T_f = \Delta T_{s+f} - \Delta T_s$. The thermal conductivity (κ_f) of a thin film is determined using Equation (16)

$$\kappa_f = \frac{Pt}{\Delta T_f \cdot S} \tag{16}$$

where P and t are heating power and film thickness, respectively.

For the 3ω method, thermal contact resistance measurements between graphene and SiO_2 based on a differential 3ω technique were made [34]. However, as the fabrication of a metal electrode with high quality and the signal extraction of the phase-locked amplifier were required, it was difficult to measure the thermal conductivity of 2D material with atomic level thickness. Zhang et al. [35] reported the thermal conductivity measurement of 100 nm thickness silicon nitride (SiN) and 64 nm thickness amorphous boron nitride (BN) based on the 3ω method. As the thermal conductivity was obtained by the frequency-dependent temperature oscillation, the 3ω method was free of the effect from contact thermal resistance between sample and substrate. Then, due to the small surface area of metal electrode, the effect of heat radiation was also limited [36]. The 3ω method also has some drawbacks that further limit its application for supported samples. The thermal conductivity of the substrate should be much higher than that of the film deposited on it to ensure a high sensitivity. A lower surface roughness of the sample is needed to prevent damage to the thin metal wires.

3.2. Opto-Thermal Techniques

Compared with electrothermal method, opto-thermal techniques, which can realize non-contact measurement with simple sample preparation, have been widely used in thermal conductivity characterization of 2D materials. Two representative methods, time-domain thermoreflectance (TDTR) method, and Raman-based methods, are introduced in detail in this section.

3.2.1. Time-Domain Thermoreflectance (TDTR) Method

The TDTR method is based on the change of surface reflectance caused by temperature change. Figure 4a shows a typical setup. The emitted laser is divided into pump light and probe light through a polarizing beam splitter (PBS). The pump light modulated by the electro-optic modulator is used to heat the sample surface. The sample surface is usually covered with a metal film in order to ensure that the pump laser is absorbed at the surface. The detection beam is delayed relative to the pump light by the mechanical delay stage and received by the photodiode detector. The converted electrical signal is extracted by the lock-in amplifier with two outputs: in-phase (V_{in}) signal and out-of-phase (V_{out}) signal, which represent the phase of the reflected beam related to the temperature response and can be written as $R = -V_{in}/V_{out}$. By continuously changing the delay time, the curve of R versus time shown in Figure 4b can be obtained. Combined with the heat transfer model established by Cahil et al. [37] in 2004, the thermal conductivity can be extracted. Schmidt et al. [38] further applied the model in anisotropic thermal conduction of highly ordered pyrolytic graphite (HOPG).

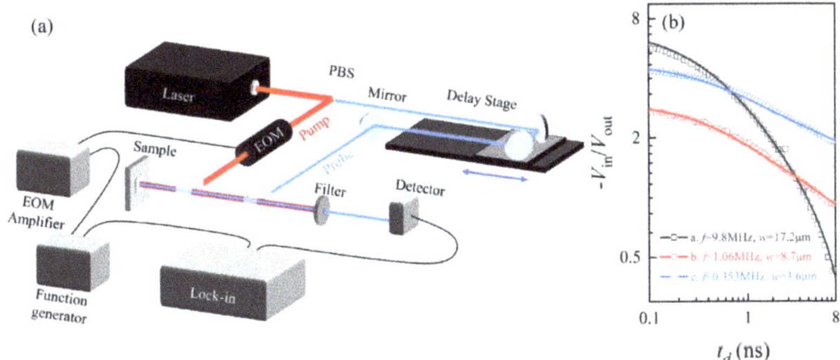

Figure 4. (**a**) Schematic of a typical TDTR setup. (**b**) The ratio between in-phase and out-of-phase signals, $-V_{in}/V_{out}$ as a function of delay time is compared with the thermal modeling to extract the thermal conductivity. Reprinted with permission from Ref. [39]. Copyright 2021, AIP Publishing.

In TDTR, due to the deposition of metal films on the sample surface, the intrinsic thermal conductivity of the sample cannot be measured accurately. The main limitation for

TDTR is the requirement for a highly smooth surface to minimize diffuse reflection and the complex experimental device. In the later development, many improvements were made based on TDTR, such as FDTR [40] TDTR based on time-resolved magneto-optical Kerr effect (TR-MOKE) [41]. In FDTR, the relationship between thermal reflection signal and modulation frequency rather than the delay time was established, in which continuous laser can be used thus it is simpler and cheaper. TDTR can also be combined with TR-MOKE to probe the sample's surface temperature, which depends on the temperature dependence of the polarization rather than the intensity of the reflected beam. This temperature measurement method allows us to use thinner ferromagnetic metal film as a transducer, reduces lateral heat flow in the metal film, and improves the accuracy of measurement results. Currently, for thermal conductivity measurement, the TDTR method is mostly used in thin films, such as transition metal dichalcogenides MX_2 (M = Mo, W and X = S, Se) [42], h-BN [43], BP [44], which requires a relatively large thickness (>100 nm). For 2D materials, this technique can realize the characterization of the interfacial heat transfer [45]. Additionally, FDTR, which is an improved TDTR method, is used in measuring the thermal conductivity of 2D materials. Rahman et al. [46] implemented frequency domain magnetooptical Kerr effect (FD-MOKE) to measure the thermal conductivity of various 2D materials, such as graphene, monolayer MoS_2, and four-layer h-BN.

3.2.2. Optothermal Raman Methods

Compared with the complex measurement device of TDTR, Raman-based methods are simpler and have been widely used in the thermal conductivity measurement of 2D materials. By constructing different heat transfer states in the time and space domain, various Raman-based measurement methods were developed. Among them, the optothermal Raman method based on steady-state heating is the most commonly used.

In this method, the sample can be heated optically or electrically. Taking optical heating as an example, Figure 5a shows the MoS_2 sample is suspended on a Si_2N_4 substrate and heated by a focused laser light. The heat can only diffuse around the sample and eventually to the substrate. As shown in Figure 5c, the Raman shift ($\Delta\omega$) of MoS_2 is linearly related to the local temperature change (ΔT) of the sample upon laser heating, and can be written as: $\Delta\omega = \chi_T \Delta T$, where χ_T is the first-order temperature coefficient. Varying laser power will also produce different thermal effects, which means that there is a similar linear relationship between Raman shift and laser power (Figure 5d). For the sample suspended on a hole with radius R, the temperature at r from the center of the hole can be calculated from the heat conduction equation as follows:

$$\kappa_{sus}\frac{1}{r}\frac{d}{dr}\left[r\frac{dT(r)}{dr}\right] + q(r) = 0, \text{ for } r \leq R \tag{17}$$

$$\kappa_{sup}\frac{1}{r}\frac{d}{dr}\left[r\frac{dT(r)}{dr}\right] + \frac{g}{t}[T(r) - T(a)] = 0, \text{ for } r \geq R \tag{18}$$

where κ_{sus}, κ_{sup}, $q(r)$, g, t and $T(a)$ are the thermal conductivity of suspended and supported structure, volume optical heating, interface thermal conductivity, thickness of sample and environmental temperature, respectively. Figure 5b shows the calculated temperature distribution of the sample. The weighted average temperature rise in the laser spot can be written as:

$$T_{calculated} \approx \frac{\int_0^R T(r)q(r)r\,dr}{\int_0^R q(r)r\,dr} \tag{19}$$

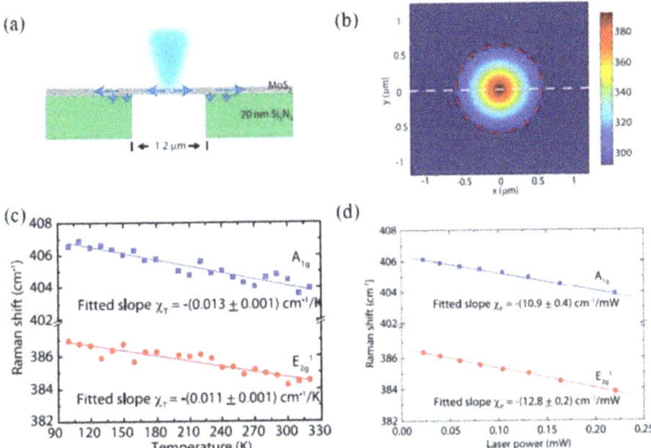

Figure 5. Illustration of optothermal Raman methods. (**a**) Schematic of the thermal conductivity measurement showing suspended MoS$_2$ flakes and excitation laser light. (**b**) Simulation of laser heating temperature rise. (**c**) Raman peak frequency shift as a function of temperature. (**d**) Experimental data for Raman shift as a function of laser power, which determines the local temperature rise in response to the dissipated power. Reprinted with permission from Ref. [47]. Copyright 2014, American Chemical Society.

By matching the calculated temperature rise ($T_{calculated} - T_a$) with the temperature rise measured by Raman spectroscopy ($\Delta T_{measured}$), the thermal conductivity κ can be extracted.

One drawback of optothermal Raman method is the measurement of absolute laser absorption power. Under laser heating, part of the energy is absorbed by the sample, while the rest of the energy is reflected by the sample or transmitted to the substrate. Currently, it is very difficult to determine the laser absorption coefficient accurately. In addition, a temperature calibration process, which is time-consuming and can introduce large errors, is also needed.

3.2.3. Time-Resolved Raman Methods

Time-domain differential Raman (TD-Raman) [48], which uses a square wave modulated laser with variable duty cycle, can be applied to measure the thermal conductivity of 2D materials. As shown in Figure 6a, the modulated laser is used for sample heating and Raman excitation, which consists of a variable excitation period t_e and a fixed thermal relaxation period t_r. Here, the thermal relaxation time t_r needs to be long enough for the sample to cool completely before the next pulse period. Figure 6b shows the corresponding temporally accumulative Raman spectra of one laser pulse cycle in 3 cases. It can be seen that longer excitation time t_e leads to higher temperature rise, and the corresponding Raman spectra also change. From cases 1 to 3, the intensity of the Raman peak increases gradually, and the softening phenomenon of Raman peak position is also observed. By analyzing the changes of Raman signals mentioned above, the average temperature rise ($\Delta \overline{T}$) of the sample in the heating zone can be determined by Raman spectroscopy. Moreover, the accumulative Raman emission for one excitation cycle ($0 \sim t_e$) is written as:

$$E_\omega(\omega, t_e) = I_0 \int_0^{t_e} (1 - A\Delta\overline{T}^*) \exp\left[-\frac{4ln2 \cdot (\omega - \omega_0 + B\Delta\overline{T}^*)^2}{(\Gamma_0 + C\Delta\overline{T}^*)^2} \right] dt \qquad (20)$$

where I_0, ω_0, Γ_0 are the corresponding Raman properties at the beginning of laser heating, A, B, C are the changing rate of Raman intensity, Raman shift, and linewidth against the normalized temperature $\Delta\overline{T}^*$. Combining with the transient heat transfer model, the thermal conductivity of the sample can be determined by fitting the variation of Raman peak with time.

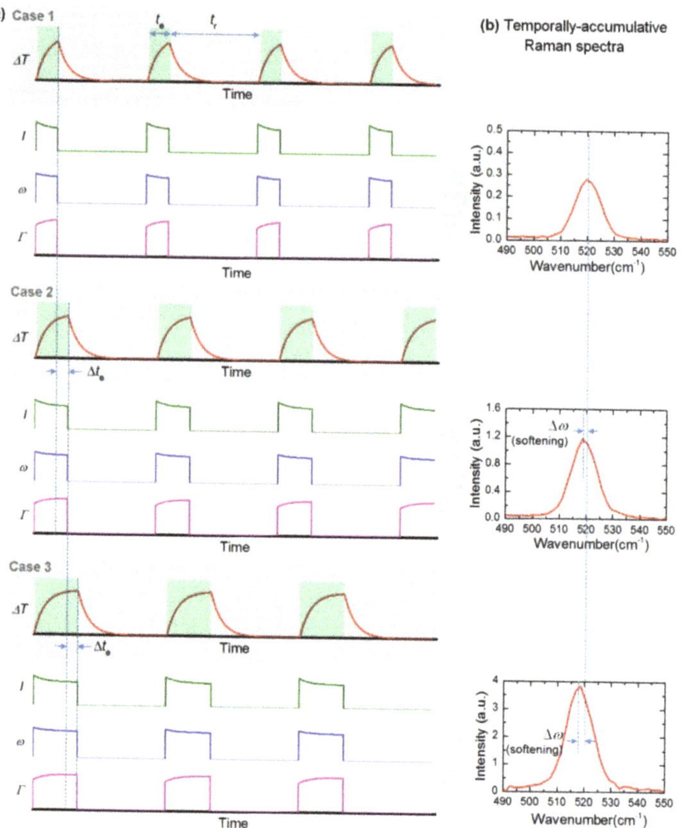

Figure 6. Concept of TD−Raman. (**a**) The change of temperature evolution(ΔT), and instant changes of Raman peak intensity (I), peak shift (ω) and linewidth (Γ). (**b**) The corresponding temporally accumulative Raman spectra of one laser pulse cycle in Case 1, 2, and 3. Reprinted with permission from Ref. [48] © The Optical Society. Copyright 2015, The Optical Society.

In TD-Raman, thermal conductivity of 2D materials is measured through the Raman characterization of transient heat transfer. However, in practice, when the heating time is too short, a long time of Raman signal acquisition is needed, which makes it hard for fast thermal transport characterization produces more environmental interference and affects the measurement accuracy. To solve this problem, Wang's lab further developed frequency-resolved (FR) Raman technique Frequency-resolved Raman for transient thermal probing and thermal diffusivity measurement [49]. As shown in Figure 7, an amplitude-modulated square-wave with different frequencies is employed to heat the sample and excite Raman signals. When the sample is irradiated by the high-frequency laser pulse, the temperature of the sample is almost constant in the whole process, which is defined, as "quasi-steady state," and the temperature rise is regarded as ΔT_{qs}. On the contrary, when low-frequency laser pulse irradiates the sample because the sample has enough time to rise to a stable state in the excitation time, the temperature of the sample is approximately regarded as a constant in the excitation time, which is defined as "steady state," and the temperature rise is regarded as ΔT_s. Here we have $\Delta T_{qs} = \Delta T_s/2$, which shows that the temperature decreases with increasing frequency. The thermal conductivity can be extracted based on the transient heat transfer model and the collected Raman signal. TD-Raman has been applied to the measurement of the anisotropic thermal conductivity of black phosphorus [50]. Compared with TD-Raman, the Raman signal collection of FR-Raman is more efficient, but the sensitivity is lower because the time between pulses is not enough to completely cool the sample.

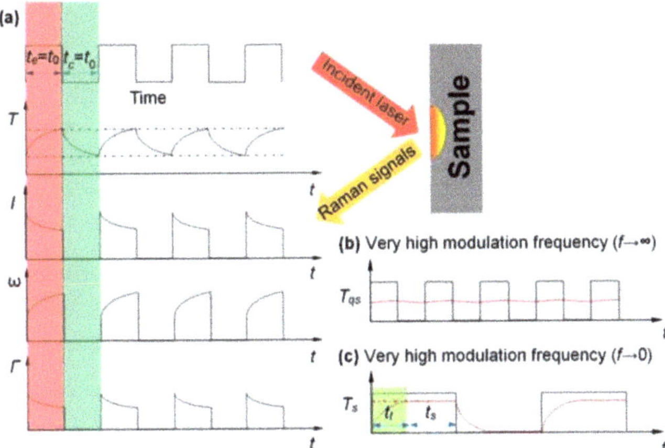

Figure 7. Concept of FR-Raman. (**a**) Time profiles of laser pulse, temperature evolution (T), Raman peak intensity (I), peak shift (ω) and linewidth (Γ). (**b**) Temperature variation (T_{QS}) at quasi-steady state. (**c**) Temperature variation (T_S) at very low frequency. Reprinted with permission from [49] © The Optical Society. Copyright 2016, The Optical Society.

3.2.4. Energy Transport State Resolved Raman (ET-Raman)

Besides the time-domain modulation, the energy transport states can also be modulated in the spatial domain. Based on this, a technique named ET-Raman was developed to measure the in-plane thermal conductivities of supported or suspended 2D materials. For supported 2D samples, both a CW laser and a picosecond laser are used. As shown in Figure 8, 5 energy transport states were constructed both in time and spatial domains [51]. Three physical processes occur with laser heating. The first is hot carrier generation, diffusion in space, and electron–hole recombination. This process introduces heat transfer and energy redistribution, which is determined by the hot carrier diffusivity (D). The subsequent process is the heat conduction by phonons, which receives energy from the hot carriers or electron–hole recombination, which mainly happens in the in-plane and depends on the thermal conductivity (κ). The third is the heat conduction from sample to substrate, and this process is dominated by the local thermal resistance (R).

By using different laser power (P), a parameter named Raman shift power coefficient (RSC) can be obtained and expressed as: $\chi = \partial\omega/\partial P$, where ω is Raman peak shift. Moreover, χ is determined by κ, D, R, laser absorption coefficient and temperature coefficient of Raman shift. According to the 5 heating states in Figure 8, 3 normalized RSC were obtained: $\Theta_n = \chi_{cw,n}/(\chi_{ps1} - \chi_{ps2})$, $n = 1, 2, 3$. The error caused by laser absorption, Raman temperature coefficient were eliminated. Meanwhile, the heat accumulation effect was removed by the difference of the heating between the 2 objectives ($50\times$, $100\times$) under picosecond pulse laser. Then, a 3D numerical model was employed to determine κ, D and R. Figure 9 shows the evolution of the distribution of $\Omega(\kappa, D, R)$. Yuan et al. measured that the in-plane thermal conductivity spans from 31.0 to 76.2 W/(m·K) of 2D few layers MoS_2 samples (thickness ranging from 2.4 nm to 37.8 nm) supported on a glass substrate by 5 state picosecond ET-Raman method.

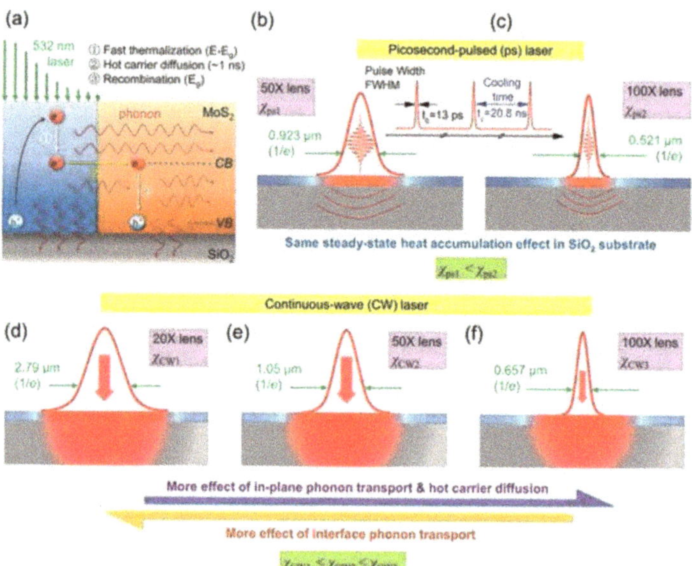

Figure 8. The Schematic diagram for mechanism of five-state energy transport state-resolved Raman (ET-Raman) technique. (**a**) The generation, diffusion, and recombination of the hot carrier in MoS$_2$ upon laser irradiating. (**b,c**) Transient state heating using picosecond laser heating under 50× and 100× objective lenses. (**d–f**) Steady state heating using CW laser with 20×, 50×, and 100× objective lenses. Reproduced from Ref. [51] with permission from the Royal Society of Chemistry. Copyright 2018, Royal Society of Chemistry.

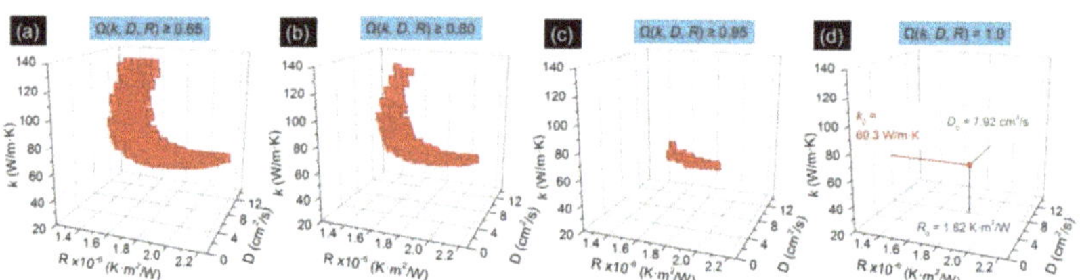

Figure 9. The evolution of distribution of $\Omega(\kappa, D, R)$. (**a**) $\Omega(\kappa, D, R) \leq 0.65$; (**b**) $\Omega(\kappa, D, R) \geq 0.80$; (**c**) $\Omega(\kappa, D, R) \geq 0.95$; (**d**) $\Omega(\kappa, D, R) = 1.0$. Reproduced from Ref. [51] with permission from the Royal Society of Chemistry.

Due to the short pulse interval, the picosecond laser, which would generate heat accumulation in the suspended structure, is replaced by a nanosecond laser. As shown in Figure 10, Zobeiri et al. measured the κ and D of suspended WS$_2$ by constructing 3 heating states with a continuous laser and a nanosecond pulse laser [52]. The influence of κ and D can be distinguished by changing the size of the heating area with a different objective lens. Similarly, 3 RSCs were defined: ψ_{CW}, ψ_{ns20} and ψ_{ns100}. Two normalized RSCs were further defined: $\Theta_{20} = \psi_{ns20}/\psi_{CW}$ and $\Theta_{100} = \psi_{ns100}/\psi_{CW}$. Theoretical values Θ under different κ and D values were obtained by temperature rise simulation under 3 states, and the matching κ and D were obtained by comparing with the experimental values. The thermal conductivity of suspended WS$_2$ was observed to increase from 15.1 to 38.8 W/(m·K) as the sample thickness increased from 13 nm to 107 nm with nanosecond ET-Raman technique.

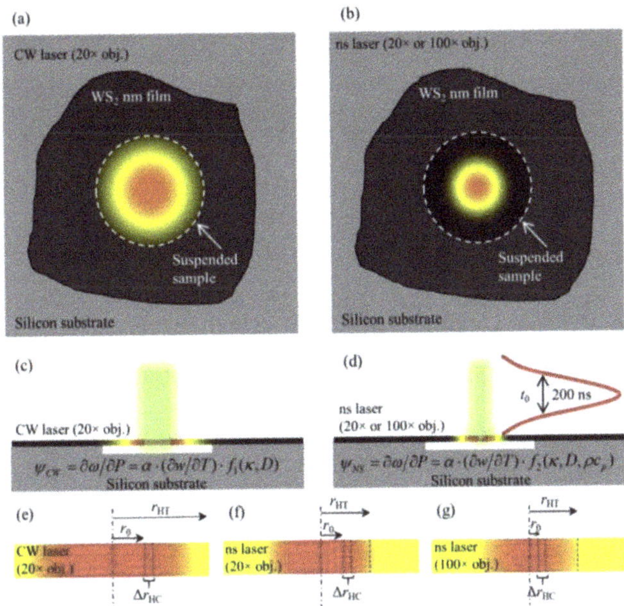

Figure 10. (**a**,**b**) Schematic diagram of suspended WS$_2$ illuminated by continuous and nanosecond lasers. (**c**,**d**) Energy transport states are constructed by continuous and nanosecond lasers in the temporal and spatial domain. (**e**–**g**) Thermal diffusion length, laser radius, and carrier diffusion length under three states. Reprinted with permission from Ref. [52]. Copyright 2019, Elsevier.

Since the Raman signal comes from optical phonons (OPs), but the heat transfer in the sample is related to acoustic phonons (APs). Considering the measurement error caused by ignoring the temperature difference between the 2 phonons, Wang et al. developed 6 heating states nanosecond ET-Raman technique by changing the objective lens: 3 steady states and 3 transient states, and realized the measurement of intrinsic κ of MoS$_2$ and MoSe$_2$ nanofilms and phonon coupling factors [53]. As shown in Figure 11a, the Raman spectrum reflects the temperature rise (ΔT_m) of OPs, which is the sum of the temperature difference (ΔT_{OA}) between OPs and APs and the temperature rise (ΔT_{AP}) of APs. Figure 11b shows that the ΔT_{OA} decreases to zero faster than ΔT_{AP}, which means that phonon coupling between OPs and APs is negligible when the laser spot is very large. Figure 11c shows the ΔT_m with different laser spot radius, which can be written as:

$$\Delta T_m = \Delta T_{OA} + \Delta T_{AP} \propto A r_0^{-2} + f(\kappa) \cdot r_0^{-n} \ (n < 2) \tag{21}$$

where r_0 is the laser spot radius, and $f(\kappa)$ is a function of thermal conductivity κ. Based on this more accurate temperature rise fitting process, the intrinsic thermal conductivity of the sample is approximately extracted.

In order to compare the different experimental methods for measuring the thermal conductivity of 2D materials much more conveniently, these methods are summarized in Table 1. The thermal conductivity values of 2D materials with a similar thickness measured by different experimental methods were quite different, which may be attributed to the differences in sample quality and different measurement methods.

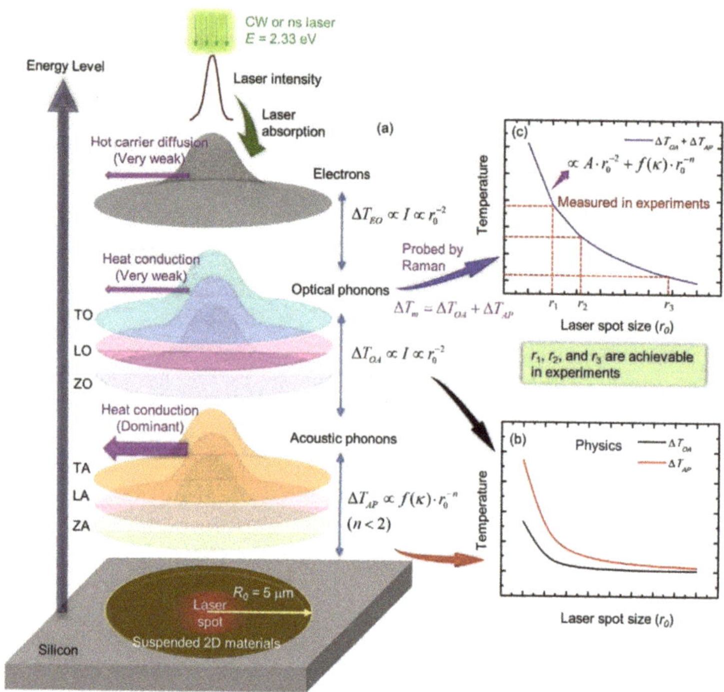

Figure 11. (**a**) Energy transport process among different energy carriers in suspended 2D materials under laser irradiation. (**b**) The temperature difference between OP and AP against laser spot size. (**c**) Acquisition of thermal conductivity of 2D materials and coupling coefficient between OP and AP. Reprinted with permission from Ref. [53]. Copyright 2020, John Wiley and Sons.

Table 1. Application and comparison of various experimental methods.

Methods	Physical Structure of Materials	Thermal Conductivity	Limitations
Suspended Micro-Bridge	Suspended	Single-layer CVD graphene [29]: 1680 ± 180 $Wm^{-1}K^{-1}$	Difficult micro-device preparation, existence of contact thermal resistance
		Bilayer h-BN [30]: 484^{+141}_{-24} $Wm^{-1}K^{-1}$	
		4L MoS_2 [31]: 44~50 $Wm^{-1}K^{-1}$	
3ω	Supported	100 nm SiN [35]: ~5 $Wm^{-1}K^{-1}$ 64 nm BN [35]: ~4 $Wm^{-1}K^{-1}$	Not applicable to few layer 2D material, deposition of metal electrodes
TDTR	Supported	Single layer graphene [1] [46]: 636 ± 140 $Wm^{-1}K^{-1}$	Complex experimental device, deposition of a metal film, not applicable to few layer 2D material
Optothermal Raman	Supported and suspended	Single layer graphene [57]: ~4840 to 5300 $Wm^{-1}K^{-1}$	The inaccurate measurement results caused by laser absorption coefficient and temperature coefficient calibration
		Few-layer h-BN [58]: 227 to 280 $Wm^{-1}K^{-1}$	
		Single layer MoS_2 [47]: 34.5 ± 4 $Wm^{-1}K^{-1}$	
ET-Raman	Supported and suspended	55 nm MoS_2 [53]: 46.9 ± 3.1 $Wm^{-1}K^{-1}$	

[1] It is measured by the variation of TDTR: FDTR.

4. Analysis of Factors Affecting Thermal Conductivity of 2D Materials

The thermal conductivity of 2D materials is affected by many factors, such as length, thickness, temperature, substrate, strain, and so on. These factors will affect the process of phonon transmission and scattering and further affect the thermal conductivity.

4.1. Size Effect

Unlike bulk materials, the thermal conductivity of nm-thick 2D materials usually exhibits an abnormal size dependence. In Zhang's work [59], the in-plane thermal conductivity of h-BCN monolayer calculated by NEMD increases with sample length increasing from 10 nm to 250 nm.

The factor for the size-dependent thermal conductivity originates in phonon scatterings at the sample boundaries. When the phonon mean free path (λ) is larger than the length (l) of the system, heat transfer is ballistic. Certain phonon modes can transmit from the heat-source to the heat-sink without scattering. When $l > \lambda$, phonon scattering is suppressed. Therefore the calculated κ results change with length l on small scales. In order to extract the thermal conductivity κ_∞ in an infinitely long system, Schelling et al. [60] proposed an extrapolation formula:

$$\frac{1}{\kappa(l)} = \frac{1}{\kappa_\infty}\left(1 + \frac{\lambda}{l}\right) \tag{22}$$

4.2. Thickness Effect

The thermal conductivity of 2D materials is also thickness-dependent. In the work of Smith et al. [61], the thermal conductivity of BP was observed to increase with the thickness increasing from 10 to 1000 nm. However, when the thickness is reduced to less than 10 nm, the thickness dependence of thermal conductivity may show the opposite trend. Yuan et al. [51] reported that the thermal conductivity of 1 to 10 layers decreases with the increase of layers. All these are related to different phonon scattering modes. In monolayer materials, the thermal conductivity is mostly affected by the boundary scattering. Moreover, Umklapp scattering is quenched. Nevertheless, Umklapp scattering has a more significant effect in thicker materials with long phonon mean free path, and the boundary scattering effect is weak which leads to low thermal conductivity.

4.3. Temperature Effect

Temperature, which can directly affect the thermal performances and cause adverse effects on the structural stability of 2D materials, is also an important factor affecting κ. Hong et al. [62] studied κ of phosphorene/graphene under different temperatures using NEMD. The result showed that the κ of phosphorene and graphene decreased with the increase of temperature, which was as expected for phonon-dominated crystalline materials. As the system temperature increases, more high-frequency phonons are activated, which accelerates heat conduction. Meanwhile, high temperature also promotes Umklapp scattering, which suppresses phonon transmission. The strong scattering effect plays a leading role in the process of heat transfer and eventually leads to the decrease of thermal conductivity. The results show that the maximum reduction of thermal conductivity κ of phosphorene and graphene from 100 K to 400 K is, respectively, 64%, 58%, 11%, and 13%. The calculated thermal conductivity is inversely proportional to the temperature, indicating that the Umklapp scattering is dominant in the temperature range.

4.4. Other Influence Factors

As the main heat carrier in 2D materials, the propagation of phonons can be adjusted by many other factors, such as lattice deformation caused by strain, substrate coupling, isotope-engineering, which leads to the change of thermal conductivity. Zhang et al. reported that a small strain has a positive effect on the heat conduction of monolayer h-BCN [59]. With further stretching, the thermal conductivity of h-BCN monolayer begins to decrease. Chen et al. reported that the thermal conductivity of SLG supported on amorphous SiO_2 substrate decreased by 40% compared with suspended SLG structure. Through spectral energy density (SED) analysis, it was found that substrate coupling inhibits the thermal transmission of ZA phonons, resulting in a significant reduction in thermal conductivity [63]. In addition, isotope engineering can also affect the thermal conductivity of 2D materials. Through photothermal Raman measurement, Li et al. reported that the in-plane thermal conductivity of isotopic pure $^{100}MoS_2$ monolayer was 50% higher than that synthesized from naturally abundant isotope mixtures. They attribute this to the former having fewer defects, which reduces phonon-defect scattering [64].

5. Conclusions and Outlook

In this paper, we systematically introduce the theoretical and experimental methods for the thermal conductivity measurement of 2D materials. The basic principles, advantages, and disadvantages are discussed in detail. Furthermore, some factors (size, temperature, thickness, strain, substrate, and isotope-engineering) that affect the thermal conductivity of 2D materials are also introduced. Based on the thorough analysis, there are many works to conduct to further develop the theoretical and experimental methods.

For the theoretical methods, the accuracy can be further improved by taking more parameters of actual materials into consideration. For example, the growth of 2D materials obtained by chemical vapor deposition (CVD) is controlled by macro physical conditions and parameters, such as partial pressures of each gas in the CVD environment, substrate, defects, furnace configuration, temperature conditions, and gas-phase reactions. One idea is to use growth kinetics and parameter settings to establish the growth model for describing the growth mechanism of the material, which makes the established model consistent with the actual growth model. Netto et al. have reported the continuous growth process of CVD diamond films using time-dependent Monte Carlo algorithm with the chemical reaction mechanism [65]. Recently, due to the high calculation requirements for theoretical methods, machine learning has been employed to accelerate the estimation of material thermal conductivity while ensuring the accuracy of measurement results. Mortazavi et al. [66] employed machine-learning interatomic potentials (MLIPs) trained over short ab initio molecular dynamics (AIMD) trajectories instead of density functional theory (DFT) calculation to evaluate anharmonic interatomic force constants, examining the thermal conductivity conveniently, efficiently, and accurately.

For experimental methods, there is also a lot of work to conduct. For suspended micro bridge devices, the contact thermal resistance is an important factor affecting the accuracy of measurement results, which is quantified in the subsequent development of electron beam self-heating method [67]. Furthermore, the suspended device can combine with TDTR for an ultrafast heat pump and probe. In this way, the influence of contact thermal resistance can be eliminated. Moreover, the non-diffusion heat transfer in 2D materials can be characterized. For the 3ω method, in order to realize its application in measuring the thermal conductivity of 2D materials, the fabrication of a metal electrode with high quality and the signal extraction of a phase-locked amplifier should be considered. Compared with other methods, the Raman method is more widely used in the measurement of 2D material thermal conductivity. However, there is still room for further improvement. First, higher spectral resolution means more accurate temperature measurement. For Raman spectrometer, the higher the grating line density, the higher the corresponding spectral resolution. The grating line density of the commonly used Raman spectrometer ranges from 300 g/mm to 1800 g/mm. If higher density gratings, such as 2400 g/mm and 3600 g/mm, are used, the temperature measurement accuracy will be improved accordingly. Besides, the spatial modulation of laser spot can be considered more. Nowadays, the modulation of laser spot size is realized by using objective lenses with different magnification. In addition, the shape of the laser spot can also be modulated to measure the thermal conductivity of anisotropic 2D materials. Moreover, aside from temporal and spatial modulation, the excitation energy can also be modulated by lasers with different wavelengths. There are few reports on the thermal conductivity of 2D materials using larger wavelength lasers such as 660 nm laser in the visible light band due to its long exposure time and low excitation efficiency. However, at the same time, the long-wavelength laser also has some advantages, such as reducing fluorescence interference and not easily damaging the sample. Therefore, its application in 2D heat transfer measurement is expected.

Author Contributions: H.D. conceived and wrote the review; R.W. conceived and revised the paper. All authors have read and agreed to the published version of the manuscript.

Funding: This research was funded by National Natural Science Foundation of China (52005367 for Ridong Wang) and National Key R&D Program of China (2020YFC2004600 for Ridong Wang).

Institutional Review Board Statement: Not applicable.

Data Availability Statement: Not applicable.

Conflicts of Interest: The authors declare no conflict of interest.

References

1. Kuang, Y.; Lindsay, L.; Shi, S.; Wang, X.; Huang, B. Thermal conductivity of graphene mediated by strain and size. *Int. J. Heat Mass Transf.* **2016**, *101*, 772–778. [CrossRef]
2. Yousefi, F.; Khoeini, F.; Rajabpour, A. Thermal conductivity and thermal rectification of nanoporous graphene: A molecular dynamics simulation. *Int. J. Heat Mass Transf.* **2020**, *146*, 118884. [CrossRef]
3. Liu, F.; Wang, Y.; Liu, X.; Wang, J.; Guo, H. Ballistic transport in monolayer black phosphorus transistors. *IEEE Trans. Electron. Devices* **2014**, *61*, 3871–3876. [CrossRef]
4. Mannix, A.J.; Zhang, Z.; Guisinger, N.P.; Yakobson, B.I.; Hersam, M.C. Borophene as a prototype for synthetic 2D materials development. *Nat. Nanotechnol.* **2018**, *13*, 444–450. [CrossRef] [PubMed]
5. Peng, B.; Zhang, H.; Shao, H.; Xu, Y.; Zhang, R.; Zhu, H. The electronic, optical, and thermodynamic properties of borophene from first-principles calculations. *J. Mater. Chem. C* **2016**, *4*, 3592–3598. [CrossRef]
6. Chen, L.; Shi, X.; Yu, N.; Zhang, X.; Du, X.; Lin, J. Measurement and analysis of thermal conductivity of Ti3C2Tx MXene films. *Materials* **2018**, *11*, 1701. [CrossRef] [PubMed]
7. Zha, X.-H.; Zhou, J.; Zhou, Y.; Huang, Q.; He, J.; Francisco, J.S.; Luo, K.; Du, S. Promising electron mobility and high thermal conductivity in Sc 2 CT 2 (T = F, OH) MXenes. *Nanoscale* **2016**, *8*, 6110–6117. [CrossRef]
8. Mortazavi, B.; Podryabinkin, E.V.; Roche, S.; Rabczuk, T.; Zhuang, X.; Shapeev, A.V. Machine-learning interatomic potentials enable first-principles multiscale modeling of lattice thermal conductivity in graphene/borophene heterostructures. *Mater. Horiz.* **2020**, *7*, 2359–2367. [CrossRef]
9. Rahman, M.H.; Islam, M.S.; Islam, M.S.; Chowdhury, E.H.; Bose, P.; Jayan, R.; Islam, M.M. Phonon thermal conductivity of the stanene/hBN van der Waals heterostructure. *Phys. Chem. Chem. Phys.* **2021**, *23*, 11028–11038. [CrossRef]
10. Mayelifartash, A.; Abdol, M.A.; Sadeghzadeh, S. Thermal conductivity and interfacial thermal resistance behavior for the polyaniline–boron carbide heterostructure. *Phys. Chem. Chem. Phys.* **2021**, *23*, 13310–13322. [CrossRef]
11. Wang, X.; Cui, Y.; Li, T.; Lei, M.; Li, J.; Wei, Z. Recent advances in the functional 2D photonic and optoelectronic devices. *Adv. Opt. Mater.* **2019**, *7*, 1801274. [CrossRef]
12. Munteanu, R.-E.; Moreno, P.S.; Bramini, M.; Gáspár, S. 2D materials in electrochemical sensors for in vitro or in vivo use. *Anal. Bioanal. Chem.* **2020**, *413*, 701–725. [CrossRef] [PubMed]
13. Dong, Y.; Wu, Z.-S.; Ren, W.; Cheng, H.-M.; Bao, X. Graphene: A promising 2D material for electrochemical energy storage. *Sci. Bull.* **2017**, *62*, 724–740. [CrossRef]
14. Krishnamoorthy, A.; Rajak, P.; Norouzzadeh, P.; Singh, D.J.; Kalia, R.K.; Nakano, A.; Vashishta, P. Thermal conductivity of MoS2 monolayers from molecular dynamics simulations. *AIP Adv.* **2019**, *9*, 035042. [CrossRef]
15. Kandemir, A.; Yapicioglu, H.; Kinaci, A.; Çağın, T.; Sevik, C. Thermal transport properties of MoS2 and MoSe2 monolayers. *Nanotechnology* **2016**, *27*, 055703. [CrossRef]
16. Brenner, D.W.; Shenderova, O.A.; Harrison, J.A.; Stuart, S.J.; Ni, B.; Sinnott, S.B. A second-generation reactive empirical bond order (REBO) potential energy expression for hydrocarbons. *J. Phys. Condens. Matt.* **2002**, *14*, 783. [CrossRef]
17. Khan, A.I.; Navid, I.A.; Noshin, M.; Uddin, H.M.A.; Hossain, F.F.; Subrina, S. Equilibrium molecular dynamics (MD) simulation study of thermal conductivity of graphene nanoribbon: A comparative study on MD potentials. *Electronics* **2015**, *4*, 1109–1124. [CrossRef]
18. Liu, G.; Gao, Z.; Li, G.-L.; Wang, H. Abnormally low thermal conductivity of 2D selenene: An ab initio study. *J. Appl. Phys.* **2020**, *127*, 065103. [CrossRef]
19. Hong, Y.; Zhang, J.; Zeng, X.C. Thermal transport in phosphorene and phosphorene-based materials: A review on numerical studies. *Chinese Phys. B* **2018**, *27*, 036501. [CrossRef]
20. Liu, G.; Wang, H.; Gao, Y.; Zhou, J.; Wang, H. Anisotropic intrinsic lattice thermal conductivity of borophane from first-principles calculations. *Phys. Chem. Chem. Phys.* **2017**, *19*, 2843–2849. [CrossRef]

21. Zulfiqar, M.; Zhao, Y.; Li, G.; Li, Z.; Ni, J. Intrinsic Thermal conductivities of monolayer transition metal dichalcogenides MX 2 (M = Mo, W.; X = S, Se, Te). *Sci. Rep.* **2019**, *9*, 1–7. [CrossRef] [PubMed]
22. Li, W.; Carrete, J.; Katcho, N.A.; Mingo, N. ShengBTE: A solver of the Boltzmann transport equation for phonons. *Comput. Phys. Commun.* **2014**, *185*, 1747–1758. [CrossRef]
23. Bouzerar, G.; Thébaud, S.; Pecorario, S.; Adessi, C. Drastic effects of vacancies on phonon lifetime and thermal conductivity in graphene. *J. Phys. Condens. Matt.* **2020**, *32*, 295702. [CrossRef] [PubMed]
24. Zhang, W.; Fisher, T.S.; Mingo, N. The atomistic green's function method: An efficient simulation approach for nanoscale phonon transport. *Num. Heat Transf. Part B Fundam.* **2007**, *51*, 333–349. [CrossRef]
25. Zhang, W.; Fisher, T.; Mingo, N. Simulation of interfacial phonon transport in Si–Ge heterostructures using an atomistic Green's function method. *J. Heat Transf.* **2007**, *129*, 483–491. [CrossRef]
26. Li, X.; Yang, R. Effect of lattice mismatch on phonon transmission and interface thermal conductance across dissimilar material interfaces. *Phys. Rev. B* **2012**, *86*, 054305. [CrossRef]
27. Kim, P.; Shi, L.; Majumdar, A.; McEuen, P.L. Thermal transport measurements of individual multiwalled nanotubes. *Phys. Rev. Lett.* **2001**, *87*, 215502. [CrossRef]
28. Shi, L.; Li, D.; Yu, C.; Jang, W.; Kim, D.; Yao, Z.; Kim, P.; Majumdar, A. Measuring thermal and thermoelectric properties of one-dimensional nanostructures using a microfabricated device. *J. Heat Transf.* **2003**, *125*, 881–888. [CrossRef]
29. Jo, I.; Pettes, M.T.; Lindsay, L.; Ou, E.; Weathers, A.; Moore, A.L.; Yao, Z.; Shi, L. Reexamination of basal plane thermal conductivity of suspended graphene samples measured by electro-thermal micro-bridge methods. *AIP Adv.* **2015**, *5*, 053206. [CrossRef]
30. Wang, C.; Guo, J.; Dong, L.; Aiyiti, A.; Xu, X.; Li, B. Superior thermal conductivity in suspended bilayer hexagonal boron nitride. *Sci. Rep.* **2016**, *6*, 1–6. [CrossRef]
31. Jo, I.; Pettes, M.T.; Ou, E.; Wu, W.; Shi, L. Basal-plane thermal conductivity of few-layer molybdenum disulfide. *Appl. Phys. Lett.* **2014**, *104*, 201902. [CrossRef]
32. Wang, Y.; Xu, N.; Li, D.; Zhu, J. Thermal properties of two dimensional layered materials. *Adv. Funct. Mater.* **2017**, *27*, 1604134. [CrossRef]
33. Liu, C.-K.; Yu, C.-K.; Chien, H.-C.; Kuo, S.-L.; Hsu, C.-Y.; Dai, M.-J.; Luo, G.-L.; Huang, S.-C.; Huang, M.-J. Thermal conductivity of Si/SiGe superlattice films. *J. Appl. Phys.* **2008**, *104*, 114301. [CrossRef]
34. Chen, Z.; Jang, W.; Bao, W.; Lau, C.N.; Dames, C. Thermal contact resistance between graphene and silicon dioxide. *Appl. Phys. Lett.* **2009**, *95*, 161910. [CrossRef]
35. Zhang, D.; Behbahanian, A.; Roberts, N.A. Thermal conductivity measurement of supported thin film materials using the 3ω method. *arXiv* **2020**, arXiv:2007.00087.
36. Cahill, D.G. Thermal conductivity measurement from 30 to 750 K: The 3ω method. *Rev. Sci. Instrum.* **1990**, *61*, 802–808. [CrossRef]
37. Cahill, D.G. Analysis of heat flow in layered structures for time-domain thermoreflectance. *Rev. Sci. Instrum.* **2004**, *75*, 5119–5122. [CrossRef]
38. Schmidt, A.J.; Chen, X.; Chen, G. Pulse accumulation, radial heat conduction, and anisotropic thermal conductivity in pump-probe transient thermoreflectance. *Rev. Sci. Instrum.* **2008**, *79*, 114902. [CrossRef]
39. Pang, Y.; Jiang, P.; Yang, R. Machine learning-based data processing technique for time-domain thermoreflectance (TDTR) measurements. *J. Applied Phys.* **2021**, *130*, 084901. [CrossRef]
40. Schmidt, A.J.; Cheaito, R.; Chiesa, M. A frequency-domain thermoreflectance method for the characterization of thermal properties. *Rev. Sci. Instrum.* **2009**, *80*, 094901. [CrossRef]
41. Liu, J.; Choi, G.-M.; Cahill, D.G. Measurement of the anisotropic thermal conductivity of molybdenum disulfide by the time-resolved magneto-optic Kerr effect. *J. Appl. Phys.* **2014**, *116*, 233107. [CrossRef]
42. Jiang, P.; Qian, X.; Gu, X.; Yang, R. Probing anisotropic thermal conductivity of transition metal dichalcogenides MX2 (M = Mo, W and X = S, Se) using time-Domain thermoreflectance. *Adv. Mater.* **2017**, *29*, 1701068. [CrossRef] [PubMed]
43. Wang, Y.; Xu, L.; Yang, Z.; Xie, H.; Jiang, P.; Dai, J.; Luo, W.; Yao, Y.; Hitz, E.; Yang, R. High temperature thermal management with boron nitride nanosheets. *Nanoscale* **2018**, *10*, 167–173. [CrossRef] [PubMed]
44. Jang, H.; Wood, J.D.; Ryder, C.R.; Hersam, M.C.; Cahill, D.G. Anisotropic thermal conductivity of exfoliated black phosphorus. *Adv. Mater.* **2015**, *27*, 8017–8022. [CrossRef] [PubMed]
45. Lu, B.; Zhang, L.; Balogun, O. Cross-plane thermal transport measurements across CVD grown few layer graphene films on a silicon substrate. *AIP Adv.* **2019**, *9*, 045126. [CrossRef]
46. Rahman, M.; Shahzadeh, M.; Pisana, S. Simultaneous measurement of anisotropic thermal conductivity and thermal boundary conductance of 2-dimensional materials. *J. Appl. Phys.* **2019**, *126*, 205103. [CrossRef]
47. Yan, R.; Simpson, J.R.; Bertolazzi, S.; Brivio, J.; Watson, M.; Wu, X.; Kis, A.; Luo, T.; Hight Walker, A.R.; Xing, H.G. Thermal Conductivity of Monolayer Molybdenum Disulfide Obtained from Temperature-Dependent Raman Spectroscopy. *ACS Nano* **2014**, *8*, 986–993. [CrossRef]
48. Xu, S.; Wang, T.; Hurley, D.; Yue, Y.; Wang, X. Development of time-domain differential Raman for transient thermal probing of materials. *Opt. Express* **2015**, *23*, 10040–10056. [CrossRef]
49. Wang, T.; Xu, S.; Hurley, D.H.; Yue, Y.; Wang, X. Frequency-resolved Raman for transient thermal probing and thermal diffusivity measurement. *Opt. Lett.* **2016**, *41*, 80–83. [CrossRef]

50. Wang, T.; Han, M.; Wang, R.; Yuan, P.; Xu, S.; Wang, X. Characterization of anisotropic thermal conductivity of suspended nm-thick black phosphorus with frequency-resolved Raman spectroscopy. *J. Appl. Phys.* **2018**, *123*, 145104. [CrossRef]

51. Yuan, P.; Wang, R.; Wang, T.; Wang, X.; Xie, Y. Nonmonotonic thickness-dependence of in-plane thermal conductivity of few-layered MoS 2: 2.4 to 37.8 nm. *Phys. Chem. Chem. Phys.* **2018**, *20*, 25752–25761. [CrossRef] [PubMed]

52. Zobeiri, H.; Wang, R.; Zhang, Q.; Zhu, G.; Wang, X. Hot carrier transfer and phonon transport in suspended nm WS2 films. *Acta Mater.* **2019**, *175*, 222–237. [CrossRef]

53. Wang, R.; Zobeiri, H.; Xie, Y.; Wang, X.; Zhang, X.; Yue, Y. Distinguishing optical and acoustic phonon temperatures and their energy coupling factor under photon excitation in nm 2D materials. *Adv. Sci.* **2020**, *7*, 2000097. [CrossRef] [PubMed]

54. Bao, H.; Chen, J.; Gu, X.; Cao, B. A review of simulation methods in micro/nanoscale heat conduction. *ES Energy Environ.* **2018**, *1*, 16–55. [CrossRef]

55. Liu, J.; Li, P.; Zheng, H. Review on techniques for thermal characterization of graphene and related 2D materials. *Nanomaterials* **2021**, *11*, 2787. [CrossRef] [PubMed]

56. Gu, X.; Yang, R. Phonon transport and thermal conductivity in two-dimensional materials. *Ann. Rev. of Heat Transf.* **2016**, *19*. [CrossRef]

57. Balandin, A.A.; Ghosh, S.; Bao, W.; Calizo, I.; Teweldebrhan, D.; Miao, F.; Lau, C.N. Superior thermal conductivity of single-layer graphene. *Nano Lett.* **2008**, *8*, 902–907. [CrossRef]

58. Zhou, H.; Zhu, J.; Liu, Z.; Yan, Z.; Fan, X.; Lin, J.; Wang, G.; Yan, Q.; Yu, T.; Ajayan, P.M.; et al. High thermal conductivity of suspended few-layer hexagonal boron nitride sheets. *Nano Res.* **2014**, *7*, 1232–1240. [CrossRef]

59. Zhang, Y.Y.; Pei, Q.X.; Liu, H.Y.; Wei, N. Thermal conductivity of a h-BCN monolayer. *Phys. Chem. Chem. Phys.* **2017**, *19*, 27326–27331. [CrossRef]

60. Schelling, P.K.; Phillpot, S.R.; Keblinski, P. Comparison of atomic-level simulation methods for computing thermal conductivity. *Phys. Rev. B* **2002**, *65*, 144306. [CrossRef]

61. Smith, B.; Vermeersch, B.; Carrete, J.; Ou, E.; Kim, J.; Mingo, N.; Akinwande, D.; Shi, L. Temperature and thickness dependences of the anisotropic in-plane thermal conductivity of black phosphorus. *Adv. Mater.* **2017**, *29*, 144306. [CrossRef]

62. Hong, Y.; Zhang, J.; Huang, X.; Zeng, X.C. Thermal conductivity of a two-dimensional phosphorene sheet: A comparative study with graphene. *Nanoscale* **2015**, *7*, 18716–18724. [CrossRef] [PubMed]

63. Chen, J.; Zhang, G.; Li, B. Substrate coupling suppresses size dependence of thermal conductivity in supported graphene. *Nanoscale* **2013**, *5*, 532–536. [CrossRef] [PubMed]

64. Li, X.; Zhang, J.; Puretzky, A.A.; Yoshimura, A.; Sang, X.; Cui, Q.; Li, Y.; Liang, L.; Ghosh, A.W.; Zhao, H.; et al. Isotope-engineering the thermal conductivity of two-dimensional MoS$_2$. *Acs Nano* **2019**, *13*, 2481–2489. [CrossRef] [PubMed]

65. Netto, A.; Frenklach, M. Kinetic Monte Carlo simulations of CVD diamond growth—Interlay among growth, etching, and migration. *Diam. Relat. Mater.* **2005**, *14*, 1630–1646. [CrossRef]

66. Mortazavi, B.; Podryabinkin, E.V.; Novikov, I.S.; Rabczuk, T.; Zhuang, X.; Shapeev, A.V. Accelerating first-principles estimation of thermal conductivity by machine-learning interatomic potentials: A MTP/ShengBTE solution. *Comput. Phys. Commun.* **2021**, *258*, 107583. [CrossRef]

67. Aiyiti, A.; Bai, X.; Wu, J.; Xu, X.; Li, B. Measuring the thermal conductivity and interfacial thermal resistance of suspended MoS 2 using electron beam self-heating technique. *Sci. Bull.* **2018**, *63*, 452–458. [CrossRef]

 *nanomaterials*

Review

Review on Techniques for Thermal Characterization of Graphene and Related 2D Materials

Jing Liu *, Pei Li and Hongsheng Zheng

College of New Materials and New Energies, Shenzhen Technology University, Shenzhen 518116, China;
2070413005@stumail.sztu.edu.cn (P.L.); 20183280058@stumail.sztu.edu.cn (H.Z.)
* Correspondence: liujing@sztu.edu.cn

Abstract: The discovery of graphene and its analog, such as MoS_2, has boosted research. The thermal transport in 2D materials gains much of the interest, especially when graphene has high thermal conductivity. However, the thermal properties of 2D materials obtained from experiments have large discrepancies. For example, the thermal conductivity of single layer suspended graphene obtained by experiments spans over a large range: 1100–5000 W/m·K. Apart from the different graphene quality in experiments, the thermal characterization methods play an important role in the observed large deviation of experimental data. Here we provide a critical review of the widely used thermal characterization techniques: the optothermal Raman technique and the micro-bridge method. The critical issues in the two methods are carefully revised and discussed in great depth. Furthermore, improvements in Raman-based techniques to investigate the energy transport in 2D materials are discussed.

Keywords: optothermal Raman technique; thermal transport; 2D materials

Citation: Liu, J.; Li, P.; Zheng, H. Review on Techniques for Thermal Characterization of Graphene and Related 2D Materials. *Nanomaterials* **2021**, *11*, 2787. https://doi.org/10.3390/nano11112787

Academic Editor: Marco Cannas

Received: 6 September 2021
Accepted: 19 October 2021
Published: 21 October 2021

1. Introduction

Since the discovery of graphene and other 2D materials such as MoS_2, various properties of 2D materials have been intensively studied [1–5]. The ultra-high thermal conductivity of graphene has led to extensive experimental research and theoretical simulations about the energy transport in it in past decades [3,6,7]. The thermal transport in other 2D materials also gains much interest for its promising applications [8,9]. However, compared with the thermal conductivity (κ) obtained from simulations, κ obtained from experiments shows large discrepancies. For example, κ of suspended single layer graphene (SLG) ranges from 1100 to 5300 W/m·K [3,10], depending on the thermal characterization method and the fabrication method of graphene. κ of supported graphene drops to hundreds W/m·K, which is also related to the substrate [6,11,12]. It is well accepted that κ of supported graphene is suppressed due to phonon leakage [6,13]. Table 1 summarizes κ of suspended and supported graphene by different experimental methods. A large discrepancy among κ can be observed. This discrepancy arises from the characterization methods and the quality of the graphene. The thermal characterization techniques of 2D materials include the optothermal Raman technique [3,11,14], micro-bridge method [6,9], time-domain thermoreflectance (TDTR) [15] and Johnson noise thermometry [16]. In this paper, we will focus on the optothermal Raman technique and the micro-bridge method. The critical issues faced in the above two methods will be discussed in depth. The issues in the optothermal Raman technique include the accuracy of the laser power absorbed by 2D materials, stress effect and inter-phonon branch nonequilibrium. When it comes to the micro-bridge method, the thermal resistance of the 2D materials should be properly chosen to guarantee measurement accuracy. These issues undermine the measurement accuracy in thermal transport characterization of 2D materials [17].

Table 1. Thermal conductivity of graphene obtained by experiments.

κ (W/m·K)	Method	Brief Description	References
~3000–5000	Raman optothermal	Suspended SLG [1], exfoliated	[3]
$2500 + 1100/ - 1050$	Raman optothermal	Suspended SLG, CVD [2]	[11]
400–1800	Raman optothermal	Suspended SLG with crystal lattice defects	[18]
$730–880 \pm 60$	Micro-bridge	Suspended bilayer graphene, PMMA [3] residues on the surface	[19]
1896 ± 390	Raman optothermal	Suspended bilayer graphene	[20]
365	Transient Thermoelectrical technique (TET)	Supported SLG on PMMA, giant scale, CVD	[12]
$370 + 650/ - 320$	Raman optothermal	Supported SLG on copper, CVD	[11]
600	Micro-bridge	Supported SLG on amorphous SiO_2 [4], exfoliated	[6]

[1] SLG: Single layer graphene. [2] CVD: Chemical vapor deposition. [3] PMMA: Polymethyl methacrylate. [4] SiO_2: Silicon dioxide.

2. Raman Optothermal Method

The characteristic peaks in Raman spectra of the 2D materials have strong temperature dependence. It is possible to make use of the Raman spectra to characterize the thermal transport in 2D materials [8,21–24]. Balandin first developed the confocal Raman spectroscopy to measure κ of suspended graphene [3]. Schematic of the optothermal Raman technique is shown in Figure 1. As the laser spot is much smaller than the suspended graphene size, the heat is propagating radially to the edges. By obtaining the Raman shift temperature coefficient (χ_T) and the Raman shift power coefficient (χ_P) of G peak, the thermal conductivity of graphene can be expressed as $\kappa = \chi_T(L/2hW)/\chi_P$ [3]. Here, L, h and W are the distance from the hot spot to the heat sink, thickness of SLG and width of the sample, respectively. The optothermal Raman technique is proven to be powerful and widely used in characterizing the energy transport in 2D materials [25]. Advantages of the optothermal Raman method include minimal sample preparation, high spatial resolution and material specificity [17]. However, it is important to point out that several critical issues should be carefully considered regarding the utilization of the Raman optothermal method.

One important parameter in the deduction of κ of graphene is the laser power (P) absorbed by the graphene. Usually, two methods are employed to obtain P. One is calculating the absorbed power based on the optical properties [3]. It is well accepted that the absorption coefficient (α_G) of SLG is 2.3% [2]. Thus, P can be described as $P = I_0A(1 - \exp(-\alpha_G\delta))$, where I_0 is the laser intensity on the surface, A is the illuminated area and δ is the thickness of SLG [3]. However, the α_G is easily affected by many factors, such as the wrinkles and the strain [26]. The optical properties can vary greatly from sample to sample, resulting in uncertainty in the laser absorption. In supported graphene, the laser absorption is significantly affected by the interface-induced optical interference [27], which leads to great uncertainty in the laser absorption calculation. Another method is directly measuring the transmitted power. Thus, the absorbed power can be obtained by subtracting the transmitted power from the total incident laser power. However, a very small proportion of the incident laser power is absorbed by graphene. Thus, even very little variation in the transmitted power can lead to great uncertainty in the absorbed power. The uncertainty in P will affect the accuracy of χ_P, which further introduces uncertainty into the derivation of κ. It is difficult to determine the uncertainty of P. If there is 10% uncertainty in χ_P, 10% uncertainty will be introduced to κ.

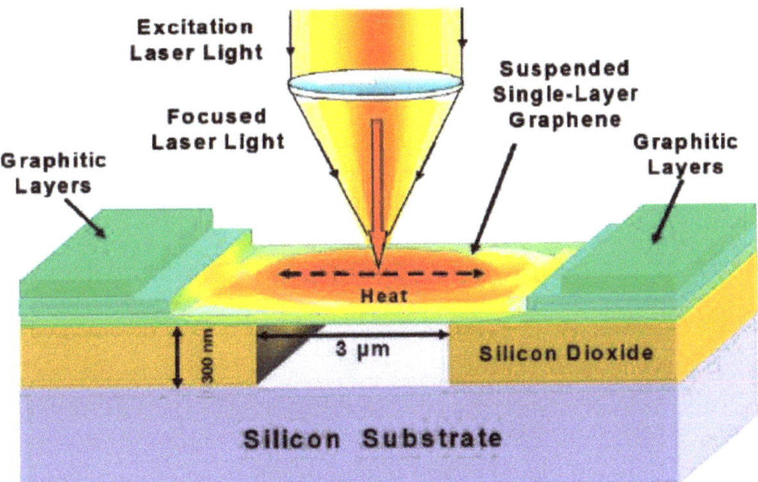

Figure 1. Schematic of the optothermal Raman technique. Reprinted with permission from ref. [3]. Copyright 2008 American Chemical Society.

Another source of uncertainty in the optothermal Raman method is the stress effect in the graphene. During the temperature coefficient calibration, the whole sample is in thermal equilibrium. However, the graphene experiences thermal nonequilibrium in the experiment. This leads to the different stress effects in the graphene during the calibration process and experiment. Thus, the temperature probed by Raman spectroscopy is not precise, which further introduces uncertainty into κ determination [28]. Apart from this, the Raman spectroscopy actually detects the temperature of the optical phonons, which is easily affected by the thermomechanical stress. The thermomechanical stress in few layers graphene (FLG) alters the interatomic-potential, which affects the energy of the optical phonons [17]. Theoretical simulation shows that the uncertainty caused by the thermomechanical stress in κ of FLG can be higher than 20% [17].

It is critically important to point out that the Raman optothermal method is based on an assumption that different phonon branches are in thermal equilibrium under the photon excitation. However, Ruan et al., first reported that the phonon branches were in strong thermal nonequilibrium by employing the density functional perturbation theory (DFPT) [29]. For example, the steady-state temperature of transverse optical phonons (T_{TO}) can be 14.8% higher than that (T_{ZA}) of out-of-plane acoustic (ZA) phonons at the center of the SLG [30]. By using the multitemperature model (MTM) developed by Ruan et al., the predicted κ of SLG is increased by 67% [30]. Ruan's theoretical simulation enlightened the experimental work about the thermal nonequilibrium among phonon branches. The temperature differences between different phonon branches in 2D materials under Raman excitation were first verified and detected by Wang's group by experiment [31]. Wang et al., distinguished the temperatures of optical (OP) and acoustic (AP) phonons under phonon excitation in 2D materials by constructing steady and nanosecond (ns) inter-phonon branch energy transport states [31]. By developing the nanosecond energy transport state-resolved Raman (ns ET-Raman) technique, the temperature difference ($\Delta T_{OP\text{-}AP}$) between OP and AP is reported to be 30% larger than the Raman-probed temperature rise in MoS_2 [31].

In most research about the energy transport in 2D materials by Raman spectroscopy, the hot carrier diffusion effect is not considered, which is more prominent as the laser spot size is smaller than 0.5 µm [28]. Here, we look at a MoS_2/c-Si structure and discuss what will happen after the laser illumination on the sample. Figure 2a shows the physical principle of the electrons and holes diffusion under the laser illumination. Subsequent to laser irradiation, the electrons and holes are generated by absorbing photons. In extremely short time (~ps), the excess energy ($\Delta E = E - E_g$) of the electrons will quickly dissipate to other unexcited electrons and the lattice. Then, the electrons and holes (hot carriers) diffuse and recombine, releasing the energy by scattering with the optical phonons. This leads to a much larger thermal source area than the excitation spot. The specific process is described in detail in the reference [32]. The electron-hole diffusion has a negligible effect on the thermal conduction in suspended 2D materials [33]. However, the effect of the hot carrier diffusion should be carefully handled when determining the interface thermal energy transport between graphene and substrate.

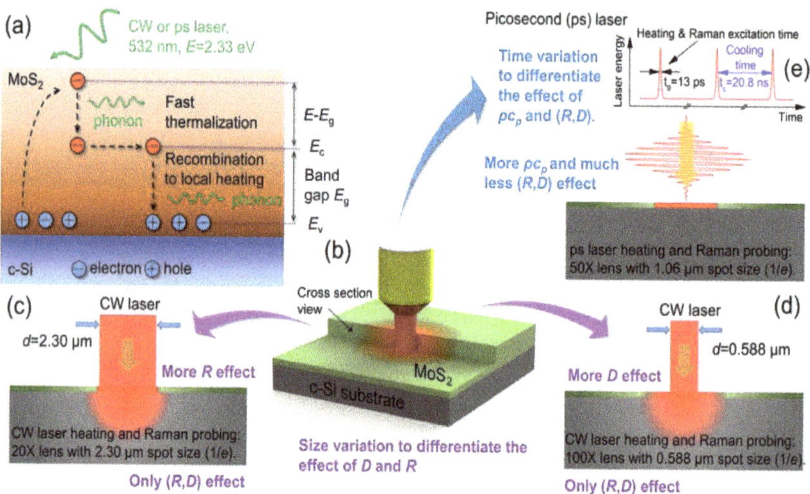

Figure 2. (a) Hot carrier diffusion in MoS₂/c-Si under laser illumination (not to scale): E_v and E_c are the valence band and conduction band, respectively, E_g is the bandgap of MoS₂, E is the photon energy of the incident laser; (b) schematic of the experiment setup (not to scale): ρc_p is the volumetric heat capacity of the sample; (c,d) continuous wave (CW) laser is used to heat the sample under 20× and 100× objective lens to achieve different hot aera size: R and D are the interface thermal resistance and hot carrier diffusion coefficient, respectively; (e) picosecond pulsed laser is used under 50× objective lens to achieve zero thermal transport state. Reprinted with permission from ref. [27]. Copyright 2017 American Chemical Society.

3. Micro-Bridge Method

Shi Li et al., first employed the micro-bridge method to measure κ of graphene supported on amorphous SiO₂ [6]. The schematic of the experiment is shown in Figure 3. There are four Au/Cr resistance thermometer (RT) lines in the setup. The two straight RT lines (RT2 and RT3) cover the two ends of the graphene. The U-shaped RT1 and RT4 separate from both the graphene and the RT2 and RT3. During the experiment, the RT1 is self-heated by applying current into it. Based on the thermal resistance circuit shown in Figure 3c, thermal resistance (R_s) of the central beam including both graphene and SiO₂ can be expressed as: $R_s = R_b \frac{\Delta T_{2,m} - \Delta T_{3,m}}{\Delta T_{3,m} + \Delta T_{4,m}}$ [6]. Here, $\Delta T_{j,m}$ ($j = 2,3,4$) is the temperature rise at the middle point of RT. R_b is the thermal resistance of each RT line with the SiO₂ beam. By measuring the R_s before and after removing the graphene, κ of graphene is determined. The accuracy of the micro-bridge method is guaranteed only as R_s is comparable to R_b. As κ of the graphene is low or the length of the graphene/SiO₂ beam is longer than tens of µm, R_s will be much larger than R_b. Thus, the heat conducting into the graphene/SiO₂ beam will be very small, which will lead to great uncertainty in the measurement of ΔT_m. This will further increase the uncertainty in the determination of κ of graphene. Overall, the micro-bridge method is feasible in principle, but its measurement accuracy is guaranteed when the sample has proper thermal resistance. In addition, it is technically challenging and time consuming to fabricate the whole measurement device.

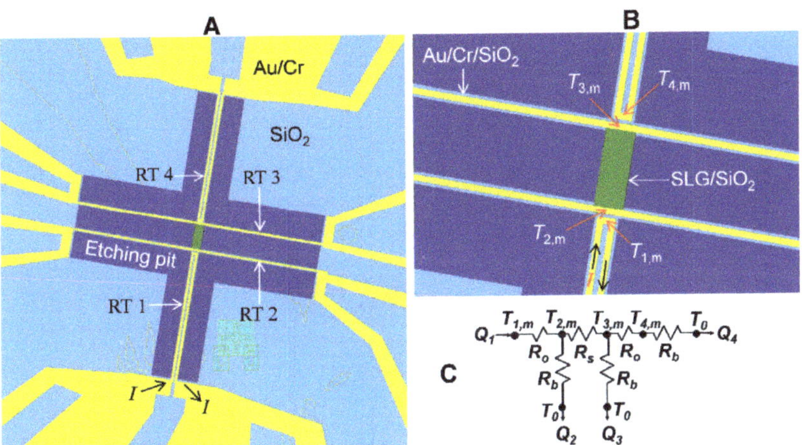

Figure 3. (**A,B**) SEM images of micro-bridge method setup; (**C**) circuit of the thermal resistance. Reprinted with permission from ref. [6]. Copyright 2010 American Association for the Advancement of Science.

The sample size tested by the Raman spectroscopy method and micro-bridge method is at the level of several µm. However, the mean free path (MFP) of phonons in graphene can be as long as hundreds of micrometers [34], surpassing the sample size. This will result in a strong phonon-edge scattering effect in the graphene. To investigate the intrinsic κ of graphene without or with minimal phonon-edge scattering, Liu et al., first developed the differential transient electrothermal technique (TET) to characterize κ of giant graphene supported by polymethyl methacrylate (PMMA) [12]. The experiment setup is shown in Figure 4. The graphene supported by PMMA is suspended between two electrodes. During the experiment, the whole sample is fed through with step current to induce Joule heating in it. The voltage evolution ($V(t)$) of the sample is recorded by an oscilloscope. The thermal diffusivity (β) of the whole sample can be obtained by fitting the $V(t)\sim t$ curve. κ_{eff} of the whole sample is calculated as $\kappa_{eff} = \beta \cdot \rho c_p$. Through simulation, it is found that the interface thermal resistance between graphene and PMMA is negligible in κ_{eff}. Thus, κ_{eff} can be written as $\kappa_{eff} = f(\kappa_p, \kappa_g, \delta_p, \delta_g)$. Here, the subscripts p and g indicate PMMA and graphene, respectively. δ is thickness. κ of SLG supported by PMMA was determined to be 365 W/m·K [12], which is only 60% of κ of graphene supported by amorphous SiO$_2$ [6]. The authors attributed the low thermal conductivity of SLG on PMMA to abundant carbon atoms in the PMMA [12]. The abundant carbon atoms lead to a strong phonon scattering effect between SLG and PMMA.

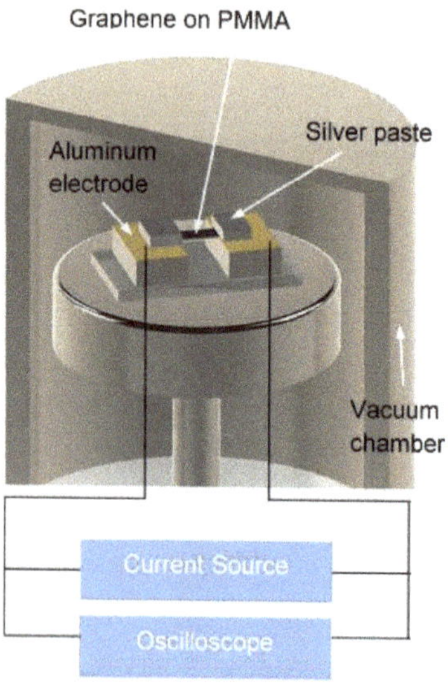

Figure 4. Experiment setup of the TET technique. Reprinted from ref. [12].

4. Improvements in the Optothermal Raman Technique

In order to resolve the challenges mentioned above in the optothermal Raman technique, various Raman-based techniques, including frequency-domain energy transport state-resolved Raman (FET-Raman) [35,36] and energy transport state-resolved Raman (ET-Raman) [33], were developed. They can free the Raman thermometry from the laser absorption and the temperature coefficient calibration. In the FET-Raman experiment, the 2D material experiences two energy transport states. The first one is the steady-state heating induced by a CW laser. By varying the incident laser power (P), the Raman shift power coefficient (RSC) $\chi_{steady\text{-}state} = \partial\omega/\partial P = \alpha\cdot(\partial\omega/\partial T)\cdot f_1(\kappa)$ is obtained. Here, α is the laser absorption coefficient, $\partial\omega/\partial T$ is the Raman shift temperature coefficient and κ is the in-plane thermal conductivity. The second energy transport state is the transient-state heating induced by a square wave-modulated CW laser. Similarly, an RSC can be obtained: $\chi_{transient} = \partial\omega/\partial P = \alpha\cdot(\partial\omega/\partial T)\cdot f_2(\kappa, \rho c_p)$, where ρc_p is the volumetric heat capacity of the sample. Since the thermal diffusion lengths in two energy states are different, a normalized RSC parameter can be defined as $\Theta = \chi_{transient}/\chi_{steady\text{-}state} = f_3(\kappa, \rho c_p)$ [35]. Thus, the effect of α and $\partial\omega/\partial T$ is eliminated. By interpolating the Θ obtained from the experiment into the Θ–κ curve obtained from a 3D numerical simulation of the MoSe$_2$ sample, κ of MoSe$_2$ is determined. The feasibility of the FET-Raman technique has been verified by employing the FET-Raman to determine κ of MoSe$_2$ and the anisotropic thermal conductivities of carbon fibers [35,36].

Inspired by the theoretical simulation by Ruan et al. [29,30,37], Wang et al., first developed ns ET-Raman to explore the inter-phonon branch non-equilibrium effect in 2D materials under photon excitation [31]. Under CW laser excitation, the local temperature rise (ΔT_m) consists of the temperature rise of acoustic phonons (ΔT_{AP}) and the temperature difference between optical phonons and acoustic phonons (ΔT_{OA}). ΔT_m can be expressed as:

$$\Delta T_m = \Delta T_{AP} + \Delta T_{OA} = \Delta T_{AP} + \delta I/G_{pp} \tag{1}$$

Here, I is the intensity of the absorbed laser at location r. δ ($0 < \delta < 1$) is the portion of the laser energy transfer from optical phonons (OP) to acoustic phonons (AP). G_{pp} is the coupling factor between OP and AP. Furthermore, the Raman intensity weighted temperature rise ($\Delta \overline{T}_m|_{CW}$) probed by the Raman spectroscopy can be expressed as [21]:

$$\Delta \overline{T}_m|_{CW} = \frac{\iint \Delta T_m I_{CW} e^{-z/\tau_L} 2\pi r dr dz}{\iint_{CW} e^{-z/\tau_L} 2\pi r dr dz}$$
$$= \Delta \overline{T}_{OA}|_{CW} + \Delta \overline{T}_{AP}|_{CW} = \frac{1}{3} \times \frac{I_0}{\tau_L} \times \frac{\delta}{G_{pp}|_{CW}} + \Delta \overline{T}_{AP}|_{CW} \tag{2}$$

Here, I_{CW} is the laser intensity distribution of the CW laser. $\Delta \overline{T}_{OA}|_{CW}$ and $\Delta \overline{T}_{AP}|_{CW}$ are the Raman intensity weighted temperature difference between OP and AP and the temperature rise of the acoustic phonons, respectively. I_0 is the absorbed laser power per unit area, and τ_L is the absorption depth. Before determining the percentages of $\Delta \overline{T}_{OA}|_{CW}$ and $\Delta \overline{T}_{AP}|_{CW}$ in $\Delta \overline{T}_m|_{CW}$, $G_{pp}|_{CW}$ should be figured out first by experiment. By constructing a 3D heat conduction model for a 55nm-thick MoS$_2$, $\Delta \overline{T}_{AP}|_{CW}$ is obtained as $\Delta \overline{T}_{AP}|_{CW} = 0.94 + 2.86e^{-1.65r_0}$. r_0 is the radius of the laser spot. The Raman shift is proportional to the temperature rise caused by unit power; thus, the Raman shift coefficient χ_{CW} can be expressed as [31]:

$$\chi_{CW} = A \times [(0.94 + 2.86e^{-1.65r_0} + \frac{1}{3} \times \frac{P}{\pi r_0^2 \tau_L} \times \frac{\delta}{G_{pp}|_{CW}})]/P \tag{3}$$

Here, A is a constant. In the experiment, three objective lenses ($20\times$, $50\times$ and $100\times$) are employed to obtain the $\chi_{CW}-r_0$ relationship. By fitting $\chi_{CW}-r_0$ relationship with Equation (3), $G_{pp}|_{CW}$ can be determined. Furthermore, the Raman intensity weighted temperature rise $\Delta \overline{T}_{OA}|_{CW}$ and $\Delta \overline{T}_{AP}|_{CW}$ can be figured out through the 3D conduction numerical calculation. It is found that the temperature difference between OP and AP accounts for more than 30% of the temperature rise detected by Raman [31]. Zobeiri et al., further characterized the thermal nonequilibrium between OP and AP under photon excitation in graphene paper [38]. The Raman intensity weighted temperature rise of OP is found to be 82.1% higher than that of AP under $100\times$ laser heating [38], which indicates the importance of taking interphonon thermal nonequilibrium effects into consideration in the optothermal Raman technique.

To consider the hot carrier diffusion effect in the thermal transport in 2D materials, Yuan et al., first developed the ET-Raman to determine the interface thermal resistance and hot carrier diffusion coefficient in MoS$_2$ supported by c-Si [27,33]. The ET-Raman includes two energy transport states: the zero thermal transport state and the steady-state thermal transport. The zero thermal transport state is obtained by applying a picosecond pulsed laser under a $50\times$ objective lens. In an extremely short pulse (~13 ps) time, only the fast thermalization process happens, so the heat conduction in the lattice can be neglected. By varying the laser power, the RSC $\chi_{ps} = \partial \omega / \partial P$ is obtained, which is more affected by the ρc_p rather than by the hot carrier diffusion coefficient (D) and interface thermal resistance (R). In the steady-state thermal transport, the RSC under $20\times$ and $100\times$ objective lenses are obtained by applying the CW laser. Both χ_{CW20} under the $20\times$ objective lens and χ_{CW100} under the $100\times$ objective lens carries the information of D and R. However, χ_{CW20} is more affected by R, while χ_{CW100} is more affected by D. Here, the normalized RSC is defined as $\Theta_1 = \chi_{CW20}/\chi_{ps}$ and $\Theta_2 = \chi_{CW100}/\chi_{ps}$. By simulating a 3D heat conduction model in the sample, the RSC contour with R and D as variables is obtained. The cross point of the Θ_1 curve and Θ_2 curve gives the value of R and D.

5. Conclusions

In summary, though facing several critical problems, the optothermal Raman technique and micro-bridge method still show suitability and feasibility in energy transport characterization in 2D materials. Much pioneering work about the thermal non-equilibrium in different phonon branches has been reported. However, the physical model and data fitting used in the pioneering work still suffer great uncertainties and make the study rather semi-quantitative. Secondly, past work has studied the thermal nonequilibrium in suspended 2D materials. However, for supported 2D materials, how the interface resistance between 2D material and substrate affects the *OP-AP* thermal nonequilibrium is unclear. Further work can be focused on the *OP-AP* thermal nonequilibrium in supported 2D materials.

Author Contributions: J.L. conceived and wrote the review; P.L. and H.Z. cooperated in bibliographic searches, studies. J.L. conceived and revised the paper. All authors have read and agreed to the published version of the manuscript.

Funding: This research was funded by the Natural Science Foundation of Top Talent of SZTU (2019209) and the Guangdong Basic and Applied Basic Research Foundation (2020A1515110389).

Institutional Review Board Statement: Not applicable.

Informed Consent Statement: Not applicable.

Data Availability Statement: No new data were created or analyzed in this review. Data sharing is not applicable to this article.

Acknowledgments: J. Liu thanks Xinwei Wang of Iowa State University for the discussion.

Conflicts of Interest: The authors declare no conflict of interest.

References

1. Ahmadi, Z.; Yakupoglu, B.; Azam, N.; Elafandi, S.; Mahjouri-Samani, M. Self-limiting laser crystallization and direct writing of 2D materials. *Int. J. Extreme Manuf.* **2019**, *1*, 015001. [CrossRef]
2. Nair, R.R.; Blake, P.; Grigorenko, A.N.; Novoselov, K.; Booth, T.; Stauber, T.; Peres, N.M.R.; Geim, A.K. Fine structure constant defines visual transparency of graphene. *Science* **2008**, *320*, 1308. [CrossRef]
3. Balandin, A.A.; Ghosh, S.; Bao, W.; Calizo, I.; Teweldebrhan, D.; Miao, F.; Lau, C.N. Superior thermal conductivity of single-layer graphene. *Nano Lett.* **2008**, *8*, 902–907. [CrossRef]
4. Yoon, D.; Son, Y.-W.; Cheong, H. Negative thermal expansion coefficient of graphene measured by Raman spectroscopy. *Nano Lett.* **2011**, *11*, 3227–3231. [CrossRef]
5. Yoon, D.; Son, Y.-W.; Cheong, H. Strain-dependent splitting of the double-resonance Raman scattering band in graphene. *Phys. Rev. Lett.* **2011**, *106*, 155502. [CrossRef]
6. Seol, J.H.; Jo, I.; Moore, A.L.; Lindsay, L.; Aitken, Z.H.; Pettes, M.T.; Li, X.; Yao, Z.; Huang, R.; Broido, D.; et al. Two-dimensional phonon transport in supported graphene. *Science* **2010**, *328*, 213–216. [CrossRef]
7. Hopkins, P.E.; Baraket, M.; Barnat, E.V.; Beechem, T.E.; Kearney, S.P.; Duda, J.C.; Robinson, J.T.; Walton, S.G. Manipulating thermal conductance at metal–graphene contacts via chemical functionalization. *Nano Lett.* **2012**, *12*, 590–595. [CrossRef]
8. Wang, R.; Wang, T.; Zobeiri, H.; Yuan, P.; Deng, C.; Yue, Y.; Xu, S.; Wang, X. Measurement of the thermal conductivities of suspended MoS_2 and $MoSe_2$ by nanosecond ET-Raman without temperature calibration and laser absorption evaluation. *Nanoscale* **2018**, *10*, 23087–23102. [CrossRef]
9. Jo, I.; Pettes, M.T.; Kim, J.; Watanabe, K.; Taniguchi, T.; Yao, Z.; Shi, L. Thermal Conductivity and Phonon Transport in Suspended Few-Layer Hexagonal Boron Nitride. *Nano Lett.* **2013**, *13*, 550–554. [CrossRef] [PubMed]
10. Chen, S.; Li, Q.; Zhang, Q.; Qu, Y.; Ji, H.; Ruoff, R.S.; Cai, W. Thermal conductivity measurements of suspended graphene with and without wrinkles by micro-Raman mapping. *Nanotechnology* **2012**, *23*, 365701. [CrossRef]
11. Cai, W.; Moore, A.; Zhu, Y.; Li, X.; Chen, S.; Shi, L.; Ruoff, R.S. Thermal transport in suspended and supported monolayer graphene grown by chemical vapor deposition. *Nano Lett.* **2010**, *10*, 1645–1651. [CrossRef]
12. Liu, J.; Wang, T.; Xu, S.; Yuan, P.; Xu, X.; Wang, X. Thermal conductivity of giant mono- to few-layered CVD graphene supported on an organic substrate. *Nanoscale* **2016**, *8*, 10298–10309. [CrossRef]
13. Ong, Z.-Y.; Pop, E. Effect of substrate modes on thermal transport in supported graphene. *Phys. Rev. B* **2011**, *84*, 075471. [CrossRef]
14. Soini, M.C.; Zardo, I.; Uccelli, E.; Funk, S.; Koblmüller, G.; I Morral, A.F.; Abstreiter, G. Thermal conductivity of GaAs nanowires studied by micro-Raman spectroscopy combined with laser heating. *Appl. Phys. Lett.* **2010**, *97*, 263107. [CrossRef]
15. Jiang, P.; Qian, X.; Yang, R. Time-domain thermoreflectance (TDTR) measurements of anisotropic thermal conductivity using a variable spot size approach. *Rev. Sci. Instrum.* **2017**, *88*, 074901. [CrossRef]
16. Waissman, J.; Anderson, L.E.; Talanov, A.V.; Yan, Z.; Shin, Y.J.; Najafabadi, D.H.; Taniguchi, T.; Watanabe, K.; Skinner, B.; Matveev, K.A.; et al. Measurement of Electronic Thermal Conductance in Low-Dimensional Materials with Graphene Nonlocal Noise Thermometry. *arXiv* **2021**, arXiv:2101.01737. Available online: https://arxiv.org/abs/2101.01737 (accessed on 10 October 2021).
17. Beechem, T.; Yates, L.; Graham, S. Invited Review Article: Error and uncertainty in Raman thermal conductivity measurements. *Rev. Sci. Instrum.* **2015**, *86*, 041101. [CrossRef]

18. Malekpour, H.; Ramnani, P.; Srinivasan, S.; Balasubramanian, G.; Nika, D.L.; Mulchandani, A.; Lake, R.K.; Balandin, A.A. Thermal conductivity of graphene with defects induced by electron beam irradiation. *Nanoscale* **2016**, *8*, 14608–14616. [CrossRef]
19. Jo, I.; Pettes, M.T.; Lindsay, L.; Ou, E.; Weathers, A.; Moore, A.L.; Yao, Z.; Shi, L. Reexamination of basal plane thermal conductivity of suspended graphene samples measured by electro-thermal micro-bridge methods. *AIP Adv.* **2015**, *5*, 053206. [CrossRef]
20. Li, H.; Ying, H.; Chen, X.; Nika, D.L.; Cocemasov, A.I.; Cai, W.; Balandin, A.A.; Chen, S. Thermal conductivity of twisted bilayer graphene. *Nanoscale* **2014**, *6*, 13402–13408. [CrossRef] [PubMed]
21. Calizo, I.; Balandin, A.A.; Bao, W.; Miao, F.; Lau, C.N. Temperature Dependence of the Raman Spectra of Graphene and Graphene Multilayers. *Nano Lett.* **2007**, *7*, 2645–2649. [CrossRef] [PubMed]
22. Wang, T.; Liu, J.; Xu, B.; Wang, R.; Yuan, P.; Han, M.; Xu, S.; Xie, Y.; Wu, Y.; Wang, X. Identifying the Crystalline Orientation of Black Phosphorus by Using Optothermal Raman Spectroscopy. *ChemPhysChem* **2017**, *18*, 2828–2834. [CrossRef] [PubMed]
23. Wang, T.; Han, M.; Wang, R.; Yuan, P.; Xu, S.; Wang, X. Characterization of anisotropic thermal conductivity of suspended nm-thick black phosphorus with frequency-resolved Raman spectroscopy. *J. Appl. Phys.* **2018**, *123*, 145104. [CrossRef]
24. Sahoo, S.; Gaur, A.P.S.; Ahmadi, M.; Guinel, M.J.-F.; Katiyar, R.S. Temperature-Dependent Raman Studies and Thermal Conductivity of Few-Layer MoS_2. *J. Phys. Chem. C* **2013**, *117*, 9042–9047. [CrossRef]
25. Malekpour, H.; Balandin, A.A. Raman-based technique for measuring thermal conductivity of graphene and related materials. *J. Raman Spectrosc.* **2017**, *49*, 106–120. [CrossRef]
26. Ni, G.-X.; Yang, H.-Z.; Ji, W.; Baeck, S.-J.; Toh, C.-T.; Ahn, J.-H.; Pereira, V.M.; Özyilmaz, B. Tuning Optical Conductivity of Large-Scale CVD Graphene by Strain Engineering. *Adv. Mater.* **2013**, *26*, 1081–1086. [CrossRef]
27. Yuan, P.; Wang, R.; Tan, H.; Wang, T.; Wang, X. Energy Transport State Resolved Raman for Probing Interface Energy Transport and Hot Carrier Diffusion in Few-Layered MoS_2. *ACS Photon.* **2017**, *4*, 3115–3129. [CrossRef]
28. Wang, R.; Wang, T.; Zobeiri, H.; Li, D.; Wang, X. Energy and Charge Transport in 2D Atomic Layer Materials: Raman-Based Characterization. *Nanomaterials* **2020**, *10*, 1807. [CrossRef]
29. Vallabhaneni, A.K.; Singh, D.; Bao, H.; Murthy, J.; Ruan, X. Reliability of Raman measurements of thermal conductivity of single-layer graphene due to selective electron-phonon coupling: A first-principles study. *Phys. Rev. B* **2016**, *93*, 125432. [CrossRef]
30. Lu, Z.; Vallabhaneni, A.; Cao, B.; Ruan, X. Phonon branch-resolved electron-phonon coupling and the multitemperature model. *Phys. Rev. B* **2018**, *98*, 134309. [CrossRef]
31. Wang, R.; Zobeiri, H.; Xie, Y.; Wang, X.; Zhang, X.; Yue, Y. Distinguishing Optical and Acoustic Phonon Temperatures and Their Energy Coupling Factor under Photon Excitation in nm 2D Materials. *Adv. Sci.* **2020**, *7*, 2000097. [CrossRef]
32. Yuan, P.; Liu, J.; Wang, R.; Wang, X. The hot carrier diffusion coefficient of sub-10 nm virgin MoS_2: Uncovered by non-contact optical probing. *Nanoscale* **2017**, *9*, 6808–6820. [CrossRef]
33. Yuan, P.; Tan, H.; Wang, R.; Wang, T.; Wang, X. Very fast hot carrier diffusion in unconstrained MoS_2 on a glass substrate: Discovered by picosecond ET-Raman. *RSC Adv.* **2018**, *8*, 12767–12778. [CrossRef]
34. Fugallo, G.; Cepellotti, A.; Paulatto, L.; Lazzeri, M.; Marzari, N.; Mauri, F. Thermal Conductivity of Graphene and Graphite: Collective Excitations and Mean Free Paths. *Nano Lett.* **2014**, *14*, 6109–6114. [CrossRef]
35. Zobeiri, H.; Wang, R.; Wang, T.; Lin, H.; Deng, C.; Wang, X. Frequency-domain energy transport state-resolved Raman for measuring the thermal conductivity of suspended nm-thick $MoSe_2$. *Int. J. Heat Mass Transf.* **2019**, *133*, 1074–1085. [CrossRef]
36. Wang, R.; Zobeiri, H.; Lin, H.; Qu, W.; Bai, X.; Deng, C.; Wang, X. Anisotropic thermal conductivities and structure in lignin-based microscale carbon fibers. *Carbon* **2019**, *147*, 58–69. [CrossRef]
37. Sullivan, S.; Vallabhaneni, A.; Kholmanov, I.; Ruan, X.; Murthy, J.; Shi, L. Optical Generation and Detection of Local Nonequilibrium Phonons in Suspended Graphene. *Nano Lett.* **2017**, *17*, 2049–2056. [CrossRef] [PubMed]
38. Zobeiri, H.; Hunter, N.; Wang, R.; Wang, T.; Wang, X. Direct Characterization of Thermal Nonequilibrium between Optical and Acoustic Phonons in Graphene Paper under Photon Excitation. *Adv. Sci.* **2021**, *8*, 2004712. [CrossRef]

MDPI
St. Alban-Anlage 66
4052 Basel
Switzerland
Tel. +41 61 683 77 34
Fax +41 61 302 89 18
www.mdpi.com

Nanomaterials Editorial Office
E-mail: nanomaterials@mdpi.com
www.mdpi.com/journal/nanomaterials

9 783036 579108